Focus Particles in German

Linguistik Aktuell/Linguistics Today (LA)

Linguistik Aktuell/Linguistics Today (LA) provides a platform for original monograph studies into synchronic and diachronic linguistics. Studies in LA confront empirical and theoretical problems as these are currently discussed in syntax, semantics, morphology, phonology, and systematic pragmatics with the aim to establish robust empirical generalizations within a universalistic perspective.

Volume 151

Focus Particles in German. Syntax, prosody, and information structure
by Stefan Sudhoff

Focus Particles in German

Syntax, prosody, and information structure

Stefan Sudhoff

John Benjamins Publishing Company
Amsterdam / Philadelphia

The paper used in this publication meets the minimum requirements of American National Standard for Information Sciences – Permanence of Paper for Printed Library Materials, ANSI Z39.48-1984.

Library of Congress Cataloging-in-Publication Data

Sudhoff, Stefan, 1977-

Focus Particles in German : syntax, prosody, and information structure / by Stefan Sudhoff.

p. cm. (Linguistik Aktuell/Linguistics Today, ISSN 0166-0829 ; v. 151)

Includes bibliographical references and index.

1. German language--Particles. 2. German language--Syntax. 3. Prosodic analysis (Linguistics) I. Title.

PF3321.S83 2010

435'.7--dc22 2009046132

ISBN 978 90 272 5534 1 (Hb ; alk. paper)

ISBN 978 90 272 8856 1 (Eb)

John Benjamins Publishing Co. · P.O. Box 36224 · 1020 ME Amsterdam · The Netherlands

John Benjamins North America · P.O. Box 27519 · Philadelphia PA 19118-0519 · USA

Boys go to Jupiter to get more stupider
Girls go to Mars, become rock stars

Sonic Youth
Nevermind (What Was It Anyway)

Table of contents

Acknowledgements

There are several people without whom this study would not have been possible. First and foremost, I would like to thank Anita Steube, Kai Alter, and Bob Ladd for their support, guidance, feedback, and advice at all stages. Further, I am indebted to Stefan Baumann, Bettina Braun, Johannes Dölling, Katharina Hartmann, Martin Schäfer, and especially Denisa Lenertová for their insightful comments and suggestions, for the time they generously spent with me answering my questions, and for the expertise they provided. Denisa Lenertová's assistance with the experimental work reported in Chapter 6 was particularly helpful. This work also benefited from suggestions and corrections made by an anonymous reviewer.

I am very grateful to Elly van Gelderen and Werner Abraham for giving me the opportunity to publish this book in the Linguistics Today series and to Kees Vaes from John Benjamins for his help in preparing the manuscript for publication.

Many thanks to those who participated in the experiments, and to Tracey S. Rosenberg and Dave Gorman for correcting what I thought was English. I do not know which of the two tasks is more annoying.

Finally, I would like to express my gratitude to both my colleagues in the DFG graduate programme "Universality and Diversity: Linguistic Structures and Processes" and at the Linguistics Department of the University of Leipzig, as well as to my parents and my friends. Without some of them, I would not have finished this book yet. Without others, I would have finished it earlier. I am equally grateful to all of them.

Abbreviations and notational conventions

Conventions used in example sentences and glosses:

- Accented syllables are printed in SMALL CAPS.
- '/' preceding an accented syllable indicates a rising pitch accent.
- $[\ \dots\ ]_{D}$ indicates the domain of a focus particle.
- Interlinear glosses are kept as simple as possible. Morphological marking is only glossed if it is relevant for the discussion at hand.

Abbreviations:

AC	associated constituent
CF	contrastive focus
F	focus
V1	verb-first
V2	verb-second
VF	verb-final
acc	accusative case
aff	affirmation
aux_f	future auxiliary
aux_p	perfect auxiliary
aux_{pass}	passive auxiliary
dat	dative case
expl	expletive
gen	genitive case
mp	modal particle
pref	separable prefix
refl	reflexive pronoun

CHAPTER 1

Introduction

> The literature on focus adverbs contains a number of valuable theoretical approaches, but at this point they must be considered as no more than avenues along which we may slowly and rather cautiously proceed towards, one hopes, that ultimate destiny, the truth. (Hoeksema & Zwarts 1991:66)

1.1 Scope and goals

The topic of the present study is the syntax, information structure, and prosody of German sentences containing words such as *nur* ('only'), *auch* ('also'), and *sogar* ('even'). One of the many terms used for such words, and the one that is chosen for this study, is *focus particles*. This term indicates two main characteristics of the elements it denotes. First, they are particles, i.e., they have an invariable form, are relatively short, and belong to the category of closed-class elements. Second, they are related to the concept of focus in a specific way; cf. the introductory examples in (1).

(1) a. Maja hat nur FElix geküsst.
Maja *aux*$_p$ only Felix kissed
b. Maja hat Felix nur geKÜSST.
Maja *aux*$_p$ Felix only kissed

The first sentence is ambiguous. It can express two things: that Maja did not kiss anyone but Felix, or that she did not do anything but kiss Felix. The second sentence unambiguously states that Maja did not do anything to Felix but kiss him. There are two obvious candidates for factors explaining the difference in meaning between (1a) and (1b). On the one hand, the sentences differ in their word order, or, more specifically, in the position of *nur*. On the other hand, they are characterized by a different location of the sentence accent.[1] These two factors, however, do not help us to explain the ambiguity of (1a) – both readings are compatible with the same word order and accentuation. Of course, the two interpretations are appropriate in different contexts. This means that they differ in their

1. Throughout this work, accents are indicated by SMALL CAPS in the examples.

information structure, i.e., in the distribution of new (or important) and given (or presupposed) information. Uttering (1a), the speaker either makes a statement (or answers a question) about the set of people kissed by Maja or about the set of things Maja has done. Information structure, in particular the partition of a sentence into a focus part and a background part, thus qualifies as a third factor influencing the meaning of a sentence containing a focus particle. There are good reasons to assume that information structure is a more elementary factor than word order and accent distribution, the last-named properties themselves being at least partly determined by information structure.

A common way to analyze the phenomenon exemplified by the sentences in (1), which is often called *focus sensitivity* or *association with focus*, is the following: A focus particle is associated with a certain part of the sentence, the focus of the particle. This association is necessary to determine the meaning contribution of the particle, as different foci result in different sentence meanings. The choice of the focus in turn imposes certain restrictions on the word order and accentuation of the sentence. While these properties thus represent cues for the identification of the elements associated with a focus particle, they do not always unambiguously determine the association, as evidenced by the different readings available for (1a).

The aim of the present study is to give a comprehensive account of the grammar of focus particle constructions in German. It will be shown how syntax, semantics, and prosody interact in sentences like those in (1), how the elements associated with the focus particles, as well as the resulting sentence meanings, are determined, what role information structure plays in this mechanism, and how the grammatical restrictions the sentences are subject to can be explained. The theory to be developed must meet the requirement of being modular, i.e., the explanations it gives must be based on principles that are independently motivated in the individual components of grammar. This is a challenge, but it also extends the relevance of the research beyond the topic of focus particles. It will become clear that focus particle constructions, among other phenomena related to information structure, present a particularly well-suited subject for the investigation of the modularity of grammar in general.

More specifically, the research questions and problems to be dealt with in this study include the following:

- What is an adequate syntactic representation of sentences containing focus particles? What categorial status do focus particles have, and how are they integrated into the syntactic structure? Are there any restrictions on the type of a focus particle's sister constituent?
- How can the relation between a focus particle and the associated elements be modeled? What are the syntactic preconditions of the association, and what information-structural prerequisites and/or effects does it have?

- Constructions with the stressed variant of the focus particle *auch* or comparable particles present a problem for most theories of the grammar of focus particle constructions. How can these constructions be accounted for?
- What prosodic properties do sentences with focus particles have, and what does the prosody of the constructions tell us about their information-structural characteristics? What is the relation between focus particles and contrast?

There is an impressive list of publications on the topic; the relevant monographs range from Altmann's (1976a, 1978) groundbreaking work over Jacobs' (1983) and Bayer's (1996) contributions to the recent studies of Nederstigt (2003) and Dimroth (2004), and are supplemented by an enormous number of articles. However, many of the questions listed above have not yet been answered satisfactorily. Hence, there is still some truth in the quote from Hoeksema & Zwarts (1991) given above, and while the present study will propose solutions for some of the problems mentioned, it will also raise several new questions to be dealt with in future research.

1.2 Organization of this study

This study can be roughly divided into a theoretical part, consisting of Chapters 2 and an empirical part, formed by Chapters 6 and 7. Chapter 2 describes the theoretical background and introduces the relevant terminology. Chapter 3 gives an overview of the semantics of focus particles. Although semantics does not belong to the central topics of this study, the results of the semantic research on focus particles serve as the basis for the investigation of syntactic and prosodic phenomena in the subsequent chapters. Chapter 4 deals with the syntax of focus particle constructions and proposes a modular account of the relation between their word order, information structure, and meaning. It is also shown how the analysis of the stressed variant of the focus particle *auch* can be integrated into this proposal. Issues of scope, which are removed from consideration in Chapter 4, are investigated in Chapter 5, the last chapter of the theoretical part.

The two empirical chapters deal with the prosodic realization of sentences containing focus particles. Chapter 6 presents a corpus study and several speech production and perception experiments examining the prosody of utterances with stressed *auch*. Chapter 7 reports two experiments on the relation between focus particles and contrast in utterances with unstressed particles. The aim of the empirical studies is twofold. On the one hand, they were carried out to obtain a more detailed picture of the prosodic realization of constructions with (and without) focus particles in German. On the other hand, they test the predictions that can be derived from the theory formulated in the first part of this work.

Chapter 8 summarizes the main results of this study and outlines possible future research directions.

CHAPTER 2

Theoretical background

This chapter sets the stage for the theoretical and empirical investigation of German focus particle constructions in the subsequent chapters. Section 2.1 gives a more detailed characterization of the object of research. The remaining sections introduce the relevant background assumptions with respect to syntax (Section 2.2), information structure (Section 2.3), and prosody (Section 2.4).

2.1 Focus particles

Although focus particles have been extensively studied in the theoretical literature in recent years,[1] there are few explicit statements about their defining criteria. Nevertheless, there is general agreement about which expressions belong to the core of this category. The most extensive lists of German focus particles are given by König (1991a, c, 1993); cf. (1).

(1) German focus particles according to König (1991a, c, 1993):
allein, auch, auch nur, ausgerechnet, ausschließlich, bereits, besonders, bloß, einzig, eben, ebenfalls, erst, gar, genau, geschweige denn, gerade, gleich, gleichfalls, insbesondere, lediglich, nicht einmal, noch, nur, schon, selbst, sogar, vor allem, wenigstens, zumal, zumindest

In the following, two ways of approaching a closer characterization of the class of focus particles will be pursued: via the superordinate categories they are considered to belong to, and via their specific properties. Focus particles are either regarded as a subclass of particles (cf. Helbig 1988; Foolen 1993) or as a subclass of adverbs (cf. König 1991a, c, 1993; Hoeksema & Zwarts 1991). Both superordinate categories, however, are quite heterogeneous and differently defined in the literature.[2]

---

1. The processing of focus particles, on the other hand, has only been addressed in a few studies; cf. Ni, Crain & Shankweiler (1996), Clifton, Bock & Radó (2000), Sedivy (2002), Heim & Alter (2006, 2007).

2. Sometimes, particles in general are categorized as a subclass of adverbs or the other way around.

Helbig (1988: 19–27) uses the following criteria to delimit the class of particles in German: (i) particles are uninflectional, synsemantic/function words, (ii) they cannot occur in the position preceding the finite verb in main clauses on their own,[3] (iii) they cannot form the answer to a question on their own, (iv) they have no effect on truth conditions and can be omitted without any dramatic consequences for the sentence meaning, and (v) they semantically or pragmatically modify sentences in a specific way. According to Helbig, expressions that usually fulfill these criteria include focus particles, modal particles, intensifiers, and negation particles, among others. While the second criterion allows for a distinction between focus particles and adverbs, the latter usually able to occur in the first position of German main clauses, the fourth criterion is problematic for at least a subset of focus particles (cf. Chapter 3). As other subgroups of particles pose problems for some of the other criteria given above, the only characterization capturing the entire range of expressions traditionally classified as particles is a negative one: particles are uninflectional words that do not belong to other uninflectional word classes such as adverbs, prepositions, and conjunctions.[4]

What are the specific characteristics of focus particles that distinguish them from the other types of particles? Two main properties are considered to facilitate a sufficiently precise definition of this subclass: their positional variability and their interaction with the focus-background partition of the sentences in which they occur (cf. König 1991c: 10). The first property is illustrated in (2). Descriptively speaking, focus particles may be located at several different places in a sentence.[5] Possible explanations for this variability, the restrictions on the positioning of focus particles, and the effects of their location on the meaning of the sentences will be discussed in Chapter 4.

(2) dass (nur) Maja (nur) ihrem Sohn (nur) den Koran (nur)
that (only) Maja (only) to_her son (only) the Koran (only)
vorgelesen hat
read *aux*$_p$

The second property, the interaction with focus structure, corresponds to the concept of focus sensitivity introduced above (cf. the discussion in Section 1.1). Focus

3. In the terminology of traditional German linguistics, this is equivalent to not having the status of a *Satzglied*.

4. "Danach wären Partikeln solche morphologisch unflektierbaren Wörter, die über keine solchen syntaktischen Funktionen verfügen, wie sie den Wörtern anderer unflektierbarer Wortklassen (z.B. den Adverbien, Modalwörtern, Präpositionen und Konjunktionen) zukommen [...]." (Helbig 1988: 20)

5. For the time being, sentences with more than one focus particle are ignored. We will return to this issue in Chapter 5.

particles are related to focused elements in the sentence, and their meaning contribution crucially depends on the choice of the focus. A detailed description of this phenomenon will be given in Chapter 3. Focus sensitivity is not restricted to constructions with focus particles. Partee (1992) lists a number of focus sensitive expressions and constructions of English. In addition to focus particles, her list includes quantificational adverbs (e.g., adverbs of frequency), counterfactuals, modals, generics, why-questions, certain clause-embedding constructions, and superlatives; cf. the examples in (3)–(9).[6]

(3) a. Mary always took JOHN to the movies.
 b. Mary always took John to the MOVies.

(4) a. If Clyde hadn't married BERtha, he would not have been eligible for the inheritance.
 b. If Clyde hadn't MARried Bertha, he would not have been eligible for the inheritance.

(5) a. DOGS must be carried.
 b. Dogs must be CARried.

(6) a. English is spoken in the SHETlands.
 b. ENGlish is spoken in the Shetlands.

(7) a. Why did Clyde marry BERtha?
 b. Why did Clyde MARry Bertha?

(8) a. It's odd that Clyde married BERtha.
 b. It's odd that Clyde MARried Bertha.

(9) a. The largest demonstrations took place in PRAGUE in November (in) 1989.
 b. The largest demonstrations took place in Prague in NOVEMber (in) 1989.

Similar examples can be given for German; cf. the overview in Geilfuß-Wolfgang (1996: 1–2). In all cases, the members of the minimal pairs of sentences differing in their focus structure have different meanings. This shows that focus sensitivity alone does not suffice as a defining criterion for focus particles; we must also refer to the superordinate category and/or to their other properties. The above considerations result in the tentative definition of focus particles given in (10), which serves as the basis for the present study.

(10) A focus particle is an uninflectional function word that shows a high positional variability and is related to one or more focused elements in the sentence, which determine its meaning contribution.

6. The examples are taken from Partee (1992), though some of them have their origin in earlier papers of other authors.

Most of the expressions that can be classified as focus particles also have other uses (cf. Jacobs 1983: 2, among others). Some of them, such as *nur* and *auch*, can serve as modal particles, others as conjunctions (cf. English *but* en Dutch *maar* 'but', but also *nur* and *auch* in German), while the particle *selbst* ('even') is homonymous with a reflexive pronoun. With the exception of the conjunctional use, which will be briefly addressed in Section 4.1, these phenomena will not be considered in the present investigation.

Although German has an impressive range of focus particles, this study will be mainly concerned with *nur* ('only'), *auch* ('also'), and *sogar* ('even'). In this respect, we follow most of the theoretical works on focus particles in German, which discuss only these three expressions or a subset of them (cf. Jacobs 1983; Bayer 1996, 1999; Dimroth & Klein 1996; Büring & Hartmann 2001; Dimroth 2004; Reis 2005). Exceptions are the works of Altmann (1976a, 1978), providing a broad descriptive survey of German focus particle constructions, and König (1991b, c), primarily dealing with the semantics of focus particles.[7]

The selection of only a few focus particles could be criticized as an unwarranted simplification. As a matter of fact, the grammatical behavior of some particles follows more complex regularities than the behavior of *nur*, *auch*, and *sogar*. However, this is not necessarily an argument against the method chosen here. The aim of the present study is not to describe the individual peculiarities of every single focus particle, but rather to identify the general grammatical mechanisms that explain the common properties of focus particle constructions and originate from the interaction of syntax, semantics, prosody, and information structure. For this purpose, the selected particles are particularly well suited. As argued by Jacobs (1983: 2–3) and accepted in most subsequent works, *nur*, *auch*, and *sogar* are fairly representative for the category as a whole. They exemplify the three main subclasses of focus particles (restrictive, additive, and scalar particles; cf. Chapter 3) and at the same time represent the most general members of these groups, i.e., they show the fewest distributional restrictions and idiosyncratic properties (cf. also Altmann 1976a). Of course, a general theory of the grammar of focus particles must ultimately be supplemented by a description of these idiosyncrasies,[8] but we endorse Jacobs' hope that broadening the range of the examined particles

7. In addition, there are several studies devoted to the description of individual focus particles or the comparison between similar German particles or between a German particle and its counterparts in other languages, e.g., Plank (1979), Foolen (1983), Primus (1992), Brauße (2000), Poljakova (2000), Penner, Tracy & Wymann (1999), and Nederstigt (2001, 2003, 2006). For the most part, however, these studies do not attempt to provide a general theory of the grammar of focus particle constructions.

8. One such attempt in the form of a lexicon of particles is made by Helbig (1988).

will not radically change the basic explanations to be given for the phenomena under discussion.

To conclude this section, a few remarks on the terminology employed in the present study are in order, as the use of different terms for the same concepts or of the same terms for different concepts has been the cause of much confusion in the literature. The term *focus(ing) particle* itself has many alternatives; in the English research tradition, *focus adverb*, *focus sensitive particle*, *focus inducer*, and *scalar particle* are the most common ones. The last-named, like its German equivalent *Gradpartikel*, refers to scalarity, a property that is not shared by all of the relevant expressions; the term is therefore avoided. Among the other terms, the choice fell on *focus particle* as it is the most common one and at the same time relatively theory-neutral.

The part of the sentence the focus particle is related to is often identified with the sentence focus. However, if one does not want to assume this correspondence from the outset, it is convenient to have an unbiased term for the associated element(s).[9] In addition to *focus*, the term *scope* (or its German counterpart *Skopus*) is sometimes used to refer to the relevant elements (cf. Altmann 1976a; Koktova 1987). Because of its different original meaning, this term is also unsuitable for our purposes. In addition, the scope of a particle will be shown to constitute an independent concept needed for the grammatical description of focus particle constructions (cf. Chapters 3 and 5). Following Nederstigt (2003), the part of the sentence related to the particle is therefore referred to as the *domain (of application)* of the particle here. In the linguistic literature, this term has not been used in other meanings to the same extent as *focus* and *scope*, and, unlike terms such as *associated constituent* or *related constituent*, it does not presuppose that the respective material has the status of a constituent. Throughout this work, the domain of a focus particle is indicated by square brackets labeled with the subscript D in the example sentences. Admittedly, the term *domain* is not used consistently in two cases. First, in the discussion of the semantic literature on focus particles in Chapter 3, we follow the prevalent terminology in this area, which means speaking of the *focus* of an operator. Second, if it is clear that the domain of a focus particle consists of one constituent only, we alternatively use the term *associated constituent*, abbreviated AC. This is mainly the case in the empirical part of this study (Chapters 6 and 7).

9. Hajičová & Sgall (2004), for instance, avoid terminological confusion by distinguishing between *focus of focalizer* and *focus of sentence*. Vallduví & Vilkuna's (1998) distinction between *kontrast* and *rheme* serves a similar purpose.

2.2 Syntax

German is a West Germanic SOV language showing the verb-second (V2) phenomenon characteristic of all Germanic languages with the exception of English. The term V2 refers to the fact that the finite verb, originating in a clause-final position, occupies the second position in German declarative main clauses (and in non-embedded wh-questions). This means that the finite verb is preceded by exactly one constituent,[10] the syntactic category or function of this constituent being irrelevant.

Grammatical descriptions of the V2-phenomenon and of German clause structure in general have existed for over a century; cf. Erdmann (1886), Drach (1937), and Bech (1955, 1957), among others. The so-called *Topological Model (Stellungsfeldermodell)* of the German clause developed in these works reveals the systematic relations between the three basic clause structures of German – verb-second clauses, verb-final (VF) clauses (mostly subordinate clauses), and verb-first (V1) clauses (yes/no questions and imperatives, among others). According to this model, clauses are structured by two relevant positions, the *left bracket* and the *right bracket (Satzklammer)*. The left bracket is the position of the conjunction in VF-clauses and of the finite verb in V1- and V2-clauses. In VF-clauses, the right bracket contains the verbal complex, i.e., the finite verb and infinite verbal elements such as infinitives and participles. In V1- and V2-clauses, the right bracket consists of the verbal complex minus the finite verb.[11] If the finite verb has a separable prefix – such as *ein-* in *einladen* ('to invite') – this prefix is located in the right bracket, even if the finite verb itself forms the left bracket.

By means of the left and the right bracket, three regions can be defined in the German clause. The region preceding the left bracket is called the *prefield (Vorfeld)*. While it is filled by a single constituent in V2-clauses (see above), it is usually empty in V1- and VF-clauses.[12] The region following the right bracket is the *postfield (Nachfeld)*. In the current terminology, the postfield is the region targeted by extraposed constituents. All remaining elements are located in the so-called *middlefield (Mittelfeld)*, the region between the left and the right bracket. Some examples of the analysis of German clauses in the Topological Model are given in

10. For (apparent) exceptions and their analysis in the framework of HPSG, see Müller (2003, 2005).

11. According to some variants of the Topological Model, the right bracket is either empty or only contains the finite verb, while the infinite verbal elements immediately precede the right bracket. This difference is immaterial here.

12. In VF-clauses, the prefield can be filled by a relative pronoun or a wh-expression.

(11)–(14).[13] Clause structure is recursive in the sense that prefield, middlefield, or postfield may in turn contain clauses that have a topological structure themselves; cf. (14).

(11) a. [ ]$_{\text{PF}}$ [dass]$_{\text{LB}}$ [Jan heute Syntax]$_{\text{MF}}$ [lernt]$_{\text{RB}}$ [ ]$_{\text{PoF}}$ (VF)
that Jan today syntax learns

b. [ ]$_{\text{PF}}$ [Lernt]$_{\text{LB}}$ [Jan heute Syntax]$_{\text{MF}}$ [ ]$_{\text{RB}}$ [ ]$_{\text{PoF}}$? (V1)

c. [Jan]$_{\text{PF}}$ [lernt]$_{\text{LB}}$ [heute Syntax]$_{\text{MF}}$ [ ]$_{\text{RB}}$ [ ]$_{\text{PoF}}$. (V2)

d. [Heute]$_{\text{PF}}$ [lernt]$_{\text{LB}}$ [Jan Syntax]$_{\text{MF}}$ [ ]$_{\text{RB}}$ [ ]$_{\text{PoF}}$. (V2)

(12) a. [ ]$_{\text{PF}}$ [dass]$_{\text{LB}}$ [Jan morgen Syntax]$_{\text{MF}}$ [gelernt haben
that Jan tomorrow Syntax learned *aux*$_p$
wird]$_{\text{RB}}$ [ ]$_{\text{PoF}}$ (VF)
aux$_f$

b. [Jan]$_{\text{PF}}$ [wird]$_{\text{LB}}$ [morgen Syntax]$_{\text{MF}}$ [gelernt haben]$_{\text{RB}}$ [ ]$_{\text{PoF}}$. (V2)

(13) a. [was]$_{\text{PF}}$ [ ]$_{\text{LB}}$ [Jan heute]$_{\text{MF}}$ [lernt]$_{\text{RB}}$ [ ]$_{\text{PoF}}$ (VF)
what Jan today learns

b. [Was]$_{\text{PF}}$ [lernt]$_{\text{LB}}$ [Jan heute]$_{\text{MF}}$ [ ]$_{\text{RB}}$ [ ]$_{\text{PoF}}$? (V2)

(14) a. [Dass Jan Syntax lernt]$_{\text{PF}}$ [ist]$_{\text{LB}}$ [bemerkenswert]$_{\text{MF}}$ [ ]$_{\text{RB}}$
that Jan syntax learns is remarkable
[ ]$_{\text{PoF}}$. (V2)

b. [Es]$_{\text{PF}}$ [ist]$_{\text{LB}}$ [bemerkenswert]$_{\text{MF}}$ [ ]$_{\text{RB}}$ [dass Jan Syntax
it is remarkable that Jan syntax
lernt]$_{\text{PoF}}$. (V2)
learns

The descriptive generalizations of the Topological Model have been reanalyzed in terms of generative syntax by den Besten (1977, 1983) and Thiersch (1978). The complementary distribution of the finite verb and the complementizer in the left bracket is explained by identifying this position with the C-head. If we consider the VF-clause structure to be the underlying structure, we can derive V1-clauses by movement of the finite verb from V^0 (= the right bracket) to C^0. The V2-order results from the subsequent movement of one constituent to [Spec,C], which is identified with the prefield. Under the assumption that CP has a single specifier, it automatically follows that only one constituent may precede the finite verb in C^0. The presented theory, amounting to the assumption that all clauses are CPs, has become the standard analysis of German clause structure (cf. Fanselow 1991; Haider 1993; Sternefeld 2006a, among many others).[14] It serves as the basis for the syntactic analyses to be given in this study.

13. PF = prefield, LB = left bracket, MF = middlefield, RB = right bracket, PoF = postfield.

14. For an alternative proposal, see Brandt, Reis, Rosengren & Zimmermann (1992).

A question that still needs to be answered is whether we must assume additional functional projections in the middlefield, such as IP or the numerous derivatives of IP (TP, AgrP, etc.) proposed since the publication of Pollock (1989). Without going into the details of their arguments, we follow Haider (1993, 1997), Abraham (1997), and Sternefeld (2006b) in not regarding the postulation of any functional projections between CP and VP as necessary for the description of the German clause. The basic syntactic assumptions adopted here are the following. First, all arguments, including the subject, are generated within VP; they do not move in order to check case or agreement features.[15] Second, the finite verb occupies its base position in VF-clauses; it does not move to the head positions of functional projections dominating VP, unless C^0 is directly targeted to derive the V1- and V2-orders. Third, this relatively 'simple' clause structure can be put down to the fact that VP is head-final in SOV languages such as German, and that the verb can uniformly license all its arguments to the left from its base position, making head movement or functional projections unnecessary for the licensing of arguments.

The last point is relevant for another aspect of German syntax: the extensive word order variation in the middlefield. That the licensing direction of the verb is to the left provides an explanation of the possibility of scrambling; cf. Rosengren (1993b, 1994), Haider & Rosengren (1998). The authors analyze scrambling as left-adjunction to VP and argue that – with respect to the licensing of arguments – there is in principle no difference between the base positions and the adjoined positions of the scrambled constituents. According to Haider & Rosengren (1998), scrambled arguments can still be licensed by the verb in clause-final position. In other words, scrambling extends the licensing domain of the verb to the left. In SVO languages such as English, on the other hand, argument licensing depends on specific structural configurations, which is why scrambling is impossible in these languages. We will return to scrambling in the next section, as it is crucially involved in the grammatical realization of information-structural properties.

2.3 Information structure

The study of information structure is concerned with the question of how sentences are embedded in coherent discourses. However, the phenomena and properties subsumed under this label are closely tied to the core modules of grammar (cf. Féry & Krifka 2008). In focus particle constructions, this link is particularly

15. The account of Sternefeld (2006b) additionally allows one to merge the subject directly in [Spec,C]. This special case is ignored here.

obvious, and an adequate grammatical description of focus particles is not possible without reference to information structure (cf. Dimroth 2004). As will be shown, this not only concerns semantics, but also syntax and phonology. The theory of information structure serving as the basis for the present study has been developed in Steube (2000), Steube & Späth (2002), and Steube, Alter & Späth (2004).[16] In this section, the model of Steube and colleagues is introduced and briefly compared to other approaches to information structure. For reasons of space, we do not discuss these alternative theories in close detail, but rather refer to the original publications.

The central idea in the model of Steube and colleagues is that information-structural properties and features have a pragmatic origin, but are specifically realized at the individual levels of grammar. Referring to Levelt's (1989) speech production model (cf. also Bierwisch & Schreuder 1992), it is assumed that, when concepts are mapped onto lexical items, the latter are enriched with the relevant information-structural features. These features are interpreted by the modules of grammar, thereby controlling the specific grammatical realization of the resulting sentence. A welcome consequence of this conception is that we need not propose a separate level of information structure interacting with the other grammatical modules, but can explain information-structural effects in the fashion of strict grammatical modularity: together with the lexical items, the features are transferred from one module to the following, each time giving rise to level-specific grammatical effects.

What kinds of information-structural features do we have to assume, and what are their grammatical effects? As for the first question, the model makes use of two pragmatic distinctions, the focus-background partition and the topic-comment partition. The *focus*, corresponding to the feature [+F], is the highlighted, important, or new information in a sentence. *Background* information, on the other hand, is given or derivable from the linguistic or situational context and therefore belongs to the common ground of speaker and hearer. It is marked with the feature [–F].

The term *topic* refers to aboutness topics in the theory of Steube and colleagues. The topic of a sentence,[17] carrying the feature [Top], denotes the entity the sentence is about (cf. Hockett 1958; Reinhart 1981). This view is opposed to the conception of topics as familiarity topics (cf. Frascarelli & Hinterhölzl 2007), which roughly correspond to background elements. The *comment* is what is said about the topic. As its definition is negative (all non-topical elements of a sentence form the comment), it is not characterized by its own information-structural

16. See also Steube (1996, 2001, 2003, 2006, 2008).

17. For the distinction between sentence topics and discourse topics, see Reinhart (1981).

feature. Although the topic often belongs to the background of a sentence, the two partitions need not necessarily coincide (cf. Molnár 1991; Steube 1996): sentences cannot have more than one topic, but they can have various background elements, and a topic may also belong to the focus. A sentence need not have a topic, and there are sentences that contain focused elements only, but sentences exclusively consisting of background material are unacceptable, as they cannot be used to convey any information.

What are the effects of information structure on the lexical and grammatical properties of sentences? We concentrate on the focus-background partition. Already the choice of the lexical items is influenced by information structure. While background elements are preferentially realized as anaphoric pronouns or definite DPs, focused constituents are often indefinites (cf. Steube 2000). The following non-exhaustive list summarizes the most important information-structural effects at the individual levels of grammar.[18]

- In *semantics*, the background is mapped onto the restrictor, and the focus onto the nuclear scope of tripartite quantificational structures (cf. Partee 1992; Hajičová, Partee & Sgall 1998a, b; Steube 2008). Information structure thus directly affects the semantic representation and may have truth-conditional effects, as exemplified in (3)–(9) above; cf. also Chapter 3 of the present study.
- In *syntax*, information structure is a decisive factor for the constituent order in the middlefield (cf. Lenerz 1977) and for the choice of the constituent located in the prefield (cf. Speyer 2004, 2007); see below.
- Information structure does not show any effects in *morphology* in German. However, morphological correlates of information-structural properties are well-attested in other languages, such as Japanese (cf. Diesing 1988) and the Chadic languages (cf. Hartmann & Zimmermann 2004, 2006, 2007).
- In *phonology*, information structure, in addition to structural rules (cf. Cinque 1993), determines accent positions and accent types (cf. Jacobs 1988; Uhmann 1991; Féry 1993; Ladd 1996; and Section 2.4 below).

The effects of information structure on word order and accent placement in German require a close look. In (15)–(19), the central claims of the model of Steube and colleagues concerning the relation between syntax, prosody, and the focus-background partition are listed. They will be discussed and compared to other approaches below.

(15) The middlefield is divided into a designated area for background elements and a designated area for the focus. The background area precedes the focus

18. For more detailed overviews, see Jacobs (1988), Steube, Alter & Späth (2004), and Féry & Krifka (2008).

area, the dividing line being the sentence adverbials. In other words, German has a syntactically defined focus domain ranging from the sentence adverbials to the end of the middlefield.

(16) All arguments and adjuncts except the sentence adverbials have their base positions in the focus domain. Background elements are preferentially moved leftward out of the focus domain, i.e., across the position of the sentence adverbials. This movement is described as an instance of scrambling, targeting positions left-adjoined to VP. Focused elements preferentially stay in their base positions to the right of the sentence adverbials.

(17) There are systematic exceptions to this general pattern: Constituents that cannot scramble for intrinsic reasons must remain inside the focus domain even if they are defocused. The finite verb and the infinite verbal elements do not participate in information structure driven movement; their positions are determined by independent syntactic requirements. The prefield may host constituents with various information-structural characteristics: topics, foci, background constituents, and even sentence adverbials. A focused prefield element may be the only focused element of the sentence or part of a larger focus.

(18) The placement of the sentence accent follows information-structural as well as independent grammatical rules. It must be located within the focus, but its exact position is structurally defined: the focus exponent (i.e., the syllable bearing the sentence accent) is the most prominent syllable of the head of the most deeply embedded focused constituent in the middlefield. If a minimally focused constituent is moved to the prefield, it takes the sentence accent along with it.

(19) Contrastive focus differs in several properties from the new information focus described so far. Contrastively focused elements are characterized by a different prosodic marking and a specific semantics, and they can occur above the sentence adverbials in the middlefield. Contrastive focus overrides the normal focus-background partition.

The first claim expresses the well-known generalization that background information usually precedes focus information in the middlefield; cf. the examples in (20). The background area corresponds to the *thematic domain* and the focus domain to the *rhematic domain* in Abraham's (1997, 2003, 2007) model. It has often been noted that the so-called *sentence adverbials* (*wahrscheinlich* 'probably', *bestimmt* 'certainly', *vielleicht* 'perhaps', *tatsächlich* 'in fact', *leider* 'unfortunately', *überraschenderweise* 'surprisingly', etc.) indicate the border between background and focus; cf. Lenerz (2001) and Haftka (1995, 2004).[19] The sentence adverbials themselves belong neither to the focus nor to the background, as they express epistemic meaning (cf. Lang 1979).

(20) a. Was ist passiert? – Peter sagt, ... ('What happened? – Peter says ...')
dass wahrscheinlich ein Kind einer Puppe ein BEIN
that probably a child a doll a leg
ausgerissen hat
torn_out *aux*$_p$

b. Was hat das Kind mit der Puppe gemacht? – Peter sagt, ...
('What did the child do to the doll?' – Peter says ...)
dass das Kind der Puppe wahrscheinlich ein BEIN ausgerissen
that the child the doll probably a leg torn_out
hat
aux$_p$

c. Was ist mit der Puppe passiert? – Peter sagt, ...
('What happened to the doll? – Peter says ...')
dass der Puppe wahrscheinlich ein Kind ein BEIN ausgerissen
that the doll probably a child a leg torn_out
hat
aux$_p$

d. Woher kommt denn dieses Bein? – Peter sagt, ...
('Where does this leg come from? – Peter says ...')
dass das Bein wahrscheinlich ein Kind einer PUPpe
that the leg probably a child a doll
ausgerissen hat
torn_out *aux*$_p$

The second claim is more controversial. In the literature, several different proposals have been made for the derivation of the word order variability in the German middlefield and its relation to information structure. One possibility is base generation. According to Abraham (1997, 2003, 2007), definite DPs are base-generated outside of VP rather than moved across the sentence adverbials. In addition to the fact that this contradicts the standard view taking all arguments to have their base positions within VP, a problem for Abraham's analysis is that the position of a definite DP or a pronoun within VP – e.g., the contrastively focused subject in (21) – must be derived by rightward movement (lowering) of the respective element (cf. Molnárfi 2007).

19. Similar proposals have been made by Frey (2000b, 2004b) and by Neeleman & Reinhart (1998) for Dutch. Frey considers all constituents to the left of the sentence adverbials to be aboutness topics, which is incompatible with our assumption that a sentence cannot have more than one aboutness topic.

(21) dass das Auto sicher der MANN / ER ausgesucht hat (..., und nicht
that the car surely the man / he chosen *aux*$_p$ and not
seine Frau)
his wife

Fanselow (2003a) goes one step further than Abraham in assuming that all observable argument orders in the middlefield are base-generated, i.e., that what has been called scrambling has nothing to do with movement at all. The problem with Fanselow's theory is that it obscures the relation between the word order variation in the middlefield and information structure. Fanselow has to abandon the concept of an unmarked constituent order. This makes it hard to explain why sentences not corresponding to this unmarked order are characterized by special information-structural properties and make greater demands on the context to be felicitously uttered.

The majority of the approaches employ some kind of leftward movement of background constituents to derive the syntactic partitioning into background and focus. Pursuing the minimalist idea that movement is always feature-driven, several authors claim that the moved constituents target specifiers of functional categories above VP, where they check uninterpretable features. Haftka (1994, 1995), for instance, considers the functional projections involved to be the agreement phrases originally proposed for case checking. Utilizing Chomsky's (1991) distinction between strong and weak features, she assumes that definite DPs must check case overtly, while indefinite DPs move to the agreement phrases only after spell-out, which explains the difference in the surface positions of definite and indefinite elements. The problem with this account, however, is that it incorrectly predicts that arguments to the left of the sentence adverbials always occur in the same order. In (22b), the order of the pronominal arguments is reversed compared to the variant with non-pronominal DPs, and in (23), both orders of the arguments are possible.[20] Moreover, as shown in (24) and (25), argument PPs and adverbials also take part in information structure driven movement, which cannot plausibly be explained as movement into agreement positions.

(22) a. dass der Puppe das Bein wahrscheinlich ein KIND ausgerissen
that the$_{dat}$ doll$_{dat}$ the$_{acc}$ leg$_{acc}$ probably a child torn_out
hat
aux$_p$

b. dass es ihr wahrscheinlich ein KIND ausgerissen hat
that it$_{acc}$ it$_{dat}$ probably a child torn_out *aux*$_p$

20. The actual order of the background elements in a sentence depends on several different but interacting factors. For optimality theoretic accounts of this phenomenon, see Müller (1999) and Haftka (2004).

(23) a. dass dem Mann die Lösung wahrscheinlich zu SPÄT
that the_{dat} man_{dat} the_{acc} $solution_{acc}$ probably too late
eingefallen ist
occurred aux_p

b. dass die Lösung dem Mann wahrscheinlich zu SPÄT
that the_{acc} $solution_{acc}$ the_{dat} man_{dat} probably too late
eingefallen ist
occurred aux_p

(24) a. dass wahrscheinlich ein Kind mit einer PUPpe gespielt hat
that probably a child with a doll played aux_p

b. dass damit wahrscheinlich ein KIND gespielt hat
that with_it probably a child played aux_p

(25) a. dass wahrscheinlich ein Mann in einem Wald ein FEUer gelegt
that probably a man in a forest a fire started
hat
aux_p

b. dass in dem Wald wahrscheinlich ein Mann ein FEUer gelegt hat
that in this forest probably a man a fire started aux_p

An alternative strategy is to introduce special categories with information-structural or semantic definitions (such as topicality, familiarity, or specificity) that attract the respective phrases; cf. Meinunger (1996, 2000), Frey (2000b, 2004b), Haftka (2004), Hinterhölzl (2004), and Frascarelli & Hinterhölzl (2007). These accounts, as well as Haftka's original proposal, face the problem that the movement operations to be explained are not always obligatory, which is unexpected in a minimalist theory of movement. Another counter-argument is given by Fanselow (2003a), who argues that information structure driven movement in the middlefield cannot be explained by feature checking, as it often has an altruistic character: "When one tries to identify the function of scrambling in German, one inevitably arrives at a *negative* formulation. A direct object is scrambled whenever the information structure linked with the clause either requires that a *different* expression is in focus, or that the object is *not* part of the focus." (Fanselow 2003a: 210) According to this view, a constituent does not move to satisfy its own needs, but to facilitate the assignment of the appropriate discourse status to the elements remaining in situ.

An approach combining Fanselow's insight with a feature-checking mechanism is suggested by Molnárfi (2003, 2004, 2007),[21] who assumes that definite DPs bear a so-called *antifocus* feature, which can be checked via movement to

21. See also Molnárfi (2002) and Abraham & Molnárfi (2002).

a functional projection above VP. The displacement of all phrases with this feature allows for the structural assignment of a neutral new information accent to the material within VP, following the rules specified by Cinque (1993).[22] While the movement of definite DPs is thus feature-driven in this model as well, its main effect concerns the elements that remain in situ, which are marked as focused by the sentence accent. The resulting derived word order is neutral in the sense that it is compatible with focus projection (cf. Höhle 1982).[23] Crucially, antifocus features are interpretable at the level of Phonological Form and therefore need not be checked before spell-out. The unchecked antifocus feature of a definite DP in situ results in a contrastive interpretation of this DP and blocks the neutral accent assignment. In this way, the occurrence of contrastively focused definite DPs and pronouns in their base positions within VP, as in (21) above, can be explained.

While this approach comes close to the view taken in the present study, it faces certain empirical problems. First of all, contrastively focused elements cannot only be found in their base positions within VP, but also to the left of the sentence adverbials (cf. Steube 2001). This remains unexplained by Molnárfi's theory, as the antifocus feature of a moved element should already be checked; as a consequence, it should have lost the ability to trigger a contrastive interpretation. Another problem of Molnárfi's approach has to do with the fact that it ties the presence of an antifocus feature to the definiteness of a phrase. As shown by Steube (2000) and Steube & Späth (2002),[24] there is only a correlation, but no one-to-one correspondence, between the definiteness/indefiniteness of a phrase and its information structural status. Under certain circumstances, which have to do with their reference, focused definites can remain in their base positions even without attracting contrastive focus; cf. (26). In these cases, they do not block focus projection, suggesting that their contextually determined discourse status rather than their lexical form is decisive for their position.

22. For a similar approach, see Zubizarreta (1998).

23. "While in Hungarian word order variation ensures that an element marked for focus gets its main stress in the prosodically prominent position at the left edge of the predicative part of the sentence, in German, scrambling for defocusing ensures maximal prosodic (and pragmatic) unmarkedness by removing all material which, on account of its referential or predicative properties, would block assignment of sentential stress and projection of wide focus. That is, to avoid unwanted pragmatic markedness, in West Germanic movement of definites is required towards the prosodically *least* prominent position in the middle field, which ensures that Cinque's (1993) Stress Assignment Rule works properly and wide focus is projected." (Molnárfi 2007: 175)

24. See also Steube & Späth (1998).

(26) dass wahrscheinlich ein Schüler den HAUSmeister beleidigt hat
that probably a pupil the janitor insulted *aux*$_p$

There are also cases of definites staying in their base positions without being focused (cf. Steube & Späth 2002; Haftka 2004): there is no difference in meaning or information structure between (27a) and (27b). While Molnárfi could deal with examples like (26) by stipulating that the definite DP for some reason does not bear an antifocus feature,[25] (27b) cannot be reconciled with his theory. As the DP *den Unfall* is definite and discourse-bound, it must be considered to bear an antifocus feature, which should either force it to move to the left or result in a contrastive interpretation. This prediction is not borne out; we are dealing with a case of true optionality here.[26]

(27) a. dass den Unfall bestimmt ein FUßgänger verursacht hat
that the accident certainly a pedestrian caused *aux*$_p$
b. dass bestimmt ein FUßgänger den Unfall verursacht hat

Examples like (27) show that theories based on feature checking – even in the modified variant of Molnárfi – must ultimately fail in their attempt to explain information structure driven movement in the German middlefield. We therefore follow Steube et al. in adopting a scrambling theory based on Rosengren (1993b, 1994) and Haider & Rosengren (1998), even if models like these are not in line with a strictly minimalist view of movement. It is assumed that arguments have base positions in a verb class specific order (cf. Haider 1993) and optionally leave these positions, left-adjoining to VP. The theory of scrambling employed here deviates from Haider & Rosengren's (1998) proposal in two respects. First, the concept of scrambling is applied not only to arguments, but also to adverbials, which are considered to have base positions defined by their c-command relations to arguments and other adverbials (cf. Frey & Pittner 1998; Frey 2000a, 2003). Second, no fundamental difference is made between scrambling of non-pronominal phrases and the movement of pronouns to the so-called *Wackernagel position* at the left edge of the middlefield (cf. Lenerz 1993). Unless they are used contrastively, anaphoric pronouns always belong to the background and therefore preferentially precede the sentence adverbials. But even in the case of pronouns, we find exceptional occurrences in the base positions, in particular after a non-pronominal subject, as in Lenerz' example (28).

25. See Molnárfi (2007: 176–178) for an argument along these lines.

26. See Haftka (2004: 136–138) for similar examples. In Dutch, definite objects also stay in their base positions in many cases (cf. van Bergen & de Swart 2009).

(28) weil ja wahrscheinlich gestern ein MÄDchen es ihm gegeben hat
because *mp* probably yesterday a girl it him given *aux*$_p$
(Lenerz 1993: 119)

The structure of the German clause according to the model described above is shown in the tree in (29), which is a slightly simplified version of the tree in Steube, Alter & Späth (2004: 27).[27] The rectangle indicates the focus domain, including the base positions of all arguments and adverbials except for the sentence adverbials.[28] The potential target positions of scrambling are located to the left of the sentence adverbials, following C^0.

(29)

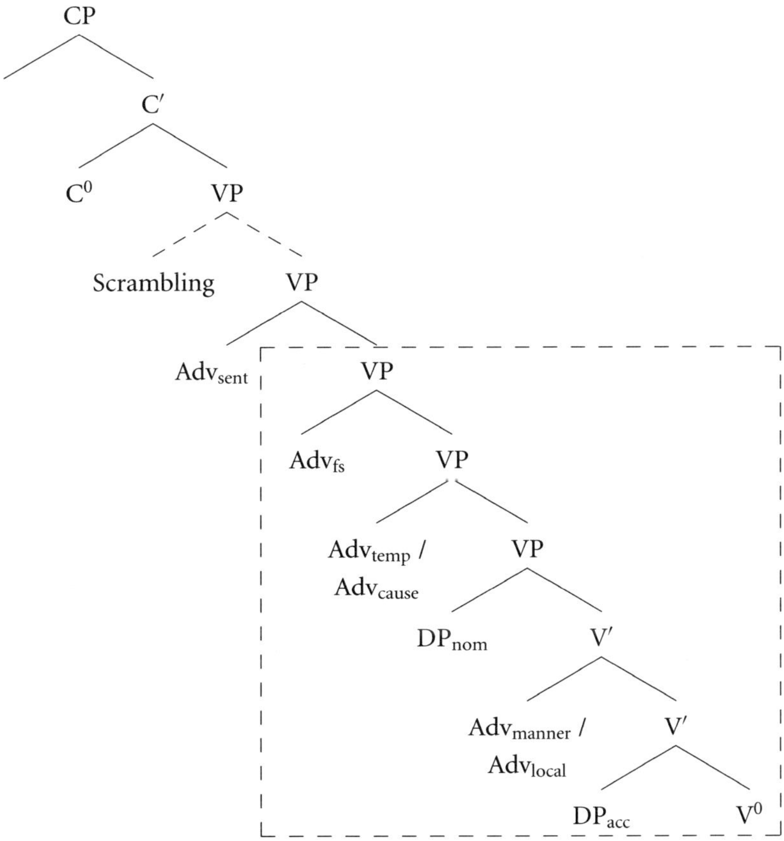

27. See also Steube (2006: 492). Adv$_{sent}$ = sentence adverbials, Adv$_{fs}$ = frame setting adverbials, Adv$_{temp}$ = temporal adverbials, Adv$_{cause}$ = causal adverbials, Adv$_{manner}$ = manner adverbials, Adv$_{local}$ = local adverbials.

28. For a more elaborate classification of adverbials and detailed assumptions about their base positions, see Frey (2003). For our purposes, the model shown in (29) is sufficient.

If we apply the model to the sentences in (20) above, they are assigned the structures given in (30). Here, the focus domain is indicated by the index [+F], attached to the labeled bracket corresponding to the left edge of the relevant VP-shell.

(30) a. dass [$_{VP}$ wahrscheinlich [$_{VP,[+F]}$ ein Kind einer Puppe ein BEIN
that probably a child a doll a leg
ausgerissen hat]]
torn_out aux_p

b. dass [$_{VP}$ [das Kind]$_i$ [$_{VP}$ [der Puppe]$_j$ [$_{VP}$ wahrscheinlich
that the child the doll probably
[$_{VP,[+F]}$ t_i t_j ein BEIN ausgerissen hat]]]]
a leg torn_out aux_p

c. dass [$_{VP}$ [der Puppe]$_i$ [$_{VP}$ wahrscheinlich [$_{VP,[+F]}$ ein Kind t_i
that the doll probably a child
ein BEIN ausgerissen hat]]]
a leg torn_out aux_p

d. dass [$_{VP}$ [das Bein]$_i$ [$_{VP}$ wahrscheinlich [$_{VP,[+F]}$ ein Kind einer
that the leg probably a child a
PUPpe t_i ausgerissen hat]]]
doll torn_out aux_p

From this syntactic representation, the focus-background partition of the sentence can be directly read off: the material within the focus domain is focused, and everything that has left the focus domain via movement to the left belongs to the background. However, this generalization does not hold without exception. In addition to the background constituents optionally remaining in the focus domain, there are several systematic exceptions, summarized in (17) above. On the one hand, certain background elements must stay in their base positions in the focus domain, as they are prevented from moving by independent syntactic principles. On the other hand, certain focused elements are forced to leave the focus domain. In the model of Steube and colleagues, background elements optionally or obligatorily remaining in the focus domain are marked with the index [–F], and focused elements outside the focus domain are indicated by the index [+F] on their traces in the base positions. In this way, only the exceptions from the default partitioning into background and focus are explicitly indicated in the syntactic representation.

Some examples are in order. The sentences in (31)–(33) show that the positions of the finite verb and the other verbal elements (such as participles) do not depend on their information-structural status (cf. Section 2.2). In the (a)-versions, which might be answers to a question such as *What does/did Maja do?*, the main verb is focused. This corresponds to its position in the focus domain in (31a) and (33a), the former being a VF-clause and the latter a V2-clause with an analytic tense, where the finite auxiliary instead of the main verb moves to the

V2-position.[29] In (32a), however, the main verb itself is forced to leave its base position. As it is focused, its trace in the focus domain is marked [+F]. In the (b)-versions of the examples, the main verb is defocused. The sentences answer a question such as *What does/did Maja buy?*, resulting in a minimal focus on the direct object. The position of the main verb is the same as in the (a)-examples, but now it must be marked [–F] in (31b) and (33b).

(31) a. dass Maja$_i$ wahrscheinlich [$_{VP,[+F]}$ t$_i$ eine GiTARre kauft]
that Maja probably a guitar buys
b. dass Maja$_i$ wahrscheinlich [$_{VP,[+F]}$ t$_i$ eine GiTARre kauft$_{[-F]}$]

(32) a. Maja$_i$ kauft$_j$ wahrscheinlich [$_{VP,[+F]}$ t$_i$ eine GiTARre t$_{j,[+F]}$] .
Maja buys probably a guitar
b. Maja$_i$ kauft$_j$ wahrscheinlich [$_{VP,[+F]}$ t$_i$ eine GiTARre t$_j$] .

(33) a. Maja$_i$ hat$_j$ wahrscheinlich [$_{VP,[+F]}$ t$_i$ eine GiTARre gekauft t$_j$] .
Maja *aux$_p$* probably a guitar bought.
b. Maja$_i$ hat$_j$ wahrscheinlich [$_{VP,[+F]}$ t$_i$ eine GiTARre gekauft$_{[-F]}$ t$_j$] .

The structure of the examples in (27) above is shown in (34). As the defocused direct object is located in the focus domain in (34b), it is marked [–F]. The sentences in (35) have a similar structure, but here, the relevant defocused element is a predicative. It is a well-known fact that predicatives, as well as directional and manner adverbials, resultative and depictive predicates, and infinite VPs, cannot scramble in German (cf. Steube 2003). As a consequence, (35a) is ungrammatical. The predicative must remain in its base position in the focus domain, even if it is defocused.[30]

(34) a. dass [den Unfall]$_i$ bestimmt [$_{VP,[+F]}$ ein FUßgänger t$_i$
that the accident certainly a pedestrian
verursacht$_{[-F]}$ hat]
caused *aux$_p$*
b. dass bestimmt [$_{VP,[+F]}$ ein FUßgänger [den Unfall]$_{[-F]}$ verursacht$_{[-F]}$ hat]

(35) a. *dass Papst$_i$ erstaunlicherweise [$_{VP,[+F]}$ ein DEUTscher t$_i$
that Pope astonishingly a German
geworden$_{[-F]}$ ist]
become *aux$_p$*
b. dass erstaunlicherweise [$_{VP,[+F]}$ ein DEUTscher Papst$_{[-F]}$ geworden$_{[-F]}$ ist]

29. The information-structural status of auxiliaries is ignored throughout this study.

30. However, (35a) is grammatical if *Papst* has the status of a contrastive topic in a so-called *bridge contour* construction and bears a rising prenuclear accent.

The sentences in (36) illustrate some possibilities to fill the prefield. The V2-property of German requires the finite verb to be preceded by exactly one constituent in German main clauses (cf. Section 2.2). However, grammar does not specify whether this constituent belongs to the focus or the background of the sentence. In (36a), it is a background constituent. In (36b), the minimally focused direct object has moved to the prefield, leaving a trace marked [+F] behind in its base position. In this case, the focus domain no longer contains any overt focused elements. The sentence adverbial *bestimmt* ('certainly'), which belongs neither to the background nor to the focus, occupies the prefield in (36c). (36d) is a fully focused sentence with the subject in the prefield.

(36) a. [Den Unfall]$_i$ hat$_j$ bestimmt [$_{VP,[+F]}$ ein Fußgänger t$_i$
the accident *aux$_p$* certainly a pedestrian
verursacht$_{[-F]}$ t$_j$] .
caused

b. [Ein Fußgänger]$_i$ hat$_j$ [den Unfall]$_k$ bestimmt [$_{VP,[+F]}$ t$_{i,[+F]}$ t$_k$
verursacht$_{[-F]}$ t$_j$] .

c. Bestimmt$_i$ hat$_j$ [den Unfall]$_k$ t$_i$ [$_{VP,[+F]}$ ein Fußgänger t$_k$ verursacht$_{[-F]}$
t$_j$] .

d. [Ein Fußgänger]$_i$ hat$_j$ bestimmt [$_{VP,[+F]}$ t$_{i,[+F]}$ einen UNFALL
a pedestrian *aux$_p$* certainly a accident
verursacht t$_j$] .
caused

To say that the prefield is not a designated position for background or focus constituents does not mean that it is not specified with respect to information structure at all. Prefield constituents are often topics, and they always play an important role for the creation of discourse coherence. The research on the conditions and characteristics of movement to the prefield in German is still in its early stages; for some recent proposals see Fanselow (2003b, 2004a, b), Frey (2004a, 2006), Speyer (2004, 2007), and Sternefeld (2006a, b).

The position of an element inside or outside the focus domain and the labels [+F] and [–F] marking exceptions from the default partitioning into the background and focus areas are directly relevant for the semantic composition. Semantic representations and syntactic surface structures are built up in a parallel fashion, and the syntactic position of an element corresponds to the place of its integration into the semantic structure (cf. Steube 2000; Steube, Alter & Späth 2004).[31] The labels [+F] and [–F] allow us to deal with the cases where the syntactic position does not reflect the information-structural status of an element. Focused

31. The necessary type-shifting operations are described in Partee (1987) and Zimmermann (1999).

constituents outside the focus domain, for instance, are interpreted in the position of their [+F]-marked traces. An exception is the verb, which is always interpreted in its base position, independently of whether it is focused or not. By means of the described mechanism, syntactic surface structures can be directly mapped onto semantic representations and the other way around, rendering a separate syntactic LF-level unnecessary (cf. Steube & Späth 2002).

We conclude this section with a few remarks on the assignment of the sentence accent and the nature of contrastive focus; cf. the claims in (18) and (19) above. The conception of the relation between focus and accentuation in the model of Steube and colleagues fundamentally differs from the view taken, e.g., by Selkirk (1984, 1995). In Selkirk's bottom-up model, focus depends on accent. The *Basic Focus Rule*, given in (37), assigns focus to accented words. The focus marking of larger constituents is achieved by the rules of *Focus Projection*, given in (38). The largest focus marked constituent of a sentence is the focus of this sentence. In other words, an accent on a certain word licenses the focus marking of a part of the relevant sentence, the maximum size of the focus being determined by phrase structural configurations.

(37) Basic Focus Rule
An accented word is F-marked.
(Selkirk 1995:555)

(38) Focus Projection
a. F-marking of the head of a phrase licenses the F-marking of the phrase.
b. F-marking of an internal argument of a head licenses the F-marking of the head.
c. F-marking of the antecedent of a trace left by NP- or *wh*-movement licenses the F-marking of the trace.
(Selkirk 1995:561)

This dependency is reversed in the theory of Rosengren (1993b). In her top-down model, a focus feature is freely assigned to a syntactic node and marks as focused all the material dominated by this node. The focus must be prosodically indicated by an accent, the location of which is determined by specific syntactic rules: in the standard case, the focus exponent is the most prominent syllable of the most deeply embedded verbal argument.[32] Thus, while phrase structure plays an important role in Rosengren's model as well, it determines the accent position (given a

32. "Fokussierung: Ein Fokusmerkmal wird einer syntaktischen oder morphologischen Konstituente frei zugewiesen. Mit dem Merkmal +F korrespondiert ein Prominenzmerkmal +P, das in PF einen oder mehrere Akzenttöne auslöst, die die overte Kennzeichnung von +F sind. Das Merkmal +F kann unter bestimmten Bedingungen projizieren. Wenn es nicht projizieren kann, ist das Ergebnis ein minimaler Fokus.

particular focus) rather than the potential size of the focus (given a particular accent position), as in Selkirk's account. In other words, while Selkirk's bottom-up theory models the view of the hearer, Rosengren's top-down theory takes up the perspective of the speaker.

Steube (2000) and Steube, Alter & Späth (2004) share Rosengren's (1993b) view that accentuation is a consequence of focus, and not the other way around. However, the authors additionally motivate focusing as pragmatically grounded and therefore need not assume that focus features are freely assigned in syntax. Lexical elements are already marked as focus or background when they enter the semantic composition and syntactic derivation. It is exactly this pragmatic characterization that – mediated by structural rules of accent assignment (cf. Cinque 1993; Jacobs 1988, 1992; Wiese 1996; Gibbon 1998) and the default focus domain in the middlefield – ultimately results in the specific prosodic realization of the sentence.[33] We dispense with giving additional examples of accent assignment, as the examples presented throughout this section already illustrate the range of relevant phenomena.

The view of the nature of contrastive focus in the model of Steube and colleagues is based on similar considerations. As opposed to the account of Molnárfi (2003, 2004, 2007), it is not seen as the result of a marked word order in the middlefield, but as a phenomenon with a pragmatic origin and specific grammatical consequences. Contrastive focus is represented by the feature [+CF], which is, like the feature [+F], assigned to lexical elements before they enter the grammatical system, and which overrides the normal focus-background partition. In most cases, the domain of contrastive focus is a single constituent, but it can also correspond to smaller or larger units, ranging from morphemes to whole sentences. The specific effects of contrastive focus at the individual levels of grammar differ from those of new information focus. Contrastive focus introduces its own characteristic meaning component (cf. Steube 2001; Späth 2007) and has special prosodic reflexes (cf. Alter, Mleinek, Rohe, Steube & Umbach 2001; see also Chapter 7 of the present study). In addition, contrastively focused elements have a higher positional variability than constituents characterized by narrow or wide new information

---

Fokusprojektion: Das Fokusmerkmal +F projiziert nach unten, wenn es einer dominierenden XP auf der Kopflinie des verbalen Kopfes zugewiesen und die relative Grundabfolge (d.h. die Basishierarchie der von +F dominierten Konstituenten) eingehalten wird. Es umfasst alles, was in seinem Dominanzbereich liegt. Das korrespondierende Merkmal +P liegt auf dem Fokusexponenten. Der Fokusexponent ist die am weitesten rechts liegende unterste verbselegierte Schwester von VP oder V′, wenn es eine solche gibt. Sonst wird +P nach bestimmten Prinzipien anderen XPs in VP zugewiesen." (Rosengren 1993b: 288–289)

33. For a similar account, see Erteschik-Shir (2006).

Table 2.1 Prosodic parameters in articulatory, acoustic, and auditory phonetics

articulatory phonetics	acoustic phonetics	auditory phonetics
vocal fold frequency	fundamental frequency	pitch
articulation time	duration	length
articulatory effort	intensity	loudness

focus; in particular, they can occur to the left of the sentence adverbials in the middlefield (cf. Steube 2001, 2003).

2.4 Prosody

The term *prosody* covers those properties of the speech signal that are tied not to individual segments, but to larger units, such as syllables or whole utterances. Following Alter (2002a), we use the term in a broad sense, referring both to the abstract phonological properties and to the concrete phonetic parameters by which they are realized. Three prosodic parameters play a central role in the experimental studies to be reported in Chapters 6 and 7: fundamental frequency (f_0), duration, and intensity. These linguistically relevant prosodic parameters are often called *suprasegmentals*; their articulatory and auditory correlates are summarized in Table 2.1 (cf. Lehiste 1970; Mayer 1997; Alter 2002a, c). From this classification, it follows that intonation, although the term is sometimes used synonymously with prosody, is only a proper subpart of the latter. It refers to those prosodic features realized by changes in fundamental frequency.

The phonological properties expressed by the mentioned prosodic parameters in intonation languages such as German are *prosodic phrasing* and *accentuation*. Prosodic phrasing is the partitioning of utterances into prosodically defined chunks of variable sizes, such as intonational and phonological/intermediate phrases. Accentuation concerns the distribution of pitch accents within these prosodic units, as well as the type of the accents. The description of the system of prosodic phonology is far from trivial: On the one hand, there is no one-to-one correspondence between phonological properties and the phonetic means of their realization. Both phrasing and accentuation arise from the complex interaction of several different factors. On the other hand, the discussed phonological properties cannot be directly mapped onto properties of other grammatical levels, or onto discourse-pragmatic and information-structural properties (cf. Alter 2002a: 23). Prosodic phrasing does not necessarily correspond to syntactic structure, and a particular pitch accent does not always mark the same information-structural category, just to mention two examples.

The theoretical framework serving as the basis for the prosodic investigations in the present study is the *Autosegmental-Metrical (AM) Theory* of prosodic phonology, initiated by Pierrehumbert's (1980) PhD thesis and further developed by Beckman & Pierrehumbert (1986), Pierrehumbert & Hirschberg (1990), and others.[34] It combines ideas of *Autosegmental Phonology* (cf. Goldsmith 1976) and *Metrical Phonology* (cf. Liberman & Prince 1977), theories dealing with the independent representation of segmental and suprasegmental information and with the determination of prominence relations on the basis of the hierarchical organization of prosodic domains, respectively.

One of the main claims of AM phonology is that *stress* and *accent* must be distinguished, and that the former can be defined independently of the latter. Stress, or prominence, results from the metrical structure of an utterance and is phonetically realized by means of a "greater force of articulation" (Ladd 1996: 58) or "greater articulatory care" (Gussenhoven 2004: 15). The interplay of the individual phonetic parameters considered to contribute to the perception of prominence – including duration, intensity,[35] vowel quality, and spectral tilt – is subject to ongoing debate. Crucially, fundamental frequency does not belong to this set of parameters. In earlier accounts, such as Bolinger (1958), the observation that perceived prominence is often accompanied by f_0-movements led to the view that the latter constitute prominence. In the AM model, however, f_0-movements are regarded as "prominence-cueing" rather than "prominence-lending" (Ladd 1996: 50).

The reason why f_0-movements can serve as cues to the location of stress becomes clear when we turn to the characteristics of accents. A pitch accent[36] is defined as an intonational event (i.e., a change in f_0) that is associated with a stressed syllable, which serves as its anchor point. While pitch accents are thus always accompanied by stress, the reverse is not always true. The last accent of an intonational phrase is called *nuclear accent*, and as intonational phrases usually correspond to whole sentences, the concept of nuclear accent can be treated as equivalent to the concept of sentence accent, which was already used in the previous section. Association of a pitch accent with a prominent syllable must be distinguished from *accent alignment* (cf. Ladd 1983b, 1996). While association is "the abstract structural property of 'belonging together' in some way", alignment is defined as "a *phonetic* property of the relative timing of events in the F_0 contour and events in the segmental string" (Ladd 1996: 55). Accent alignment is included in the prosodic analyses in Chapter 6 as a separate prosodic parameter.

---

34. The term *AM phonology* goes back to Ladd (1996), who also gives a comprehensive overview of this theory and its development.

35. Gussenhoven (2004) argues against the relevance of intensity for the realization of stress.

36. The terms *accent* and *pitch accent* are used synonymously.

Not all intonational events correspond to pitch accents. Changes of f_0, among other parameters, also contribute to the delimitation of prosodic constituents. The so-called *boundary tones* are not associated with prominent syllables, but with boundaries of intonational or intermediate phrases.

Another central claim of the AM model is that intonational patterns can be analyzed as sequences of high and low tones, indicated by H and L, respectively. These so-called *level tones* are the target points of f_0-movements, i.e., local f_0-maxima and -minima, and it is assumed that these targets, rather than the transitions between them, represent the relevant intonational primitives (cf. Bruce 1977). The two level tones may serve as high and low boundary tones, and they are the building blocks of pitch accents. In Pierrehumbert's (1980) original proposal, as well as in most later versions of the AM theory, pitch accents are either monotonal or bitonal, i.e., they consist of at least one, but not more than two level tones. The single tone of a monotonal accent, as well as one of the two tones of a bitonal accent, is associated with the stressed syllable; this tone is marked with an asterisk (*) following the H or L. The second tone in a bitonal accent is called *leading tone* if it precedes the starred tone and *trailing tone* if it follows it. If we assume that bitonal accents must consist of two different tones, this gives us six possible pitch accents: the high accent H* (peak), the low accent L* (valley), the two rising accents L*H and LH* (valley + peak), and the two falling accents H*L and HL* (peak + valley).

A further differentiation was achieved by introducing a separate feature for *downstep*, i.e., the phenomenon that the peak height of an H tone is often reduced relative to the peak height of a preceding H tone within the same intonational phrase. Ladd (1983b) argues that downstep is not a matter of phonetic realization, but a phonological phenomenon that must be included in the representation of intonational patterns.[37] As a convention, downstepped H tones are indicated by an exclamation mark preceding the H in monotonal and bitonal accents (e.g., !H* or L!H*). Crucially, as downstep can be iterated (each H tone is lowered relative to the immediately preceding one), it may serve as an explanation of the global downtrend of f_0 across utterances, i.e., *declination* (cf. Ladd 1996: Sections 2.4 and 3.3.1).

We conclude this brief overview of AM theory by mentioning two consequences of its view of prosodic phenomena. First, the phonological nature of prosodic entities implies that they combine to 'prosodic morphemes' with a constant meaning. Pitch accents are good candidates for such meaningful elements, and in the history of AM phonology, many attempts have been made to describe their meanings, usually in terms of information structure.[38] Second, a

37. For potential arguments against this claim, see Gussenhoven (2004: Chapter 6).

38. For a recent proposal, see Steedman (2000, 2007).

phonological theory of prosodic properties such as the AM model must be complemented by a theory of the phonetic implementation of the proposed phonological entities, of the mapping between "categorically distinct entities" and "continuously varying parameters" (Ladd 1996: 11). Abstract H and L tones, for instance, can be mapped onto f_0-values of an extremely broad spectrum, the concrete phonetic realization depending, among other factors, on the speaker, the language, and the paralinguistic meaning conveyed by the same signal. These issues cannot be dealt with in more detail here.[39]

The AM theory serves as the basis for a labeling system for English prosody called ToBI – *Tones and Break Indices* (cf. Silverman, Beckman, Pitrelli, Ostendorf, Wightman, Price, Pierrehumbert & Hirschberg 1992). This system is a set of conventions for the transcription of pitch accents and prosodic boundaries. On the model of the original ToBI system, several labeling standards for languages other than English have been developed, among them the German version GToBI (cf. Grice & Baumann 2002; Grice, Baumann & Benzmüller 2005).[40] The inventory of GToBI consists of six pitch accents (H*, L*, L*H, LH*, HL*, and H!H*), five boundary tones (high and low boundary tones associated with the right edge of intermediate (H- and L-) and intonational phrases (H% and L%) and a high boundary tone associated with the left edge of intonational phrases (%H)), and the break indices 3 and 4, corresponding to boundaries of intermediate and intonational phrases, respectively. It is further assumed that any H tone can be subject to downstep, which results in a number of additional pitch accents and boundary tones.

In Chapters 6 and 7 of the present study, a slightly modified version of GToBI is used for the classification of pitch accents.[41] We deviate from the original conventions specified by Grice et al. in two details. First, the accent H*L is included in the inventory. In GToBI, it is replaced by the combination of a high accent and a low boundary tone, i.e. H* L-. However, as noted by the authors themselves, this is still a controversial issue. Without going into the details of the theoretical discussion, we choose the 'simpler' notation used in traditional descriptions of German intonation such as Uhmann (1991) and Féry (1993). Second, downstep is dealt with independently from accent type. This reduces the number of descriptive categories and is in line with Ladd's (1996) claim that downstep and accent type must be kept apart: "The *shape* of accents can be expressed by means of the tonal

39. For discussion, see Ladd (1996) and Gussenhoven (2004).

40. GToBI is not the first attempt to describe German prosody within the framework of AM phonology. Other systems, mainly differing in their inventories of pitch accents and boundary tones, include Wunderlich (1988), Uhmann (1991), and Féry (1993).

41. As prosodic phrasing is immaterial to the issues to be discussed, boundary tones and break indices are neglected.

analysis (H*+L, H*, L*+H, etc.), but downstep must be treated as an independently selected 'feature' of each accent that can be present or absent independently of the choice of accent type itself." (Ladd 1996:91)

2.5 Summary

Figure 2.1 gives an overview of the relation between the modules of grammar dealt with in the previous sections. This model follows Steube et al.'s (2004) conception of grammatical modularity, assuming that lexical elements are combined to semantic representations, the *Semantic Forms* (cf. Bierwisch 1988, 1989), and that these are mapped onto morphosyntactic surface representations, which in turn serve as the input for the phonological system. Grammar as a whole is located between the conceptional-intentional (C-I) system and the articulatory-perceptual (A-P) system, its function being to establish a relation between meaning and sound. As mentioned above, information structure does not have the status of a separate module in this conception of grammar. It is represented by the pragmatically motivated features that enter the grammatical system together with the lexical elements, and its specific effects at the individual levels of grammar are considered to be triggered by these features.

In the remaining chapters of the present study, we will extend the presented model with a detailed description of the grammar of focus particles. We will look into the semantic, syntactic, and prosodic properties of focus particle constructions, as well as into the specific way focus particles interact with the information-structural features at each grammatical level.

C-I interface
↓
Lexicon
↓
Semantic Form
↓
Syntactic Surface Structure
↓
Phonological Form
↓
A-P interface

Figure 2.1 The structure of grammar according to Steube et al. (2004)

CHAPTER 3

The semantics of focus particles

This chapter gives a short overview of phenomena and theories related to the semantics of focus particles. Semantics is the aspect of the grammar of focus particles that has received the most attention and has been studied for the longest time.[1] For this reason, we will not offer new insights into this topic, but will instead summarize and compare the different approaches that can be found in the literature. As the meaning of focus particles is comparable across languages, we will not only consider works about German, but also relevant publications about other languages, mainly English and Dutch. In addition, some concepts and terminology relevant for the analyses to be presented in the subsequent chapters will be introduced.

Section 3.1 describes the factors that determine the contribution a focus particle makes to the meaning of a sentence. The remainder of the chapter is mainly devoted to the interaction between focus particles and the focus-background structure. Section 3.2 discusses how the meaning of constructions with focus particles can be derived compositionally with reference to focus. The two main frameworks, Alternative Semantics and Structured Meanings, are briefly compared, and the question is addressed as to what kind of meaning focus particles express. Section 3.3 deals with the lexical semantics of focus particles and their classification on the basis of semantic criteria.

3.1 Overview

It has often been noted that the meaning contribution of focus particles is variable. On the one hand, this is due to the different lexical meanings of the elements belonging to this class (cf. Section 3.3). On the other hand, the meaning of a sentence containing a focus particle varies with the focus-background partition of the sentence, its accentuation, and its word order (in particular, the relative order of the particle and other elements); cf. Taglicht (1984) and Jacobs (1983), among others.

1. The study of the meaning of *only*, for instance, goes back at least to the Middle Ages; cf. the overview given by Horn (1996).

Jacobs (1983) calls this dependency *Bezugsvariation* ('variation of reference') and identifies three relevant factors: focus, the scope of the particle, and its c-command domain.[2]

The interaction of focus particles with the focus-background structure, i.e., their focus sensitivity, is their key property. Focus particles establish a specific relation between the meaning of their domain and its relevant alternatives, where the particles' domain is equated with the focus (cf. Dimroth 2004; Hajičová, Partee & Sgall 1998a; König 1991a, c).[3] We can distinguish between a quantificational and a scalar use of focus particles (cf. Altmann 1976a; Bayer 1996; Helbig 1988; Jacobs 1983). Quantificational focus particles such as *nur* and *auch* in (1a) and (1b) quantify over the set of alternatives of the focus: (1a) says that Maja insulted Felix and that she did not insult any other contextually relevant person. In other words, the alternatives of Felix are excluded from the set of people that Maja insulted. (1b), on the other hand, says that Maja hugged Felix and that there is at least one proper alternative to Felix who was hugged by Maja. Scalar focus particles such as *sogar* in (1c) assign their domain an extreme position on a scale formed of its contextually relevant alternatives (cf. König 1991a, c). In the example, the speaker characterizes Felix as an unlikely person for Maja to invite.

(1)	a.	Maja	hat	nur	[FElix $]_F$	beleidigt.
		Maja	aux_p	only	Felix	insulted
	b.	Maja	hat	auch	[FElix $]_F$	umarmt.
		Maja	aux_p	also	Felix	hugged
	c.	Maja	hat	sogar	[FElix $]_F$	eingeladen.
		Maja	aux_p	even	Felix	invited

The comparison between the examples in (1) and (2) shows that the meaning contribution of focus particles depends on the (size of the) focus. If the focus is expanded to the entire material following the particle – which does not result in different word order or accentuation in this case – the specific meaning component introduced by the focus particle changes. Felix is no longer compared to other people, but Maja's actions are related to relevant alternative actions. (2a) says that Maja did not do anything other than insult Felix (e.g., she did not break the window), while (2b) tells us that, in addition to hugging Felix, Maja did something

2. See Jacobs (1982, 1991) for the interaction of these factors with negation.

3. For the time being, constructions with stressed additive particles, which present a problem to this assumption, are removed from consideration. For a discussion of this pattern, see Section 4.5. To ensure compatibility with the semantic literature on focus particles, the domain/focus of a particle is indicated by the index F throughout this chapter. See the remarks on terminology in Section 2.1.

else (e.g., she kissed Konrad). By (2c), inviting Felix is characterized as an unlikely action for Maja to carry out.

(2) a. Maja hat nur [FElix beleidigt]$_F$.
Maja *aux*$_p$ only Felix insulted
b. Maja hat auch [FElix umarmt]$_F$.
Maja *aux*$_p$ also Felix hugged
c. Maja hat sogar [FElix eingeladen]$_F$.
Maja *aux*$_p$ even Felix invited

The focus thus determines the part of the sentence that is 'semantically affected' by a focus particle. In most cases, of course, a change of the focus is accompanied by a change in the location of the accent and/or a change in word order.[4]

The scope of a focus particle is characterized by König (1991c: 31) as "the semantic counterpart of that part of a sentence that is relevant for spelling out [the particle's] contribution." In other words, what is meant by scope is the scope of the operator corresponding to the focus particle (one of the quantifiers ∃ and ∀; see below) in the semantic representation of the sentence (cf. Jacobs 1983: 9). The effect of a particle's scope on the meaning of a sentence can best be illustrated by some examples. Although (3a) and (3b) are parallel in structure, (3a) can be paraphrased by (4a), but (3b) cannot be paraphrased by (4b).

(3) a. Maja hat nur [die SeMANtikklausur]$_F$ bestanden.
Maja *aux*$_p$ only the semantics_exam passed
b. Mindestens 3 Studenten haben nur [die SeMANtikklausur]$_F$ bestanden.
At_least 3 students *aux*$_p$ only the semantics_exam passed

(4) a. Only for x = semantics exam: Maja passed x.
b. Only for x = semantics exam: At least 3 students passed x.
c. For at least 3 students: Only for x = semantics exam: They passed x.

Sentence (3b) can still be true if four students passed the exam in syntax. What is important is that there are at least three students who passed no exam apart from that in semantics. The correct paraphrase for (3b) is thus (4c). The difference between (3a) and (3b) is not due to the focus-background partition, which is identical in the two sentences. Rather, the difference is that *Maja* is in the scope of *nur* in the former example, while *mindestens 3 Studenten* ('at least 3 students') in the latter is not, the reason being that *mindestens 3 Studenten*, in contrast to *Maja*,

4. For an optimality theoretic account of the identification of the element associated with a focus particle on the basis of word order and (de-)accentuation, see Hendriks (2004).

is a scope-bearing element itself. Therefore, its syntactic position relative to the focus particle is decisive for the scope relations.

A similar phenomenon can be observed in complex sentences like those in (5). Here, the interpretation depends on whether the focus particle is located in the matrix clause or in the embedded clause. The paraphrases for (5a) and (5b), which again have an identical focus, are given in (6a) and (6b), respectively.

(5) a. Ich hoffe nur, dass [MAja]$_F$ singt.
    I hope only that Maja sings
  b. Ich hoffe, dass nur [MAja]$_F$ singt.

(6) a. Only for x = Maja: I hope that x sings.
  b. I hope: Only for x = Maja: x sings.

In (5b), *nur* does not have scope over the matrix verb *hoffen* ('to hope'). Thus, by uttering this sentence, the speaker expresses the hope that no one apart from Maja sings. The scope of the particle is restricted to the embedded clause. In (5a), on the other hand, *nur* has scope over the matrix verb, resulting in the interpretation that the only proposition of the form *x sings* of which the speaker hopes that it is true is the proposition *Maja sings*.

The above examples show that the scope of a focus particle is relevant for the interpretation of a sentence if this sentence contains other scope-bearing elements (such as quantificational DPs) or if there are syntactic nodes that restrict the scope of the particle (such as the CP node of an embedded clause). These phenomena will be dealt with in Chapter 5. In the remainder of this chapter and in Chapter 4, problems of scope are removed from consideration. This is achieved by restricting the attention to simplex sentences without scope-bearing elements apart from the focus particles themselves. We assume that in this subset of constructions with focus particles, the particle always has scope over the whole sentence.

The third factor identified by Jacobs (1983), the c-command domain of the focus particle, does not affect the meaning of the respective sentence directly. Instead, it influences the scoping options of the particle and constrains the distribution of focus and background. The interaction between the c-command domain of a focus particle and its focus will be extensively discussed in Chapter 4; the interaction between c-command and scope will be looked at in Chapter 5. The remainder of this chapter deals with the question of how focus particles interact with the focus structure of sentences, i.e., to what extent their meaning contribution depends on the focus and how this dependency can be theoretically modeled.

3.2 Compositional semantics: Association with focus

Since Jackendoff (1972), the relation between a focus particle and the corresponding focus has been known under the term *association with focus*: the particle associates with a focus (i.e., one or more focused elements), which plays a crucial role in explicating what the particle contributes to the meaning of the sentence. In other words, the meaning of the particle must somehow refer to the meaning of the focus. If the sentence meaning were derived without reference to the focus, the difference between the sentences in (1) and the corresponding sentences in (2) above could not be accounted for. But what exactly does *association with focus* mean? How can a focus particle identify the (size of the) focus? Rooth's (1985) PhD thesis is only one attempt to describe the nature of the relation between a focus particle and its associated focus. In the following subsection, we will give a brief overview of the different theoretical approaches to association with focus (or focus sensitivity) that can be found in the literature.

3.2.1 Syntactic, semantic, and pragmatic theories

Theories of association with focus can be classified into syntactic, semantic, and pragmatic theories, depending on the way they describe the relation between a focus particle and its focus.[5] Syntactic theories, such as Anderson (1972), Chomsky (1976), Drubig (1994), Karttunen & Peters (1979), and Sgall, Hajičová & Panevová (1986), assume that a focus particle and its focus must form a constituent or appear in a specific configuration (e.g., a spec-head configuration) at some level of syntactic structure. However, the relevant syntactic level cannot be surface structure, as focus particles frequently do not occur in positions fulfilling the proposed requirements. This is particularly obvious in English, where focus particles associated with the direct object can precede the finite verb instead of occurring adjacent to the focus; cf. (7a). As the same surface-syntactic configuration is compatible with a domain that includes the finite verb – cf. (7b) – the intended association cannot directly be read off from surface word order.

(7) a. Maja only hugged [FElix]$_F$.
b. Maja only [hugged FElix]$_F$.

Therefore, syntactic theories of association with focus either assume that the relevant restrictions must be fulfilled at some underlying structural level and that the particle is subsequently moved to its surface position, or that the required

5. For surveys of the relevant literature, see Aloni, Beaver & Clark (1999), Beaver & Clark (2003), Kratzer (1991), Krifka (2004a), Rooth (1992), and von Stechow (1991a).

configuration is only formed after surface structure has been spelled out, e.g., by LF movement. In both cases, semantic interpretation is based on this configuration, which syntactically encodes association with focus. The described syntactic theories have been subject to much criticism, mainly for two reasons (cf. Rooth 1985; Bayer 1996). First, they cannot straightforwardly account for cases where a focus particle is associated with more than one constituent. Second, the involved movement operations must be of a special type, as they violate well-established syntactic principles such as Ross' (1967) island constraints.[6]

Semantic and pragmatic theories of association with focus are similar in that they do not presuppose a certain syntactic configuration that identifies the element(s) associated with a focus particle.[7] This renders it unnecessary to employ the movement operations mentioned above, which is why the relevant theories are often called *in-situ theories* of association with focus. In semantic theories, such as Jackendoff (1972), Jacobs (1983), Rooth (1985), König (1991c), and Krifka (1992a, b, 1993), different focus-background partitions of a given structure in the scope of a focus particle give rise to different semantic representations of that structure. When these representations are combined with the semantic representation of the particle, the encoded information about focus and background can be used to specify the meaning contribution of the particle (cf. Section 3.2.2). Association with focus is thus seen as a phenomenon of compositional semantics.[8]

Pragmatic theories of association with focus are represented by Rooth (1992) and von Fintel (1994).[9] Unlike semantic accounts, these theories do not assume a direct, grammatical link between focus and semantics. Rather, it is argued that the interpretation of a focus particle, or more precisely, its domain, is specified pragmatically, and that focus is only one factor influencing this specification: "The null hypothesis about such phenomena [focus sensitivity] is this: the pragmatics is seen to supply the value of a free variable quantifier domain and various factors, among them topic/focus-articulation and presuppositional information, are simultaneously at play that function as partial clues as to what domain is intended. There are no rules of grammar that make reference to focus or presuppositions." (von Fintel 1994: 36) This approach predicts that association with focus is not

6. For more recent accounts defending the syntactic approach to association with focus against this criticism, see Drubig (1994) and Krifka (2006).

7. A syntactic requirement assumed in some form by most theories is that the particle c-commands its domain. However, this constraint, which goes back to Jackendoff (1972), does not ensure the possibility of a structural identification of the domain; cf. (1) and (2) again.

8. Of course, this point of view is not per se incompatible with the syntactic approaches presented above. See Krifka (2006) for a combination of a syntactic and a semantic approach.

9. See also von Fintel (2004).

obligatory. Focus may, but need not, play a role in restricting the domain of quantification; if it does, this is achieved only indirectly by an anaphoric link between a variable introduced by focus and a free variable in the lexical meaning of the focus sensitive operator (cf. Rooth 1992). As a consequence, different focus-background partitions of the scope of a focus particle do not result in different semantic representations: "In association with focus, according to the free parameter hypothesis, things (the semantic values of phrases in LF or in an analysis tree) are put together in just one way, resulting in a meaning with a free parameter which can be constrained using focus." (Rooth 1992: 97–98)[10]

While Rooth (1985) is a semantic theory of association with focus, Rooth (1992) is a pragmatic theory, although both belong to the same theoretical framework, namely, Alternative Semantics (cf. Section 3.2.2.1). This difference corresponds to Rooth's (1992: 107–108) distinction between a weak theory, "one which [...] leaves it to particular lexical items or semantic interpretive rules to say how focus is used semantically", and a strong theory of association with focus, "a theory which does not contemplate construction-specific stipulation of focus effects". In addition, Rooth (1992: 110–112) considers an intermediate theory saying that association with focus is obligatory in some cases, but not in others.[11]

The last-named idea can also be found in a series of papers by David Beaver and colleagues (cf. Aloni, Beaver & Clark 1999; Beaver & Clark 2002a, b, 2003; Beaver 2004). The authors argue that expressions analyzed as focus sensitive in the literature do not form a homogeneous class and that different mechanisms are at work in two subclasses of these elements. Beaver et al. compare the focus particle *only* to the quantificational adverbial *always*. The examples in (8) and (9) show that the two expressions have a similar meaning (represented by the universal quantifier) and seemingly exhibit comparable effects of focus sensitivity.

(8) a. Sandy always feeds [Fido]$_F$ Nutrapup.
    b. Sandy only feeds [Fido]$_F$ Nutrapup.
    c. $\forall$x [feed(sandy,x,nutrapup) $\rightarrow$ x = fido]
       'Everything Sandy feeds Nutrapup to is Fido.'
    (Beaver & Clark 2003: 325)

(9) a. Sandy always feeds Fido [Nutrapup]$_F$.
    b. Sandy only feeds Fido [Nutrapup]$_F$.

10. As the domain of a focus particle can influence the truth conditions of a sentence (cf. Sections 3.2.2 and 3.2.4), pragmatic accounts of association-with-focus phenomena pose problems for the traditional view of the semantics-pragmatics distinction identifying the subject of semantics with the truth-conditional content of sentences. For a general discussion of this issue, see Levinson (2000) and Carston (2004a, b, c).

11. See also Hajičová & Sgall (2004).

c. $\forall x$ [feed(sandy,fido,x) $\rightarrow$ x = nutrapup]
'Everything Sandy feeds to Fido is Nutrapup.'
(Beaver & Clark 2003: 325)

However, unlike *only*, *always* occurs in constructions where it is not associated with focus. In (10), it shows the so-called *association-with-presupposition* effect discussed by Rooth (1999). This is not possible for *only*; cf. (11).

(10) Mary always managed to complete her [EXAMS]$_F$.
a. 'Whenever Mary took exams, she completed them.'
b. ?'Whenever Mary completed something, it was invariably an exam.'
(Beaver & Clark 2003: 335)

(11) Mary only managed to complete her [EXAMS]$_F$.
a. *'What Mary did when taking exams was complete them and do nothing else.'
b. 'What Mary completed was an exam and nothing else.'
(Beaver & Clark 2003: 335)

Beaver et al. argue that the observed non-obligatory focus sensitivity of *always* calls for a pragmatic account. The application of such an account to *only*, on the other hand, is demonstrated to be highly problematic. From a broad range of data (e.g., the fact that *only* cannot associate with weak pronouns or extracted elements), the authors conclude that association with focus is obligatory for *only* and must be grounded in the lexical meaning of the particle: "At a more general level, anyone advancing a purely pragmatic theory of focus sensitivity has a lot of explaining to do in cases where configurational changes in a sentence, e.g., changes resulting from extraction, have a dramatic effect on the interpretation of a focus sensitive operator." (Beaver & Clark 2003: 347)

As Beaver and colleagues convincingly show, focus sensitive expressions must be split into two categories. In one subgroup, including *only*, focus sensitivity is based on a grammatical mechanism. These expressions are *focus functional* operators. In the other subgroup, including *always*, effects of focus sensitivity result from pragmatic processes. These expressions are *non-focus-functional.* A unified account of these two categories of expressions, such as Koktova (1987), fails to explain the relevant differences. In the following, we assume that at least the core cases of focus particles examined here (*nur*, *auch*, *sogar*) belong to the group of focus functional operators and that their focus sensitivity can best be described in a semantic framework.[12] In the next subsection, two influential semantic theories

12. For additional data supporting this claim, see Shaer (2004) and Geilfuß-Wolfgang (1996: 14–16).

of association with focus will be introduced in more detail: Alternative Semantics and Structured Meanings.

3.2.2 *John only introduced Bill to Sue*: Alternative Semantics and Structured Meanings

Rooth (1996) summarizes the general program of semantic theories of association with focus as follows: "We somehow modify our way of modeling the semantics of phrases so that phrases differing in the location of focus have different semantic values. We then state semantic and pragmatic rules for focus sensitive constructions and discourse configurations in terms of such focus-influenced semantic values." (Rooth 1996: 275)[13] Alternative Semantics and Structured Meanings are two theoretical frameworks that realize this program in different ways. While Alternative Semantics introduces additional focus semantic values, Structured Meanings directly represents the focus-background partition by dividing semantic representations into a focus part and a background part.

3.2.2.1 *Alternative Semantics*

The basic idea behind Alternative Semantics as introduced by Rooth (1985)[14] is that focus evokes alternatives. In a sentence like (12), the focus on *Felix* signals that alternatives to *Felix*, but not to *Maja* or *kissed*, are under consideration.

(12) Maja kissed [FElix]$_F$.

This intuition is incorporated into the theory by assigning every linguistic expression α two different denotations: its ordinary semantic value $[[\ \alpha\ ]]^o$ and its focus semantic value $[[\ \alpha\ ]]^f$. The focus semantic value of an expression α is a set of denotations with the same type as α's ordinary semantic value, a so-called *p-set* or *alternative set*. This set is obtained from $[[\ \alpha\ ]]^o$ by substituting the parts corresponding to focused expressions in α by elements of the same semantic type. Rooth (1985: 14) recursively defines focus semantic values along the following lines: If α is a focused expression, its focus semantic value is the domain of the type of $[[\ \alpha\ ]]^o$;

---

13. The idea goes back to Dretske (1972: 412): "If *C(U)* is a linguistic expression in which *U* is embedded, and *U* can be given different contrastive foci (say U_1 and U_2), then it often makes a difference to the meaning of *C(U)* whether we embed U_1 or U_2. Linguistically this is important because it means that any adequate semantical theory, one that is capable of exhibiting the source of semantical differences between complex expressions, between $C(U_1)$ and $C(U_2)$, will have to be provided with the resources for distinguishing between U_1 and U_2."

14. What we present here is a simplified version of Rooth's (1985) theory. For reasons of brevity and readability, we disregard intensionality, and the formal conventions employed are those of Rooth (1992, 1996) rather than those used in the original version of the theory.

cf. (13a). As non-focused expressions do not evoke alternatives, the focus semantic value of a simple non-focused element is the singleton set of its ordinary semantic value; cf. (13b). The focus semantic value of a complex non-focused expression is obtained by combining the focus semantic values of its components; cf. (13c). The ordinary semantic value is insensitive to focus, thus $[[\ \alpha_F\ ]]^o = [[\ \alpha\ ]]^o$.

(13) a. $[[\ \alpha_F\ ]]^f = D_{type([[\ \alpha\ ]]^o)}$
b. $[[\ \alpha\ ]]^f = \{[[\ \alpha\ ]]^o\}$
c. $[[\ \alpha(\beta)\ ]]^f = \{A(B) \mid A \in [[\ \alpha\ ]]^f, B \in [[\ \beta\ ]]^f\}$

With respect to the example in (12), this definition yields the semantic values given in (14).

(14) $[[$ Maja $]]^o$ = maja $[[$ Maja $]]^f$ = {maja}
$[[$ FElix$_F$ $]]^o$ = felix $[[$ FElix$_F$ $]]^f$ = {felix, maja, phillip, henry, ...}
$[[$ kissed $]]^o$ = λyλxKISS(x,y) $[[$ kissed $]]^f$ = {λyλxKISS(x,y)}
$[[$ kissed [FElix $]_F$ $]]^o$ = λxKISS(x,felix)
$[[$ kissed [FElix $]_F$ $]]^f$ = {λxKISS(x,felix), λxKISS(x,maja), λxKISS(x,phillip), λxKISS(x,henry), ...}
$[[$ Maja kissed [FElix $]_F$ $]]^o$ = KISS(maja,felix)
$[[$ Maja kissed [FElix $]_F$ $]]^f$ = {KISS(maja,felix), KISS(maja,maja), KISS(maja,phillip), KISS(maja,henry), ...}

How do focus semantic values help us in explaining the focus sensitivity of particles such as *only*? Rooth (1985: Chapter 3) analyzes focus particles as crosscategorial operators, i.e., operators that can be combined with elements of different types. This is achieved by defining a basic operator operating on propositions for each particle, from which a crosscategorial family of operators can be derived. The basic operator for *only* is given in (15) (cf. Rooth 1985: 120).

(15) $[[\ only_S\ ]] = \lambda p\ [\ p\ \&\ \forall q\ [\ (\ q \in C\ \&\ q\ ) \rightarrow q = p\ ]]$

According to (15), *only* applied to a proposition p means that p is true and that all true propositions q from a set C of propositions are identical to p.[15] C is the domain-of-quantification variable of the operator; it denotes the set of elements the operator quantifies over. The corresponding operator for *only* adjoined to VP is given in (16). According to this definition, *only* applied to a property P denotes the set of individuals that have P and no other properties from the set C.

(16) $[[\ only_{VP}\ ]] = \lambda P \lambda x\ [\ P(x)\ \&\ \forall Q\ [\ (\ Q \in C\ \&\ Q(x)\ ) \rightarrow Q = P\ ]]$

15. For the time being, we are not differentiating between assertion and presupposition. See Section 3.2.4.

Crucially, the domain-of-quantification variable C must somehow be constrained. What kinds of other propositions or properties are excluded by *only*? We already know that it must be the focus that controls this domain restriction. Here, the focus semantic value comes into play. Focus is interpreted at the level of the phrase *only* is adjoined to, i.e., the focus semantic value of the particle's sister constituent is computed. Then, C is simply identified with this focus semantic value. As a consequence, *only* quantifies over the alternatives evoked by the focus. The alternative set is only a subset of the set of elements matching the denotation of the particle's sister constituent in type. This mechanism is illustrated by Rooth's well-known examples in (17).

(17) a. John only introduced [BILL $]_F$ to Sue.
b. John only introduced Bill to [SUE $]_F$.

The two variants have distinct truth conditions. In a situation where John introduced Bill to Sue and Mary and no other introductions took place, (17a) is true and (17b) is false. This must be reflected in the semantic representation. (18) shows the derivation of the meaning of (17a). As *only* is arguably adjoined to VP here, we use the operator given in (16).

(18) $[\![$ John $]\!]^o$ = john $[\![$ John $]\!]^f$ = {john}
$[\![$ BILL$_F$ $]\!]^o$ = bill $[\![$ BILL$_F$ $]\!]^f$ = {bill, john, sue, mary, ...}
$[\![$ Sue $]\!]^o$ = sue $[\![$ Sue $]\!]^f$ = {sue}
$[\![$ introduced $]\!]^o$ = λzλyλxINTR(x,y,z)
$[\![$ introduced $]\!]^f$ = {λzλyλxINTR(x,y,z)}
$[\![$ introduced [BILL $]_F$ to Sue $]\!]^o$ = λxINTR(x,bill,sue)
$[\![$ introduced [BILL $]_F$ to Sue $]\!]^f$
= {λxINTR(x,bill,sue), λxINTR(x,john,sue), λxINTR(x,sue,sue), λxINTR(x,mary,sue), ...}
$[\![$ only introduced [BILL $]_F$ to Sue $]\!]^o$
= λx [INTR(x,bill,sue) & ∀Q [(Q ∈ $[\![$ introduced [BILL $]_F$ to Sue $]\!]^f$ & Q(x)) → Q = λxINTR(x,bill,sue)]]
= λx [INTR(x,bill,sue) & ∀Q [(Q ∈ {λxINTR(x,bill,sue), λxINTR(x,john,sue), λxINTR(x,sue,sue), λxINTR(x,mary,sue), ...} & Q(x)) → Q = λxINTR(x,bill,sue)]]
$[\![$ John only introduced [BILL $]_F$ to Sue $]\!]^o$
= INTR(john,bill,sue) & ∀Q [(Q ∈ $[\![$ introduced [BILL $]_F$ to Sue $]\!]^f$ & Q(john)) → Q = λxINTR(x,bill,sue)]
= INTR(john,bill,sue) & ∀Q [(Q ∈ {λxINTR(x,bill,sue), λxINTR(x,john,sue), λxINTR(x,sue,sue), λxINTR(x,mary,sue), ...} & Q(john)) → Q = λxINTR(x,bill,sue)]

(19) shows the result of the corresponding derivation for (17b). As can be seen, the two representations differ in the domain of quantification of the focus particle. This gives us the desired difference in truth conditions.

(19) $[\![$ John only introduced Bill to [Sue $]_F$ $]\!]^o$
$= \text{INTR}(\text{john,bill,sue}) \mathbin{\&} \forall Q\, [\, (\, Q \in [\![$ introduced Bill to [Sue $]_F$ $]\!]^f \mathbin{\&} Q(\text{john})\,) \rightarrow Q = \lambda x\text{INTR}(x,\text{bill,sue})\,]$
$= \text{INTR}(\text{john,bill,sue}) \mathbin{\&} \forall Q\, [\, (\, Q \in \{\lambda x\text{INTR}(x,\text{bill,sue}), \lambda x\text{INTR}(x,\text{bill,bill}), \lambda x\text{INTR}(x,\text{bill,john}), \lambda x\text{INTR}(x,\text{bill,mary}), \ldots\} \mathbin{\&} Q(\text{john})\,) \rightarrow Q = \lambda x\text{INTR}(x,\text{bill,sue})\,]$

3.2.2.2 *Structured Meanings*

While the basic idea of the Structured Meanings approach goes back to Jackendoff's (1972) *presuppositional sets*, the theory itself was developed and applied to focus particles in various publications by von Stechow, Krifka, and Jacobs, among others (cf. von Stechow 1991b; Krifka 1992a, b, 1993; Jacobs 1983). Unlike Alternative Semantics, the Structured Meanings approach does not employ a second semantic value to represent the focus-background partition in semantics; instead, the regular semantic representation is divided into a background part and a focus part. The meaning of an expression containing a focus is represented as a pair of meanings $\langle\alpha, \beta\rangle$, where α corresponds to the background and β to the focus of the expression. As α is derived from the standard denotation by λ-abstracting over the element in focus, α can be applied to β, yielding the standard denotation $\alpha(\beta)$ again.

As the information about the focus-background partition of an expression must be preserved in the course of the semantic composition, functional application must be redefined to capture focus-background structures (cf. Krifka 1992a). The most important rules, application of a simple denotation A to a structured meaning $\langle\alpha, \beta\rangle$ and application of a structured meaning $\langle\alpha, \beta\rangle$ to a simple denotation A, are given in (20). Krifka (1992a:25) also gives a rule for cases where both the functor and the argument are structured meanings of the form $\langle\alpha, \beta\rangle$.

(20) a. $A(\langle\alpha, \beta\rangle) = \langle\lambda X\, [\, A(\alpha(X))\,]\,, \beta\rangle$
b. $\langle\alpha, \beta\rangle(A) = \langle\lambda X\, [\, \alpha(X)(A)\,]\,, \beta\rangle$

With these rules, the meaning of (12) above, repeated here as (21), can be derived as demonstrated in (22). If we apply the background to the focus in the last line of (22), we get the regular denotation KISS(maja,felix).

(21) Maja kissed [FElix $]_F$.

(22) $[\![$ Maja $]\!]$ = maja
$[\![$ FElix$_F$ $]\!] = \langle\lambda y\, [\, y\,]\,, \text{felix}\rangle$
$[\![$ kissed $]\!] = \lambda y \lambda x \text{KISS}(x,y)$

$[\![$ kissed [Felix $]_F$ $]\!]$ = ⟨λyλxkiss(x,y) , felix⟩
$[\![$ Maja kissed [Felix $]_F$ $]\!]$ = ⟨λykiss(maja,y) , felix⟩

How does the theory account for the meaning contribution of focus particles? They are translated into operators operating on structured meanings of the form ⟨α, β⟩. In other words, they take two arguments: the background and the focus of the expression they are combined with. As in Alternative Semantics, we need different operators for focus particles in different syntactic positions. (23) shows the propositional operator for the particle *only*, and (24) the operator corresponding to *only* adjoined to VP. Here, alt is a function that yields the set of alternatives of its argument. *Only* applied to a structured proposition consisting of a background α and a focus β means that α applied to β is true and that all alternatives to β that yield a true proposition when α is applied to them are identical to β.

(23) $[\![\text{only}_S]\!] = \lambda\langle\alpha,\beta\rangle\ [\ \alpha(\beta)\ \&\ \forall A\ [\ (\ A \in \text{ALT}(\beta)\ \&\ \alpha(A)\ ) \rightarrow A = \beta\ ]]$
(24) $[\![\text{only}_{VP}]\!] = \lambda\langle\alpha,\beta\rangle\lambda x\ [\ \alpha(\beta)(x)\ \&\ \forall A\ [\ (\ A \in \text{ALT}(\beta)\ \&\ \alpha(A)(x)\ ) \rightarrow A = \beta\ ]]$

How does the Structured Meanings approach handle Rooth's examples in (17), repeated in (25)? The meaning derivation for (25a) is given in (26); the result of the derivation for (25b) is shown in (27). The operator used for the representation of *only* is (24). As with the mechanism provided by Alternative Semantics, we ultimately get different truth conditions for the two sentences.

(25) a. John only introduced [Bill $]_F$ to Sue.
b. John only introduced Bill to [Sue $]_F$.

(26) $[\![$ John $]\!]$ = john
$[\![$ Bill_F $]\!]$ = ⟨λy [y] , bill⟩
$[\![$ Sue $]\!]$ = sue
$[\![$ introduced $]\!]$ = λzλyλxintr(x,y,z)
$[\![$ introduced [Bill $]_F$ to Sue $]\!]$ = ⟨λyλxintr(x,y,sue) , bill⟩
$[\![$ only introduced [Bill $]_F$ to Sue $]\!]$
= λx [intr(x,bill,sue) & ∀y [(y ∈ alt(bill) & intr(x,y,sue)) →
y = bill]]
$[\![$ John only introduced [Bill $]_F$ to Sue $]\!]$
= intr(john,bill,sue) & ∀y [(y ∈ alt(bill) & intr(john,y,sue)) →
y = bill]

(27) $[\![$ John only introduced Bill to [Sue $]_F$ $]\!]$
= intr(john,bill,sue) & ∀z [(z ∈ alt(sue) & intr(john,bill,z)) →
z = sue]

3.2.2.3 *Comparison*

According to the Structured Meanings approach, the meaning of a focus particle has direct access to the meaning of the focus and the meaning of the background. They can be seen as arguments of the particle, which quantifies over the alternatives of the focus. It was shown above, for instance, that *only*, applied to a structured proposition, means that the focus, but no other element from its set of alternatives, yields a true proposition when combined with the background. In Alternative Semantics, focus and background are not directly accessible to the operator. Instead, association with focus is mediated by the focus semantic value of the element the particle is applied to. The operator establishes a relation between the ordinary semantic value and the focus semantic value of this element, which contains the focus, but need not be identical to it. In this view, propositional *only* says that a proposition p, but no other proposition in its set of alternatives, is true, the nature of this set being determined by the focus of the sentence corresponding to p. In both theories, a range of operators for focus particles combining with elements of other semantic types can be derived from the basic propositional operators.

Parallel to the examples discussed above, association with focus can be described for other focus particles such as *also* and *even* and their German equivalents. For instance, (28) and (29) represent the basic operators corresponding to *also* in Alternative Semantics and Structured Meanings, respectively.

(28) $[\![\text{also}_S]\!] = \lambda p\ [\ p\ \&\ \exists q\ [\ q \in C\ \&\ q \neq p\ \&\ q\ ]]$

(29) $[\![\text{also}_S]\!] = \lambda\langle\alpha, \beta\rangle\ [\ \alpha(\beta)\ \&\ \exists A\ [\ A \in \textsc{alt}(\beta)\ \&\ A \neq \beta\ \&\ \alpha(A)\ ]]$

As shown above, both theories give us the correct truth conditions in relatively simple cases of association with focus like those presented above. There is still controversy about which theory is more appropriate when it comes to more complex cases (cf. von Stechow 1991a, b; Rooth 1996; Krifka 2006).[16] Crucially, both theories demonstrate that a semantic treatment of focus sensitivity is possible in principle.

3.2.3 The restriction of the alternatives

From what has been said so far, it should be clear that the alternatives of the focus play a central role in determining the meaning contribution of a focus particle. However, we have not yet addressed the question of what the set of alternatives of a given focus exactly contains. There is general agreement that the alternatives must

16. What has not been considered here, for instance, is the fact that focus particles themselves may belong to the focus or to the background of a sentence and can even be part of the domain of another operator. We will briefly return to this issue in Section 5.2.3.

somehow be restricted (cf. Rooth 1985, 1992; Krifka 1992a, 1993; Umbach 2001). In the previous subsection, it was shown that they must be of the same semantic type as the focus. In addition, if the focused element is an argument, the alternatives must satisfy the selectional restrictions imposed by the corresponding verb, deverbal noun, or adjective (cf. Umbach 2001). But this is still not enough. Another important criterion is that the alternatives must be contextually relevant. In (30a), for instance, the relevant alternatives do not include all people in the world, but only people Maja could have plausibly invited, i.e., a subset of the people she knows. The problem is even more obvious in (30b). Here, the focus corresponds to a property, but the sentence cannot be interpreted as saying that Maja has no other properties apart from watching TV. This would make the sentence false in every model, as Maja necessarily has many other properties, e.g., the property of being identical to herself and the property of being Maja (cf. Rooth 1985:42).

(30) a. Maja only invited [Felix and JOHANnes $]_F$ to the party.
b. Maja only [watches TV $]_F$.

The question is how the contextual restriction of the alternatives can be incorporated into a theory of association with focus. Within pragmatic accounts of focus sensitivity effects, this is straightforward: according to these theories, the domain of quantification of a focus particle is fixed pragmatically, the location of the focus being only one factor among others. But how do semantic theories of association with focus allow for the restriction of alternative sets? Discussing a possible revision of his earlier account, Rooth (1992) suggests that we do not identify the domain-of-quantification variable C with the focus semantic value of the relevant constituent, but rather that we let the former be a subset of the latter. This is what his *focusing adverb constraint* claims: "If C is the domain of quantification of a focusing adverb with argument α, then $C \subseteq [\![\alpha]\!]^f$." (Rooth 1992:85) In the Structured Meanings account, the alternatives must be restricted to the contextually relevant ones by the function ALT, which forms the alternative set. In both theories, the mechanism that actually determines the relevant alternatives is pragmatic in nature; the restriction lies outside the scope of semantics.

Umbach (2001) attempts to put the mechanisms involved in the restriction of the alternatives in more concrete terms. Interpreting alternative sets as presuppositions/anaphora in DRT (cf. van der Sandt 1992), Umbach shows that in many cases, the alternative set is discourse-semantically constrained. In the most plausible interpretation of (31), the definite DP *dem Professor* ('the professor') is linked via bridging to the research team mentioned in the context sentence. This anaphoric link restricts the alternative set to members of the team: Anna may have talked to other people than the professor, but these people must not belong to the research team for the sentence to be true. The explanation Umbach gives is that the alternative set evoked by the DP *dem Professor* is bound by the already existing discourse referent for the research team.

(31) Das Forschungsteam war erschöpft von der langen Reise. ('The research team was exhausted by the long journey.')

Anna	hat	nur	mit	dem	[Professor]$_F$	gesprochen.
Anna	*aux*$_p$	only	to	the	professor	talked

(Umbach 2001: 186)

While this shows that part of the restrictions on alternative sets can be captured in (discourse) semantics, the employed mechanism does not help us in cases like (30) above, where no discourse referent able to bind the alternative set exists. The solution van der Sandt's (1992) presuppositions-as-anaphora approach offers us for such cases is accommodation of a suitable antecedent, but the question of what this antecedent should look like can again only be answered by entering pragmatic territory.

Umbach (2001) proposes another constraint on alternatives, which is closely related to the ideas presented above. The alternatives must comply with Lang's (1977, 1984) conditions for conjuncts in coordinate structures. First, they must have a so-called *Common Integrator*, i.e., fall under the same superordinate concept. Second, they may not subsume each other. In other words, the alternatives must be somehow similar, but not identical or overlapping (cf. also Krifka 1993). As Umbach notes, not every superordinate concept qualifies as a Common Integrator. Since the alternatives must be of the same semantic type, one will always find a common superordinate concept if only the level of abstraction is high enough. Finding a suitable Common Integrator for the alternatives of a focus is comparable to accommodating a discourse referent that can serve as an antecedent for the alternative set. It is an important task for further research to specify the pragmatic mechanisms involved in this process.

3.2.4 Assertions, presuppositions, implicatures

It is sometimes claimed that focus particles do not contribute anything to the truth conditions of the sentences in which they occur (cf. Bos 1994; Helbig 1988). The examples with *only* discussed in Section 3.2.2 clearly show that this cannot be true: sentences containing *only* have different truth conditions than the corresponding sentences without the particle, and the truth conditions of the former additionally depend on the location of the focus, while the truth conditions of sentences without focus particles normally do not depend on the focus-background partition.[17] What has led to disagreement in the literature is most likely that the individual focus particles show a different behavior with respect to truth conditions. To shed more light on this issue, it is necessary to distinguish between the different aspects of meaning observable in sentences with focus particles: their assertions/entailments, presuppositions, and implicatures.

A good starting point for the discussion is the well-known fact that the meaning of a sentence with a focus particle always includes the meaning of the corresponding sentence without the particle (cf. König 1991c, 1993).[18] (32b) follows from all three variants of (32a). In addition, each variant of (32a) has a second meaning component, which depends on the respective focus particle. In the representations discussed in Section 3.2.2 above, the two meaning components were conjoined. As will be shown, this is a simplification. The meaning components of sentences containing focus particles differ in their status, and the question of the actual status of the components must be answered differently for the individual particles.

(32) a. Maja only / also / even kissed [FELIX]$_F$.
b. Maja kissed Felix.

The most influential study on this topic is Horn (1969). One of its central claims is that a sentence containing *only* presupposes the corresponding sentence without the particle. Thus, while (33a) asserts (33b), (33c) is a presupposition of the sentence. A schematic representation of these relations is given in (34).

(33) a. Only [Maja]$_F$ kissed Felix.
b. No one distinct from Maja kissed Felix.
c. Maja kissed Felix.

(34) Only [A]$_F$ is B.
Assertion: No one distinct from A is B.
Presupposition: A is B.

The standard tests for presuppositions confirm this analysis. The second meaning component is invariant if the sentence is negated or transformed into a question:

17. But see Section 2.1.

18. Of course, this only holds in cases where the particle has scope over the whole sentence, i.e., in the constructions to which we have restricted our attention here (cf. Section 3.1). As the scope of *only* in (i-a) is limited to the embedded clause, (i-b) is not part of the meaning of the sentence.

(i) a. Felix does not believe that Maja only kissed [HENRY]$_F$.
b. Felix does not believe that Maja kissed Henry.

(33c) follows from both (35a) and (35b), while (33b) does not follow from either of them.

(35) a. It is not the case that only Maja kissed Felix.
b. Did only Maja kiss Felix?

Comparing *only* to *even*, Horn shows that the meaning components of sentences with the latter particle cannot be treated in the same way. Here, the corresponding sentence without the particle represents the assertion, while the specific contribution of the particle is presupposed. (36a) asserts (36b) and presupposes (36c). In addition, (36a) has another meaning component, roughly corresponding to (36d). This part of the meaning is not discussed in detail by Horn; it will be shown below that it can best be analyzed as a conventional implicature. A general scheme for the meaning components of sentences with *even* is given in (37).

(36) a. Even [Maja $]_F$ kissed Felix.
b. Maja kissed Felix.
c. Someone distinct from Maja kissed Felix.
d. Maja is unlikely to kiss Felix.

(37) Even [A $]_F$ is B.
Assertion: A is B.
Presupposition: Someone distinct from A is B.
(Conventional implicature: A is unlikely to be B.)

Although Horn (1969) does not give an analysis of *also/too*, it is obvious what such an analysis should look like in his system. *Also* and *too* have similar meanings as *even*, but lack the third meaning component. (38a) asserts (38b) and presupposes (38c), which is schematically represented in (39).[19]

(38) a. [Maja $]_F$ also kissed Felix.
b. Maja kissed Felix.
c. Someone distinct from Maja kissed Felix.

(39) [A $]_F$ is also B.
Assertion: A is B.
Presupposition: Someone distinct from A is B.

We now return to the question of the relation between focus particles and truth conditions. As demonstrated above, the specific meaning contribution of focus particles – the component they add to the corresponding sentence without a particle – can be situated on different levels of meaning: according to Horn (1969),

19. We disregard the differences in syntactic distribution between *only, even, also,* and *too*. See Jackendoff (1972) and Taglicht (1984) for the relevant generalizations with respect to the English data.

this component is an assertion in the case of *only* and a presupposition in the case of *also/too* and *even*. Consequently, *only* is relevant for the truth conditions of a sentence, while the other particles discussed above are not. In Section 3.3, these regularities will be generalized to apply to larger groups of focus particles.

Horn's presuppositional analysis has become the standard analysis of the meaning of focus particles; the majority of the subsequent works on the topic have adopted his view (cf. Altmann 1976a; König 1991a, c; Krifka 1992a, 1993; Braußе 2000; Dimroth 2004, among many others). Krifka (1993) shows how the distinction between assertion and presupposition can be incorporated into the Structured Meanings account of association with focus. However, many authors (including Horn himself) have cast doubt on the correctness of the original account. In the remainder of this subsection, we give a short overview of alternative theories.

The most controversial issue is the status of *A is B* in sentences of the form *Only A is B*. This component is analyzed as part of the assertion by Taglicht (1984), as a conventional implicature by Karttunen & Peters (1979), and as a generalized conversational implicature by Horn (1992). A radical view had been advanced by Geach (1962), who assumes that it is not part of the meaning of *Only A is B* at all. In a number of papers, Atlas (1991, 1993, 1996) argues that the assertion of *Only A is B* is *Exactly one individual, and no other than A, is B*. Under this view, *A is B* is not part of the semantic representation of *Only A is B*, but it is an entailment of the meaning of this sentence.

Horn (1996) starts out from the common assumptions that *only* corresponds to a universal quantifier in the semantic representation (this was tacitly assumed in the discussion of the examples in Section 3.2.2) and that universal quantifiers come with an "existential inference" (Horn 1996: 10), i.e., the inference that the set corresponding to the restrictor is non-empty. The consequence is that *Only A is B* has the presupposition *Someone is B.*[20] Together with the assertion *No one distinct from A is B*, this yields the inference *A is B*, which is thus neither a presupposition nor part of the assertion. Geurts & van der Sandt (2004) go one step further than Horn, assuming that the presupposition *Someone is B* is not triggered by *only* or the corresponding universal quantifier, but by the focus on the domain of the particle. This is an effect of their *Background Presupposition Rule*, claiming that every focus comes with the presupposition that the corresponding background holds of some individual. What theories such as Horn (1996) and Geurts & van der Sandt (2004) must explain is of course why negative sentences of the form *Not only A is B* also give rise to the inference *A is B* (cf. also Beaver 2004). This is a natural

20. Horn makes no explicit statement as to whether this inference is indeed a presupposition or, as advanced in his 1992 paper, an implicature. However, Horn's (1996: 16) assumption that the inference is accommodated suggests that he considers it to be a presupposition.

consequence of Horn's original account, but it does not straightforwardly follow from the theories based on existential inferences.

Ippolito (2008) argues that *only* triggers a presupposition, but not the one assumed by Horn (1969). In Ippolito's account, *Only A is B* presupposes *If someone is B, A is B*, while *A is B* is an implicature of the sentence. As such, it can be suspended in certain contexts. In negative sentences of the form *Not only A is B*, however, the truth of the proposition *A is B* follows from the conditional presupposition triggered by *only* combined with the negative assertion of the sentence.

With respect to sentences containing *also*, *too*, and *even*, it is the meaning component *Someone distinct from A is B* that has been the center of attention. While Horn (1969) ascribed it the status of a presupposition, Taglicht (1984) and Karttunen & Peters (1979) analyze it as a conventional implicature. Atlas (1991) claims that it is part of the assertion, which according to him is *At least two individuals, one of whom is A, are B*. Geurts & van der Sandt (2004) essentially follow Horn's (1969) presuppositional analysis, but maintain that only one part of the presupposition – the part saying that some individual distinct from A exists – is due to the meaning of the focus particle, while the second part – that this individual is B – is again a presupposition of the focus resulting from the *Background Presupposition Rule*. Dealing with *sogar*, the German counterpart of *even*, Schwarz (2005) argues that *Someone distinct from A is B* is not necessarily part of the meaning of sentences containing this particle. In their elaborate analysis of German *auch*, Reis & Rosengren (1997) argue that *Someone distinct from A is B* is a conventional implicature, but that the particle also "contributes a non-implicated, truth-relevant meaning element, which we call ADD (for 'in addition')" (Reis & Rosengren 1997: 273).[21] We will return to this account in Section 4.5.

3.3 Lexical semantics: Subgroups of focus particles

So far, the meaning of focus particles has been discussed at the level of the individual particles. However, this way of approaching the issue misses important generalizations. It is possible and worthwhile to classify focus particles with respect to semantic criteria, yielding several subgroups of particles, the members of which can be captured by a unified semantic analysis.

---

21. See also Krifka (1999) for a similar claim.

3.3.1 The traditional classification

Traditionally, focus particles are subdivided into restrictive/exclusive, additive/inclusive, and scalar particles (cf. Altmann 1976a; Jacobs 1983; Krifka 1999; Dimroth 2004; Ippolito 2007).[22] The terms *restrictive* and *additive* refer to the quantificational use of focus particles: as formulated in the Structured Meanings approach, the particles quantify over the set of alternatives, excluding elements distinct from the focus from the set of elements that yield a true proposition when the background is applied to them (restrictive particles), or including them in this set (additive particles).

With respect to their meaning, restrictive focus particles form a relatively homogeneous class. The description of the lexical meaning of the prototypical member *only* given in Sections 3.2.2 and 3.2.4 (cf. (15), (23), and (34) above) can be transferred to the rest of the group, including English *merely* and German *allein*, *bloß* etc. The differences between the individual particles are mainly of a stylistic nature. The same can be said of additive focus particles with their prototype *also*, the meaning description of which (cf. (28), (29), and (39) above) characterizes the whole group as well. Examples of other additive particles are English *too*, *either* and German *ebenfalls*, *ebenso* etc. In sum, while the syntactic distribution of the individual restrictive and additive particles differs both within and between the two languages, their semantics, including the division between the asserted and presupposed meaning components, is fairly constant within the two groups.

The defining criterion for scalar focus particles is that they arrange the alternatives of the focus on a scale and assign the value of the focus an extreme position on this scale (cf. König 1991c; Jacobs 1983; Poljakova 2000). In Section 3.2.4, a schematic characterization of the meaning of the scalar particle *even* was given (cf. (37) above). Can this meaning description be generalized to cover the entire group of scalar particles?

In analogy to sentences containing *also*, sentences of the form *Even A is B* were considered to assert *A is B* and to presuppose *Someone distinct from A is B*. Crucially, the meaning of *even* involves a third component, which cannot be observed in the case of *also*. This component – roughly corresponding to *A is unlikely to be B* – makes *even* a scalar particle. As indicated by the paraphrase, the scale on which it is based is one of likelihood (cf. Karttunen & Peters 1979; Francescotti 1995; Krifka 1999).[23] *Even* says that the application of the background to the focus yields a proposition the truth of which is less likely than the truth of any proposition that

22. The members of the two word pairs *restrictive/exclusive* and *additive/inclusive* are used synonymously.

23. See Kay (1990) for a different approach, based on informativity instead of likelihood, and Francescotti (1995) for a criticism of this approach.

can be obtained by applying the background to an alternative of the focus. This is linked to the expression of unexpectedness or surprise by the speaker, which is why *even* is said to convey epistemic meaning (cf. Francescotti 1995: 172). Arguably, the third meaning component is a conventional implicature (cf. König 1991c; Primus 1992; Francescotti 1995): On the one hand, it resembles a presupposition in that it is not relevant for the truth conditions of the sentence. On the other hand, it shows a different projection behavior than presuppositions and, unlike the latter, expresses an attitude (cf. König 1991c: 55–58).

When we compare *even* to other scalar focus particles, we see that its meaning cannot be equated with the meaning of scalar particles in general. In the examples in (40), *only* occurs in a scalar use.

(40) a. Maja is only [a NURSE]$_F$.
b. Maja only called [TWICE]$_F$.

First, as discussed above, the distribution of the asserted and presupposed meaning components in sentences with *only* is different from that in sentences with *even*. The corresponding sentence without the particle is presupposed by (40a) and (40b), while the restrictive meaning component introduced by *only* is asserted. Hence, the group of scalar particles is not homogeneous with respect to the status of the meaning of the underlying sentence and with respect to the distribution of assertion and presupposition in general.

Second, the relevant scales in (40) clearly differ from the likelihood scale involved in the meaning of sentences with *even*: the scale in (40a) is one of professional status, while the scale in (40b) is a frequency scale. Thus, the scales differ between the individual focus particles, as well as between different uses of the same particle, making an explicit and uniform characterization of the scale for the entire group of scalar particles impossible. Abstracting from the idiosyncratic and context-dependent aspects of the scales, König (1991c) gives a more general description of the scalar meaning component, amounting to the generalization that "a particle may evaluate its focus as a 'maximal' or 'minimal' value of the relevant partially ordered set" (König 1991c: 45). König's formal representations, which are based on the Structured Meanings approach, are shown in (41).[24]

(41) a. $\text{Max}_c(\langle\alpha, \beta\rangle)$
b. $\text{Min}_c(\langle\alpha, \beta\rangle)$

The index c indicates the context-dependency of the involved scales. A question that will not be addressed here is whether the nature of the scales is entirely

24. According to Francescotti's (1995) description of *even*, the focus need not necessarily be assigned an end point of the scale; it is sufficient if it has a higher/lower value than most of its alternatives.

determined by the context, or whether the particles themselves contribute to their selection, as suggested by the description of *even* given above.[25]

3.3.2 A cross-classification of focus particles

The discussion of the properties of scalar particles in the previous subsection has revealed a number of drawbacks of the traditional division of focus particles into an additive, a restrictive, and a scalar group. For one thing, the three categories are not mutually exclusive: *even* is both scalar and additive (cf. (37) above), and the restrictive particle *only* is also scalar in many of its uses. Furthermore, the German additive particle *auch*, unlike *also*, has a scalar use (cf. Plank 1979; Nederstigt 2001). In (42), it is synonymous with *sogar* and corresponds to English *even* rather than *also*.

(42)	Dieses	Auto	ist	auch	[für	Bill	GATES]$_F$	zu	teuer.
	this	car	is	even	for	Bill	Gates	too	expensive

A closely related problem for the traditional classification is that particles such as *only/nur* and *auch* have a scalar as well as a non-scalar use. One could assume that we are dealing with cases of polysemy here, but from the point of view of linguistic economy, this is an unattractive assumption, and it obscures the role of the context in determining whether a particle is scalar or not in a given sentence.

The last problem is that – as shown above – scalar focus particles do not form a homogeneous group with a uniform meaning, in particular with respect to the distribution of the asserted and presupposed meaning components. The decisive factor is whether a focus particle is additive or restrictive, while scalarity can best be seen as an additional feature introducing another meaning component.

A natural solution to these problems is to reinterpret the labels *additive*, *restrictive*, and *scalar* as semantic features and to separate the first two from the last. Such a description is suggested by König (1991a, c) and more explicitly formulated by Foolen (1993). In his analysis of the Dutch focus particle system, Foolen captures the additive/restrictive distinction by a binary feature [+/–restrictive], where [–restrictive] denotes the group of additive particles. A second feature [+/–scalar] distinguishes between the scalar and non-scalar particles within the groups established by the first feature. The resulting system of Dutch focus particles is given in Table 3.1.

However, this classification does not solve the problem of particles that have a scalar as well as a non-scalar use, such as *only/nur* and *auch*. Contrary to what Table 3.1 suggests, the Dutch additive particle *ook*, like its German counterpart

25. For a discussion of this issue, see König (1991c:69–76) and Jacobs (1983:Chapter 4).

Table 3.1 A cross-classification of Dutch focus particles, taken from Foolen (1993:149)

	[–scalar]	[+scalar]
[–restrictive]	ook 'also'	zelfs 'even'
[+restrictive]	alleen 'only'	maar 'only'

Table 3.2 A cross-classification of German (GE), Dutch (DU), and English (EN) focus particles

	[–scalar]	[α scalar]	[+scalar]
[–restrictive]	ebenso (GE) evenzo (DU) also (EN)	auch (GE) ook (DU)	sogar (GE) zelfs (DU) even (EN)
[+restrictive]	allein (GE) alleen (DU) purely (EN)	nur (GE) slechts (DU) only (EN)	maar (DU)

auch, has a scalar use as well.[26] An example of an additive particle that is always non-scalar is Dutch *evenzo*, corresponding to German *ebenso*. In addition, Dutch has a restrictive focus particle with a scalar and a non-scalar use, namely, *slechts*. The Dutch particle system nicely shows that focus particles can be (i) always non-scalar (*evenzo, alleen*), (ii) always scalar (*zelfs, maar*), or (iii) scalar or non-scalar, depending on the context (*ook, slechts*). A plausible assumption is that the third group is underspecified with respect to scalarity (cf. König 1991c:42, 100). A cross-classification of focus particles incorporating this group is given in Table 3.2. Where possible, the Dutch particles are supplemented by their German and English counterparts.[27]

Another complication is that certain focus particles, including German *ausgerechnet* ('X of all Ys'), *eben/genau* ('exactly'), and *gerade* ('just') are neither addi-

26. *Ook* and *auch* behave similarly in many respects; cf. Bergsma (2006).

27. An intriguing asymmetry depending on the specification of the feature [+/–scalar] is exemplified in (i). While in the case of scalar additive particles, the alternatives of the focus can be easily accommodated (cf. (i-a)), they must be given in the context in the case of non-scalar additive particles (cf. (i-b), where *auch* is preferentially interpreted as non-scalar). See also Zeevat (1992) and Tovena (2005).

(i) Ich war mit einigen Freunden im Kino. ('I went to the cinema with some friends.')

a. Der Film war so langweilig, dass sogar [HENRY]$_F$ eingeschlafen ist.
the film was so boring that even Henry fallen_asleep *aux*$_p$

b. *Der Film war so langweilig, dass auch [HENRY]$_F$ eingeschlafen ist.
the film was so boring that also Henry fallen_asleep *aux*$_p$

tive nor restrictive. A discussion of these particles, which differ from the particles described so far in other properties as well, is provided by König (1991b).

3.4 Summary

This chapter provided an overview of the semantics of focus particles, in particular of the phenomenon of focus sensitivity and its formal analysis. It was shown how the actual meaning contribution of a focus particle in a given sentence can be derived from its interaction with the sentence's focus-background partition, represented either in the format of Alternative Semantics or in that of the Structured Meanings approach. In both theories, the derivation of a semantic representation that correctly reflects the meaning of the sentence does not depend on a specific syntactic configuration of the particle and its domain. As a consequence, a uniform semantic description of focus particle constructions – adapted only to the peculiarities of the semantic subclasses of particles described in Section 3.3 – is possible, although the syntax of the constructions may vary both within one language and between languages. As the choice between the two formats of semantic representation is immaterial to the analysis of the syntactic, prosodic, and information-structural properties of the constructions in the remainder of this work, no such choice is made.

CHAPTER 4

Focus particles, syntax, and information structure

The present chapter deals with two general questions concerning the grammar of focus particle constructions in German. First, what is an adequate syntactic representation of the sentences? Important issues include the categorial status of focus particles, their integration into the syntactic structure, and the type of their sister constituents. Second, what information-structural properties do sentences with focus particles have, and how do the particles interact with the grammatical reflexes of information structure in syntax and prosody? In particular, what constraints does the choice of a particle's domain impose on word order and accent placement in the respective sentences, and how can these constraints be explained? The main goal of this chapter is to develop a modular account of the relevant data that is based on independently motivated assumptions about the grammatical realization of information structure in German. Ideally, such an account does not make reference to principles and restrictions that must be stipulated specifically for the description of focus particles. By examining focus particle constructions from the point of view of the information-structural model introduced in Section 2.3, it will be shown that information structure not only plays a central role for their semantics, but also goes a long way towards explaining their syntactic and prosodic peculiarities.

The chapter is organized as follows: Section 4.1 provides an overview of the usage patterns of focus particles in German. It is followed by a brief review of previous syntactic analyses in Section 4.2, which shows that none of the accounts in the literature is fully satisfactory. An alternative proposal is outlined in Section 4.3; the remainder of the chapter substantiates and justifies this new approach to the grammar of focus particles in German. It is argued that a large part of the relevant phenomena can be explained by analyzing focus particles as adjuncts to VP and AP (Section 4.4), that stressed additive focus particles preceding their domains can straightforwardly be integrated into this account (Section 4.5), and that adjunction to phrases different from VP and AP is possible, but restricted to certain well-defined cases and tied to a special information structure (Section 4.6). Section 4.7 summarizes the results and conclusions.

4.1 Focus particles in German: A descriptive survey

This section gives a descriptive overview of the various ways in which focus particles can be integrated into German clauses. In the first two subsections, this description will be confined to non-contrastive uses of the particles; their contrastive counterparts will be addressed in Section 4.1.3. The primary goal is to determine which positions in the clause focus particles occupy, where they are located relative to their domains, and whether a particle and its domain must be adjacent.

4.1.1 Positions of focus particles and their domains

In the following, 11 usage patterns of focus particles will be identified using the Topological Model (*Stellungsfeldermodell*) of the German clause introduced in Section 2.2.[1] At this point, no detailed syntactic analyses of these patterns will be given; the collection of the data serves to show the range of phenomena to be accounted for by an adequate syntactic theory of German focus particle constructions.

Pattern 1: Unstressed focus particle in the middlefield preceding its domain. The pattern often assumed to be the most basic one involves a focus particle in the middlefield followed by its domain. In the examples in (1), the domain is a single constituent. However, it can also consist of one or more constituents and the verb (or a part of the verb cluster) in clause-final position, or of a (finite or infinite) verb alone, cf. (2) and (3).[2]

(1) a. dass Maja nur / auch / sogar [FElix $]_D$ eine Blume gab
that Maja only / also / even Felix a flower gave
b. dass Maja Felix nur / auch / sogar [eine BLUme $]_D$ gab

(2) a. dass Maja Felix nur / auch / sogar [eine BLUme gab $]_D$
that Maja Felix only / also / even a flower gave
b. dass Maja nur / auch / sogar [Felix eine BLUme gab $]_D$

(3) a. dass Maja Felix nur / auch / sogar [KÜSSTE $]_D$
that Maja Felix only / also / even kissed
b. dass Maja Felix nur / auch / sogar [geKÜSST $]_D$ hat
that Maja Felix only / also / even kissed *aux*$_p$

---

1. For a similar survey of focus particles in Dutch, see Foolen, van Gerrevink, Hogeweg & Prawiro-Atmodjo (2009).

2. In the examples, we return to the notation introduced in Section 2.1, indicating the domain of a focus particle by square brackets labeled with the subscript D.

c. dass nur / auch / sogar [gesUNgen]$_D$ wurde
that only / also / even sung aux_{pass}

Without context information, sentences can be ambiguous with respect to the domain of the focus particle. (4), for instance, has the readings given in (1b) and (2a) above (cf. also the discussion in Section 1.1).

(4) dass Maja Felix nur / auch / sogar eine BLUme gab
dass Maja Felix only / also / even a flower gave

There are also cases where a focus particle is associated with two or more elements in the middlefield that do not form a constituent; cf. (5).

(5) a. dass nur / auch / sogar [Maja FElix]$_D$ küsste
that only / also / even Maja Felix kissed

b. dass nur / auch / sogar [Maja eine GIRAFfe]$_D$ streichelte
that only / also / even Maja a giraffe stroked

In all examples considered so far, the focus particle immediately precedes its domain. As shown by the sentences in (6), intervening elements often result in ungrammaticality. However, as noted by Büring & Hartmann (2001), the focus particle and its domain need not (and, in fact, must not) be adjacent in certain cases; cf. (7)–(9).

(6) a. *dass Maja nur Felix [eine BLUme]$_D$ gab
dass Maja only Felix a flower gave

b. *dass sogar Maja Felix [KÜSste]$_D$
that even Maja Felix kissed

(7) a. dass Maja sogar auf den Berg [RANNte]$_D$
that Maja even onto the hill ran

b. *dass Maja auf den Berg sogar [RANNte]$_D$

(8) a. dass Maja sich nur in Sicherheit [GLAUBte]$_D$
that Maja herself only in safety believed

b. *dass Maja sich in Sicherheit nur [GLAUBte]$_D$

(9) a. dass Maja auch schlafen [WOLLte]$_D$
that Maja also to_sleep wanted

b. *dass Maja schlafen auch [WOLLte]$_D$

Pattern 2: Unstressed focus particle in the middlefield between parts of a discontinuous domain. The second pattern comprises cases where a focus particle is located in the middlefield, while its domain is split into a part that precedes it and one that follows it. Elements to the left of the particle that belong to the domain may occur in the prefield or at the left edge of the middlefield; cf. (10). In (10d), the whole sentence except the particle itself forms the domain.

(10) a. Sicher [läuten]$_D$ nur / auch / sogar [die
certainly ring only / also / even the
KIRCHturmglocken]$_D$.
church_bells

b. [Jemand]$_D$ besitzt nur / auch / sogar [ein Pony]$_D$.
someone owns only / also / even a pony

c. Felix hat [sich]$_D$ nur / auch / sogar [rasIERT]$_D$.
Felix *aux$_p$* himself only / also / even shaved

d. [Jemand spült]$_D$ nur / auch / sogar [das GeSCHIRR]$_D$.
someone washes only / also / even the dishes

Example (11) demonstrates that elements not belonging to the domain of the particle may occur in the middlefield between the two parts of the domain. These elements behave like their counterparts in the sentences of Pattern 1: they usually precede the focus particle.

(11) [Maja liest]$_D$ ihm nur / auch / sogar [ein BUCH vor]$_D$.
Maja reads to_him only / also / even a book *pref*

Pattern 3: Unstressed focus particle in the middlefield, domain in the prefield. If a focus particle in the middlefield is associated with a single constituent, this element can occupy the prefield, as in (12). In addition to DPs, PPs, and adverbials, possible domains in the prefield include VPs, infinitives, participles, and even whole clauses.

(12) a. [SUshi]$_D$ hat Maja nur / auch / sogar gegessen.
sushi *aux$_p$* Maja only / also / even eaten

b. [SUshi gegessen]$_D$ hat Maja nur / auch / sogar.
sushi eaten *aux$_p$* Maja only / also / even

c. [Essen]$_D$ wollte sie das Sushi nur / auch / sogar.
to_eat wanted she the sushi only / also / even

d. [GeGEssen]$_D$ hat sie das Sushi nur / auch / sogar.
eaten *aux$_p$* she the sushi only / also / even

e. [Dass FElix kommt]$_D$ hat Maja nur / auch / sogar gehofft.
that Felix comes *aux$_p$* Maja only / also / even hoped

Pattern 4: Unstressed focus particle in the middlefield, domain = finite verb in the V2-position. In V2-clauses without any (modal) auxiliaries, the finite main verb itself must move to the V2-position (cf. Section 2.2). There it is still a possible domain of a focus particle in the middlefield; cf. (13).

(13) Maja [KÜSSTE]$_D$ Felix nur / auch / sogar.
Maja kissed Felix only / also / even

Pattern 5: Stressed or unstressed focus particle in the middlefield, domain = extraposed clause. Embedded clauses are often extraposed in German; for finite clauses, extraposition is even obligatory. The examples in (14) demonstrate that focus particles located in the middlefield can associate with extraposed finite or infinite clauses. If there is overt material after the base position of the extraposed clause, such as parts of the verb cluster, the particle and its domain end up non-adjacent; cf. (14b). As noted by Altmann (1976a: 151–159), the focus particle may be accented in the pattern under discussion, but the sentence accent is invariably located within its domain.[3] The variants of (14a) and (14b) with a stressed focus particle also differ from the variants without stress on the particle in that they show a clear intonational break between the matrix clause and the embedded clause. Unlike *nur* and *auch*, the particle *sogar* can only occur in an unstressed form; cf. (14c).

(14) a. Maja hofft nur / NUR / auch / AUCH, [dass FElix kommt]$_D$.
Maja hopes only / also that Felix comes
b. dass Maja nur / NUR / auch / AUCH hofft, [rechtzeitig
that Maja only / also hopes in_time
ANzukommen]$_D$.
to_arrive
c. Maja hofft sogar / *SOGAR, [dass FElix kommt]$_D$.
Maja hopes even that Felix comes

Pattern 6: Stressed focus particle in the middlefield following its domain. This pattern is restricted to the additive focus particle *auch* and a few other particles (such as *gleichfalls* 'likewise' and *ebenfalls*/*ebenso* 'as well'), which have a more restricted distribution, but are semantically equivalent to *auch*. If these particles follow their domains, they may be stressed. Crucially, in the sentences of Pattern 6, the focus particle carries the sentence accent, while its domain – located either in the prefield or at the left edge of the middlefield – is unaccented or carries a rising prenuclear accent; cf. (15).[4] The overall intonation thus clearly differs from that of Pattern 3, where the focus particle is unaccented.

(15) a. [/FElix]$_D$ hat AUCH / Ebenfalls Sushi gegessen.
Felix *aux$_p$* also / as_well sushi eaten
b. [/Sushi gegessen]$_D$ hat Felix AUCH / Ebenfalls.
sushi eaten *aux$_p$* Felix also / as_well

3. Constructions with the sentence accent on the focus particle either belong to Pattern 6 or involve a contrastive use of the particle.

4. Rising accents are indicated by "/" preceding the accented syllable in the examples.

c. dass [/FElix]$_D$ gestern AUCH / Ebenfalls Sushi gegessen hat
that Felix yesterday also / as_well sushi eaten aux_p

As opposed to the patterns described so far, the domain of the focus particle need not be overtly realized in Pattern 6. In (16a), the domain has undergone topic drop, and in the control construction (16b), *auch* is associated with the *PRO*-subject of the embedded infinitival clause. Still, the positions arguably occupied by the non-overt domains precede the focus particle.

(16) a. [Ø]$_D$ Ist AUCH schon fertig.
is also already finished

b. Maja versprach Felix, [Ø]$_D$ AUCH zu singen.
Maja promised Felix also to sing

Pattern 7: Unstressed focus particle preceding its domain in the prefield. In this pattern, the focus particle and its domain occupy the prefield together. Exactly those elements qualify as the domain of the particle in this position that can occur in the prefield on their own: DPs, PPs, adjectives, adverbials, VPs, participles, infinitives, and whole clauses, among others. The domain adjacently follows the unstressed particle; cf. (17).

(17) a. Nur / Auch / Sogar [MAja]$_D$ hat Sushi gegessen.
only / also / even Maja aux_p sushi eaten

b. Nur / Auch / Sogar [SUshi gegessen]$_D$ hat Maja.
only / also / even sushi eaten aux_p Maja

c. Nur / Auch / Sogar [geGEssen]$_D$ hat Maja das Sushi.
only / also / even eaten aux_p Maja the sushi

d. Nur / Auch / Sogar [Essen]$_D$ wollte Maja das Sushi.
only / also / even to_eat wanted Maja the sushi

e. Nur / Auch / Sogar [dass FElix kommt]$_D$ hat Maja gehofft.
only / also / even that Felix comes aux_p Maja hoped

f. Nur / Auch / Sogar [intelliGENT]$_D$ ist Felix.
only / also / even intelligent is Felix

Pattern 8: Unstressed focus particle adjacently following its domain. Jacobs (1983) gives examples of constructions with unstressed focus particles immediately following their domains in the prefield or middlefield; cf. (18). There is controversy in the literature about the status of such sentences; sometimes they are assumed to be outdated or even ungrammatical (cf. Büring & Hartmann 2001). However, the acceptability of this construction type depends heavily on the focus particle involved. Jacobs himself considers the variants of (18a) with *nur* and *sogar* more acceptable than the variant with *auch*; the examples in (19) are even better. In any case, the described pattern cannot generally be ruled out.

(18) a. [Die TOCHter]$_D$ nur / auch / sogar entkam den Flammen.
the daughter only / also / even escaped the flames
b. Der Vater verriet [der TOCHter]$_D$ nur das Geheimnis.
the father told the daughter only the secret
c. Der Vater hat [an die TOCHter]$_D$ nur gedacht.
the father aux_p of the daughter only thought
(Jacobs 1983:95–100)

(19) a. [Seit JAnuar]$_D$ erst / schon ist Maja arbeitslos.
since January only / already is Maja unemployed
b. [Zu WEIHnachten]$_D$ noch / bereits hatte Maja Arbeit.
at Christmas still / already had Maja work
c. [Ihre MIEte]$_D$ wenigstens konnte sie bezahlen.
her rent at_least could she pay

Pattern 9: Unstressed focus particle within DP or PP. The occurrence of focus particles within DPs or PPs is highly restricted in German. The examples in (20), for instance, are all ungrammatical. However, a focus particle can occur within a DP or a PP if it is associated with, and adjacent to, an adjective, a numeral, or a part of an AP; cf. (21).

(20) a. *der nur / auch / sogar [GewINNer]$_D$
the only / also / even winner
b. *die berühmten nur / auch / sogar [PHYsiker]$_D$
the famous only / also / even physicists
c. *der Mantel nur / auch / sogar [des PiaNIsten]$_D$
the coat only / also / even the_{gen} $pianist_{gen}$
d. *mit nur / auch / sogar [MAja]$_D$
with only / also / even Maja

(21) a. das nur [LAUwarme]$_D$ Wasser
the only lukewarm water
b. für nur [ZWEI]$_D$ Euro
for only two euros
c. der nur / auch / sogar [auf seine FrisUR]$_D$ stolze Linguist
the only / also / even of his hairstyle proud linguist

Examples like (22), taken from Kleemann (2006), are exceptions to this generalization. Here, *nur* precedes the whole genitive complement of the noun *Absage* ('cancelation'); the phrase structurally resembles (20c) rather than (21a). According to Kleemann, this structure is only possible if the head noun is a deverbal event nominalization. That this still cannot be the correct generalization is evidenced by the fact that (23), where the head noun is not deverbal, is also acceptable.[5]

(22) die Absage nur des [FRÜHen]$_D$ Termins
the cancelation only the$_{gen}$ early$_{gen}$ appointment$_{gen}$
(Kleemann 2006: 105)

(23) der Tod nur [des ANführers]$_D$
the death only the$_{gen}$ leader$_{gen}$

Pattern 10: Unstressed focus particle as the only prefield element. A focus particle can occur as the only element preceding the finite verb in V2-clauses. Its domain seems to be the remainder of the clause in these cases, though this is not always easy to determine. In (24a) and (24b), examples are given for *nur* and *auch*, respectively; (24c) shows that *sogar* cannot be used in this pattern.[6]

(24) a. Nur [hat mir das niemand geSAGT]$_D$.
only *aux$_p$* me that no_one told
b. Auch [wollte ich niemanden beLEIdigen]$_D$.
also wanted I no_one to_insult
c. *Sogar [habe ich den ersten PREIS gewonnen]$_D$.
even *aux$_p$* I the first prize won

Although *nur* and *auch* in (24a) and (24b) share some properties with their counterparts in the other patterns, their semantic contribution is different in the construction type under discussion. This is particularly obvious in the case of *nur*, which does not have its typical restrictive meaning in (24a). In Pattern 10, but not in the other patterns, it can be substituted by *allerdings* ('though') or *jedoch* ('however'). *Auch* in (24b), on the other hand, has an additive meaning. The whole proposition is added to another, contextually given proposition. However, the particle shows similar peculiarities as *nur* with respect to its replaceability: while *auch* can be substituted by *außerdem* ('besides') and *darüber hinaus* ('apart from that') in Pattern 10, this is impossible in the other patterns. The instances of *nur* and *auch* in (24) and similar examples have more in common with conjunctions than with the other uses of focus particles in German; cf. Altmann (1976a: Section 4.2.1).[7] We follow Altmann in assuming that we are dealing with a different, albeit

5. See also the discussion in Sections 4.6.2 and 5.1.

6. The anonymous reviewer notes that examples with *sogar* as the only prefield element can be found on the internet. While the possibility of *sogar* in this position would facilitate a more uniform treatment of the focus particles under discussion, we consider the relevant constructions extremely marginal.

7. See also Büring & Hartmann (2001: 241, Footnote 7).

related, grammatical phenomenon here and that a theory of focus particles need not cover cases like (24). From Section 4.2 on, the constructions of Pattern 10 will be excluded from consideration.

Summary. The generalizations in (25) and (26) summarize the overview of possible positions of focus particles and their domains.

(25) A focus particle usually precedes its domain.

(26) A focus particle is usually adjacent to its domain.

These generalizations have often been formulated in a similar way in the literature; cf. Altmann (1976a: 297), Jacobs (1983: 86, 113), Büring & Hartmann (2001: 236–237, 266), and Jaeger & Wagner (2003: 4–5), among others. As indicated by the word *usually*, they only describe the default and allow for exceptions. Stressed *auch* and comparable particles obligatorily follow their domains in Pattern 6. In these cases, adjacency of the focus particle and its domain is not necessary (if the domain is located in the middlefield) or even impossible (if it is located in the prefield). Unstressed focus particles can follow (parts of) their domains if one or more elements have moved to the left across the particle (Patterns 2–4), or if the domain immediately precedes the particle in the prefield or middlefield (Pattern 7). Patterns 3–5 can deviate from the adjacency default to meet movement requirements of the particle's domain, while in Pattern 1, adjacency is necessary in many cases, but impossible in others.

4.1.2 The location of the sentence accent

On the basis of the data presented so far, we can address the relation between the domain of a focus particle and the sentence accent.[8] With few exceptions, the sentence accent is located within the domain of the particle, its exact position being determined by structural rules of accent assignment. As shown in (4) above, the sentence accent does not always unambiguously identify the domain of a focus particle.[9] In this respect, the domain behaves like the sentence focus: the latter also interacts with, but cannot directly be read off from, the accentuation of the sentence; the ambiguity observed in (4) is analogous to focus ambiguities resulting from the possibility of focus projection (cf. Section 2.3). The generalization in (27) describes the prototypical case of accent placement in focus particle constructions.

8. The phenomenon of second occurrence focus (cf. Section 5.2.3), which is accompanied by a special accentuation pattern, is ignored for the time being.

9. See also the discussion of the examples in (1) and (2) in Chapter 3.

(27) The sentence accent of a focus particle construction is usually located within the domain of the particle.

Two of the usage patterns identified in the previous subsection deviate from this default. In the constructions of Pattern 6, the focus particle itself carries the sentence accent, while its domain optionally carries a rising prenuclear accent. Under certain circumstances, however, the domain cannot be accented. This is the case in sentences where it is not overtly realized, as in (16) above, but also occurs when the particle is associated with an element that never receives any stress in German, such as the weak pronoun *es* ('it') in (28).

(28) [Es $]_D$ ist AUCH kaputtgegangen.
it aux_p also broken

The phrases of Pattern 9 (cf. (21)–(23) above) involve an accent within the domain of the focus particle, but this accent does not necessarily end up as the sentence accent when the phrase is integrated into a larger structure. If the sentence accent is located elsewhere, the domain of the particle carries a secondary accent; cf. (29).[10]

(29) a. dass Felix für nur [ZEHN $]_D$ Euro einen PulLOver bekommen hat
that Felix for only ten euros a pullover got aux_p

b. dass Maja mit einem sogar [auf seine FrisUR $]_D$ stolzen Linguisten in den TIERpark gegangen ist
that Maja with a even of his hairstyle proud linguist to the zoo gone aux_p

4.1.3 Contrastive uses of focus particles

Contrastive uses of focus particles will be removed from consideration in the remainder of this work. To complete the picture, they are nevertheless included in the descriptive overview. After some general remarks, the usage patterns established in Section 4.1.1 will be tested for their compatibility with contrastively used focus particles, showing that the possibility of a contrastive use depends on the choice of the particle, as well as on the position of its domain.

The relevant constructions have two characteristic properties. First, the focus particle bears a contrastive accent, while its domain is unaccented. Second, the meaning of the particle is contrasted with the meaning of another focus particle

10. Similarly, the domain of the focus particle (or the particle itself) can carry a secondary accent in the constructions of Patterns 7 and 8; cf. Section 5.3.

or a similar expression.[11] In the authentic sentence in (30), for instance, *nur* is contrasted with the focus sensitive adverb *hauptsächlich* ('mainly').

(30) Die expressionistische Architektur spielt sich hauptsächlich in Skizzen ab.
('The expressionist architecture takes place mainly in sketches.')
Eigentlich spielt sie sich NUR [in Skizzen]D ab.
actually takes_place it *refl* only in sketches *pref*

As shown above, constructions of Pattern 5 sometimes involve an accented focus particle. In these cases, however, it does not necessarily get a contrastive interpretation. Altmann (1976a: 153) assumes that the accent on the particle only compensates for the lack of an accent that would normally occur on a placeholder element for the extraposed clause, but cannot be realized due to the deletion of this placeholder. In his view, (31a) is an elliptical variant of (31b), where the placeholder *dann* ('then') is accented. The two sentences do not differ in their meaning.

(31) a. Eine Ursache kann begrifflich NUR gegeben sein, [wenn eine
a cause can conceptually only given be if a
FoLge vorliegt]D .
consequence exists
b. Eine Ursache kann begrifflich nur [DANN]D gegeben sein, [
a cause can conceptually only then given be
wenn eine FoLge vorliegt]D .
if a consequence exists
(Altmann 1976a: 256)

The question is why the placeholder element in (31b) is accented in the first place. This has nothing to do with the presence of a focus particle, but is a more general phenomenon observable in constructions with extraposed clauses (cf. Breindl 1989). The accent on the placeholder indicates that the extraposed clause is focused. Extraposition of an embedded clause that forms the focus of the matrix clause results in a structure where the sentence accent is not located in its normal position at the end of the middlefield of the matrix clause. The accent on the placeholder, which remains in the base position of the extraposed clause, stands in for this 'missing' accent.

A stressed focus particle in Pattern 5 thus need not indicate contrast. However, as will be shown below, a contrastive use of the particle is nevertheless possible. In Pattern 6, on the other hand, the accent on the particle never indicates contrast,

11. We do not consider cases involving metalinguistic contrast/correction (e.g., the correction of an incorrect pronunciation), as this type of contrast is grammatically nearly unrestricted (cf. Steube 2001) and does not allow conclusions to be drawn about the grammar of focus particle constructions.

which is why this pattern will be ignored in the remainder of this subsection. The function of the accent on the focus particle in constructions of Pattern 6 will be dealt with in Section 4.5.

We turn to the contrastive uses of the individual particles, starting with *nur*. If *nur* is stressed, it often contrasts with *auch*, emphasizing the exclusion of alternatives. The contrastive use of *nur* is possible in Patterns 1, 5, 7, and 9; cf. (32)–(34).

(32) Kommt morgen auch Felix? ('Will Felix come tomorrow, too?')
  a. Morgen kommt NUR [Felix]$_D$. (Pattern 1)
     tomorrow comes only Felix
  b. NUR [Felix]$_D$ kommt morgen. (Pattern 7)

(33) Hat Maja auch gesagt, dass etwas geschehen muss?
  ('Did Maja also say that something must happen?')
     Maja hat NUR gesagt, [dass etwas geschehen
     Maja *aux*$_p$ only said that something happen
     muss]$_D$. (Pattern 5)
     must

(34) ... der auch auf seine Frisur stolze Linguist ...
  ('... the linguist also proud of his hairstyle ...')
     ... der NUR [auf seine Frisur]$_D$ stolze Linguist ... (Pattern 9)
     the only of his hairstyle proud linguist

In the remaining patterns, the contrastive use of *nur* is much less acceptable or impossible, as evidenced by (35)–(39).[12]

(35) Läuten auch die Kirchturmglocken? ('Do the church bells ring, too?')
     ??Sicher [läuten NUR die Kirchturmglocken]$_D$. (Pattern 2)
     certainly ring only the church_bells

(36) Kommt morgen auch Felix? ('Will Felix come tomorrow, too?')
     *[Felix]$_D$ kommt morgen NUR. (Pattern 3)
     Felix comes tomorrow only

(37) Hat Maja Felix auch geküsst? ('Did Maja also kiss Felix?')
     *Maja [küsste]$_D$ Felix NUR. (Pattern 4)
     Maja kissed Felix only

(38) Entkam auch die Tochter den Flammen?
  ('Has the daughter escaped the flames, too?')

---

12. (35) is fully acceptable if the domain is restricted to the subject *die Kirchturmglocken* ('the church bells'). Then, of course, the sentence is an instance of Pattern 1.

*[Die Tochter]$_D$ NUR entkam den Flammen. (Pattern 8)
the daughter only escaped the flames

(39) Auch hat ihm das niemand gesagt. ('In addition, no one has told him that.')
*NUR [hat ihm das niemand gesagt]$_D$. (Pattern 10)
only *aux$_p$* him that no_one told

An apparent counterexample to the claim that contrastive *nur* cannot associate with the finite verb in the V2-position is given in (40a). However, *nur* is used in an exceptional way here: it contrasts with *oft* ('often'), its meaning corresponding to *always* or *all the time* rather than *only*. In a context that necessitates the normal meaning of *nur* (i.e., where it contrasts with *auch*), the sentence is extremely marginal; cf. (40b). This difference receives a plausible explanation if we assume *nur* in (40b), but not in (40a), to be a focus functional operator in the sense of Beaver & Clark (2003). According to these authors, the focus sensitivity of non-focus-functional operators is based on pragmatic processes, which is why the respective constructions are subject to less grammatical restrictions than constructions involving association with focus grounded on semantic mechanisms (cf. Section 3.2.1 above).

(40) a. Streiten deine Eltern OFT? ('Do your parents often argue?')
Meine Eltern [streiten]$_D$ NUR (noch).
my parents argue only still
b. STREIten deine Eltern auch? ('Do your parents also argue?')
??Meine Eltern [streiten]$_D$ NUR.

The data presented so far suggests the following generalization about the contrastive use of focus particles.

(41) If a focus particle is used contrastively, it must precede its domain.

With the exception of Pattern 10, the generalization in (41) accounts for the (im)possibility of contrastive *nur* in all patterns. Sentences of Pattern 10 are ungrammatical if *nur* is stressed, even though the particle precedes its domain. Again, this results from the exceptional use of *nur* in connection with a special meaning in this pattern (cf. Section 4.1.1). In all other cases, the contrastive use of *nur* is clearly degraded or impossible if the domain partly or as a whole precedes the particle. The reason probably lies in the accentuation of the sentences. If a focus particle is used contrastively, it attracts the sentence accent. The domain, on the other hand, is deaccented, which means that no accentual information is available for its identification. In this situation, the default applies: the domain is assumed to be located to the right of the particle.

The distribution of contrastive *auch* substantially mirrors that of contrastive *nur* – it is compatible with Patterns 1, 5, 7, and 9. However, the relevant sentences, exemplified in (42)–(44), are slightly less acceptable than their counterparts with *nur*.

(42) Kommt morgen nur Felix? ('Will only Felix come tomorrow?')

a. ?Morgen kommt AUCH [Felix]$_{\text{D}}$. (Pattern 1)
tomorrow comes also Felix

b. ?AUCH [Felix]$_{\text{D}}$ kommt morgen. (Pattern 7)

(43) Hat Maja nur gesagt, dass etwas geschehen muss?
('Did Maja only say that something must happen?')

?Maja hat AUCH gesagt, [dass etwas geschehen
Maja aux_p also said that something happen
muss]$_{\text{D}}$. (Pattern 5)
must

(44) ... der nur auf seine Frisur stolze Linguist ...
('... the linguist only proud of his hairstyle ...')

?... der AUCH [auf seine Frisur]$_{\text{D}}$ stolze Linguist ... (Pattern 9)
the also of his hairstyle proud linguist

Contrastive *auch* is unacceptable in all other patterns; cf. (45)–(49). If *auch* is stressed in Pattern 3, the outcome resembles the constructions of Pattern 6. However, the unacceptability of the discourse in (46) shows that the stressed particle cannot have a contrastive interpretation in these cases.

(45) Läuten nur die Kirchturmglocken? ('Do only the church bells ring?')

*Sicher [läuten AUCH die Kirchturmglocken]$_{\text{D}}$. (Pattern 2)
certainly ring also the church_bells

(46) Kommt morgen nur Felix? ('Will only Felix come tomorrow?')

*[Felix]$_{\text{D}}$ kommt morgen AUCH. (Pattern 3)
Felix comes tomorrow also

(47) Hat Maja Felix nur geküsst? ('Has Maja only kissed Felix?')

*Maja [küsste]$_{\text{D}}$ Felix AUCH. (Pattern 4)
Maja kissed Felix also

(48) Entkam nur die Tochter den Flammen?
('Has only the daughter escaped the flames?')

*[Die Tochter]$_{\text{D}}$ AUCH entkam den Flammen. (Pattern 8)
the daughter also escaped the flames

(49) Nur hat ihm das niemand gesagt. ('No one has told him that, though.')

*AUCH [hat ihm das niemand gesagt]$_{\text{D}}$. (Pattern 10)
also aux_p him that no_one told

Why is the contrastive use of *auch* (cf. (42)–(44)) generally less acceptable than that of *nur* (cf. (32)–(34))? We can only give a speculative answer to this question. As shown in Section 3.2.4, the distribution of the presupposed and asserted meaning components is different in constructions with *nur* and *auch*. A sentence with *nur* presupposes the meaning of the respective sentence without the particle; the restrictive meaning component introduced by *nur* is asserted. In the case of *auch*, it is the other way around: the underlying sentence is asserted, while the additive meaning component contributed by the particle is a presupposition. This difference might have an effect on the acceptability of the contrastive uses of the particles. In the case of *nur*, the contrast is established by means of the assertion of the sentence. The contrastive accent on the particle in (32a) above, for instance, emphasizes that no one apart from Felix will come. By means of the contrastive use of *auch* in (42a), on the other hand, it is emphasized that other people will come. This contrasting part of the meaning, however, is only a presupposition of the sentence. Arguably, it is easier to establish a contrast by means of the assertion of a sentence than by means of its presupposition. As sentences with contrastive *auch* instantiate the latter variant, they are more marked than sentences with contrastive *nur*.

Apart from cases involving metalinguistic contrast, the focus particle *sogar* does not have a contrastive use and never carries the sentence accent. Illustrating examples can be dispensed with here; the sentences resulting from the substitution of *auch* by accented *sogar* in (42)–(49) are ungrammatical without exception. We will return to this issue in Section 4.5.2 below.

4.2 Syntactic analyses of focus particle constructions

In the literature, a number of different syntactic accounts of German focus particle constructions have been proposed. The most influential ones are briefly reviewed in this section. An adequate syntactic (and information-structural) theory of focus particles must cover the entire range of data presented in Section 4.1, and it should answer the following questions:

- What categorial status do focus particles have? Are they to be analyzed as (functional) heads or maximal projections?
- How are focus particles integrated into the syntactic structure? Is there a designated position for focus particles (e.g., in the specifier of a functional projection), or can they be merged at different stages of the derivation?
- Are there any restrictions on a focus particle's syntactic sister? Can focus particles combine with maximal and non-maximal projections, and is the category of the sister of any relevance?

- Must a focus particle and its domain enter into a specific syntactic configuration? How do syntax, prosody, and the information-structural properties expressed on these grammatical levels interact to identify the domain?
- Can the domain of a focus particle be equated with the sentence focus? If so, how are constructions with stressed *auch* to be analyzed, where the focus particle itself seems to be focused?

The existing syntactic analyses of German focus particle constructions can be roughly classified into two groups, which we call *adverbial analyses* and *adjunction-to-XP analyses.*[13] Proponents of the first type of analysis include Jacobs (1983, 1986, 1988), Primus (1992), and Büring & Hartmann (2001). They consider focus particles to be a subgroup of adverbials, i.e., modifiers of verbal projections. Advocates of the second type of theory, such as Bayer (1996), Reis & Rosengren (1997), and Nederstigt (2003), analyze focus particles as crosscategorial operators, i.e., elements that can have maximal projections of any kind as their sister constituents. As noted by Büring & Hartmann (2001:231), sentences like (50a) are compatible with both analyses, the reason being that the left edge of the particle's domain coincides with the left edge of VP. The decision whether (50b) or (50c) represents the correct analysis of (50a) must therefore be made on the basis of criteria other than surface word order.

(50) a. Ich habe nur [einen ROMAN]$_D$ gelesen.
I *aux*$_p$ only a novel read
b. Ich habe [$_{VP}$ nur [$_{VP}$ [$_{DP}$ einen Roman] gelesen]] .
c. Ich habe [$_{VP}$ [$_{DP}$ nur [$_{DP}$ einen Roman]] gelesen] .
(Büring & Hartmann 2001:231)

As will be shown below, both types of analyses have advantages as well as disadvantages, and König's (1993:985) assessment of the situation has not lost its validity more than fifteen years later: "The debate is still open."

4.2.1 Focus particles as adverbials

An assumption common to all variants of the adverbial analysis is that focus particles syntactically behave like adverbials, i.e., that they are maximal projections adjoined to a node on the projection line of the verb. As noted by König (1993:983), this characterization "gets some cross-linguistic support from the fact that focus particles often have typically adverbial endings such as *-ly* in English

13. For an overview, see König (1993) and Hoeksema & Zwarts (1991).

(*only*, *merely*, *especially*) or *-ment* in French (*seulement*, *également*)."[14] The exact definition of possible adjunction sites in the individual analyses depends on the chosen syntactic framework.

Jacobs (1983, 1986, 1988). Jacobs' account, developed within the theoretical frameworks of Montague grammar and GPSG, is the first formal account of the syntax of focus particle constructions in German. Jacobs introduces the hypothesis that focus particles do not minimally c-command the element they immediately precede in a sentence, but a node of the verbal projection that contains this element.[15] Accordingly, (51a) is assigned the structure in (51b).[16]

(51) a. (dass) Luise nur / sogar / auch ihrem ARZT ein Auto
that Luise only / even / also her doctor a car
vermachte
bequeathed

b.

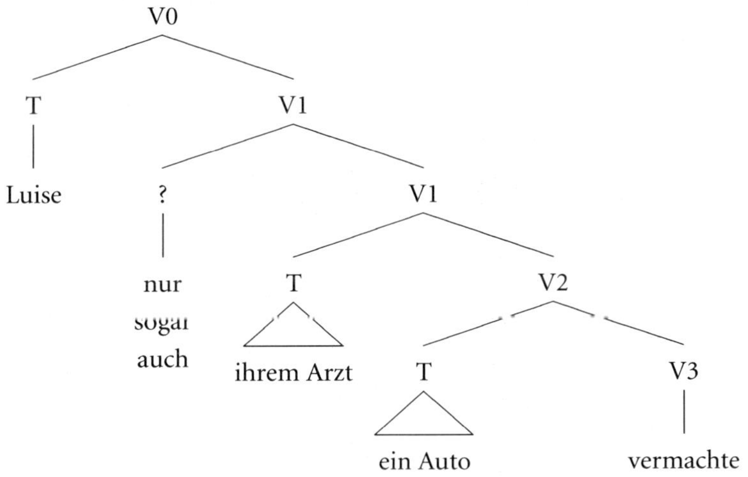

(Jacobs 1983:42)

14. Focus particles morphologically marked as adverbs actually exist in a broad range of languages, including many Romance and Slavic languages, and can also be observed in non-Indo-European languages (Alena Witzlack-Makarevich, p.c.).

15. "Ich gehe davon aus, dass im Allgemeinen der syntaktische Bereich von Gradpartikeln *nicht* das auf der Verbendstellungsstufe unmittelbar folgende Satzglied ist (auch wenn es den Fokusakzent trägt), sondern *die ganze auf der Verbendstellungsstufe auf die Gradpartikel folgende null- bis dreistellige Verbalphrase*." (Jacobs 1983:41–42)

16. *T* is the abbreviation for *term*, which is equivalent to DP; *Vn* stands for a verbal category with *n* unsaturated argument slots.

Jacobs (1983: Section 3.2.1.2) offers a number of arguments in favor of this structure, which are only listed here and will be discussed in more detail below. First, it seems that the combination of a focus particle and an immediately following DP cannot serve as the complement of a preposition or be coordinated with another DP (cf. (52a) and (52b), respectively), suggesting that the particle and the DP do not form a constituent. Second, as focus particles cannot be extraposed together with an embedded clause (cf. (52c)), they do not seem to be able to form a constituent with a CP argument, either. Third, the domain of a focus particle may consist of more than one constituent, as shown in (5) above. For obvious reasons, the particle cannot be adjoined to its domain in these cases.

(52) a. *Luise wurde von nur ihrem ARZT vor dem Rauchen
Luise *aux*$_{pass}$ by only her doctor against the smoking
gewarnt.
warned

b. ??dass Peter und nur / sogar / auch LUISE sich in Straßburg trafen
that Peter and only / even / also Luise *refl* in Straßburg met

c. *dass er bedauerte nur / sogar / auch dass GERDA nicht
that he regretted only / even / also that Gerda not
gekommen war
come *aux*$_{p}$

(Jacobs 1983: 42–46)

There are two exceptions to Jacobs' generalization that focus particles may only adjoin to verbal projections. In the final version of the theory, potential adjunction sites include adjective phrases and determiners. The first extension is needed to account for examples like those in (21) above. While structures involving a focus particle within a DP are usually ungrammatical, they are possible if the DP contains an AP that can serve as the adjunction site of the particle. In order to cover these cases, Jacobs (1983: 66) formulates a metarule postulating a general similarity between verbal and adjectival projections. The second extension is made to explain sentences like (53a), where, according to Jacobs, the focus particle is adjoined to the determiner *einem* rather than to the whole DP *einem Täter*. This view is supported by the fact that focus particles cannot adjoin to DPs without determiner, as evidenced by (53b).

(53) a. Die Polizei geht von nur EINem Täter aus.
the police assume of only one culprit *pref*

b. *Peter träumt von nur GERda.
Peter dreams of only Gerda

(Jacobs 1983: 69)

However, this second modification of the theory is unnecessary, as *einem* in (53a) is not the indefinite determiner ('a'), but the homonymous numeral ('one'). As such it can be treated as an adjective or the head of a quantifier phrase (cf. Büring & Hartmann 2001: 275–276; Bayer 1996: 23–24). An analysis along these lines also offers an explanation of the fact that other determiners, such as the definite article in (54) or the possessive pronoun in (52a) above, are incompatible with focus particles in the structures under discussion, as noticed by Jacobs (1983: 70) himself.

(54) *von nur dem Täter
of only the culprit
(Jacobs 1983: 70)

A consequence of Jacobs' theory is that focus particles need not minimally c-command their domains. As shown in (1)–(6) above, however, the domain must immediately follow the focus particle in most cases. Jacobs (1983: 86) accounts for this fact by postulating a filter mechanism that excludes sentences where the distance between the focus particle and its domain is too large. What counts as 'too large' is defined by Jacobs' (1983: 86) *Principle of Maximal Closeness to the Focus (Prinzip der maximalen Fokusnähe, PMF)*, saying that a focus particle must be located as close as possible to its domain while still complying with certain scope restrictions and the requirement that the domain must be c-commanded by the particle. Additional filters are necessary to rule out sentences with a derived word order within a complex domain and to ensure that the domain of a sentence-initial focus particle does not extend beyond the prefield; cf. (55).

(55) a. ?Peter wollte auch [die Stadt seiner MUTter zeigen]$_D$.
Peter wanted also the city his mother to_show
b. ??Nur [mein NACHbar schlägt da seine FRAU]$_D$.
only my neighbor beats there his wife
(Jacobs 1983: 88–89)

For the analysis of constructions with focus particles following (parts of) their domains, Jacobs makes use of insertion rules specific to his theoretical framework. In this context, the PMF is generalized to the *Principle of Latest Possible Positioning (Prinzip der maximalen Spätstellung, PMS)*, saying that a focus particle must occur as late as possible in a sentence (cf. Jacobs 1983: 113). This modification is needed to account for the fact that focus particles following their domains must be maximally distant rather than maximally close to the domain; cf. (56). As the insertion rules employed by Jacobs are incompatible with modern generative syntactic theories, constructions with focus particles following their domains are often problematic for more recent versions of the adverbial analysis. We will return to this point below.

(56) a. Das Auto hat er ihr AUCH geschenkt.
the car aux_p he her also given
b. ??Das Auto hat er AUCH ihr geschenkt.
(Jacobs 1983:112)

One of the strongest objections to the adverbial analysis is already anticipated by Jacobs (1983:49) himself: given that the focus particle and its domain do not form a constituent in a sentence like (57), such constructions violate the V2-generalization of German, which says that the finite verb may only be preceded by one constituent in main clauses. Jacobs' reply to this objection is simply that the relevant focus particle constructions are exceptions to this generalization.

(57) Nur LUISE vermachte ihrem Arzt ein Auto.
only Luise bequeathed her doctor a car
(Jacobs 1983:49)

Büring & Hartmann (2001). In their paper, Büring & Hartmann reconsider and modify Jacobs' hypotheses. However, they share the basic assumption that focus particles behave like adverbials and only adjoin to verbal projections, which include in their argument VP, IP, and CP. Büring & Hartmann's (2001) reformulation of Jacobs' proposal is given in (58).

(58) a. FPs must be adjoined to an extended verbal projection.
b. FPs must be adjoined to a maximal projection.
c. FPs must c-command the focus.
d. FPs are as close to the focus as possible.
(Büring & Hartmann 2001:237)

Sentences like those in (3) above, where the focus particle immediately precedes the verb, are derived by leftward movement of all intervening constituents. The theory correctly predicts that constituents that cannot scramble (predicatives and directional adverbials, among others) may intervene between a focus particle and its domain in the middlefield, as in (7) and (8) above. Jacobs' PMS is replaced by the *Closeness Principle* (58d), requiring a focus particle "to be as 'low in the tree' as possible while still c-commanding the focus, in other words: to be as close to the focus as possible" (Büring & Hartmann 2001:237). The authors present additional arguments for the adverbial analysis, in particular for the claim that sentence-initial focus particles do violate the V2-generalization. Their central argument, the so-called *(no) reconstruction argument*, will be addressed in Chapter 5. It will be shown that it does not stand up to close examination.

Taking into account that focus particles cannot adjoin to argument CPs, as demonstrated by Jacobs' example in (52c) above, Büring & Hartmann (2001:266) modify their theory in such a way that it allows only non-arguments as adjunction sites. After this modification, potential sister constituents of focus particles include APs, while argument CPs, DPs, and PPs are excluded. The final version of the proposal is given in (59).

(59) For any node α marked F in a phrase marker P, let the set of f-nodes of α consist of all nodes β in P such that
a. β is a non-argument
b. β is a maximal projection
c. β dominates α or is identical to α
d. there is no EP [= extended projection] β′ of the same head that β is an EP of such that β dominates β′ and β′ meets [(59b)] and [(59c)].

A FP must be left-adjoined to an f-node of its focus.
(Büring & Hartmann 2001:266)

We briefly address two drawbacks of Büring & Hartmann's (2001) analysis; a more detailed discussion is postponed to the subsequent sections. First, the analysis cannot account for focus particles immediately following their domains in the prefield or middlefield; cf. the examples of Pattern 8 above.[17] The authors consider sentences like those in (18) and (19) to be unacceptable and remove them from consideration: "we do not intend our analysis to cover cases like [(18)]" (Büring & Hartmann 2001:240). This is an unwarranted limitation of the theory's scope. Second, it remains unexplained why the domain of a sentence-initial focus particle must not extend beyond the prefield. In particular, the theory has no means to exclude cases like (55b), where the particle's domain is the remainder of the sentence. A smaller domain in the middlefield is ruled out by the *Closeness Principle*, but (55b), for the exclusion of which Jacobs (1983) employs a special filter mechanism, does not violate any of Büring & Hartmann's (2001) constraints.

4.2.2 Focus particles as crosscategorial operators

In contrast to adverbial analyses, adjunction-to-XP analyses share the assumption that a focus particle may occur as a sister constituent of any maximal projection, including DP and PP. This view is adopted from the literature on English focus particles (e.g., Taglicht 1984), the exact conception of the syntactic relationship differing from author to author.

17. The other patterns where the domain partly or completely precedes the focus particle, i.e., Patterns 2, 3, 4, and 6, are not covered by the theory in its present form, either. However, this shortcoming can be overcome by minor changes in the formalization; cf. Sections 4.4.3 and 4.5.2, and Büring & Hartmann (2001:241, Footnote 9).

Bayer (1996). Taking up a proposal by Rothstein (1991), Bayer analyses focus particles as minor functional heads, "which subcategorize, but do not have θ-grids, do not bind θ-positions, and do not project category features" (Rothstein 1991: 107–108). They can take any XP as their complement, forming another instance of the same XP-type. Even though the complement projects its category, certain semantic features of the particle are inherited by the upper XP-node. This is indicated by the superscript *q* in Bayer's representation; cf. (60). Although this analysis does not involve adjunction in the strict sense of the term, the predictions it makes are similar to those derivable from an account where the focus particle is adjoined to XP, for which reason it is classified as an adjunction-to-XP analysis. Like Büring & Hartmann (2001), Bayer does not analyze focus particles immediately preceding the verb in its base position as attached to a non-maximal projection. The relevant constructions are considered to involve VP attachment and scrambling of all intervening VP internal material.

(60)

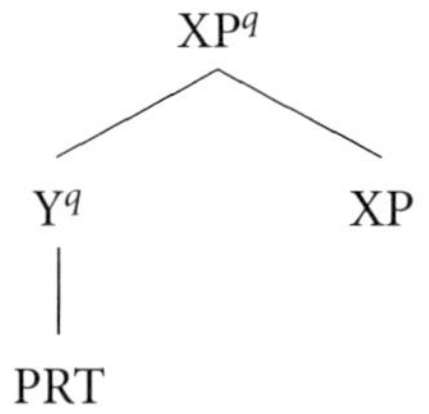

(Bayer 1996: 15)

Although Bayer's theory allows focus particles to attach to XPs of any kind, it does not make the claim that the phrase minimally c-commanded by the particle always coincides with the particle's domain. The proposed relation between a focus particle and its domain is expressed by the generalizations in (61).

(61) a. A focusing particle must c-command a focused constituent.
b. The focused constituent may be unboundedly far away from the focusing particle.
(Bayer 1996: 16)

A clear benefit of Bayer's analysis is that it leaves the V2-generalization unaffected: sentence-initial focus particles are assumed to be part of the prefield constituent rather than to c-command the whole CP. As a consequence, they can associate with the immediately following constituent, but not with the whole clause. In the latter case, the c-command condition (61a) is not fulfilled. Bayer's criticism of Jacobs' (1983) analysis is not entirely justified, though. With respect to the examples in (62), he states the following: "In Jacobs' theory it is an accident that *sogar* associates with HANS in [(62a)]. There is no reason why it should not associate with some other focus constituent." (Bayer 1996: 22)

(62) a. Sogar HANS gab seiner Tochter ein neues Fahrrad.
even Hans gave his daughter a new bike
b. *Sogar Hans GAB seiner Tochter ein neues Fahrrad.
c. *Sogar Hans gab SEIner Tochter ein neues Fahrrad.
d. *Sogar Hans gab seiner TOCHter ein neues Fahrrad.
e. *Sogar Hans gab seiner Tochter ein NEUes Fahrrad.
f. *Sogar Hans gab seiner Tochter ein neues FAHRrad.
(Bayer 1996: 22)

Jacobs's analysis, however, excludes most of the ungrammatical sentences by means of the PMS, which requires the focus particle to occur as close as possible to its domain. In (62b)–(62e), the location of the sentence accent blocks focus projection, resulting in a violation of the PMS. The only problematic case is (62f), which should be compatible with a domain corresponding to the whole remaining clause, as indicated in (63). It is this type of construction that Jacobs (1983: 90) must rule out by stipulating an additional, language-specific filter mechanism.[18]

(63) *Sogar [Hans gab seiner Tochter ein neues FAHRrad $]_D$.
even Hans gave his daughter a new bike

The distributional restrictions of focus particles considered by Jacobs (1983) to support his analysis – e.g., the ban on focus particles within PPs and DPs and the impossibility of extraposing a focus particle together with a clausal argument – are explained by Bayer through movement restrictions that prevent the relevant structures from getting interpretable LFs.[19] As shown by Büring & Hartmann (2001), this argument has several problems. A more detailed discussion cannot be provided here.

Reis & Rosengren (1997). In their paper, Reis & Rosengren discuss the grammar of the focus particle *auch*. They attempt to explain the distribution and characteristics of the stressed and unstressed variants of the particle, in particular the exceptional behavior of stressed *auch* following its domain; cf. the examples of Pattern 6 above. Regarding the V2-constraint as inviolable, Reis & Rosengren conclude that focus particles are crosscategorial operators that take all kinds of XPs as their sister constituents. *Auch* itself is considered to be a non-expanding maximal projection of its own kind (*AuchP*); cf. (64).

18. For a similar misinterpretation of Jacobs' analysis, see Reis & Rosengren (1997: 302–303, Footnote 21).

19. See also Bayer & Grosu (2000).

(64)

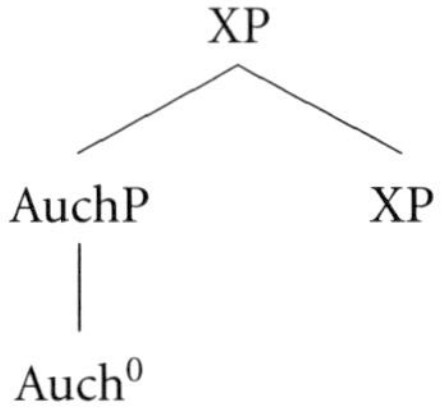

(Reis & Rosengren 1997: 262)

Another central assumption of Reis & Rosengren's theory is given in (65).[20] This generalization rules out occurrences of the focus particle within PPs and DPs not containing an AP, the ungrammaticality of which is considered by Jacobs (1983) as evidence against the adjunction-to-XP analysis.

(65) *Auch* divides its host proposition such that the *Auch* phrase is always an immediate constituent on the projection line of the predicate.
(Reis & Rosengren 1997: 260)

Nederstigt (2003). Nederstigt investigates the focus particles *auch* and *noch* ('also, still, another, else'). With respect to *noch* and the unstressed variant of *auch*, her syntactic analysis is similar to those proposed by Bayer (1996) and Reis & Rosengren (1997). The particles are regarded as adjuncts to XPs of any kind; cf. the structure in (66).[21]

(66)

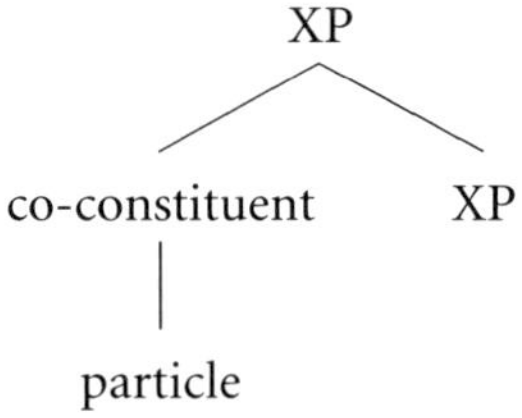

(Nederstigt 2003: 199)

20. *Auch phrase* refers to the combination of *auch* and its sister constituent, i.e., $[_{XP}$ auch XP$]$, and predicate projections include verbal as well as adjectival and small clause projections (cf. Reis & Rosengren 1997: 258).

21. Nederstigt's terminology is somewhat confusing here. The particle is argued to be a *co-constituent* of its domain in (66): "we will assume that in *auch*-utterances, the particle is a co-constituent of the phrase that functions as domain of application for the particle rather than being an adjunct to this phrase" (Nederstigt 2003: 199). In the case of stressed *auch*, on the other hand, where Nederstigt argues for an analysis in terms of a functional projection (cf. (67) below), she uses the term *adjunction*: "this analysis assumes that AUCH is an adjunct to the VP" (Nederstigt 2003: 196). In recapitulating Nederstigt's theory, we keep to the more commonly used terminology, referring to the focus particle as an adjunct in (66) and as a functional head in (67).

A crucial difference to the variants of the adjunction-to-XP analysis discussed so far is Nederstigt's claim that the XP serving as the adjunction site of the focus particle is always identical to the particle's domain. This assumption, which is explicitly argued against by Bayer (1996: 16) and Reis & Rosengren (1997: 242), has the consequence that the analysis cannot account for cases where the domain does not consist of a single constituent or where the particle is not adjacent to its domain; cf. the examples in (5) and (7)–(9) above.

The stressed variant of *auch* following its domain (Pattern 6) is analyzed in a different way, namely, as the head (or the specifier) of a functional projection AuchP located between VP and IP. The resulting syntactic structure is given in (67). In contrast to the account proposed by Reis & Rosengren (1997), Nederstigt's (2003) analysis presupposes the existence of two different lexicon entries for *auch*.

(67)

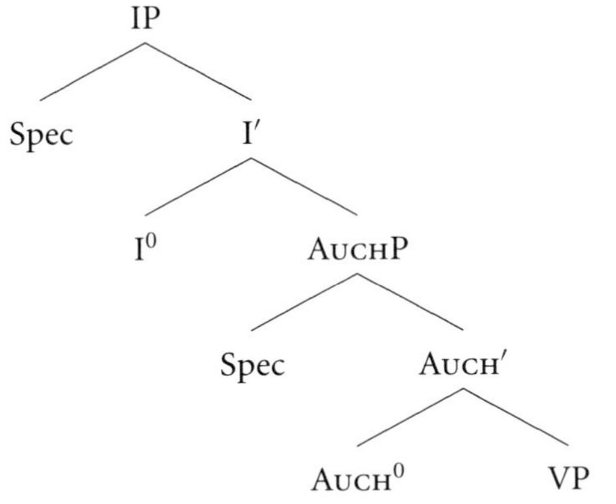

(Nederstigt 2003: 197)

4.2.3 The role of information structure

In the literature, information structure has been assigned an important status within the grammar of focus particle constructions.[22] However, the individual analyses differ with respect to the way it is integrated into the description. The term *focus particle* indicates the particular relevance of the focus-background partition, and, as mentioned above, most authors identify the domain of a focus particle with the focus of the respective sentence. This view is already present in the groundbreaking work of Altmann (1976a, 1978) and serves as the basis for semantic theories of association with focus, such as Jackendoff (1972) and Rooth (1985).

22. See, for instance, Dimroth (2004).

Regarding the question of how association with focus is established in grammar, two main theoretical lines can be distinguished. Proponents of the so-called *relational theory of focus* (Taglicht 1984; Jacobs 1983, 1986, 1988; Altmann 1993; Foolen 1993; Drubig 1994; Bayer 1996) consider focus particles to be operators responsible for the creation of a focus-background structure in the respective sentences. According to this theory, a particle assigns a focus feature to its domain, which results in the prosodic marking of the domain by means of a focus accent. The central claim is that the partition into focus and background is not independently given, but only exists in relation to some focus-inducing element, or, as Jacobs puts it: "A focus (background) in a sentence always is the focus (background) of some linguistic element in that sentence. This element I call the FOCUS INDUCER. Within this view the meaning of focus and background depends on the choice of the focus inducer." (Jacobs 1986: 104) As a consequence of this assumption, the presence of a phonologically empty operator must be postulated for sentences that do not contain any overt focus inducers. Another common claim connected with the relational view on focus is that focus particles induce contrastive focus; cf. Altmann (1976a, b) and Foolen (1993). According to these authors, the domain of a focus particle is always contrasted with some contextually given or derivable alternative, resulting in an interpretation comparable to a correction.

The alternative view of the relation between focus particles and information structure is taken by Büring & Hartmann (2001), Dimroth & Klein (1996), and Dimroth (2004), among others. Their basic assumption is that focus particles do not create a focus-background partition themselves, but interact with an independently given one. The particles are analyzed as focus sensitive operators rather than focus inducers in the sense of Jacobs; their meaning contribution depends on the actual choice of the focus. Dimroth (2004), for instance, characterizes focus particles as optional elements operating on the initial structure (*Ausgangsstruktur*) of the sentences in which they occur. The initial structure corresponds to the respective sentence without particle and is already divided into focus and background parts, i.e., it comes with a specified information structure. While the individual analyses within this second line of research differ in their conceptions of how focusing works (cf. the possibilities discussed in Section 2.3), they share the view that it does not depend on the presence of an overt or covert operator. In addition, this view predicts that focus particles can associate with both contrastive and new information foci, depending on the information-structural status of the particle's domain in the initial structure.

Constructions with the stressed variant of *auch* (Pattern 6) pose a serious problem for both of the views described above, and, as a consequence, also for the semantic theories of association with focus discussed in Chapter 3. In sentences with stressed *auch*, the domain of the particle need not be prosodically marked (in fact, it need not even be overtly realized), while the particle itself carries the sentence accent. The focus structure in these sentences thus crucially differs from that in other focus particle constructions, and focus does not fulfill its normal function. In the literature, two ideas have been pursued to account for this phenomenon. Reis & Rosengren (1997) abandon the concept of association with focus. In their view, the domain is identified with the help of the context: "the division of the *Auch* proposition into RC [= related constituent] and the rest of the proposition is not determined by its focus structure (as previously assumed), but by comparing it with some contextually given proposition in the same set of alternatives" (Reis & Rosengren 1997: 240). A consequence of this approach, which comes close to von Fintel's (1994) pragmatic fixing of quantifier domains, is that the term *focus particle* is essentially inappropriate for the elements under discussion. Krifka (1999) and Dimroth (2004), on the other hand, acknowledge the importance of information structure, but argue that, in the case of stressed *auch*, the relevant concept is (contrastive) topic rather than focus. Krifka's *Contrastive Topic Hypothesis* is given in (68).[23]

(68) *Contrastive Topic Hypothesis:*
The associated constituent of stressed postponed additive particles is the contrastive topic of the clause in which they occur.
(Krifka 1999: 113)

Contrastive topics, like foci, are able to supply the alternatives necessary for the determination of a focus particle's meaning contribution. Hence, association with focus is not abandoned by Krifka and Dimroth, but complemented with an alternative mechanism one might call *association with contrastive topic*. A crucial assumption is that although the domain of stressed *auch* is a contrastive topic, it need not be prosodically marked as such, as, in most cases, it can be identified on the basis of syntactic information alone.

The different attempts to account for the properties of constructions containing the stressed variant of *auch* or one of its equivalents indicate that these particles are not easy to integrate into a general syntactic and information-structural theory of focus particles in German. However, the conclusion that completely independent mechanisms are at work in cases with stressed *auch* and unstressed focus particles is premature, and a uniform account, explaining the distribution and behavior of the two variants on the basis of independent factors, still remains a valid option. The peculiarities of *auch* and their consequences for the grammatical description of focus particles will be discussed in more detail in Section 4.5.

23. Krifka attributes this hypothesis to an unpublished M.A. thesis by A. Kowalski (1992). However, a similar proposal had already been made by Jacobs (1983: Section 3.2.3.2). See also Tanaka (2000).

4.2.4 Summary

In this section, two types of syntactic analyses of focus particle constructions were briefly reviewed: adverbial analyses and adjunction-to-XP analyses. It was shown that both types are problematic, as the individual approaches are unable to explain the relevant distributional restrictions or fail to cover the entire range of data. A particular challenge is the stressed variant of the particle *auch*, which is often ignored (cf. Bayer 1996; Büring & Hartmann 2001) or only accounted for by introducing ad hoc assumptions about the reasons for its exceptional behavior (cf. Nederstigt 2003). Additional shortcomings of the existing accounts will be discussed in the subsequent sections.

4.3 An alternative proposal

In the present section, an alternative theory of the grammar of focus particle constructions in German is outlined. Based on the insight that neither adverbial analyses nor adjunction-to-XP analyses are fully satisfactory, the merits of both theories are combined. The resulting hybrid account considers focus particles to be adverbial-like (i.e., modifiers of verbal projections) in the standard case, but allows for exceptions under certain well-defined information-structural conditions. In subsequent sections, the claims and predictions of this new proposal will be discussed in detail and compared to those of the former accounts. It will be shown that the most relevant properties of focus particle constructions, such as the position of the particle relative to its domains and the size and type of the domain, follow without stipulation from independently motivated principles. In addition, parallels will be drawn between the grammar of focus particles and the grammar of German (non-contrastive and contrastive) negation.

The theoretical framework of the analysis, in particular the underlying conception of the grammatical realization of information structure, was introduced in Chapter 2. On the basis of these assumptions, we formulate the following hypotheses about the syntax and information structure of focus particle constructions in German:

- Focus particles have the status of phrasal categories. Like adverbs, they form non-expanding, maximal projections.
- In the standard case, focus particles adjoin to VP. They c-command the focus domain and are c-commanded by the sentence adverbials, as shown in (69). Adjunction of focus particles to the root CP is impossible.

(69)

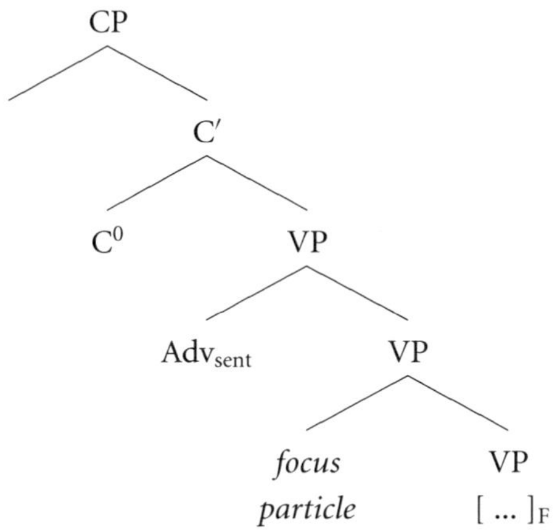

- The domain of a focus particle adjoined to VP corresponds to the sentence focus. As focused elements preferentially stay in their base positions in the focus domain, and as defocused elements preferentially leave the focus domain via movement to the left (either to a position adjoined to the maximal VP above the sentence adverbials, or to the prefield), a focus particle usually c-commands its domain and only its domain. Exceptions to this generalization (elements that are not part of the domain, in spite of being c-commanded by the particle, and elements that belong to the domain, but are not c-commanded by the particle) result from independently motivated movement restrictions or movement requirements.
- Focus particles interact with a focus-background partition that is independently given. They do not induce focus in the sense described by Jacobs (1983, 1986, 1988).
- Owing to their similarity to VPs, adjectival projections are also potential adjunction sites for focus particles. The restrictions on the placement of focus particles and the behavior of their domains are the same in VPs and APs.
- Constructions with the stressed focus particle *auch* following its domain can be derived from the same underlying structure as constructions with unstressed focus particles. The exceptional properties of this pattern follow from the special information structure it involves.
- Focus particles may adjoin to phrases other than VP and AP if these are contrastively focused. In addition to (69), the structures in (70), among others, are possible in German, parallelling structures with contrastive negation.

(70)

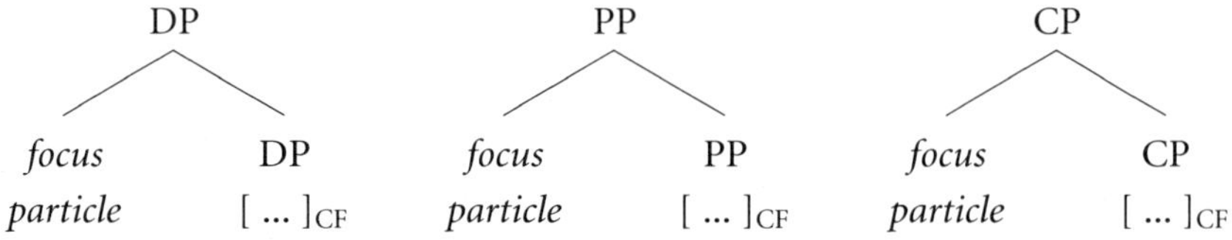

With these hypotheses, the main claims of the theory of focus particle constructions advocated in this chapter are outlined. Throughout the remainder of the chapter, they will be specified and substantiated. Section 4.4 shows that, for the most part, the relevant constructions can be accounted for by a modified version of Büring & Hartmann's (2001) adverbial analysis. In Section 4.5, it is argued that cases with stressed *auch* do not require a separate treatment, but are subject to the same principles and regularities. Section 4.6 deals with constructions that are not accounted for by a pure adverbial analysis.

4.4 Focus particles as adjuncts to VP and AP

The present section begins by dealing with occurrences of focus particles preceding their domain in the German middlefield, and asks how they can be integrated into the model of information structure introduced in Section 2.3. The analysis, which considers the particles to be adjuncts to VP, is then extended to cases where a focus particle is arguably adjoined to AP.

4.4.1 The syntactic status and the position of focus particles

In large part, the claim that focus particles are maximal projections adjoining to VP corresponds to the adverbial analyses of Jacobs (1983, 1986) and Büring & Hartmann (2001). This assumption requires some elaboration. If focus particles have the status of phrases, they should be able to occur in the prefield on their own, i.e., to serve as the only preverbal element in V2-clauses. Büring & Hartmann (2001: 240–241) interpret the sentences in (71) as confirming this prediction.

(71) a. Auch war ich sehr MÜDE.
also was I very tired
b. Nur WEISS das keiner.
only knows that nobody
(Büring & Hartmann 2001: 241)

However, as argued in Section 4.1.1, the usage of *nur* and *auch* in such constructions, which instantiate Pattern 10 of our descriptive survey, differs from that in the other patterns; the elements resemble conjunctions rather than focus particles and are characterized by a different meaning.[24] As a consequence, this type of data is of questionable value in determining the syntactic status of focus particles. In addition, it remains unexplained why *sogar* cannot be used in the same way; cf. (24c) above.[25] As the alternative view, i.e., that focus particles are functional heads, is not supported by conclusive evidence, either (cf. Reis & Rosengren 1997: 261–262), we nevertheless keep to the simpler assumption that focus particles are adverb-like maximal projections. The question of why a focus particle in its normal use, like the negation particle *nicht* and certain adverbials, cannot normally serve as the only prefield element must be left for further research.

Under this premise, and assuming that VP is the only possible adjunction site, the default position of focus particles in the middlefield can be easily determined. On the one hand, they must c-command the VP node that dominates the base positions of all arguments and adverbials (except the sentence adverbials). In other words, focus particles must c-command the focus domain. Only in this position are they compatible with a maximal domain, one that includes all middlefield elements, as in (72a). If any adverbials or arguments precede the particle in the middlefield, as in (72b), these elements are interpreted as not belonging to the particle's domain. In the next subsection, it will be argued that they have left the focus domain via movement to the left. If the domain is as large as indicated in the example, *sogar* cannot be placed between the other middlefield elements.

(72) a. Es hat sogar [neulich jemand in der Innenstadt einen
expl *aux*$_p$ even recently someone in the city_center a
streunenden FUCHS gesehen]$_D$.
stray fox seen

b. Es hat [neulich (*sogar) jemand (*sogar) in der Innenstadt (*sogar) einen streunenden FUCHS gesehen]$_D$.

On the other hand, focus particles must be c-commanded by the sentence adverbials, which do not belong to the focus; cf. (73). (73b), where the particle precedes the sentence adverbial *wahrscheinlich* ('probably'), would only be acceptable with an accent on the adverbial, accompanied by the deaccentuation of *Flasche* ('bottle'). This, however, restricts the particle's domain to the sentence adverbial itself, resulting in a contrastive interpretation.

24. See Foolen, van Gerrevink, Hogeweg & Prawiro-Atmodjo (2009) for a similar analysis of sentence initial focus particles in Dutch.

25. See also Büring & Hartmann (2001: 241, Footnote 7).

(73) a. Es hat wahrscheinlich nur [jemand eine FLAsche
expl aux_p probably only someone a bottle
umgeworfen $]_D$.
knocked_over

b. *Es hat nur wahrscheinlich [jemand eine FLAsche umgeworfen $]_D$.

In the standard case, focus particles are thus located in the middlefield between the sentence adverbials and the left edge of the focus domain. This is also the position of the negation particle *nicht* ('not'), if it expresses sentence negation (cf. Steube 2005, 2006). The relation between focus particles and the negator will be discussed in Section 5.2.1.

4.4.2 Association with the sentence focus

Another assumption to be defended here is that the domain of a focus particle corresponds to the sentence focus. In other words, an element belongs to the domain of the particle if and only if it is focused. If it is true that focus particles have a designated position to the left of the VP containing the base positions of all arguments and adverbials except the sentence adverbials, that they c-command the sentence focus, and that the sentence focus forms the domain of the particle, then the question arises: how can association of focus particles with domains of different sizes be explained? The answer follows without stipulation from the theory of information structure introduced in Section 2.3: Defocused elements preferentially leave the focus domain via movement to the left; they are either scrambled to a middlefield position above the sentence adverbials or moved to the prefield. As background constituents, they no longer belong to the domain of the focus particle. The examples in (74), which instantiate Pattern 1, illustrate this mechanism.

(74) a. Es hat$_i$ $[_{VP,[+F]}$ auch $[_{VP}$ gestern ein Mann einen HUND
expl aux_p also yesterday a man a dog
geschlagen t_i]] .
beaten

b. Es hat$_i$ gestern$_j$ $[_{VP,[+F]}$ auch $[_{VP}$ t_j ein Mann einen HUND geschlagen t_i]] .

c. Gestern$_i$ hat$_j$ $[_{VP,[+F]}$ auch $[_{VP}$ t_i ein Mann einen HUND geschlagen t_j]] .

d. Gestern$_i$ hat$_j$ [der Mann $]_k$ $[_{VP,[+F]}$ auch $[_{VP}$ t_i t_k einen HUND
yesterday aux_p the man also a dog
geschlagen t_j]] .
beaten

e. Gestern$_i$ hat$_j$ [der Mann $]_k$ [den Hund $]_l$ $[_{VP,[+F]}$ auch $[_{VP}$ t_i
yesterday aux_p the man the dog also
t_k t_l geschLAgen t_j]] .
beaten

In (74a), no element except the finite auxiliary has moved out of the focus domain. The temporal adverbial *gestern* ('yesterday'), both arguments, and the main verb belong to the domain of *auch*. The whole proposition – that a man beat a dog on the day before – is added to another, contextually given proposition. For a felicitous use of (74a), the two propositions must be relevant alternatives of each other (see below). In the example, the presupposed proposition could, for instance, refer to another act of cruelty to animals. In (74b) and (74c), the temporal adverbial has left the focus domain. As part of the background of the sentences, it is excluded from the domain of *auch*.[26] Both sentences state that, in addition to some presupposed event on the previous day, a man beat a dog. In (74d), the subject has also left the focus domain. Its position, as well as the use of the definite article, indicates its status of belonging to the background. The sentence asserts that some contextually anchored man beat a dog on the day before, and it presupposes that this man did something else that is a relevant alternative to beating a dog. In (74e), the only element left in the focus domain is the main verb, which forms the domain of *auch* on its own. The presupposition of this sentence is that a contextually anchored man did something different from beating to some contextually anchored dog on the previous day; its assertion is that he beat it. The last example shows that our model can account for cases where the domain only consists of the verb in clause-final position without allowing the particle to adjoin to a non-maximal element such as V^0. This analysis is corroborated by the fact that a focus particle cannot move to the V2-position together with the finite verb, as shown in (75).[27]

(75) *Felix [nur SCHLUG]$_i$ den Hund t$_i$.
Felix only beat the dog

Our claim is thus that the particle always adjoins to VP in constructions like (74e), and that all defocused VP-internal elements move to the left across the particle. Similar solutions have already been proposed by Bayer (1996), Reis & Rosengren (1997), and, most explicitly, by Büring & Hartmann (2001). However, in the view taken here, the 'altruistic' movement of the elements originally intervening between the particle and its domain receives a natural explanation, based on independently motivated principles of information structure. In Büring & Hartmann's (2001) analysis (cf. (59) above), a focus particle is forced to adjoin to the lowest possible maximal projection that is a non-argument and dominates or is identical to the focus. Maximal closeness between the particle and

26. As noted in Section 2.3, the prefield differs from the target positions of scrambling in the middlefield in that it cannot only host background constituents, but also focused elements. For the time being, we assume that prefield constituents such as *gestern* in (74c) are indeed defocused. We will return below to examples where this is not the case.

27. See also Reis & Rosengren (1997:254–255) and Büring & Hartmann (2001:241).

its domain is guaranteed by permitting different adjunction sites for the particle (CP, IP, and VP), and by the requirement that of the potential positions, the lowest still complying with the c-command condition is chosen. In this way, the correct word order is predicted in many cases, e.g., in sentences with a defocused subject like (76). According to Büring & Hartmann's analysis, the subject *Peter* is located in [Spec,I] in this case, forcing *nur* to adjoin to VP. Adjunction of the particle to IP is ruled out when the domain consists of the direct object only, as VP is a lower adjunction site dominating the focus.

(76) weil Peter nur [MARIA]$_D$ küsste
because Peter only Maria kissed

The theory runs into problems, though, with ordering restrictions within one of the phrases serving as adjunction sites of focus particles. A case in point are sentences where the particle is associated with the verb in clause-final position, as in Büring & Hartmann's own example (77a). The authors propose the structure given in (77b), assuming that the focus particle adjoins to VP (a lower adjunction site not being available) and that the direct object is scrambled. However, scrambling of the object intervening between the particle and the focused verb is neither motivated nor enforced by the theory. In fact, the ungrammatical sentence (78) is not ruled out by (59).

(77) a. weil Peter Maria nur [KÜSSTE]$_D$
because Peter Maria only kissed
b. weil [$_{IP}$ Peter [$_{VP}$ Maria [$_{VP}$ nur [$_{VP}$ t$_{Maria}$ KÜSSTE]]]]
(Büring & Hartmann 2001:241–242)

(78) *weil Peter nur Maria [KÜSSTE]$_D$
because Peter only Maria kissed

One could argue that an additional principle enforcing scrambling of the direct object in (77) can easily be integrated into Büring & Hartmann's proposal. As a consequence, however, the fact that a focus particle usually immediately precedes its domain in the middlefield would be explained on the basis of two different mechanisms: the constraint that the particle adjoins as low as possible in the tree, and – in case there is still intervening material – the requirement that this material is scrambled across the particle. In contrast, only one constraint is necessary in our theory, namely, that all defocused elements must, if possible, leave the c-command domain of the particle, which has a fixed position at the left edge of the focus domain.

The analysis outlined above, in particular the claim that focus particles are associated with the sentence focus, makes two predictions. First, focused elements that must leave the focus domain for independent grammatical reasons, and that are therefore not c-commanded by the particle, nevertheless belong to its domain.

Second, defocused elements that cannot move for independent grammatical reasons are not part of the domain of a focus particle, although they remain within the focus domain and are c-commanded by the particle. The first prediction will be dealt with in the next subsection; the second, which is directly relevant for the constructions of Pattern 1, is addressed here.

We consider finite and infinite verb forms first. In German declarative main clauses, the finite verb obligatorily moves to the V2-position, while all other parts of the verb cluster (infinitives and participles) remain in their clause-final base positions; in verb-final clauses, the finite verb also stays in its base position (cf. Section 2.2). The distribution of the verbal elements is determined by purely syntactic principles and does not allow for exceptions. As a consequence, it is independent of the information-structural partition of the respective sentence: a (finite or infinite) verb in its base position in the focus domain may be focused or not, and the same holds for a finite verb in the V2-position. The theory of information structure introduced in Section 2.3 handles this phenomenon by marking all defocused verbal elements in their VP-internal base positions with the index [–F], which overrides the default principle that all elements in the focus domain are focused. This mechanism is relevant for the interpretation of focus particle constructions. In (79a), the participle *geschlagen* ('beaten') cannot leave the focus domain. However, as a defocused element, it does not belong to the domain of *nur*. The only focused element is the direct object *einen Hund* ('a dog'); the sentence states that Felix did not beat anyone/anything but a dog. The change from perfect to past tense left aside, (79a) has the same interpretation as (79b), where the defocused finite main verb has left the focus domain. In the subordinate clause (79c), the finite main verb remains in its base position, but again, it does not belong to the domain of *nur*, as it is marked [–F].

(79) a. Felix$_i$ hat$_j$ [$_{VP,[+F]}$ nur [$_{VP}$ t$_i$ einen HUND geschlagen$_{[-F]}$ t$_j$]] .
Felix *aux$_p$* only a dog beaten

b. Felix$_i$ schlug$_j$ [$_{VP,[+F]}$ nur [$_{VP}$ t$_i$ einen HUND t$_j$]] .
Felix beat only a dog

c. dass Felix$_i$ [$_{VP,[+F]}$ nur [$_{VP}$ t$_i$ einen HUND schlug$_{[-F]}$]]
that Felix only a dog beat

The examples in (80) demonstrate that the model can account for cases where the domain of a focus particle consists of two or more elements in the middlefield that do not form a constituent (cf. also the examples in (5) above). In both sentences, the main verb and the adverbial *gestern* ('yesterday') are defocused, and the domain of the particle consists of the remaining VP-internal elements, i.e., the subject and the direct object. A strict version of the adjunction-to-XP analysis claiming that focus particles always adjoin to their domains (cf. Nederstigt 2003) cannot explain such data. The analyses of Bayer (1996) and Reis & Rosengren (1997), on the other hand, would have to assume adjunction to VP here, confirming the prediction of the adverbial analyses.

(80) a. Gestern$_i$ hat$_j$ [$_{VP,[+F]}$ sogar [$_{VP}$ t$_i$ Maja FElix geküsst$_{[-F]}$ t$_j$]] .
yesterday *aux$_p$* even Maja Felix kissed

b. Gestern$_i$ küsste$_j$ [$_{VP,[+F]}$ sogar [$_{VP}$ t$_i$ Maja FElix t$_j$]] .
yesterday kissed even Maja Felix

In addition to finite and infinite verb forms, there are several other elements that violate the generalization that the focus domain only contains focused material. As observed by Büring & Hartmann (2001), these elements may intervene between a focus particle and its domain in the middlefield. Cases in point are directional adverbials, manner adverbials, resultative predicates, depictive predicates, predicatives, and infinite VPs; cf. (81)–(86). These elements are known to be unable to scramble in German (cf. Steube 2003: 170).[28] In the examples, they must remain within the focus domain, even though they are defocused. Again, the information-structural status of the elements is indicated by the index [–F]. As predicted, they do not belong to the domain of the particle, which is associated with the accented verb only. The sentences in (81)–(86) instantiate another construction type that is not accounted for by Nederstigt's (2003) theory. The data may be covered by the less restrictive versions of the adjunction-to-XP analysis, but again, the adverbial analysis facilitates a more straightforward explanation of the phenomenon.

(81) a. dass Maja$_i$ [$_{VP,[+F]}$ sogar [$_{VP}$ t$_i$ [auf den Berg]$_{[-F]}$ geRANNT
that Maja even onto the hill run
ist]]
aux$_p$

b. *dass Maja$_i$ [auf den Berg]$_j$ [$_{VP,[+F]}$ sogar [$_{VP}$ t$_i$ t$_j$ geRANNT ist]]

(82) a. dass Maja$_i$ sich$_j$ [$_{VP,[+F]}$ nur [$_{VP}$ t$_i$ t$_j$ freundlich$_{[-F]}$ verHALten
that Maja *refl* only friendly behaved
hat]]
aux$_p$

b. *dass Maja$_i$ sich$_j$ freundlich$_k$ [$_{VP,[+F]}$ nur [$_{VP}$ t$_i$ t$_j$ t$_k$ verHALten hat]]

(83) a. dass Maja$_i$ [das Zimmer]$_j$ [$_{VP,[+F]}$ sogar [$_{VP}$ t$_i$ t$_j$ rot$_{[-F]}$
that Maja the room even red
gesTRIchen hat]]
painted *aux$_p$*

b. *dass Maja$_i$ [das Zimmer]$_j$ rot$_k$ [$_{VP,[+F]}$ sogar [$_{VP}$ t$_i$ t$_j$ t$_k$ gesTRIchen hat]]

---

28. In addition to the elements listed here, finite subordinate clauses cannot scramble. However, as they are obligatorily extraposed in German, they never intervene between a focus particle and its domain.

(84) a. dass Maja$_i$ [$_{VP,[+F]}$ sogar [$_{VP}$ t$_i$ nackt$_{[-F]}$ heRUMlief]]
that Maja even naked walked_around
b. *dass Maja$_i$ nackt$_j$ [$_{VP,[+F]}$ sogar [$_{VP}$ t$_i$ t$_j$ heRUMlief]]

(85) a. dass Maja$_i$ [$_{VP,[+F]}$ sogar [$_{VP}$ t$_i$ Weltmeisterin$_{[-F]}$ WURde]]
that Maja even world_champion became
b. *dass Maja$_i$ Weltmeisterin$_j$ [$_{VP,[+F]}$ sogar [$_{VP}$ t$_i$ t$_j$ WURde]]

(86) a. dass Maja$_i$ [$_{VP,[+F]}$ nur [$_{VP}$ t$_i$ [zu schlafen]$_{[-F]}$ SCHIEN]]
that Maja only to sleep seemed
b. *dass Maja$_i$ [zu schlafen]$_j$ [$_{VP,[+F]}$ nur [$_{VP}$ t$_i$ t$_j$ SCHIEN]]

The examples in (87) demonstrate that sentences where a background element optionally remains within the focus domain (cf. Section 2.3) also show the expected behavior. The defocused direct object *den Unfall* ('the accident') may scramble to the background area at the left edge of the middlefield, but it can also occur in its base position immediately preceding the verb. In neither case does it belong to the domain of the focus particle.

(87) a. dass [den Unfall]$_i$ [$_{VP,[+F]}$ nur [$_{VP}$ ein Fußgänger t$_i$
that the accident only a pedestrian
verursacht$_{[-F]}$ hat]]
caused *aux$_p$*
b. dass [$_{VP,[+F]}$ nur [$_{VP}$ ein Fußgänger [den Unfall]$_{[-F]}$ verursacht$_{[-F]}$ hat]]

To sum up, one of the central claims of the theory advocated here is that focus particles associate with the sentence focus, which, in the standard case, corresponds to the syntactically determined focus domain in the middlefield. Association of focus particles with domains of varying sizes normally involves movement of the defocused material to the left across the particle (and the sentence adverbials). However, this movement is not specific to focus particle constructions, but a general means of the syntactic realization of information structure in German. In the default case, the particle therefore c-commands its domain and only its domain. One exception are background elements that do not (or cannot) leave their base positions. These elements are marked [–F], which excludes them from the domain of the particle.[29] In the following subsection, the complementary phenomenon will be addressed: elements that leave the focus domain although they are focused.

29. In addition to the reasons discussed here, a defocused element can remain within the focus domain for reasons of scope. This phenomenon will be addressed in Section 5.2.

4.4.3 Movement of (parts of) a focus particle's domain

In German, certain elements undergo movement for reasons independent of information structure (cf. Section 2.2), which sometimes causes parts of the focus to leave the focus domain. The framework introduced in Section 2.3 deals with such moved focused elements by assuming that they leave traces marked [+F] behind in their base positions. These traces are responsible for the fact that the moved parts are interpreted as belonging to the focus and, as a consequence, to the domain of a focus particle. In this way, we can account for sentences where a focus particle's domain or parts of it are not c-commanded by the particle, i.e., the constructions of Patterns 2, 3, 4, and 5 from the descriptive overview in Section 4.1.1. What counts is that the focus particle c-commands the base positions of all elements belonging to its domain; it need not c-command their surface positions (cf. also Jacobs 1986: 120).

Again, we consider the positions of verbal elements first. As there are no auxiliary verbs, the finite main verb must move to C^0 in the V2-clauses in (88), although it is focused. Its trace being marked [+F], it nevertheless belongs to the domain of *nur*. (79b) above is almost identical to (88b); the only difference is that the verb is defocused in the former case and focused in the latter. As predicted, the two sentences differ in their meanings, although this cannot be read from their word order or intonation, but must be determined with the help of the context. Given the information structure indicated in the examples, (79b) says that the only thing that Felix beat was a dog, while (88b) says that the only thing that Felix did was to beat a dog.

(88)	a.	Sicher	läuten$_i$	[$_{VP,[+F]}$	nur	[$_{VP}$	die	KIRCHturmglocken	t$_{i,[+F]}$	]] .
		certainly	ring		only		the	church_bells		
	b.	Felix$_i$	schlug$_j$	[$_{VP,[+F]}$	nur	[$_{VP}$ t$_i$	einen	HUND	t$_{j,[+F]}$	]] .
		Felix	beat		only		a	dog		

In addition to the finite verb in the V2-position, the element occupying the prefield is relevant in the present context. In (88a), the prefield element is a sentence adverbial, which does not take part in the focus-background partition. In (88b), the background constituent *Felix* is placed in the prefield. However, the prefield can also be filled by a focus constituent, and if all potential prefield elements are focused, there is no choice but to use one of them to satisfy the V2-constraint. In the unmarked case, this is the subject, but other elements, such as temporal adverbials, are possible as well. The focused prefield element leaves a trace marked [+F] behind in its base position and belongs to the domain of the focus particle in sentences like those in (89) and (90).

(89)	a.	Jemand$_i$	besitzt$_j$	[$_{VP,[+F]}$	sogar	[$_{VP}$	t$_{i,[+F]}$	ein	Pony	t$_j$	]] .
		someone	owns		even			a	pony		

b. Felix$_i$ schlug$_j$ [$_{VP,[+F]}$ nur [$_{VP}$ t$_{i,[+F]}$ einen HUND t$_j$]] .
Felix beat only a dog

(90) a. Jemand$_i$ spült$_j$ [$_{VP,[+F]}$ sogar [$_{VP}$ t$_{i,[+F]}$ das GESCHIRR t$_{j,[+F]}$]] .
someone washes even the dishes

b. Felix$_i$ schlug$_j$ [$_{VP,[+F]}$ nur [$_{VP}$ t$_{i,[+F]}$ einen HUND t$_{j,[+F]}$]] .
Felix beat only a dog

In (89), the finite verb in the V2-position is defocused; in (90), it belongs to the focus. As a consequence, the sentences in (90) do not contain any background elements, and the focus particle is associated with the whole proposition. Are focus particles acceptable in such fully focused sentences? As demonstrated at length in Chapter 3, a focus particle establishes a relation between its domain and the relevant alternatives of the domain, which must be contextually given or derivable. Two propositions are relevant alternatives of each other if they have a so-called *Common Integrator* (cf. Lang 1977, 1984), i.e., if they make a contribution to the same discourse topic. Thus, for the constructions under discussion to be felicitously uttered, the context must meet comparatively specific requirements. An additional complication is that fully focused sentences usually occur discourse-initially, while focus particle constructions often require some preceding discourse in which the alternatives of the particle's domain are established. These circumstances could lead to the conclusion that focus particles can never occur in fully focused sentences. However, if the context meets the decisive conditions, the respective sentences are perfectly acceptable. In the case of (90a), for instance, a suitable context would be (91).[30] We will return to fully focused sentences with focus particles in the next subsection.

(91) In unserer WG ist heute alles anders als sonst: Die Katze ist friedlich, das Bad ist aufgeräumt, und jemand spült sogar das Geschirr.
'In our shared flat, everything is different today: the cat is calm, the bathroom is tidy, and someone even washes the dishes.'

In the constructions considered so far, a part of the focus leaves the focus domain via movement to the prefield or, in case of the finite verb, to the V2-position. Movement of focused elements within the middlefield, on the other hand, is usually assumed to be impossible. However, as observed by Jacobs (1983:79) and Jaeger & Wagner (2003), unstressed pronouns (e.g., reflexive and reciprocal pronouns) must precede the particle in the middlefield, even if they belong to the focus, cf. (92) and (93).

30. See Altmann (1976a) and Jacobs (1983) for additional examples.

(92) a. Felix$_i$ hat$_j$ sich$_k$ $[_{VP,[+F]}$ nur $[_{VP}$ t$_i$ t$_{k,[+F]}$ rasIERT t$_j$]] .
Felix *aux$_p$* himself only shaved
b. *Felix$_i$ hat$_j$ $[_{VP,[+F]}$ nur $[_{VP}$ t$_i$ sich rasIERT t$_j$]] .

(93) a. [Felix und Maja]$_i$ haben$_j$ einander$_k$ $[_{VP,[+F]}$ sogar $[_{VP}$ t$_i$ t$_k$
Felix and Maja *aux$_p$* each_other even
geKÜSST t$_j$]] .
kissed
b. *[Felix und Maja]$_i$ haben$_j$ $[_{VP,[+F]}$ sogar $[_{VP}$ t$_i$ einander geKÜSS t$_j$]] .

Examples like these represent an exceptional pattern. In the default case, pronouns are background elements. If they are minimally focused, they bear the sentence accent and follow the focus particle, as evidenced by (94). In (92) and (93), the pronouns are also focused – (92a), for instance, answers a question such as *Was hat Felix getan?* ('What did Felix do?') – but here, they are only a proper part of the focus. In this case, it is impossible to put the sentence accent on the pronoun, even if it is placed in the standard accent position to the left of V^0. Unstressed pronouns, however, almost always move to the so-called *Wackernagel position* at the left edge of the middlefield in German, and this holds for defocused as well as for focused pronouns. Under the assumption that the movement of unstressed pronouns has an independent motivation, the phenomenon can be easily integrated into our model: as the moved pronouns in (92a) and (93a) are co-indexed with traces marked [+F] in the focus domain, they are interpreted as belonging to the domain of the focus particle.

(94) Felix$_i$ hat$_j$ $[_{VP,[+F]}$ nur $[_{VP}$ t$_i$ SICH rasiert$_{[-F]}$ t$_j$]] .
Felix *aux$_p$* only himself shaved

The examples in (88)–(93) show how our model accounts for sentences where a focus particle occurs between the parts of a discontinuous domain, i.e., the constructions of Pattern 2. In Pattern 3, the domain consists of the prefield constituent only, and in Pattern 4, the particle is associated with the finite verb in the V2-position. In contrast to Pattern 2, the focused element preceding the particle obligatorily bears the sentence accent in these cases, as there is no focused material left in the focus domain. Analyses of sentences exemplifying Patterns 3 and 4 are given in (95) and (96), respectively. As in the examples of Pattern 2, the association of the particle with its domain is mediated by the [+F]-traces in the base positions of the moved elements.

(95) a. MAja$_i$ kam$_j$ $[_{VP,[+F]}$ sogar $[_{VP}$ t$_{i,[+F]}$ t$_j$]] .
Maja came even
b. SUshi$_i$ hat$_j$ Maja$_k$ $[_{VP,[+F]}$ nur $[_{VP}$ t$_k$ t$_{i,[+F]}$ gegessen$_{[-F]}$ t$_j$]] .
sushi *aux$_p$* Maja only eaten

(96) Maja$_i$ KÜSSTE$_j$ Felix$_k$ [$_{VP,[+F]}$ auch [$_{VP}$ t_i t_k $t_{j,[+F]}$]] .
Maja kissed Felix also

The sentences in (79), (88)–(90), (92), and (93) above are ambiguous with respect to the size of the domain of the particle, if they are encountered without a disambiguating context. In (95) and (96), on the other hand, the accentuation pattern suffices to identify the domain. The sentence accent on the moved element outside the focus domain indicates that this element is minimally focused and, as a consequence, serves as the domain of the focus particle by itself.

In Pattern 5, a finite subordinate clause serving as the domain of a focus particle is extraposed. By assumption, the embedded clause moves to the right and adjoins somewhere higher in the tree (cf., for instance, Büring & Hartmann 1995). We will not speculate about the exact adjunction site here. If extraposition targets a position within the focus domain, i.e., in the c-command domain of the focus particle, the mechanism involved in the interpretation is the same as in Pattern 1: the particle associates with the focused elements that it c-commands. If, on the other hand, the clause leaves the focus domain and adjoins above the particle, its focus status must be indicated by a trace marked [+F] in its base position, as in Patterns 2–4. The latter possibility is shown in (97).

(97) Maja$_i$ hat$_j$ [$_{VP,[+F]}$ nur [$_{VP}$ t_i $t_{k,[+F]}$ gehofft$_{[-F]}$ t_j]] [dass FELIX
Maja *aux$_p$* only hoped that Felix
kommt]$_k$.
comes

It was claimed above that a focus particle normally c-commands its domain. The examples discussed in this subsection demonstrate that the c-command condition (cf. Jacobs 1983, 1986; Büring & Hartmann 2001) can be violated under certain circumstances: focused elements that must leave the focus domain for independent grammatical reasons are treated as if they had remained in their base positions. In our model, this is indicated by the index [+F] on their traces in the focus domain. In Section 4.5, a similar analysis will be proposed for constructions with stressed additive focus particles following their domains (Pattern 6).

In the present subsection and in the preceding one, the generalization that a focus particle c-commands its domain and only its domain was complemented with explanations for the observed exceptions (parts of the domain not c-commanded by the particle; elements that are c-commanded by the particle, but do not belong to its domain). As a consequence, the model is now able to account for relatively complex cases of association with focus particles, such as those in (98). The surface word order of the sentence in (98a) is compatible with at least the focus-background partitions and corresponding accentuation patterns and interpretations given in (98b)–(98e).

(98) a. Maja hat nur Felix verraten, dass es regnet.
Maja *aux*$_p$ only Felix told that it rains
b. Maja$_i$ hat$_j$ [$_{VP,[+F]}$ nur [$_{VP}$ t$_i$ FElix t$_k$ verraten$_{[-F]}$ t$_j$]] [dass es regnet]$_k$.
'The only person Maja told that it rains is Felix.'
c. Maja$_i$ hat$_j$ [$_{VP,[+F]}$ nur [$_{VP}$ t$_i$ Felix t$_{k,[+F]}$ verraten t$_j$]] [dass es REGnet]$_k$.
'The only thing Maja did was to tell Felix that it rains.'
d. Maja$_i$ hat$_j$ [$_{VP,[+F]}$ nur [$_{VP}$ t$_i$ Felix t$_{k,[+F]}$ verraten$_{[-F]}$ t$_j$]] [dass es REGnet]$_k$.
'The only pair <x,y>, such that Maja told y to x, is the pair <Felix, that it rains>.'
e. Maja$_i$ hat$_j$ [$_{VP,[+F]}$ nur [$_{VP}$ t$_{i,[+F]}$ Felix t$_{k,[+F]}$ verraten t$_j$]] [dass es REGnet]$_k$.
'The only thing that happened is that Maja told Felix that it rains.'

4.4.4 An argument against adjunction to the root CP

This subsection contrasts a prediction of Büring & Hartmann's (2001) variant of the adverbial analysis with one that can be derived from the account advocated here, showing that the relevant data supports our proposal. The predictions concern the position of focus particles in fully focused sentences. As noted in Section 4.2.2, Bayer (1996: 22) criticizes Jacobs' (1983) theory of focus particle constructions, claiming that it does not explain why a sentence-initial focus particle can only associate with the immediately following prefield constituent. Though Bayer's criticism is not fully justified (cf. the discussion of the examples in (62) and (63) above), its valid part carries over to Büring & Hartmann's (2001) analysis. Like Jacobs, Büring & Hartmann assume that a sentence-initial focus particle adjoins to the root CP rather than to the prefield constituent. Their *Closeness Principle* (cf. (58d) and (59d) in Section 4.2.1) correctly predicts that the particle cannot associate with a constituent located in the middlefield. However, it is not clear why the particle must not be associated with the whole remaining clause, either. Sentences like those in (99), which are clearly ungrammatical, are not ruled out by Büring & Hartmann's account. Here, the root CP is a non-argument, it is a maximal projection, it corresponds to the focus, and there is no adjunction site further down in the tree that fulfills these conditions. As a consequence, a fully focused CP should be a possible adjunction site of a focus particle. Büring & Hartmann (2001: 234, Footnote 3) reject Bayer's criticism of the adverbial analysis, claiming that Jacobs' (1983) theory, as well as their own, does account for the restriction under discussion. However, in their argumentation, they replace Bayer's example with one where the focus particle is placed in the middlefield and say nothing about sentences like those in (99).

(99) a. *Sogar [jemand spült das GESCHIRR]$_D$.
even someone washes the dishes

b. *Nur [Felix schlug einen HUND]$_D$.
   only Felix beat a dog

Furthermore, the position of the particle in (99) is not only permitted by Büring & Hartmann's theory, but actually predicted to be the only possible position in fully focused sentences. This is evident when we look at the phenomenon from the opposite perspective: if a focus particle is intended to associate with a whole clause, the rules in (59) above force it to adjoin to the root CP, as adjunction of the particle within its domain is not an option. Our model, on the other hand, predicts that the particle adjoins to VP, no matter what the size of the focus is. In fully focused V2-sentences, the finite verb subsequently moves to the V2-position, and a focused constituent fills the prefield. Both elements are co-indexed with [+F]-traces in the focus domain, which indicate that they belong to the domain of the particle. The resulting structure is exemplified by the grammatical sentences given in (90) above; these sentences cannot be derived in Büring & Hartmann's theory.

The argument put forward in this subsection supports the claim that adjunction of focus particles to the root CP is impossible in German. In Section 4.6, an alternative analysis of sentence-initial focus particles will be presented.

4.4.5 Focus particles as adjuncts to AP

As noted above, the occurrence of focus particles within DPs is highly restricted in German, but it is normally possible if the DP contains a modifier in the form of an AP; cf. (21) in Section 4.1.1 (Pattern 9). Jacobs (1983) and Büring & Hartmann (2001), among other proponents of the adverbial analysis, assume that this follows from the fact that APs are similar to VPs in many respects and, as a consequence, can also serve as adjunction sites of focus particles. In the present subsection, we take a brief look at this argument, concluding that the proposed extension of the adverbial analysis is justified.

Verbal and adjectival projections share many grammatical properties in German (cf., for instance, Zimmermann 1985, 1989): Both are head-final and can be modified by various types of adverbials (including sentence adverbials), which occur in the same order in APs and VPs, cf. (100).[31] Moreover, scrambling, which was described for VP internal elements in Section 2.3, can also be observed in APs, where it has comparable information-structural effects; cf. (101).

31. The examples are based on (21) and (22) in Zimmermann (1989: 20).

(100) a. der [$_{AP}$ wahrscheinlich [$_{AP}$ seit seiner Kindheit [$_{A'}$ in gewisser
the probably since his childhood in certain
Weise [$_{A'}$ seiner Mutter [$_{A'}$ sehr ähnliche]]]]] Sohn
way his mother very similar son

b. der Sohn, der [$_{VP}$ wahrscheinlich [$_{VP}$ seit seiner Kindheit
the son who probably since his childhood
[$_{V'}$ in gewisser Weise [$_{V'}$ seiner Mutter [$_{V'}$ sehr ähnelt]]]]]
in certain way his mother very resembles

(101) a. der [$_{AP}$ wahrscheinlich [$_{AP}$ seit vielen Jahren [$_{A'}$ auf seine
the probably since many years of his
Frisur stolze]]] Linguist
hairstyle proud linguist

b. der [$_{AP}$ [auf seine Frisur]$_i$ [$_{AP}$ wahrscheinlich [$_{AP}$ seit vielen Jahren [$_{A'}$ t$_i$
stolze]]]] Linguist

Given this similarity, it comes as no surprise that focus particles can also adjoin to APs in German, and that they show the same behavior in VPs and APs. In (102) and (103), the focus particle is an adjunct to the maximal AP below the sentence adverbials, its domain being the focused elements it c-commands. The adjectival head may, but need not, belong to the particle's domain: the linguist in (102a) is proud of his hairstyle and has some other relevant property, while the one in (102b) is proud of his hairstyle and of something else. Elements that have been scrambled across the particle and the sentence adverbials, such as the complement in (103b), do not belong to the particle's domain, and background constituents able to scramble normally must not intervene between the particle and its domain, as evidenced by (103c).

(102) a. der wahrscheinlich auch [auf seine FrisUR stolze]$_D$ Linguist
the probably also of his hairstyle proud linguist

b. der wahrscheinlich auch [auf seine FrisUR]$_D$ stolze Linguist

(103) a. der wirklich nur [seinem VORgängermodell]$_D$ ähnliche Wagen
the really only his previous_model similar car

b. der seinem Vorgängermodell wirklich nur [ÄHNliche]$_D$ Wagen

c. *der wirklich nur seinem Vorgängermodell [ÄHNliche]$_D$ Wagen

In sum, the presented data supports the adverbial analysis rather than invalidates it. The ability of focus particles to modify adjectival projections shows once more that they behave like adverbials in many respects. Furthermore, as suggested by Büring & Hartmann (2001: 275–276), the analysis of focus particles as adjuncts to AP can also be applied to cases where the particle is associated with a quantifier expression or a numeral, as in (21b) or in Jacobs' example (53a) above.

4.4.6 Summary

In this section, it was argued that focus particles are maximal projections that, in the default case, adjoin to VP below the position of the sentences adverbials. They associate with the sentence focus, which normally corresponds to the syntactically determined focus domain, i.e., the material c-commanded by the particle. Exceptions to this generalization (defocused elements within and focused elements outside the c-command domain of the particle) were shown to be independently motivated by syntactic movement requirements and movement restrictions. It was also demonstrated that our model predicts the correct position of focus particles in fully focused sentences and that the adverbial analysis can be extended to focus particles adjoining to adjectival projections.

Up to this point, our analysis has mainly been based on Jacobs' (1983) and Büring & Hartmann's (2001) variants of the adverbial analysis, but differs from these approaches in a number of respects. In particular, it was argued that the grammatical properties of constructions with focus particles for the most part follow from their information structure. Under the assumption that focus particles have a fixed position to the left of the focus domain and that the movement operations driven by information structure apply just as in sentences without the particles, we are able to derive the correct word order and accentuation patterns without having to postulate rules specific to focus particle constructions. This view also suggests that a focus particle does not determine the information structure of a sentence, as claimed by Jacobs (1983, 1986, 1988), but interacts in a modular way with independently (i.e., pragmatically) specified information-structural properties. We will return to this point in Chapter 7. So far, we have given analyses for Patterns 1–5 and partly for Pattern 9 of the descriptive overview in Section 4.1.1. In the following sections, we will discuss the remaining patterns, thereby extending the scope of our theory.

4.5 Stressed additive focus particles

This section deals with constructions containing the stressed variant of the additive focus particle *auch* or one of its equivalents (*gleichfalls* 'likewise', *ebenfalls*/*ebenso* 'as well', among others). The exceptional behavior of these particles has already been noticed by Altmann (1976a), and since then, it has created difficulties for the theoretical description of German focus particles. The relevant constructions, which belong to Pattern 6 of our classification (cf. (15) and (16) above), have two important properties in common. First, the focus particle does not c-command its domain, which precedes the particle and is either placed in the prefield or at the left edge of the middlefield. The particle itself always occurs in the middlefield; it need not immediately follow its domain. Second, the particle carries the sentence accent, while its domain may, but need not, be marked by an additional accent. This is hard to reconcile with the analysis of focus particles as focus sensitive, i.e., as associating with the focused part of a sentence. Owing to these characteristics, constructions with stressed additive particles lie beyond the scope of many theories of focus particles, such as Bayer (1996) and Büring & Hartmann (2001). The approaches that try to incorporate them, on the other hand, differ considerably in their analyses and in the conclusions they draw for a general account of focus particle constructions. After briefly reviewing the hypotheses brought forward in the literature – in particular regarding the question of whether sentences with stressed *auch* can be derived from the corresponding sentences with its unstressed counterpart – we will propose and motivate an analysis that is based on such a derivation. The special syntactic and prosodic properties of the constructions will be argued to follow from their special information structure.

4.5.1 Previous analyses

Jacobs (1983). The fact that a focus particle may follow its domain without being adjacent to it is considered by Jacobs as an argument against adjunction-to-XP analyses. On the basis of his claim that focus particles adjoin to VP only, he argues that there is no fundamental difference between constructions with stressed and unstressed *auch*, and that the former can be derived from the latter by a syntactic infixation rule.[32] Although this solution is incompatible with current syntactic theories, the consequences of Jacobs' claims are worth discussing. First, it follows that constructions with stressed *auch* are not necessarily exceptions to the generalization that focus particles c-command their domains. The derivation proposed by Jacobs (1983: Section 3.2.3.2) corresponds to an analysis involving movement of the associated element out of the c-command domain of *auch* in our theory, and as shown above, the traces of moved elements can satisfy the c-command condition under certain circumstances. The possibility of such a movement analysis has been rejected by most authors who discuss Jacobs' analysis. The second consequence, which is no less controversial, is that constructions with stressed *auch* and the corresponding sentences with the unstressed variant of the particle are

32. "Nach meinem Vorschlag gibt es dagegen zwischen den beiden Anordnungsmustern keinen über den Reihenfolgeunterschied hinausgehenden strukturellen Unterschied und entsprechend [...] auch keine abweichenden syntaktischen Bindungen der Gradpartikeln. Der ganze Unterschied besteht nach dieser Interpretation darin, dass die Partikeln in der zweiten Gruppe von Sätzen als *juxtaponiert*, in der ersten dagegen als *infigiert* zu betrachten sind. Dabei ist der syntaktische Bereich jeweils derselbe, nämlich eine null- bis dreistellige Verbalphrase." (Jacobs 1983: 102)

predicted to be synonymous (cf. Jacobs 1983:106). We will return to both of these issues below.

A serious drawback of Jacobs' analysis is that it cannot explain the complementary distribution of stressed and unstressed *auch*, which becomes apparent if one relates the relative order of the particle and its domain to the accentuation of the sentence: it is always the last element of the pair consisting of *auch* and its domain that carries the sentence accent (cf. Reis & Rosengren 1997:243). This seems to be inconsistent with the claim that the domain of a focus particle corresponds to the focus of the sentence. In addition, it remains unexplained why *auch* and other additive particles have stressed variants following their domains, while particles such as *nur* and *sogar* do not.

Reis & Rosengren (1997). A critical examination of Jacobs' hypotheses leads Reis & Rosengren (1997) to the conclusion that a movement analysis of constructions with stressed *auch* is not tenable. The authors argue (i) that there is no derivational link between sentences with the stressed and unstressed variants of the particle, (ii) that there is nevertheless only one lexical item *auch* underlying both usages, and (iii) that the complementary distribution is a consequence of the modular interaction of syntax, semantics, and prosody. In order to reconcile their version of the adjunction-to-XP analysis with the special characteristics of stressed *auch*, Reis & Rosengren claim that this variant of the particle is syntactically more restricted than its unstressed counterpart. In particular, they consider only predicate projections to be possible adjunction sites of stressed *auch*, thus adopting the basic assumption of the adverbial analysis in this case. Another distinctive feature of their model concerns the question of what is actually 'added' by an additive particle. According to the authors, this is either the associated element, as assumed in most other accounts, or some defocused predicative material that is repeated from an utterance occurring earlier in the discourse. Sentences like (104) are considered to exemplify the second possibility. In Reis & Rosengren's view, Felix is not added to the set of singing people here, but an event of singing is added to a contextually given event of the same type, which, however, has a different agent and is therefore distinct from the singing event referred to by (104).

(104) Felix singt AUCH.
Felix sings also

Reis & Rosengren argue that what is added by *auch* does not depend on the information-structural partition of the sentence, but on the material in the particle's c-command domain, and that the two possibilities – adding the associated element and adding defocused predicative material – give rise to different utterance meanings of *auch*, namely, 'furthermore' and 'likewise' (cf. also Féry, to appear). As noted by Reis & Rosengren (1997:294) themselves, however, the two meanings do not correspond directly to the unstressed and stressed variants of the particle, which is why the distinction is ignored for the time being. We will discuss the utterance meanings of *auch* in more detail at the end of Section 4.5.2. Like Jacobs (1983), Reis & Rosengren have no answer to the question of why restrictive and scalar focus particles cannot occur in the constructions of Pattern 6.

Nederstigt (2003). Advancing a more far-reaching hypothesis than Reis & Rosengren (1997), Nederstigt (2003) assumes that the stressed and unstressed variants of *auch* represent different lexical items. While she considers stressed *auch* to be the head (or the specifier) of a functional projection AUCHP, its unstressed counterpart is analyzed as an adjunct to XPs of all kinds (cf. Section 4.2.2 above). Of course, such an approach excludes the possibility of deriving one usage pattern of *auch* from the other. In Nederstigt's theory, the domain of stressed *auch* is always the whole utterance, not just an element to the left of the particle. This amounts to the claim that what is added by the particle is a complete answer to an (implicit) discourse question – the *Quaestio* in Klein & von Stutterheim's (1987, 1992) model.

Krifka (1999). In his paper on stressed additive particles, Krifka (1999) argues that the element associated with stressed *auch* is a contrastive topic, which is not necessarily marked as such by the typical rising contrastive accent (cf. the Contrastive Topic Hypothesis given in (68) above).[33] As this account is of particular relevance for the syntactic description to be given in the next subsection, it is discussed here in somewhat more detail. Krifka's starting point is the observation that one common prosodic realization of sentences containing stressed *auch* is the so-called *bridge contour*, an accentual pattern consisting of a rising contrastive accent and the normal falling sentence accent (cf. Jacobs 1997; Molnár & Rosengren 1997; Mehlhorn 2001; Steube 2003; van Hoof 2003). The very same pattern is typical of sentences with contrastive topics; cf. (105). The prosodic similarity of the two constructions is mirrored by a correspondence in their semantics: elements associated with stressed *auch*, as well as contrastive topics in sentences like (105b), presuppose the existence of relevant alternatives. Krifka concludes that the domain of a stressed additive particle is in fact a contrastive topic, and he considers this analysis to predict that the particle associates with exactly one constituent to its left.

(105)	a.	/PETER	hat	die Ausstellung	wahrscheinlich	AUCH	besucht.
		Peter	*aux*$_p$	the exhibition	probably	also	visited

33. See Rullmann (2003) for an application of Krifka's Contrastive Topic Hypothesis to the English focus particles *too* and *either*.

b. /PEter hat die AUSstellung besucht (und /PIa ist EINkaufen
Peter aux_p the exhibition visited and Pia aux_p shopping
gegangen).
gone
(Krifka 1999: 113)

However, the rising contrastive accent is not obligatory in constructions with stressed *auch*. This is particularly obvious in sentences with weak pronouns as associated elements, like those in (106), and in sentences where the particle is associated with a non-overt element, like in the examples in (16) above. The weak pronoun *es* is never accented in German,[34] and phonologically empty elements cannot receive any accentual marking, either. Nevertheless, both may serve as the domain of stressed *auch*, and they semantically behave like contrastive topics. Krifka (1999) argues that the prosodic marking can be dispensed with, as the special construction type, in particular the accent on the particle, facilitates an unambiguous identification of the domain in most cases. Historically, the pattern may have emerged in the following way: "First, contrastive topics can associate with stressed additive particles [...]. Second, a construction pattern consisting of a clearly marked contrastive topic and a stressed additive particle gets established. Third, the marking of the contrastive topic becomes redundant, to a certain degree, as stressed additive particles occur more or less exclusively with contrastive topics, and the context of utterance can determine which constituent is a contrastive topic." (Krifka 1999: 118)

(106) a. Es ist wahrscheinlich AUCH runtergefallen.
it aux_p probably also fallen_down
b. weil es wahrscheinlich AUCH runtergefallen ist
because it probably also fallen_down aux_p
(Krifka 1999: 116)

The semantic properties common to the constructions under discussion deserve a closer look. A contrastive topic is always accompanied by the presupposition of a set of alternatives. In (105b), for instance, this set consists of Peter and Pia. As shown in Chapter 3, the same is true for the domain of *auch*: (105a) cannot be felicitously uttered unless there is some person different from Peter who visited the exhibition. In both cases, the sentences are only partial answers to (implicit)

34. See, for instance, Sudhoff (2003: Chapter 2).

questions; they fulfill Büring's (1997a; 1997b) *Condition of Disputability* (COD), given in (107).[35]

(107) *Condition of Disputability:*
Given a sentence *A* containing a Topic, there must be at least one disputable element in $[[A]]^t$ after uttering *A*.
Disputability: A set of propositions *P* is disputable wrt a set of worlds CG (the *Common Ground*) if there is at least one element *p* in *P* such that both *p* and $\neg p$ could informatively and coherently be added to CG.
(Büring 1997a: 178)

According to Krifka (1999), another constraint applies to sentences with contrastive topics, the (relatively weak) *Condition of Distinctiveness*; cf. (108). This condition, which is most likely of a pragmatic nature, says that the predication made of a contrastive topic must be different from the predications made of its alternatives. As Krifka points out, it may be circumvented by the use of a stressed additive particle, which explicitly indicates that the same predication holds of both the contrastive topic and its alternatives. The difference is illustrated by the English examples in (109); German shows the same behavior in this respect.

(108) *Condition of Distinctiveness:*
If [... T_F ... C_F ...] is a contrastive answer to a question Q, then there is no alternative T′ of T such that the speaker is willing to assert [... T′ ... C ...].
(Krifka 1999: 122)

(109) What did Peter and Pia eat?
a. */PEter ate PAsta, and /PIa ate PAsta.
b. /PEter ate PAsta, and /PIa ate pasta, TOO.
(Krifka 1999: 122)

Krifka (1999) offers an explanation of the fact that the focus particle itself, rather than its domain, carries the sentence accent in the constructions of Pattern 6.[36] On the one hand, *auch* is the last accentable element in the sentence. The predication made of the contrastive topic consists of background information only; it must be given in the prior discourse (cf. Reis & Rosengren 1997: 285). On the other hand, Krifka assumes that postponed additive particles are focused, as "they realize an affirmative element explicitly, just like *did* and *certainly* in [(110)]" (Krifka 1999: 124). As focused elements, they must of course have alternatives.

35. Büring's *Topic* refers to contrastive topics, and $[[A]]^t$ is the *topic value* of *A*, i.e., a set of sets of propositions. See Krifka (1999: 122–123) for a discussion of the *problem of the last answer* arising in this context.

36. See also Féry (2006), Féry (to appear).

Krifka (1999: 124–125) discusses several possibilities: simple affirmation, simple negation, and a negating element that has the same presupposition as *auch*.

(110) Did Peter eat pasta?
  a. (Yes,) Peter DID eat pasta.
  b. (Yes,) Peter CERtainly ate pasta.
  (Krifka 1999: 124)

Krifka also explains why restrictive and scalar focus particles are impossible in the constructions of Pattern 6. The reason for the ungrammaticality of sentences like (111) – with the intended interpretation that Felix kissed Maja and that nobody else kissed her – is the COD. Once we know that Felix is the only person who kissed Maja, we also know that all other people who are relevant alternatives to Felix did not kiss her. Thus, after uttering (111), there are no disputable sets of propositions left in the topic value of the sentence. The existence of such sets (the so-called *residual topics*), however, is required by the disputability condition. In other words, sentences where a restrictive focus particle is associated with a contrastive topic are ruled out because the COD, activated by the contrastive topic, is incompatible with the lexical meaning of the particle.

(111) *[/FElix]$_D$ hat Maja NUR geküsst.
   Felix *aux$_p$* Maja only kissed

Scalar particles, such as *sogar* in (112), are excluded as well. According to Krifka (1999), this is due to the fact that they can never be stressed or focused (cf. also Section 4.1.3 above). This claim is supported by an observation made by Altmann (1976a: 261): the particle *auch*, which has a scalar use if it is unstressed (cf. Section 3.3), is always non-scalar in the constructions of Pattern 6. While *auch* corresponds to *even* in (113a), it can only be translated with *also* in (113b).

(112) *[/FElix]$_D$ hat Maja SOGAR geküsst.
   Felix *aux$_p$* Maja even kissed

(113) a. Auch der SCHNELLste Computer kann diese Aufgabe nicht lösen.
   even the fastest computer can this task not solve
  b. Der /SCHNELLste Computer kann diese Aufgabe AUCH nicht lösen.
   the fastest computer can this task also not solve
  (Krifka 1999: 112)

4.5.2 A movement account of stressed *auch*

Jacobs' (1983) account of constructions containing stressed additive focus particles can be regarded as a predecessor of a movement analysis that derives the sentences under discussion from their counterparts with unstressed particles preceding their domains. However, as noted above, it fails to explain why the particle is accented, and why *nur* and *sogar* cannot be used in the same way. Krifka's (1999) theory, on the other hand, answers these question, but leaves open how the constructions can be analyzed syntactically. The present subsection argues that a comprehensive view of stressed additive focus particles can be achieved by combining Krifka's claims with a syntactic theory of bridge contour constructions, such as Steube (2003). If sentences with stressed *auch* can be shown to have the same underlying structure as sentences with unstressed focus particles, we are no longer forced to assume that different mechanisms are at work in constructions with the stressed and unstressed variants of the particle (cf. Reis & Rosengren 1997), or that the variants represent different lexical items (cf. Nederstigt 2003). The main hypothesis to be defended here is that the element associated with stressed *auch* has its base position in the focus domain (where it is c-commanded by the particle), but must be moved to the left, as it has the status of a contrastive topic.

The domain of stressed auch. Following Krifka (1999), we assume that the elements associated with stressed *auch* are contrastive topics. The consequences of this claim for the semantic and syntactic description of the constructions will be discussed throughout this section; the issue of their prosodic realization will be addressed in Chapter 6. One central semantic aspect was mentioned in the review of Krifka's account: a contrastive topic presupposes the existence of relevant alternatives; it represents a member of a contextually given or inferable set. In sentences traditionally considered to involve a contrastive topic, such as (105b) above, different things must be predicated of the contrastive topic and its alternatives; cf. Krifka's distinctiveness condition given in (108) above.[37] Van Hoof (2003: 521) argues against this restriction. Crucially, the counterexample she gives is one with stressed *auch*; cf. (114). Here, the particle is used to emphasize the fact that the same predication holds of the contrastive topic and of its alternatives. We follow Krifka in assuming that the affirmation of precisely this fact is focused in constructions with stressed *auch*, and that this focus is indicated by the accent on the particle.

(114) Die /MÄNNER haben ein REZITATIV geprobt, und die /FRAUEN haben
the men *aux$_p$* a recitative rehearsed and the women *aux$_p$*
AUCH ein Rezitativ geprobt.
also a recitative rehearsed
(van Hoof 2003: 521)

37. See also Steube (2003: 177).

In Krifka's (1999) theory, contrastive topics form a subset of aboutness topics. However, the term *contrastive topic* is also used in a broader sense in the literature, referring to the elements bearing the rising contrastive accent in bridge contour constructions.[38] Contrastive topics in the latter sense do not necessarily fall under the traditional concept of topic, a precondition of which is referentiality (cf. Reinhart 1981).[39] As noted by Steube (2003) and van Hoof (2003), non-referential elements – such as manner adverbials, resultative and depictive predicates, predicatives, subjects of existential sentences, quantified DPs such as *niemand* ('nobody'), infinite VPs, finite verbs, and even separable verb prefixes – can also function as contrastive topics in the broad sense; cf. the examples in (115) and (116).[40] Apart from the fact that they cannot be interpreted as aboutness topics, these elements show the same semantic properties as referential contrastive topics. In particular, the sentences are also only partial answers to (implicit) questions relevant in the discourse.

(115) a. [/FREUNDlich]$_{CT}$ hat er sich NICHT benommen.
friendly aux_p he *refl* not behaved

b. [Aka/DEmiker]$_{CT}$ wollen VIEle werden.
academics want many to_become

c. [/AN]$_{CT}$ hat auf alle Fälle PEter das Licht gemacht.
on aux_p in any case Peter the light turned

(Steube 2003: 170–171)

(116) [/NIEmand]$_{CT}$ hat er NICHT beleidigt, [ein /PAAR Gäste]$_{CT}$
nobody aux_p he not insulted a few guests
SCHON.
aff
(van Hoof 2003: 525)

Steube (2003) and van Hoof (2003) conclude (contra Büring 1997b) that the relevant information-structural concept characterizing the element bearing the rising accent in bridge contour constructions is contrastive focus rather than contrastive topic in the narrow sense of the term. In this view, the sentences have a discontinuous focus: the rising accent marks a contrastively focused element, which can, but need not, have the status of a topic,[41] while the falling accent marks the non-contrastive sentence focus. From what has been said, it follows that, strictly

38. The same is true for the alternative term *I-topic*, where the *I* stands for *intonation*.

39. See also the discussion in Jacobs (2001).

40. CT = contrastive topic.

41. The notions of topic and focus do not exclude each other (cf. Section 2.3).

speaking, the term *contrastive topic* in its broad sense is inadequate. We nevertheless continue using it for the present purpose, as it has become the standard term for the elements under discussion.

How do the elements associated with stressed *auch* behave with respect to referentiality? Krifka (1999) only discusses referential elements. However, most of the non-referential contrastive topics mentioned by Steube (2003) and van Hoof (2003) can also be associated with the particle. The domain of *auch* is a manner adverbial in (117a), a predicative in (117b), and a separable verb prefix in (117c). Some non-referential elements that can be contrastive topics are unable to associate with stressed *auch* because of their semantics: they give rise to a contradiction between a presupposition of the sentence and its assertion. A case in point is *niemand* ('nobody') in (117d). If nobody kissed Maja, the presupposition of *auch* – that someone did kiss her – cannot be satisfied. Crucially, the data in (117a)–(117c) shows that Krifka's (1999) assumption that the element associated with stressed *auch* must be an aboutness topic is not correct. If we want to maintain the Contrastive Topic Hypothesis, it must be considered to refer to contrastive topics in the broad sense of the term.

(117) a. [/FREUNDlich]$_D$ hat sich Maja AUCH benommen.
friendly *aux$_p$* *refl* Maja also behaved

b. [Aka/DEmiker]$_D$ wollte Felix AUCH werden.
academic wanted Felix also to_become

c. [/AN]$_D$ hat Maja das Licht AUCH gemacht.
on *aux$_p$* Maja the light also turned

d. *[/NIEmand]$_D$ hat Maja AUCH geküsst.
nobody *aux$_p$* Maja also kissed

Another consequence of Steube's (2003) and van Hoof's (2003) view on contrastive topics is that the concept of focus sensitivity, which is abandoned by Reis & Rosengren (1997) and Féry (to appear), can be re-established in the analysis of stressed *auch*. As in other focus particle constructions, the particle is associated with a focused element, and the alternatives evoked by the focus determine the domain of quantification of the particle (cf. Chapter 3). In contrast to Reis & Rosengren's approach, where the alternatives necessary for the interpretation must be determined on the basis of a pragmatic mechanism (cf. Section 4.2.3), the account of stressed *auch* envisaged here is compatible with a semantic theory of association with focus. This is a welcome result, as it facilitates a uniform semantic treatment of constructions with stressed and unstressed focus particles, although they differ considerably in their information-structural properties.

Split domains. Having shown that the elements associated with stressed *auch* need not be aboutness topics, we can now reconsider Krifka's (1999) claim that the particle cannot associate with more than one constituent, i.e., that split domains are impossible in constructions with stressed additive focus particles. Reis & Rosengren (1997) also argue that the domain of stressed *auch* must not be split; however, the authors only discuss sentences where the particle is located between the two parts of its domain. The ungrammaticality of such constructions is expected under the Contrastive Topic Hypothesis, as contrastive topics always occur in the left periphery of the clause (see below). This still leaves open the possibility that *auch* associates with two elements to its left, both being contrastive topics. That a sentence may contain more than one contrastive topic is demonstrated both by Krifka (1999) and by van Hoof (2003); cf. the examples in (118) and (119).

(118) What about Peter and Pia? Did they get any gifts from Mary or Sue?

/PIa	hat	von	/MAry	einen	BALL	geschenkt	bekommen.
Pia	aux_p	from	Mary	a	ball	as_a_present	gotten

(Krifka 1999: 114)

(119)

Die	/MÄNner	haben	die	Rezita/TIVE	GRÜNDlich	geprobt.
the	men	aux_p	the	recitatives	thoroughly	rehearsed

(van Hoof 2003: 519)

However, according to Krifka, the two contrastive topics are not ranked equally in these sentences. They are so-called *stacked topics*, one of which has scope over the other: "the speaker selects one discourse entity as a main topic at which a piece of information is to be stored, but structures this piece of information further into a secondary topic and a comment" (Krifka 1999: 114). If an instance of stressed *auch* occurs in a sentence with two stacked topics, it cannot associate with both of them, but takes the lower topic as its domain. This is the case in Reis & Rosengren's (1997) example (120).[42]

(120) Mensch, Paul besitzt einen Gauguin! ('Boy, Paul possesses a Gauguin!')

Einen	Gau/GUIN	besitzt	/PEter	AUCH,
a	Gauguin	possesses	Peter	also

aber ihm fehlen andere Impressionisten.
('but he doesn't have other impressionists.')
(Reis & Rosengren 1997: 253)

Can a sentence have two contrastive topics that are ranked equally? Krifka (1999) argues that such *complex topics*, the counterparts of *complex foci*, do not exist, the

42. Reis & Rosengren (1997) use this example to argue against the claim that stressed *auch* associates with contrastive topics. In their view, a sentence can only have one topic, which is *einen Gauguin* ('a Gauguin') in (120). The particle, however, is associated with the subject *Peter*.

reason being that topics serve as anchor points for information. As a consequence, split domains of stressed *auch* should be impossible: "If there are no complex topics, and if postposed additive particles under stress associate with contrastive topics, then we should assume that they can associate only with one constituent, and not with two. This should contrast with the regular case of additive particles, which can associate with a complex focus [...]." (Krifka 1999: 115) Krifka considers the data in (121) as a confirmation of this prediction. The English focus particle *too*, which behaves similar to stressed *auch*, cannot be associated with both *Mo* and *soup* in (121c). The German version of the sentence, given in (122), is equally ungrammatical.

(121) a. Jo had fish and Mo had fish TOO.
b. Jo had fish and Jo had soup TOO.
c. *Jo had fish and Mo had soup TOO.
(Krifka 1999: 115)

(122) *Maja hat Fisch gegessen, und Felix hat Suppe AUCH gegessen.
Maja *aux*$_p$ fish eaten and Felix *aux*$_p$ soup also eaten.

The problem is that Krifka's argumentation is based on the aboutness concept of topics: a sentence cannot have more than one topic because it can only be 'about' one entity. As shown above, however, the aboutness concept is irrelevant for the domains of stressed *auch* and for contrastive topics in general. This has an important consequence: if contrastive topics need not be aboutness topics, the Contrastive Topic Hypothesis no longer predicts that stressed *auch* associates with exactly one constituent to its left. The sentences in (123) to (126) demonstrate that this is a welcome result. Contrary to Krifka's assumption, the domain of the particle may be split, i.e., stressed *auch* can associate with two equally ranked constituents to its left.

(123) Ich liebe dich. ('I love you.')
[Ich]$_D$ liebe [dich]$_D$ AUCH.
I love you also

(124) Warum sollte sich Maja keinen neuen Fernseher kaufen? Nur weil sie zur Zeit kein Geld hat? ('Why shouldn't Maja buy a new TV set? Only because she doesn't have the money right now?')
[Felix]$_D$ hat [sein Auto]$_D$ doch AUCH auf Raten gekauft.
Felix *aux*$_p$ his car *mp* also in instalments bought

(125) Warum finden es alle so schlimm, dass Henry Nele betrogen hat?
('Why does everyone reproach Henry for having cheated on Nele?')

[Maja $]_D$ hat [Felix $]_D$ damals AUCH betrogen,
Maja aux_p Felix then also cheated_on
und niemanden hat es gestört. ('and nobody cared about it.')

(126) Iss deinen Fisch! Du kannst nicht immer nur essen was du magst.
('Eat your fish! You cannot only eat the things you like.')
[Felix $]_D$ hat [seine Suppe $]_D$ schließlich AUCH gegessen,
Felix aux_p his soup after_all also eaten
obwohl er sie nicht mag. ('though he doesn't like it.')

These sentences share a pair of elements that is added to a set of pairs by means of the focus particle. The parts of the split domain are ranked equally; they form a 'complex contrastive topic'.[43] This is particularly evident if one compares (126) to the ungrammatical sentence in (122). The two sentences have a similar structure; in (122), however, the subject and the direct object cannot be interpreted as a pair of contrastive topics. This is due to the parallel make-up of the two conjoined clauses. The first one is clearly structured into the topic *Maja* and the comment *hat Fisch gegessen* ('ate fish'), and the indefinite direct object *Fisch* is interpreted as belonging to the non-contrastive sentence focus. This information-structural partition is transferred to the second clause (the whole sentence is interpreted as a pair-list answer to a question such as *Who ate what?*), where it conflicts with the requirement that the object *Suppe* ('soup') has the status of a contrastive topic. (126) shows that, in an appropriate context, the second clause of (122) is perfectly acceptable. We conclude that stressed *auch* can be associated with more than one element to its left, if the information-structural requirements imposed by the particle can be met. In the remainder of this chapter, split domains of stressed *auch* are removed from consideration. In Chapter 6, we will briefly return to this phenomenon, showing that the discussed constructions can be found in natural language data.

Movement of the associated element. Contrastive topics have their base positions in the focus domain, but obligatorily move to the left, either to the prefield or to a position at the left edge of the middlefield, i.e., above the sentence adverbials. In their surface positions, they must c-command the sentence focus (cf. Steube 2003; Sudhoff, Steube & Hogrefe 2004). Applied to constructions with stressed *auch*, this means that the associated element is generated in the c-command domain of the particle, just like in sentences with unstressed focus particles. The only difference is that it has the status of a contrastive topic, which enforces its movement to the left periphery. The particle itself is the only focusable element remaining in the focus

43. For a similar line of reasoning, see Repp (2008).

domain and bears the falling accent marking the regular sentence focus; other foci are excluded by the meaning of *auch*. The described mechanism is exemplified in (127).

(127) a. /FElix$_{i,[+CF]}$ hat$_j$ Maja$_k$ sicher [$_{VP,[+F]}$ AUCH [$_{VP}$ t$_{i,[+CF]}$ t$_k$
Felix *aux$_p$* Maja certainly also
geküsst$_{[-F]}$ t$_j$]] .
kissed

b. dass /FElix$_{i,[+CF]}$ Maja$_j$ sicher [$_{VP,[+F]}$ AUCH [$_{VP}$ t$_{i,[+CF]}$ t$_j$
that Felix Maja certainly also
geküsst$_{[-F]}$ hat]]
kissed *aux$_p$*

Unlike, e.g., scrambled elements, contrastive topics can undergo long distance movement in German, i.e., they systematically cross clause boundaries (cf. Haider & Rosengren 1998; Steube 2003; Frey 2006). The same is true for the domain of stressed *auch*, independently of whether the particle itself belongs to the matrix clause or to the embedded clause, as shown in (128). This data corroborates the analysis of constructions with stressed *auch* in terms of the Contrastive Topic Hypothesis.

(128) a. /BEATles-Platten$_{i,[+CF]}$ weiß ich AUCH, dass Felix zu Hause t$_{i,[+CF]}$
Beatles-records know I also that Felix at home
hat.
has

b. /BEATles-Platten$_{i,[+CF]}$ weiß ich, dass Felix AUCH zu Hause t$_{i,[+CF]}$ hat.

The proposed movement analysis explains why the fact that the domain of stressed *auch* is not c-commanded by the particle does not result in ungrammaticality. As demonstrated in Section 4.4.3, the c-command condition may be violated if a focused element must leave the focus domain for independent grammatical reasons. Preposing a contrastive topic is such an independently motivated movement operation. As the moved element is focused, it leaves a [+F] trace (strictly speaking, a [+CF] trace) behind in its base position in the focus domain. This trace facilitates the association of the particle and its domain, the involved mechanism being the same as in cases with unstressed focus particles.

Another argument for an analysis deriving constructions with stressed and unstressed focus particles from the same underlying structure is the placement of background constituents relative to the particle. As noted by Jacobs (1983), background constituents show a similar behavior in both types of focus particle constructions: they preferentially precede the particle. In both (129) and (130), the variant where the defocused subject *Felix* has not left the focus domain is clearly less acceptable.[44] On the basis of such data, Jacobs (1983: 113) generalizes his *Principle of Maximal Closeness to the Focus*, saying that unstressed focus particles must be placed as close as possible to their domains, to the *Principle of Latest Possible Positioning*. The latter principle requires focus particles – independently of whether they are stressed or not – to occur as late as possible in a sentence (cf. Section 4.2.1).

(129) a. /GEstern$_{i,[+CF]}$ hat$_j$ Felix$_k$ [$_{VP,[+F]}$ AUCH [$_{VP}$ t$_{i,[+CF]}$ t$_k$ gesungen$_{[-F]}$ t$_j$]] .
yesterday *aux$_p$* Felix also sung

b. ??/GEstern$_{i,[+CF]}$ hat$_j$ [$_{VP,[+F]}$ AUCH [$_{VP}$ t$_{i,[+CF]}$ Felix$_{[-F]}$ gesungen$_{[-F]}$ t$_j$]] .

(130) a. Sicher hat$_i$ Felix$_j$ [$_{VP,[+F]}$ auch [$_{VP}$ GEstern t$_j$ gesungen$_{[-F]}$ t$_i$]] .
certainly *aux$_p$* Felix also yesterday sung

b. ??Sicher hat$_i$ [$_{VP,[+F]}$ auch [$_{VP}$ GEstern Felix$_{[-F]}$ gesungen$_{[-F]}$ t$_i$]] .

Crucially, the very same correspondence between constructions with the stressed and unstressed variants of *auch* can be observed in cases where a defocused element remains within the focus domain for independent reasons. In (131) and (132), scrambling of the direct object *eine Birne* ('a pear') is strongly dispreferred. Outside the focus domain, the indefinite DP gets a specific interpretation (cf. Lenerz 2002; Steube 2006), which is extremely implausible in these examples. If sentences with stressed *auch* can be derived from the same underlying structure as sentences with unstressed focus particles, and if there is no difference in the syntactic status and position of the particle, background constituents are expected to behave identically in the two patterns. Hence, the data supports a unified account of stressed and unstressed *auch*.

(131) a. /FElix$_{i,[+CF]}$ hat$_j$ [$_{VP,[+F]}$ AUCH [$_{VP}$ t$_{i,[+CF]}$ [eine Birne]$_{[-F]}$ gegessen$_{[-F]}$ t$_j$]] .
Felix *aux$_p$* also a pear eaten

b. ??/FElix$_{i,[+CF]}$ hat$_j$ [eine Birne]$_k$ [$_{VP,[+F]}$ AUCH [$_{VP}$ t$_{i,[+CF]}$ t$_k$ gegessen$_{[-F]}$ t$_j$]] .

(132) a. Sicher hat$_i$ [$_{VP,[+F]}$ auch [$_{VP}$ FElix [eine Birne]$_{[-F]}$ gegessen$_{[-F]}$ t$_i$]] .
certainly *aux$_p$* also Felix a pear eaten

b. ??Sicher hat$_i$ [eine Birne]$_j$ [$_{VP,[+F]}$ auch [$_{VP}$ FElix t$_j$ gegessen$_{[-F]}$ t$_i$]] .

44. However, (129b) and (130b) are possible in certain contexts, in particular if *Felix* is not completely deaccented. These cases involve second occurrence focus, similar to constructions with more than one focus particle (cf. Section 5.2.3).

Restrictive and scalar particles. As noted in Section 4.5.1 above, Krifka's (1999) Contrastive Topic Hypothesis explains why restrictive particles cannot be used in the constructions of Pattern 6: the respective sentences violate Büring's (1997a) Condition of Disputability. More specifically, the meaning contribution of *nur* is incompatible with a particular presupposition of sentences containing contrastive topics, namely, that there are disputable sets of propositions in the topic value of the sentence. As for scalar particles such as *sogar*, Krifka assumes that they are excluded because they can never be stressed. But why is this the case? In another paper, Krifka (1992a) suggests that scalar particles modify the assertion operator of the clause in which they occur and – as they are, "in a sense, [...] part of that operator" (Krifka 1992a: 37) – cannot be focused themselves. This account, which is not fully worked out, will not be followed up here. Instead, we discuss another possible explanation, based on certain similarities of scalar focus particles and epistemic sentence adverbials.

In contrast to the so-called *verficational* or *positional* sentence adverbials (cf. Haftka 1995, 2003; Pittner 1999), such as *tatsächlich* ('in fact'), *wirklich* ('really'), and *keinesfalls* ('under no circumstances'), epistemic sentence adverbials, such as *leider* ('unfortunately'), *überraschenderweise* ('surprisingly'), and *möglicherweise* ('possibly'), cannot be focused.[45] Lang (1979) attributes this to the fact that they express non-propositional meaning: they express an attitude of the speaker, which is not part of the denotation of the respective sentence.[46] Taking a similar view, Steube (1995) claims that epistemic expressions "do not belong to the proposition representing a situation but refer to the speaker's cognitive structures only" (Steube 1995: 120). However, epistemic sentence adverbials can be substituted by expressions with propositional meaning. The resulting difference is illustrated in (133), taken from Lang (1979).

(133) a. Peter trinkt noch einen Schnaps, weil er leider /
Peter drinks another liquor because he unfortunately /
bedauerlicherweise süchtig ist.
regrettably addicted is

45. Metalinguistic contrast is left out of consideration.

46. "[M]it der durch den Satz *s* ausgedrückten Proposition *p* bezieht sich der Sprecher eines Äußerungsvorkommens von *s* auf die aktuale Welt, mit der durch ein Sadv [= sentence adverbial] ausgedrückten propositionalen Einstellung bezieht sich der Sprecher auf seine eigene Kognition. In diesem Fall wird durch *p* etwas denotiert, über das gesprochen wird, mit dem Sadv hingegen wird etwas ausgedrückt. Einstellungen ausdrücken ist nicht dasselbe, wie über Einstellungen sprechen." (Lang 1979: 212)

b. Peter trinkt noch einen Schnaps, weil es bedauerlich ist, dass
Peter drinks another liquor because it regrettable is that
er süchtig ist.
he addicted is
(Lang 1979: 210)

According to (133a), Peter drinks because he is addicted to alcohol, and the speaker is unhappy about Peter's addiction. (133b), on the other hand, says that Peter drinks because he is unhappy about his addiction, which is not necessarily an addiction to alcohol in this case. As the sentence adverbial *leider/bedauerlicherweise* ('unfortunately/regrettably') in (133a) is non-propositional, it is irrelevant for the causal connection (cf. Lang 1979: 210). The paraphrase *es ist bedauerlich* ('it is regrettable') in (133b) is propositional; consequently, it is interpreted as the reason for Peter's drinking. In Lang's view, the fact that epistemic sentence adverbials are non-propositional results in a number of other properties of these elements: they cannot be negated, corrected, or focused/accented.[47] The last-named property is exemplified in (134).

(134) *Felix hat Maja LEIder / möglicherWEIse geküsst.
Felix *aux*$_p$ Maja unfortunately / possibly kissed

The same reasoning can be applied to scalar focus particles, which, like sentence adverbials, convey epistemic meaning. By using *sogar*, for instance, the speaker expresses surprise or astonishment (cf. Section 3.3). Scalar focus particles can also be substituted by a propositional paraphrase; cf. (135). The substitution results in the same meaning difference as in (133) above. According to (135a), the reason for Felix' happiness is that he has been awarded the Nobel prize. The astonishment expressed by *sogar* relates to the speaker, not to Felix. In contrast, (135b) says that Felix is happy because it is surprising that he has been awarded the prize. In parallel to Lang's examples in (133), this difference should be due to the fact that *sogar* expresses non-propositional meaning, while the paraphrase *es ist erstaunlich/überraschend* ('it is astonishing/surprising') does not. However, *sogar* differs from epistemic sentence adverbials in that its meaning contribution is not entirely of a non-propositional nature. Its additive meaning component, which would be lost in (135b) if *auch* was not included in the embedded clause, is propositional. The meaning contribution of non-scalar restrictive and additive focus particles, on the other hand, is exclusively propositional; cf. (136). *Nur* and *auch* are relevant for the causal relationship in this example.

(135) a. Felix ist glücklich, weil er sogar den Nobelpreis bekommt.
Felix is happy because he even the Nobel_prize gets

47. See also Brandt, Reis, Rosengren & Zimmermann (1992: 66–71).

b. Felix ist glücklich, weil es erstaunlich / überraschend ist, dass
Felix is happy because it astonishing / surprising is that
er (auch) den Nobelpreis bekommt.
he (also) the Nobel_prize gets

(136) Felix ist glücklich, weil er nur / auch den Nobelpreis bekommt.
Felix is happy because he only / also the Nobel_prize gets

If Lang (1979) is right in assuming that the property of expressing non-propositional meaning prevents an expression from being focused and accented, and if *sogar* has a non-propositional meaning component, we have a straightforward explanation of the fact that *sogar* cannot be used like stressed *auch*. As argued above, the constructions of Pattern 6 require the focus particle to be focused itself, and this is incompatible with the semantics of *sogar* and other scalar particles. An argumentation along these lines also explains why *auch* in its scalar use is obligatorily unstressed (cf. Section 4.5.1), why there is no contrastive use of *sogar* (cf. Section 4.1.3), and why *sogar* cannot occur in the scope of negation (cf. Section 5.2.1 below).

To sum up, it has been shown that restrictive and scalar focus particles cannot be used in the constructions of Pattern 6 and that this has different, albeit similar, reasons in the semantics of the particles: the meaning of restrictive particles is incompatible with the domain being a contrastive topic, and the meaning of scalar particles is incompatible with the particle being focused. These two information-structural characteristics, however, represent the key properties of Pattern 6. As a consequence, *auch* (in its non-scalar use) and its equivalents are the only particles possible in this pattern.

At this point, it is worthwhile to compare stressed *auch* to unstressed focus particles following their domains, in particular in the constructions of Pattern 3; cf. the examples in (12) above. In Jacobs' (1983) approach, the constructions of Patterns 3 and 6 are derived by the same mechanism, namely, by syntactic infixation rules. While the analysis advocated here shares Jacobs' assumption that there is no fundamental syntactic difference between the two patterns, it also stresses the fact that they crucially differ in their information structure. Pattern 3 involves movement of a minimally focused constituent to the prefield; the focus particle itself remains unstressed. In Pattern 6, on the other hand, a contrastive topic is moved to the left periphery, resulting in a different accent pattern – an optional rising accent on the associated element and the falling sentence accent on the particle – and a special semantics.

Compared to Jacobs' approach, our information structure based analysis has two advantages. First, it explains why postponed *auch* can be stressed, while postponed *nur* and *sogar* cannot, and why the domain of *auch* often bears a rising contrastive accent, while the domain of *nur* and *sogar* is always marked by a falling focus accent, even if it precedes the particle. As noted by Jacobs (1983: 109), *auch* is also possible in Pattern 3; cf. (137a). However, constructions with postponed unstressed *auch* are more marked than their counterparts with *nur* and *sogar*. This is probably due to their similarity to the constructions of Pattern 6, which are very frequent in German (cf. Nederstigt 2003). As shown above, a comparable intervening pattern does not exist in the case of *nur* and *sogar*. Our model gives a straightforward explanation of the described distribution of *auch*, *nur*, and *sogar*: all three particles allow the movement of their domain to the prefield, but only *auch* has the additional option of associating with a contrastive topic, as in (137b); the other particles are impossible in this pattern for semantic reasons.

(137) a. GERda kommt auch.
Gerda comes also
b. /GERda kommt AUCH.
(Jacobs 1983: 109–110)

Second, our analysis accounts for differences in acceptability, depending on the exact position of a preposed element associated with a focus particle. Again, the relevant observations go back to Jacobs (1983). The domain of stressed *auch* may occur in the prefield or at the left edge of the middlefield; cf. (138a) and (138b). Both positions are well attested for contrastive topics in German (cf. Steube 2003). Preposed domains of unstressed focus particles, on the other hand, are fully acceptable only in the prefield, while the middlefield position is highly marked; cf. (138c) and (138d). This follows from the assumption that the domain is not contrastively focused in these cases, but corresponds to the non-contrastive sentence focus. While the prefield is a good position for minimal non-contrastive foci (cf. Speyer 2004; Frey 2004b), they usually do not move within the middlefield; cf. (139).

(138) a. [Seine /MUTter $]_D$ kommt morgen AUCH.
his mother comes tomorrow also
b. Ich vermute, dass [seine /MUTter $]_D$ morgen AUCH kommt.
I suspect that his mother tomorrow also comes
c. [Seine MUTter $]_D$ kommt morgen nur / sogar.
his mother comes tomorrow only / even
d. ??Ich vermute, dass [seine MUTter $]_D$ morgen nur / sogar
I suspect that his mother tomorrow only / even
kommt.
comes
(Jacobs 1983: 108)

(139) Wen hat Felix geküsst? (‘Who did Felix kiss?’)

a. Er_i hat_j wahrscheinlich $[_{VP,[+F]}$ t_i MAja $geküsst_{[-F]}$ t_j] .
he aux_p probably Maja kissed

b. $MAja_i$ hat_j er_k wahrscheinlich $[_{VP,[+F]}$ t_k $t_{i,[+F]}$ $geküsst_{[-F]}$ t_j] .

c. ??Er_i hat_j $MAja_k$ wahrscheinlich $[_{VP,[+F]}$ t_i $t_{k,[+F]}$ $geküsst_{[-F]}$ t_j] .

The difference in acceptability between (138b) and (138d) cannot easily be accounted for in Jacobs’ theory. Jacobs (1983: 108) assumes that it is due to idiosyncratic properties of the individual focus particles. However, this is an unsatisfactory solution, particularly as (138d) does not improve if the unstressed variant of *auch* is used instead of *nur* or *sogar*. If the different information-structural properties of the two patterns are taken into consideration, it can be shown that the relevant restrictions are of a more general nature and do not directly relate to the focus particles.

Information structure and the meanings of auch. Do the two variants of *auch* differ in their meanings? The movement analysis proposed above predicts that the meaning of constructions with stressed *auch* does not fundamentally differ from that of their counterparts with the unstressed variant of the particle. This corresponds to Jacobs’ (1983) synonymy hypothesis.[48] However, given the information-structural differences between the two patterns, we do not expect them to be completely equivalent, at least if properties of information structure are subsumed under meaning.[49]

As noted by Reis & Rosengren (1997), *auch* has two different utterance meanings: ‘in addition/furthermore’ and ‘likewise’.[50] At first sight, the former seems to correspond to unstressed *auch*, and the latter to the stressed variant of the particle; cf. (140). However, as Reis & Rosengren’s (1997) own example (141) shows, there is no one-to-one correspondence between the usage patterns of the particle and the utterance meanings: in spite of being stressed, *auch* has the ‘furthermore’ interpretation here.

(140) a. Gestern hat auch [FElix $]_D$ gesungen. (‘furthermore’)
yesterday aux_p also Felix sung

b. [/FElix $]_D$ hat gestern AUCH gesungen. (‘likewise’)

48. “Mit den Ableitungen [...] wird sich, da die Insertionsregeln genauso interpretiert werden wie die entsprechenden Phrasenstrukturregeln, die Synonymie der abgeleiteten Sätze [...] ergeben.” (Jacobs 1983: 106)

49. For a detailed proposal along these lines, see Dimroth (2004).

50. See also Marschall (2001) and Féry (to appear).

(141) Paul war gestern im Kino. ('Paul went to the cinema yesterday.')

[Ge/ARbeitet$_i$]$_D$	hat	Paul	gestern	AUCH	t_i	.	('furthermore')
worked	*aux$_p$*	Paul	yesterday	also			

(Reis & Rosengren 1997: 294)

According to Reis & Rosengren (1997), the utterance meaning of (stressed or unstressed) *auch* depends on the status of the material c-commanded by the particle: if *auch* c-commands focused material or traces of focused elements, the utterance meaning is 'furthermore'; if the c-command domain of the particle only contains defocused material or traces of background elements, the utterance meaning is 'likewise'. Of course, this generalization is compatible with the data in (140) and (141) only if stressed *auch* c-commands the base position of its domain in cases like (141), but not in cases like (140b). In contrast, the movement analysis advocated here, which derives constructions with the stressed and unstressed variants of *auch* from the same underlying structure, presupposes that the elements associated with stressed *auch* always originate in the c-command domain of the particle. This means that we need a different generalization about the particle's utterance meanings. A plausible candidate is (142). It is also based on the information structure of the sentences, but accounts for the distribution of the two meanings in a simpler way.

(142) If *auch* is associated with an aboutness topic, it has the utterance meaning 'likewise' (stressing the aspect of correspondence); in all other cases, its utterance meaning is 'furthermore' (stressing the aspect of addition).

According to (142), the unstressed variant of *auch* always has the utterance meaning 'furthermore', as it never associates with an aboutness topic. Stressed *auch*, on the other hand, should occur with either of the two meanings, the choice depending on whether its domain is an aboutness topic. The examples discussed so far are accounted for both by (142) and by Reis & Rosengren's generalization. Crucially, the two approaches make different predictions with respect to examples like those in (143). Here, *auch* is associated with a preposed direct object, which, according to Reis & Rosengren, has its base position outside the c-command domain of the particle. Consequently, the particle should have the utterance meaning 'likewise'. This prediction, however, is only borne out by (143a), where the domain of *auch* qualifies as an aboutness topic. The non-specific DP *irgendein beliebiges Buch über Satanismus* ('some arbitrary book on Satanism') in (143b) is not compatible with this information-structural status. (142) correctly predicts that *auch* has the utterance meaning 'furthermore' in this sentence. Giving up the claim that *auch* does not c-command the base position of its domain in cases like (140b) and (143a) would not save Reis & Rosengren's account, as the different meaning of the particle in (143a) and (143b) could still not be accounted for.

(143) a. [Die /BUDdenbrooks]D will Maja AUCH lesen. ('likewise')
the Buddenbrooks wants Maja also to_read

b. [Irgendein beliebiges Buch über Sata/NISmus]D will Maja
some arbitrary book on Satanism wants Maja
AUCH lesen. ('furthermore')
also to_read

4.5.3 Arguments against a movement account

There are several potential objections to the movement analysis of constructions with stressed *auch* presented above. This subsection addresses these counter-arguments, showing that they are inconclusive and that the observations they are based on also support alternative explanations. It has already been shown that the strongest objections to Jacobs' (1983) original version of the movement account do not apply to our approach based on the Contrastive Topic Hypothesis. First, our analysis does not presuppose that focus and sentence accent are separated in the constructions under discussion; the accent on the particle marks the focus on its affirmative meaning component. Second, no stipulations are needed to account for the fact that *nur* and *sogar* do not have a stressed postponed variant; the observed restrictions follow from their semantic properties. Third, the movement of the particle's domain is neither unmotivated nor special in any other respect, as contrastive topics must always be placed in the left periphery of the clause.

An objection that must be taken more seriously is made by Reis & Rosengren (1997: 249). The authors claim that the domain of stressed *auch* may be base-generated to the left of the particle. If this turned out to be true, a unified account of stressed and unstressed *auch* would no longer be tenable. As the subject *Peter* follows the modal particle *ja* in (144), Reis & Rosengren argue, it must be in its base position. Referring to observations made by Lenerz (1993), the authors treat modal particles on a par with sentence adverbials and assume that movement in the middlefield (i.e., scrambling or the preposing of a contrastive topic) always crosses the position of these elements (cf. also Abraham 1991; Brandt, Reis, Rosengren & Zimmermann 1992). Several points can be made against this way of reasoning. First of all, the position of the modal particle in Reis & Rosengren's example is not the most natural one. (144) is much more marked than (145), where *ja* follows the weak pronouns. The difference is more obvious if the modal particle is replaced by a sentence adverbial such as *sicher* ('certainly'); cf. (146).

(144) weil ja [Peter]D es ihm AUCH zeigen wollte
because *mp* Peter it him also to_show wanted
(Reis & Rosengren 1997: 249)

(145) weil [Peter]D es ihm ja AUCH zeigen wollte
because Peter it him *mp* also to_show wanted

(146) a. weil [Peter $]_D$ es ihm sicher AUCH zeigen wollte
because Peter it him certainly also to_show wanted
b. ??weil sicher [Peter $]_D$ es ihm AUCH zeigen wollte

Nevertheless, (144) is not ungrammatical. One possibility of bringing it into line with a movement analysis is to allow scrambling in the middlefield below the sentence adverbials and modal particles, as suggested by Frey (2004b). However, this type of movement should have no information-structural effects; the subject *Peter* and the weak pronouns *es* and *ihm* are predicted to be in the focus domain in (144). In the theory advocated here, this conflicts with the fact that these elements precede the focus particle, which is assumed to mark the left edge of the focus domain. In addition, the subject *Peter*, as a contrastive topic, should not be allowed in the focus domain at all.

Another possible way out is to give up the assumption that modal particles behave like sentence adverbials and that constituents to the right of them have not left the focus domain. This solution is corroborated by sentences like (147), where both the subject *Felix* and the direct object *den Brief* ('the letter') are background constituents and must have left their base positions: they precede the sentence adverbial *sicher* ('certainly'), and the relative order of indirect and direct object is reversed. Nevertheless, both elements follow the modal particle *ja*. As modal particles usually precede the sentence adverbials in the middlefield (cf. Lindner 1991; Brandt, Reis, Rosengren & Zimmermann 1992), constituents to the left of a modal particle must have been moved. This, however, does not mean that constituents to the right of a modal particle may not have been moved; cf. (147).[51] Hence, (144) cannot be considered as evidence against a movement analysis of constructions with stressed *auch*.

(147) weil ja $Felix_i$ [den Brief $]_j$ sicher t_i einem Polizisten t_j
because *mp* Felix the letter certainly a policeman
gezeigt hat
shown aux_p

Nederstigt (2003) also deals with (144). Following Reis & Rosengren, she assumes that the subject *Peter* and the two object pronouns are in their base positions (cf. Nederstigt 2003:204). The focus particle *auch*, on the other hand, is considered to be the head of a functional projection above VP (cf. (67) above). However, if *Peter*, *es* and *ihm* precede the focus particle and are in their base positions at the same time, it remains obscure where these base positions are located. The analysis implies that the direct and the indirect object as well as the subject are generated outside of VP. In addition, it conflicts with Nederstigt's assumption (given in a

51. The same conclusion can be drawn from Lenerz' (1993) argumentation.

later chapter of her book) that the constituent associated with stressed *auch* does move.[52] Because of its obvious shortcomings, Nederstigt's analysis of (144) will not be pursued here any further.

As noted by Reis & Rosengren (1997) and Nederstigt (2003), sentences with stressed *auch* cannot always be transformed into sentences with the unstressed counterpart of the particle, and vice versa. The authors interpret this fact as a central argument against a unified account of the two patterns. Some of the relevant examples are given in (148)–(150). Under the assumption that constructions with stressed *auch* can be derived by leftward movement of the particle's domain, the ungrammaticality of (148b) and (148d) is unexpected. Conversely, the sentences in (149) and (150a) should, but do not, have counterparts with the unstressed variant of the particle.

(148) a. und zwar so dass man die Beschreibung auch [LEsen kann]$_D$
and actually so that one the description also read can
b. *und zwar so dass man die Beschreibung [lesen kann]$_D$ AUCH
c. aber manche Männer sind dann so neugierig und wollen einfach
but some men are then so curious and want simply
dabei sein [...] oder auch [ihre MEInung sagen]$_D$
there to_be or also their opinion to_give
d. *[...] oder [ihre Meinung sagen]$_D$ AUCH
(Nederstigt 2003: 185)

(149) a. [Ø]$_D$ Hab ich AUCH schon erledigt.
aux$_p$ I also already finished
b. Kommt bitte [*pro*]$_D$ AUCH.
come please also
c. Er bat ihn, [*PRO*]$_D$ AUCH zu kommen.
he asked him also to come
(Reis & Rosengren 1997: 249)

(150) Ich stand vor dem Eingang. ('I stood at the entrance.')
a. Und [wer]$_D$ stand da plötzlich AUCH?
and who stood there suddenly also
b. *Auch [WER]$_D$ stand da plötzlich?
(Reis & Rosengren 1997: 249)

On closer examination, however, this data does not provide evidence against a uniform analysis, as in each case, the impossibility of using the complementary pattern can be attributed to independent factors. In (148a), movement of the

52. "In *AUCH*-utterances, the particle does not move, but given that the particle is always following the contrasted element in the utterance, *AUCH*-utterances require the movement of this contrasted element out of the VP to a position preceding the particle." (Nederstigt 2003: 334)

particle's domain is syntactically blocked. Here, the domain is the verb cluster of the embedded clause, which must remain in its base position.[53] But even if the embedded clause is turned into a main clause, the infinitive *lesen* ('read') and the finite modal auxiliary *kann* ('can') do not move together, as the finite verb (and only it) obligatorily moves to the V2-position (cf. Section 2.2). As for (148c), the elliptic coordination by means of *oder* ('or') requires the two conjuncts to have a parallel syntax and information structure. In the first conjunct, the predicate *dabei sein* ('to be there') corresponds to the sentence focus and has not been moved. The predicate in the second conjunct must share these properties, which is not the case in (148d). After slight modifications – i.e., the insertion of an additional modal auxiliary in (148a) and the elimination of the coordination structure in (148c) – the sentences can be turned into constructions with stressed *auch*; cf. (151).

(151)	a.	[Lesen	können	$]_D$ soll	man	die	Beschreibung	AUCH.		
		read	can	shall	one	the	description	also		
	b.	[Ihre	Meinung	sagen	$]_D$ wollen	manche	Männer	AUCH.		
		their	opinion	to_give	want	some	men	also		

The examples in (149) have in common that the domain of stressed *auch* is not overtly realized. Information-structural principles prevent the same in constructions with unstressed *auch*. The differences in information structure between sentences with the two variants of the particle were described in detail above. Being a contrastive topic, the domain of stressed *auch* can already be established in the preceding context. This, as well as the fact that it need not be accented (cf. Section 4.5.1), is a precondition for the non-overt realization of the domain. In addition, the focus particle itself is focused in the relevant constructions; that the particle's domain is phonologically empty does not mean that the sentence has no overt focus. In sentences with unstressed focus particles, on the other hand, the domain of the particle is not given or derivable, but corresponds to the new information focus and is obligatorily marked by the sentence accent. It cannot be omitted, as every sentence must at least have one overt focused element (cf. Steube, Alter & Späth 2004).

We briefly address the examples in (149) one by one. In (149a), the prefield element serving as the domain of *auch* has been dropped. Nevertheless, (149a) is interpreted as a declarative V2-clause; it answers a question such as *What about washing the dishes?* The possibility of *topic drop*, as the phenomenon is called, is relatively restricted in German: it mainly occurs in spoken language, the dropped constituent must be sentence-initial, and, most importantly, it must be contextually given (cf. Huang 1984; Fries 1988; Hoffmann 1997; Schulz 2006). As the

53. This also explains the ungrammaticality of Nederstigt's (2003: 185) example (5.11c).

last-named requirement is not met by the domain of unstressed *auch*, this element cannot undergo topic drop.

The subject of an imperative like (149b), i.e., the addressee, can always be identified in the situation of utterance. To leave it implicit is not only possible, but represents the preferred option. In cases where the addressee is associated with a focus particle, however, the covert realization is only possible if the particle itself is focused, i.e., in constructions with the stressed variant of *auch*. Imperatives like (149b) do have counterparts with unstressed *auch*; cf. (152a). For the reasons indicated above, the addressee must be realized overtly here. Furthermore, imperatives with stressed *auch* may have an overt subject associated with the focus particle; cf. (152b). As predicted, the only ungrammatical case is (152c), which does not have an overt focus.

(152) a. Komm auch [DU]$_D$. / Werden auch [SIE]$_D$ reich und berühmt.
come also you / become also you rich and famous

b. Komm [du]$_D$ bitte AUCH.
come you please also

c. *Komm bitte auch [*pro*]$_D$.
come please also

Interestingly, the domain of *auch* obligatorily precedes the particle *bitte* ('please') in (152b), as evidenced by the ungrammaticality of (153a). Irrespective of the exact status of *bitte*, this shows that the domain of stressed *auch* must be located in the left periphery of the clause, and in analogy to (152b), *pro* in Reis & Rosengren's example (149b) should also be located to the left of *bitte*. Another intriguing point is the difference in acceptability between (153b) and (153c). Although subjects of imperatives are usually highly marked in the prefield, this position is much more acceptable if the subject is associated with stressed *auch*. We consider both observations as additional support for the Contrastive Topic Hypothesis: as a contrastive topic, the domain of stressed *auch* is licensed in the left periphery, and it is licensed only there.

(153) a. *Komm bitte [du]$_D$ AUCH.
come please you also

b. [Du]$_D$ komm bitte AUCH.

c. ??Du komm bitte.

Control constructions like (149c) do not have alternative variants where the controlled element (*PRO*) is overtly realized. According to common assumptions, the infinite verb of the embedded clause does not license an overt subject. As a consequence, cases with overt and non-overt domains cannot directly be compared here. However, the impossibility of using the unstressed variant of *auch* in (149c) follows from the same regularities as in the cases discussed so far: *PRO* as the particle's domain is incompatible with the requirement that an unstressed focus particle is associated with an overt focus.

We must leave open the question of whether the non-overt domains of *auch* in (149b) and (149c) are moved out of the c-command domain of the focus particle or whether they are base-generated to its left. If topic drop in examples like (149a) can be analyzed in terms of *pro*, as suggested by Junghanns (2002), it is plausible that at least *pro* is able to move.[54] Reis & Rosengren (1997:249) argue against this assumption, claiming that *PRO* and *pro* do not move in general. However, this is not necessarily an argument against a unified account of stressed and unstressed *auch*. Most likely, the movement account proposed above could be modified in such a way that it does not require the movement of non-overt elements such as *PRO* and *pro*.

The contrast in grammaticality between the wh-questions in (150) is also predicted by our theory: The focus particle and the question word do not form a constituent in their base positions in the middlefield. As a consequence, they cannot undergo wh-movement together, which is why (150b) is ruled out. A variant where unstressed *auch* precedes the wh-element in the middlefield is not possible either, as it would not satisfy the wh-criterion. However, (150b) is acceptable as an echo question. We will return to this observation in Section 4.6.3, showing that it is compatible with our theory.

A last argument brought forward by Reis & Rosengren (1997:250) against a movement analysis is based on sentences like (154a), where the associated element is excluded from the c-command domain of *auch*. Reis & Rosengren's reasoning is as follows: The focus particle is located inside a predicate phrase in (154a). The domain *Petra* cannot have its base position within this phrase, as shown by the ungrammaticality of (154b). Hence, (154a) cannot be derived by movement of *Petra* out of the c-command domain of the focus particle.

(154) a. [Petra]$_D$ gilt als AUCH sehr ehrgeizig.
Petra counts as also very ambitious
b. *Es gilt als auch [PEtra]$_D$ sehr ehrgeizig.
expl counts as also Petra very ambitious
(Reis & Rosengren 1997:250)

While we consider Reis & Rosengren's conclusion to be correct, we question the grammaticality of (154a) with the intended meaning, i.e., with *Petra* as the domain

54. On the other hand, an analysis of imperatives like (149b) in terms of *pro* cannot be taken for granted (cf. Rosengren 1993a, among others).

of *auch*.[55] The grammatical variant of (154a) is (155a). Here, the focus particle c-commands the whole predicate phrase, and a movement analysis is no longer impossible. The sentence has a grammatical counterpart with unstressed *auch*; cf. (155b). The difference in grammaticality between (154a) and (155a) is even more evident when the compositionally derived meaning of the sentences is considered: (155a) says that Petra is regarded as ambitious (assertion) and that someone else is regarded as ambitious (presupposition). (154a) would have the same assertion; its presupposition, however, would be that Petra is attributed the property that another person is ambitious. Since this is not a property of Petra, the sentence does not make sense. In our model, the ungrammaticality of (154a) in the reading intended follows from the ungrammaticality of (154b).

(155)	a.	[Petra]$_D$	gilt	AUCH	als	sehr	ehrgeizig.			
		Petra	counts	also	as	very	ambitious			
	b.	Es	gilt	auch	[PEtra]$_D$	als	sehr	ehrgeizig.		
		expl	counts	also	Petra	as	very	ambitious		

To sum up: The objections brought forward by Reis & Rosengren (1997) and Nederstigt (2003) against a unified account of constructions with stressed and unstressed *auch* are not conclusive. Most of the authors' observations can be traced back to independent syntactic, semantic, or information-structural principles. While some of the remaining points require a closer look, they do not provide sound arguments against a movement analysis of constructions with stressed *auch*, either.

4.5.4 Summary

Section 4.5 dealt with the group of stressed additive focus particles, in particular with its prototypical member *auch*. It was argued that constructions containing the stressed variant of this particle, which always follows its domain, can be derived from the same underlying structure as constructions with unstressed *auch*. A central assumption is that the associated element is a contrastive topic obligatorily moving to the left periphery of the clause. The special characteristics of the pattern – concerning focusing and accentuation, word order, and the limitation to additive particles – were shown to follow from its information structure. The main conclusion is that constructions of Pattern 6 do not require an independent treatment, as suggested by Reis & Rosengren (1997) and, even more radically, by Nederstigt (2003), but can straightforwardly be integrated into the analysis

55. This was confirmed by three informants, all of which judged the sentence to be ungrammatical.

proposed in Section 4.4. Additional prosodic evidence for the claim that stressed *auch* associates with contrastive topics will be presented in Chapter 6.

4.6 Focus particles as adjuncts to XP

Which usage patterns of the classification in Section 4.1.1 can the proposed model of the grammar of focus particle constructions cope with so far? In Section 4.4, it was argued that our version of the adverbial analysis covers Patterns 1–5 and parts of Pattern 9. The goal of the previous section was to demonstrate that the constructions of Pattern 6 can be integrated into this analysis. Due to the special status of the particles in Pattern 10, this pattern had already been excluded from consideration in Section 4.1.1. What our theory still fails to cope with are Patterns 7 and 8, as well as the remaining constructions of Pattern 9. As the root CP is no longer considered a possible adjunction sites of focus particles, Pattern 7 (unstressed particle preceding its domain in the prefield) presents a problem for the analysis that did not emerge in Büring & Hartmann's (2001) theory. Pattern 8, where an unstressed particle adjacently follows its accented domain in the prefield or middlefield, is neither accounted for by an adverbial analysis along the lines of Büring & Hartmann (2001) nor by the model proposed here. The same is true for those constructions of Pattern 9 where the focus particle cannot be analyzed as an adjunct to an adjective or quantifier phrase. We will argue that it is unavoidable to employ assumptions of the adjunction-to-XP analysis to overcome this problem.

The present section is structured as follows. In a first step, we expound how the necessary extension of the theory could look like. Next, the arguments against the adjunction-to-XP analysis brought forward in the literature are reconsidered. Corpora of German are consulted to reveal empirical problems of the existing accounts, independently of whether they belong to the group of adverbial analyses or to the group of adjunction-to-XP analyses. Lastly, we address the question of how the proposed extension of the theory can be motivated, i.e., why adjunction of focus particles to projections other than VP and AP is possible in certain well-defined cases. The answer can once more be found in the information structure of the relevant constructions.

4.6.1 Adjunction to DP, PP, and CP

Pattern 7, as well as the hitherto unexplained cases of Pattern 9, can be accounted for if one allows focus particles to adjoin to maximal projections other than VP and AP. Potential adjunction sites include DPs, PPs, and embedded CPs. Examples of the resulting structures are given in (156) and (157).[56]

(156) a. Nur [MAja $]_D$ hat eine Birne gegessen.
only Maja *aux*$_p$ a pear eaten

b.

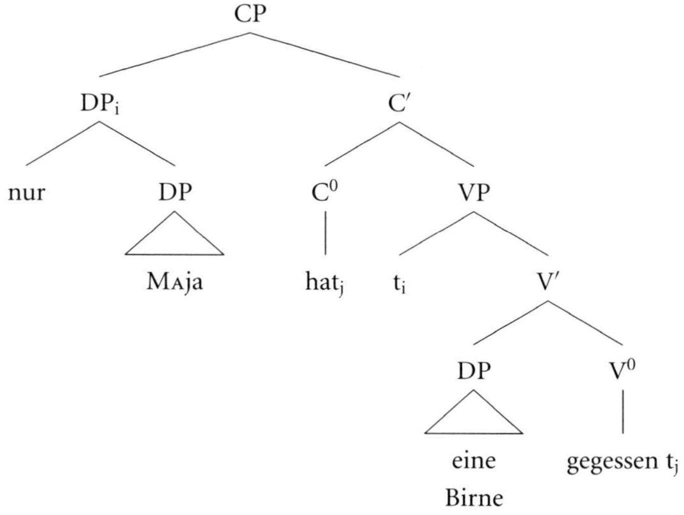

c. $[_{PP}$ Auch $[_{PP}$ auf FElix $]]_i$ hat_j Maja t_i gewartet t_j.
also for Felix *aux*$_p$ Maja waited

d. $[_{CP}$ Sogar $[_{CP}$ dass FElix kommt $]]_i$ hat_j Maja t_i gehofft t_j.
even that Felix comes *aux*$_p$ Maja hoped

(157) der Tod $[_{DP}$ nur $[_{DP}$ des ANführers]]
the death only the_{gen} $leader_{gen}$

To treat focus particles as adjuncts to non-verbal projections in the constructions of Pattern 7 is desirable for two reasons. First, the well-motivated V2-generalization of German, saying that the finite verb in main clauses may be preceded by only one constituent, need not be given up. Pure adverbial analyses have to assume adjunction of the focus particle to the root CP in the examples in (156), with the consequence that the sentences represent V3-structures. If, however, the focus particle is adjoined to the element that serves as its domain, the resulting constituent is the only preverbal element. Second, we have an explanation of the fact that the focus particles in (156) can only be associated with the immediately following constituent. As shown in Section 4.4.4, Büring & Hartmann's account fails to explain why a sentence-initial particle cannot be associated with

56. Examples like (157), the grammaticality of which has often been questioned in the literature, will be addressed in more detail in Section 4.6.2.

the whole remaining clause. If focus particles may not adjoin to the root CP, the reason is obvious: being a part of the prefield constituent, a sentence-initial focus particle does not c-command the remainder of the clause. Association with focus, however, presupposes that the particle c-commands (the base positions of) all elements belonging to its domain.

In Pattern 8, an unstressed focus particle immediately follows its domain in the prefield or middlefield. The relevant examples from Jacobs (1983) are repeated in (158). These sentences, in particular (158a), call for an analysis where the focus particle and its domain form a constituent. There are two potential ways to adjust our theory in such a way that it accounts for cases like (158). One possibility is to allow right adjunction of focus particles to maximal projections, as in (159). With respect to adverbials, Ernst (2002, 2003) argues – contra Kayne (1994) and Cinque (1999) – that right adjunction is possible. If this analysis can be transferred to focus particles, a parallel treatment of Pattern 7 and 8 is conceivable.

(158) a. [Die TOCHter $]_D$ nur / auch / sogar entkam den Flammen.
the daughter only / also / even escaped the flames
b. Der Vater verriet [der TOCHter $]_D$ nur das Geheimnis.
the father told the daughter only the secret
c. Der Vater hat [an die TOCHter $]_D$ nur gedacht.
the father aux_p of the daughter only thought
(Jacobs 1983: 95–100)

(159)
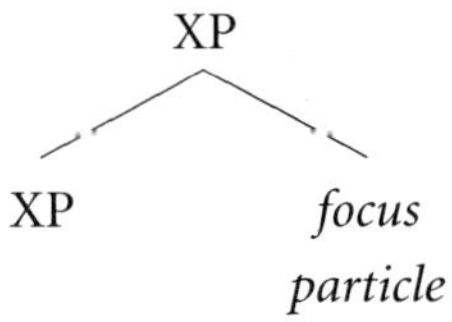

Ernst (2002) argues that the availability of right adjunction depends on whether the host projection is left- or right-headed. Among other things, it is predicted that adverbials can only right-adjoin to left-headed VPs, i.e., VPs in VO-languages such as English. For the present problem, this means that right adjunction of focus particles should be possible if the domain is a DP, PP, or CP, but impossible if it is a VP, as VP is head-final in German. For DP-, PP-, and VP-domains, these predictions are borne out; cf. (158) above and (160a). However, contrary to the expectations, a focus particle immediately following a CP-domain in the prefield is also ungrammatical, as shown by (160b).

(160) a. *[Eine BIRne gegessen $]_D$ nur hat sie.
a pear eaten only aux_p she
b. ??[Dass er KOMMT $]_D$ nur habe ich erwartet.
that he comes only aux_p I expected

The second possibility to integrate constructions of Pattern 8 into our theory is to propose a different structure for a focus particle forming a constituent with its domain. Instead of adjunction of the particle to the domain, as in (156) and (159), one could assume that the associated element is the complement of the particle in these cases. Postponed focus particles could then be explained by movement of the domain to the specifier of the focus particle phrase (FPP); cf. (161). It is not clear, however, how the involved movement operation, which is also extensively employed by Kayne (1994) and other authors working within the antisymmetric framework, could be motivated. Another disadvantage of this proposal is that the resulting phrase does not have the same category as the particle's domain. Alternatively, focus particles could be treated as minor functional heads not projecting their category features, as suggested by Bayer (1996); cf. Section 4.2.2.

(161)

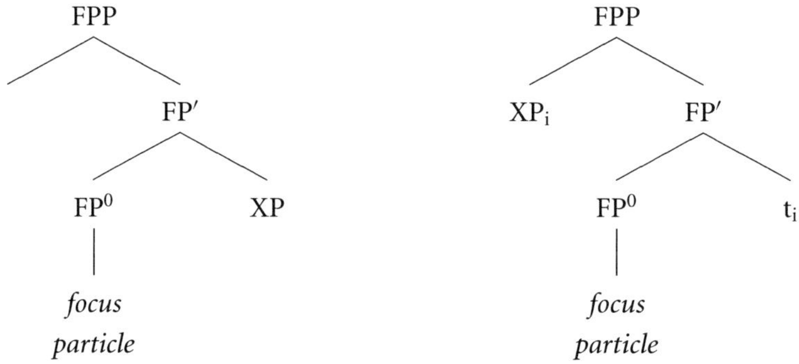

Both of the presented possibilities to integrate constructions of Pattern 8 into our analysis require modifications of the syntactic theory, although the first calls for less radical changes than the second. The construction type under discussion requires more detailed research; what has been shown is that our theory, in contrast to Bürger & Hartmann's (2001) account, is potentially compatible with unstressed focus particles immediately following their domains in the prefield or middlefield.

4.6.2 Arguments against adjunction to XP

In the literature, several arguments have been brought forward against adjunction of focus particles to DPs and embedded CPs. The following list gives an overview of these arguments, which at first sight suggest that a pure adverbial analysis of focus particle constructions is preferable.[57]

57. Bürger & Hartmann's (2001) *(no) reconstruction argument* against adjunction to XP will be discussed in Chapter 5.

– A focus particle does not form a constituent with a subsequent DP, as the combination of a focus particle and a DP is impossible as the complement of a preposition (Jacobs 1983: 42; Bayer 1996: 18; Büring & Hartmann 2001: 233); cf. (162).

(162) a. *mit nur Hans
 with only Hans
 b. *gegen sogar den Präsidenten
 against even the president
 (Büring & Hartmann 2001: 233)

– A focus particle does not form a constituent with a subsequent DP, as the combination of a focus particle and a DP is impossible as a genitive complement of a noun (Bayer 1996: 18; Büring & Hartmann 2001: 233); cf. (163).

(163) a. *der Bruder nur des Grafen
 the brother only the_{gen} $count_{gen}$
 b. *die Proklamation sogar der Unabhängigkeit
 the proclamation even the_{gen} $independence_{gen}$
 (Büring & Hartmann 2001: 233–234)

– A focus particle does not form a constituent with a subsequent DP, as the combination of a focus particle and a DP cannot be coordinated with another DP (Jacobs 1983: 45–46; Bayer 1996: 18–19); cf. (164).

(164) a. ??dass Peter und nur Luise spazierengehen
 that Peter and only Luise go_for_a_walk
 b. ??dass Gerd Peter und sogar Luise traf
 that Gerd Peter and even Luise met
 (Bayer 1996: 19)

– A focus particle does not form a constituent with a subsequent embedded CP, as the combination of a focus particle and a CP cannot be extraposed as a whole (Jacobs 1983: 46–47; Bayer 1996: 17); cf. (165).

(165) *dass Hans gesagt hat nur dass der Kanzler zu dick sei
 that Hans said aux_p only that the chancellor too fat is
 (Bayer 1996: 17)

If these arguments were shown to be valid, they would strongly suggest that a focus particle and a following DP or embedded CP cannot form a constituent together, which would in turn support an adverbial analysis of focus particle constructions.[58] However, the validity of the arguments is questioned by proponents of

58. A similar argument can be constructed on the basis of adjunction of focus particles to PPs. We will return to this point below.

the adjunction-to-XP analysis. Bayer (1996), for instance, attributes the observed restrictions to an independent factor. He argues that a focus particle and its domain cannot undergo LF-movement out of DP/PP (in case of the combination of a focus particle and a DP) or VP (in case of the combination of a focus particle and an embedded CP) together.[59] According to Bayer, movement of this kind is necessary for the sentence to be interpretable, but impossible if the dominating projection has the status of a barrier. Whether a phrase is a barrier is determined by Koster's (1987) *Condition of Global Harmony* requiring "that all the governors involved in a sequence (i.e. a *chain* of governors) point in the same direction" (Bayer 1996: 43). A similar solution is proposed by Reis & Rosengren (1997): in their theory, the ungrammatical sentences in (162)–(165) are ruled out by an additional constraint saying that the constituent resulting from adjunction of a focus particle to an XP must always be the daughter of a node on the predicate's projection line.[60]

While Bayer (1996) and Reis & Rosengren (1997) give alternative explanations for the observed restrictions, König (1993) questions the empirical validity of the arguments given above. Discussing examples like those in (166), König concludes that "there are no syntactic constraints precluding the occurrence of particles within genitive constructions or the coordination of bare NPs and NPs modified by particles" (König 1993: 984). The ungrammaticality of examples like those in (163) and (164) is attributed to semantic mismatches.

(166) a. Die Auflösung nur der Universitäten wäre nicht sinnvoll.
the dissolution only the$_{gen}$ universities$_{gen}$ would_be not sensible
b. Paul, Peter und sogar Fritz werden kommen.
Peter Paul and even Fritz *aux$_f$* come
(König 1993: 984)

In the first place, the question of whether the arguments against adjunction to XP are valid is thus an empirical question. To determine the possibility of focus particles in the configurations described above (i.e., configurations incompatible with an analysis in terms of adjunction to VP, AP, or root CP), two corpora of German were consulted: the *DeReKo* corpus (Deutsches Referenzkorpus; Institut für Deutsche Sprache Mannheim),[61] which mainly consists of written texts, and

59. See also Bayer & Grosu (2000).

60. See (65) above and the summary in Reis & Rosengren (1997: 267).

61. See http://www.ids-mannheim.de/kl/projekte/korpora/. For most enquiries, only the morphosyntactically annotated part of this corpus was used.

the *Verbmobil* corpus (Institut für Maschinelle Sprachverarbeitung Stuttgart),[62] which consists of transcriptions of dialogs. As it proved impossible to search for the relevant constructions systematically in the corpora, we cannot give a quantitative analysis of the corpus data. As a consequence, the results presented below only have an exploratory character and must be confirmed by further research. We first discuss the configurations listed above, before we turn to another relevant case, which has not been addressed in the literature: focus particles adjoined to PPs.

Few instances of a focus particle and a DP serving as the complement of a preposition could be found. In all cases, the particle was *nur*; cf. (167) and (168).[63] Due to the extreme rareness of this pattern, no statement can be made about its grammaticality.

(167) Weg vom Streben *nach nur Konsum und materieller*
away from_the striving for only consumption and material
Verbesserung, mahnt der Papst.
betterment admonishes the pope
(DeReKo, MMM/105.15042)

(168) *Mit "nur" einer Platzwunde am Kopf* kam dieser Serbe davon,
with only a laceration on_the head got this Serbian away
als aufgebrachte Kroaten die serbischen Flüchtlinge mit Steinen
when outraged Croatians the Serbian refugees with stones
bewarfen.
threw_at
(DeReKo, MMM/508.12568)

However, Bouma, Hendriks & Hoeksema (2007) argue that focus particles are possible within PPs in German, as they are in English and Dutch. The authors provide some examples found on the internet; cf. (169) and (170). The rareness of this pattern in German is explained as a consequence of the strong tendency of German prepositions to appear adjacent to their complements. This hypothesis is spelled out by Bouma, Hendriks & Hoeksema (2007) within an optimality theoretic framework.

(169) Wahlweise kann man sich die Maschine mit nur dem Piloten oder
optionally can one *refl* the machine with only the pilot or
1–3 Passagieren auswählen [...].
1–3 passengers select
(Bouma, Hendriks & Hoeksema 2007: 14–15)

62. See http://www.ims.uni-stuttgart.de/projekte/verbmobil/Dialogs/.

63. The relevant parts of the corpus examples are printed in italics.

(170) Symbol: Zeigt Ihnen die ganze Ziffer an oder reduziert die
symbol shows you the whole number *pref* or reduces the
Auswahl auf nur diese Ziffer.
choice to only this number
(Bouma, Hendriks & Hoeksema 2007: 15)

Combinations of a focus particle and a DP serving as genitive complements or attributes of nouns were much more frequent. Although no instances with *sogar* could be found, the corpora contained many examples with *nur* and *auch*, a small selection of which is given in (171)–(176). This data suggests that the pattern under discussion exists in German.

(171) Schluderei und *Unachtsamkeit nur der Firmen*?
sloppiness and inattentiveness only the$_{gen}$ companies$_{gen}$
(DeReKo, MMM/602.08833)

(172) Auch *die Beibehaltung nur der privaten Vermögensteuer* wies
also the retention only the$_{gen}$ private$_{gen}$ wealth_tax$_{gen}$ rejected
Waigel zurück.
Waigel *pref*
(DeReKo, MMM/610.28892)

(173) Wenn die schrecklichen Erlebnisse nicht verarbeitet, sondern
if the dreadful experiences not overcome but
abgespalten und unterdrückt werden, drängen sie aus den Tiefen
split_off and suppressed aux_{pass} push they from the depths
der Seelen nicht nur der Opfer immer wieder nach
the$_{gen}$ souls$_{gen}$ not only the$_{gen}$ victims$_{gen}$ always again to
oben.
the_surface
(DeReKo, S93/H38.04602)

(174) Sie bemühen sich derzeit um *die Unterstützung auch der*
they endeavor *refl* at_the_moment for the support also the$_{gen}$
europäischen Staaten.
European$_{gen}$ countries$_{gen}$
(DeReKo, MMM/508.11531)

(175) Längst ist Aids in Cagliari *eine Erkrankung auch der*
for_a_long_time is AIDS in Cagliari a disease also the$_{gen}$
heterosexuellen Nichtdrogenabhängigen.
heterosexual$_{gen}$ non-drug-addicts$_{gen}$
(DeReKo, S93/H28.03392)

(176) Das Fernsehen knabbert an *den Marktanteilen auch der*
the television gnaws at the market_shares also the$_{gen}$
Printmedien.
printed_media$_{gen}$
(DeReKo, S93/H44.05346)

The third pattern examined – the coordination of the combination of a focus particle and a DP with another DP – was also represented in the corpora. It is remarkable that there were few examples with *nur*, but many cases with *auch* and *sogar*; cf. (177)–(182).

(177) Diese Richtlinien wurden inhaltlich von *einzelnen*
these guidelines *aux$_{pass}$* as_regards_content by individual
Bundesländern und auch Hochschulen übernommen.
states and also universities taken_on
(DeReKo, LIM/LI1.00264)

(178) *Sponsoren und auch die Stadt* helfen beim Kauf der
sponsors and also the city help with_the purchase the$_{gen}$
nötigen Materialien.
necessary$_{gen}$ materials$_{gen}$
(DeReKo, MMM/104.04804)

(179) *Der fünfzehnte März und auch der sechzehnte* würden mir beide sehr
the fifteenth March and also the sixteenth would me both very
gut passen.
well suit
(Verbmobil, g095axx0_004_ANS_011050)

(180) Da wandern *Sofakissen und Kämme, Geschirr, Fußmatten und*
there move sofa_cushions and combs tableware doormats and
sogar bedruckte Kondome in Windeseile aus den Vorräten der
even printed condoms in no_time from the stocks the$_{gen}$
Verkäufer in die Taschen der Fans.
sellers$_{gen}$ into the pockets the$_{gen}$ fans$_{gen}$
(DeReKo, MMM/104.02017)

(181) Erstmals gab es *ausreichend Toiletten und sogar*
for_the_first_time were there sufficient toilets and even
Duschwagen ausschließlich für Frauen.
shower_wagons exclusively for women
(DeReKo, MMM/506.01704)

(182) *Frostige Temperaturen und sogar Schneeflocken* begleiten den
frosty temperatures and even snowflakes accompany the
Wochenbeginn.
beginning_of_the_week
(DeReKo, MMM/603.11552)

Interestingly, the few examples with *nur* that were found in the corpora share the property that the two coordinated DPs are identical; cf. (183) and (184). This observation sheds new light on the examples used to argue against an adjunction-to-XP analysis, like (164a) above. As suggested by König (1993), semantic incompatibilities are responsible for the ungrammaticality of such sentences: the focus particle *nur* excludes alternatives to its domain; the coordination structure, however, explicitly introduces an alternative. The meaning of (164a), for instance, has the contradictory components that Peter went for a walk and that Luise is the only person who went for a walk. There are two ways to avoid this inconsistency. One is to keep the two coordinated DPs identical, as in (183), (184), and König's example (185). In such constructions, which are used to emphasize the uniqueness of the particle's domain, the coordination does not introduce a genuine alternative.

(183) Sie haben dem Mann die Hilfe verweigert, die *Sie und nur Sie*
you aux_p the man the help refused that you and only you
hätten leisten können.
aux_p given could
(DeReKo, S94/H11.01266)

(184) *Sie und nur sie* bestimmt die Forschungsrichtung und
it and only it determines the research_trend and
Einzelthemen.
individual_topics
(DeReKo, S94/H25.03032)

(185) Paul und nur Paul ist für die Aufgabe geeignet.
Paul and only Paul is to the task suited
(König 1993: 984)

The second possibility of saving coordination structures with *nur* adjoined to the second conjunct is to insert *sonst* or *ansonsten* ('else/other') before the particle; cf. (186)–(188). This has the effect that not all alternatives to the domain of *nur* are excluded, but only those that have not been mentioned before, so that the semantic contradiction is resolved. The relevant constructions were numerously represented in the corpora, showing that a DP modified by *nur* can be coordinated with another DP if there is nothing against it from a semantic point of view. The examples in (186)–(188) become ungrammatical if *sonst* is omitted.

(186) Ein Gemälde mit Sprintern im Bühnenhintergrund [...] verweist
a painting with sprinters in_the stage_background refers
auf jene Lebensrealität, in der es *einen Sieger und sonst nur*
to that reality in which there one winner and else only
Verlierer gibt.
losers is
(DeReKo, R99/APR.30431)

(187) *Kein Ass, eine Karo-Dame und sonst nur Luschen* – mit
no ace one queen_of_diamonds and else only low_cards with
solch miesen Karten kann auch ein ausgebuffter Pokerspieler den
such bad cards can even a shrewd poker_player the
fetten Pott nicht abräumen.
fat pot not win
(DeReKo, M03/304.27536)

(188) An der zentralen Avenida Nuevo Leon [...] wartet das "Rexo",
at the central Avenida Nuevo Leon waits the Rexo
Mexikos schönste Bar, eine Neuschöpfung aus *schwarzen*
Mexico's nicest bar a new_creation made_of black
Stahlträgern und sonst nur Glas auf drei ineinander greifenden
steel_girders and else only glass on three engaging
Ebenen.
levels
(DeReKo, P00/JUL.28848)

A similar semantic incompatibility is responsible for the ungrammaticality of Jacobs' (1983) example (189). The variant with *nur* is excluded for the reason discussed above. With *auch* or *sogar*, however, the sentence is equally unacceptable. At first sight, this is unexpected. On closer examination, it appears that the meaning of the verb plays a crucial role here. *Treffen* ('to meet') is a collective verb; it requires its subject to refer to a plural entity. Adding *Luise* by means of *auch* or *sogar* in (189), on the other hand, implies that Peter also could have met alone, which results in a contradiction. In Bayer's (1996) version of the sentence, given in (164b) above, *treffen* is used as a non-reflexive transitive verb. Its direct object can refer to a singular or a plural entity. Contrary to Bayer's judgement, the use of *auch* or *sogar* (but not *nur*) is possible in this case. Altogether, the corpus data and the additional examples discussed above show that coordination of two DPs, one of which is modified by a focus particle, is possible in German.

(189) ??dass Peter und nur / sogar / auch Luise sich in Straßburg trafen
that Peter and only / even / also Luise *refl* in Straßburg met
(Jacobs 1983:45)

No instances of a focus particle and an embedded CP extraposed together were found in the corpora. Bayer (1996) and Büring & Hartmann (2001) argue that this pattern is possible if the CP is an adjunct; cf. (190) and (191). However, the status of these examples is unclear. On the one hand, (190) is marked; the sentence is much better when the subordinate clause is extraposed alone, leaving the focus particle in the middlefield of the matrix clause. On the other hand, the constructions in (191) are fully acceptable only with a clear intonational break between matrix clause and embedded clause, suggesting that the latter is a separate unit rather than a fully integrated part of the matrix clause. This data deserves further research, as does the question of why extraposition of an argument clause together with a focus particle is impossible.

(190) dass Hans hereingekommen wäre nur wenn alle geschlafen
that Hans entered *aux*$_p$ only if everybody slept
hätten
aux$_p$
(Bayer 1996: 204)

(191) a. Peter will ihm nicht die Hand geben, sogar nachdem er sich
Peter wants him not the hand to_shake even after he *refl*
entschuldigt hat.
apologized *aux*$_p$
b. Maria will kommen, auch wenn sie nicht eingeladen ist.
Maria wants to_come even if she not invited is
(Büring & Hartmann 2001: 269)

A pattern that has not been considered in the literature so far, but that also provides an argument for the existence of adjunction-to-XP structures, is the coordination of a PP modified by a focus particle with another PP. The corpora contained many sentences instantiating this pattern; some examples are given in (192)–(194).

(192) Japaner lernen *für den Job und nur für ihn.*
Japanese learn for the job and only for it
(DeReKo, S93/H15.01713)

(193) Wir haben auch schon *bei Kaffeemaschinen und Computern für*
we *aux*$_p$ also already for coffee_machines and computers for
Schulen und sogar bei Feuerwehrautos Rabatte rausgeschlagen.
schools and even for fire_engines discounts got
(DeReKo, MMM/602.09586)

(194) Ich denke, ich werde mich dann *um die Hotels und auch um die*
I think I *aux*$_f$ *refl* then after the hotels and also after the
Fahrkarten kümmern [...].
tickets look
(Verbmobil, m148ach2_029_HAS_470010)

To sum up: Two of the patterns that have been claimed to be ungrammatical in the literature (focus particle + DP within DP; focus particle + DP coordinated with another DP) could be shown to exist in German. In addition, the existence of a third pattern predicted to be ungrammatical by a pure adverbial analysis (focus particle + PP coordinated with another PP) was demonstrated. The examination of the two remaining patterns (focus particle + DP within PP; extraposition of focus particle + embedded CP) did not yield clear results. Crucially, some of the arguments brought forward against adjunction-to-XP analyses have now turned into arguments against a pure adverbial analysis. In the examples discussed above, the focus particles cannot be adjoined to verbal or adjectival projections, but must be analyzed as adjuncts to DP or PP. Hence, the employment of adjunction-to-XP structures need not be stipulated for the constructions of Patterns 7 and 8 alone; they are needed on independent grounds. Moreover, the corpus data not only provides arguments against pure adverbial analyses of German focus particle constructions such as Jacobs (1983) and Büring & Hartmann (2001); it also shows that the accounts of Bayer (1996) and Reis & Rosengren (1997) – which are in the spirit of the adjunction-to-XP analysis, but exclude the constructions discussed above by independent means – are too restrictive. At least two issues call for a more detailed examination. First, the semantic restrictions involved in determining whether focus particles may adjoin to DPs and PPs have only been touched on very briefly. Second, it is still unclear why a focus particle and an embedded CP cannot be extraposed together.

4.6.3 Adjunction to XP and information structure

This subsection deals with the information-structural peculiarities of the constructions that are analyzed here as involving adjunction of focus particles to non-predicate projections. This issue is relevant inasmuch as information structure provides a motivation for the special syntactic structure, which deviates from the standard case described in Section 4.4, i.e., adjunction to VP. While there is no difference in truth-conditional semantics between sentences like (195a) and (195b), they differ in their conditions of use. It will be argued that these differences are closely connected to the different syntax of the sentences.

(195) a. Gestern hat nur [FELIX]$_D$ gesungen.
yesterday *aux*$_p$ only Felix sung
b. Nur [FELIX]$_D$ hat gestern gesungen.

We start with some observations. First, the sentence focus, which normally corresponds to the syntactic focus domain (i.e., the VP below the sentence adverbials; cf. Section 2.3), is put out of force in the constructions under discussion. The sister constituent of the focus particle is always narrowly focused. This is not surprising, given that the domain of a focus particle must be focused and that the particle must c-command its domain. Second, the behavior of focus particles adjoined to DPs, PPs, and embedded CPs shows obvious parallels to the behavior of contrastive negation in sentences like (196).[64] Like focus particles, contrastive negation frequently occurs in the prefield preceding a focused element. In such constructions, the negation particle *nicht* ('not') can be analyzed as an adjunct to the constituent to its right, which corresponds to the negated part of the sentence (cf. Steube 2005). This use of negation must be distinguished from its non-contrastive use. In the latter case, *nicht* is mostly analyzed as a VP-adjunct or as the head (or the specifier) of a designated functional projection (NegP or PosP) in the middle-field (cf. Haftka 1994, 1995, 2003; Steube, Alter & Späth 2004; Späth & Trautwein 2004; Steube 2005, 2006). This non-contrastive, 'adverbial-like' use of negation corresponds to the VP-modifying focus particles discussed in Section 4.4.

(196) Nicht FElix hat gestern gesungen.
not Felix aux_p yesterday sung

Third, constructions of Patterns 7 and 8 – like constructions with contrastive negation – have a contrastive interpretation. This is particularly evident when natural continuations of sentences like (195b) and (196) are considered; cf. the examples in (197). In both cases, the focused constituent of the first clause contrasts with an element explicitly mentioned in the second (elliptic) clause, either correcting an earlier statement or expressing a contrast to an implicit assumption or expectation.

(197) a. Nur FElix hat gestern gesungen, und nicht MAja / und sonst NIEmand.
only Felix aux_p yesterday sung and not Maja / and else no_one

b. Nicht FElix hat gestern gesungen, sondern MAja.
not Felix aux_p yesterday sung but Maja

Our conclusion is the following: if a focus particle is adjoined to a DP, PP, or embedded CP, this constituent is contrastively focused. In the literature, it has often been shown that contrastive focus differs from new information focus in several respects, including (i) its prosodic realization (categorical and gradual properties; cf. Bannert 1985; Alter, Mleinek, Rohe, Steube & Umbach 2001; Alter 2002b; Toepel & Alter 2004; Baumann, Grice & Steindamm 2006; Becker, Schröder & Barry 2006), (ii) its semantic effects (presupposition of the existence of relevant alternatives in the context, closed alternative set; cf. Steube 2001; Molnár 2006; Späth 2007), and (iii) its effects on word order (higher positional variability of contrastively focused elements; cf. Steube 2001, 2003). We consider it to

64. See also Jacobs (1982, 1983, 1991).

be another property of contrastive focus that it licenses the adjunction of focus particles to non-predicate projections. In other words, an exception to the generalization that focus particles are adjuncts to VP or AP is claimed to be possible only if the particle is associated with a contrastively focused constituent. The different usage patterns of focus particles thus parallel the usages of (contrastive and non-contrastive) negation in German: like *nicht*, focus particles can adjoin to predicate projections (the standard case) or to phrases characterized by contrastive focus. If this claim, which is a mere conjecture at this stage of the investigation, proved to be well-motivated, information structure could be shown to play another important role in the grammar of focus particle constructions.

In Section 4.5.3, it was noted that the focus particle *auch* normally cannot precede a wh-element in the prefield (cf. Reis & Rosengren 1997). The same is true for other focus particles; cf. (198). However, sentences with an initial focus particle followed by a question word can be used as echo questions. This observation can be connected with the claim that focus particles are able to adjoin to contrastively focused XPs of any kind. The question word in an echo question behaves like a contrastive focus in many respects. It prosodically differs from wh-words in non-echo questions, and it presupposes the existence of alternatives in the context.[65] The only difference to most other contrastive foci is that the contrast evoked by an echo question is situated on a metalinguistic level: the question word contrasts with a part of an utterance preceding the echo question in the discourse. If we assume that wh-words in echo questions are characterized by contrastive focus, our model correctly predicts that focus particles can adjoin to these elements. Wh-words in non-echo questions, on the other hand, are characterized by new information focus and thus do not allow the adjunction of focus particles.

(198) *Nur / Auch / Sogar [WER]$_D$ hat geantwortet?
only / also / even who *aux*$_p$ answered

In the remainder of this subsection, the proposed analysis is related to two claims about contrast from the literature. Frey (2004a, 2006) argues that focused elements in the prefield or at the left edge of the middlefield that have reached their surface position via true Ā-movement always have a contrastive interpretation in German. Nothing will be said here about the appropriateness of this hypothesis in general; however, it is compatible with the view of XP-adjoined focus particles presented above. Frey's account, as well as ours, predicts that the particle's domain is contrastively focused in the constructions of Pattern 7. In addition, Frey's theory predicts a contrastive interpretation of the prefield element in Pattern 3 (unstressed focus particle in the middlefield, domain in the prefield), but not in

65. For a more detailed characterization of echo questions and the pragmatic *echo effect*, see Reis (1999).

Pattern 2 (fully focused sentences with a focus particle in the middlefield). According to Frey, the syntactic operation filling the prefield in the latter case is not true Ā-movement, but Formal Movement,[66] which moves the highest middlefield constituent to the prefield without producing any semantic or pragmatic side effects.

Another view held in the literature – most explicitly formulated by Altmann (1976a, b) and Foolen (1993) – is that focus particles are *always* associated with contrastively focused elements. This claim is incompatible with our theory, which is based on the assumption that a focus particle interacts with an independently given focus-background partition instead of inducing (contrastive) focus itself. According to the model proposed above, the domain of a focus particle can, but need not, be a contrastive focus, the actual choice depending on the information structure of the sentence, which is in turn determined by the linguistic and non-linguistic context. This issue will be addressed from a prosodic point of view in Chapter 7.

4.6.4 Summary

In this section, it was argued that neither Bürger & Hartmann's (2001) version of the adverbial analysis nor the model presented in Section 4.4 is able to account for the full range of focus particle constructions in German, and that it is unavoidable to employ adjunction-to-XP structures in certain cases (the constructions of Patterns 7 and 8 and part of the constructions of Pattern 9). Under the proposed analysis, which involves adjunction of focus particles to DPs, PPs, and embedded CPs, constructions with sentence-initial focus particles do not violate the V2-generalization of German. In addition, the analysis explains the fact that only the prefield constituent, but not the whole remaining clause, can serve as the particle's domain in these cases. With the help of corpus data, it was shown that some of the arguments brought forward against adjunction-to-XP analyses are not valid and can in fact be turned into arguments against a pure adverbial analysis. Lastly, it was claimed that adjunction to projections other than VP and AP is only possible if the respective phrases are contrastively focused. The different usage patterns of focus particles were shown to parallel the behavior of contrastive and non-contrastive negation.

66. See also Bhatt (1999).

4.7 Summary

In the following, we summarize the hypotheses about the grammar of focus particle constructions in German we argued for in this chapter.

- Focus particles are non-expanding maximal categories adjoining to VP (or AP) in the standard case. They syntactically behave like adverbials and have a fixed position in the German clause immediately below the position of the sentence adverbials.
- A focus particle is sensitive to the focus-background partition of the sentence in which it occurs. The focus-background partition is independently given and does not depend on the presence of the particle. The domain of a focus particle corresponds to the sentence focus, which normally coincides with the syntactic focus domain, i.e., the topmost VP-shell c-commanded by the particle. As defocused material preferentially leaves the focus domain via movement to the left, focus particles mostly, but not always, end up adjacent to their domains. Focused elements may also leave the syntactic focus domain, e.g., in order to fulfill the V2-requirement of German. Nevertheless, these elements belong to the domain of a focus particle linearly following them. In any case, the particle must c-command all elements belonging to its domain or – if they have moved – their base positions. The association of a focus particle with focused elements occurring outside the syntactic focus domain on the surface is mediated by the [+F]-traces left behind by these elements.
- The domain of a stressed additive focus particle is a contrastive topic, which obligatorily leaves the focus domain via movement to the left periphery of the clause. The particle occupies its standard position in these cases, and the respective constructions can be derived from the same underlying structure as constructions with unstressed focus particles. The special properties of this usage pattern (accent on the focus particle, reverse order of the particle and its domain) follow from its special information structure.
- In addition to VPs and APs, possible adjunction sites of focus particles include contrastively focused DPs, PPs, and embedded CPs. An analysis employing adjunction-to-XP structures in a limited set of cases allows us to maintain the V2-generalization of German, and it explains the fact that a sentence-initial focus particle can only be associated with the immediately following constituent. The inadequacy of a pure adverbial analysis also follows from data strictly excluding an analysis in terms of adjunction to VP or AP: focus particles modifying genitive complements or attributes of nouns and focus particles modifying DPs or PPs in coordination structures.

It was shown that both the adverbial analysis (cf. Jacobs 1983, 1986; Büring & Hartmann 2001) and the adjunction-to-XP analysis (cf. Bayer 1996; Reis &

Rosengren 1997; Nederstigt 2003) face several conceptual and empirical problems. As none of the accounts proposed in the literature is able to account for the entire range of relevant data, a new approach, which combines the merits of both theories, was developed. The central insight is that two types of focus particle constructions must be distinguished. As opposed to the analysis of Nederstigt (2003), however, the difference between them is not attributed to the particles themselves, but to their usage in different linguistic contexts: the dividing line is drawn between focus particles adjoined to VP (and AP), which interact with the partition of the sentence into new information focus and background, and focus particles adjoined to XPs of any kind, which associate with contrastive foci.

One of the main goals of this chapter was to demonstrate the necessity of referring to notions of information structure in the grammatical description of focus particle constructions. Although its relevance is implied by the term *focus particle*, the important role of information structure, which is also emphasized by Dimroth (2004), has not been sufficiently explicated in the literature. The results presented here can be seen as a first step into the direction of a comprehensive syntactic and information-structural theory of the grammar of focus particles in German.

CHAPTER 5

The scope of focus particles

This chapter deals with phenomena related to the scope of focus particles and shows possible ways to account for them. So far, we have restricted our attention to cases where a focus particle has scope over the whole sentence. However, as shown by some examples in Chapter 3, there are also cases where the scope of a focus particle is limited to a proper subpart of the sentence. The scope can be divided into a focus part and a background part (cf. Jacobs 1983; Sgall 1994; Hajičová, Partee & Sgall 1998a), which are essential for determining the particle's meaning contribution. Elements outside the scope of a focus particle, on the other hand, do not have any effect on its meaning. The importance of scope for a correct analysis of focus particles has often been stressed (cf. Jacobs 1983; König 1991c; Reis & Rosengren 1997). Analyses that explicitly deny the relevance of what we are defining as the scope of a focus particle, such as Koktova (1987), are not able to correctly derive the meaning of the relevant sentences.[1]

The main question to be answered in this chapter is what determines the scope of a focus particle in German. Section 5.1 discusses the restriction of a particle's scope by certain syntactic nodes. Section 5.2 takes a closer look at the relative scope of focus particles an other scope-bearing elements, such as negation, certain adverbials, and quantified DPs, and briefly deals with multiple occurrences of focus particles in one sentence. Section 5.3 addresses Büring & Hartmann's (2001) (no) reconstruction argument against adjunction-to-XP analyses of focus particles, as this argument is based on scope relations and the resulting (un)availability of certain readings. Section 5.4 summarizes the results and discusses their consequences for the analysis of focus particles presented in the previous chapter.

5.1 Syntactic restrictions on the scope of focus particles

A comprehensive source of generalizations on scope restrictions in German is Jacobs (1983). One of Jacobs' observations, termed *Bereichsabsorption*, is that the

1. Koktova (1987:181) discusses examples taken from Jacobs (1983). We will return to this type of sentences in Section 5.2. See also Dimroth (2004:47–48).

scope of a focus particle is restricted to the minimal clause in which it occurs (cf. also Sgall 1994; König 1991c; Reis & Rosengren 1997). An example of this phenomenon was given in Chapter 3; it is repeated in (1) for convenience.

(1) a. Ich hoffe nur, dass [MAja $]_D$ singt.
I hope only that Maja sings
Only for x = Maja: I hope that x sings.
b. Ich hoffe, dass nur [MAja $]_D$ singt.
I hope: Only for x = Maja: x sings.

In the previous chapter, it was argued that focus particles are adjuncts to VP in the German middlefield. In complex sentences, this gives us two possible adjunction sites: the VP of the matrix clause and the VP of the (extraposed) embedded clause. The respective structures are shown in (2). Together with the assumption that the scope of a focus particle cannot be larger than the minimal clause it is contained in, these structures explain the difference in meaning between the two sentences: in the first, *nur* has matrix scope; in the second, its scope is limited to the embedded CP. The meaning difference has nothing to do with focus, which is on the same element (*Maja*) in (1a) and (1b).

(2) a. Ich_i $hoffe_j$ $[_{VP}$ nur $[_{VP}$ t_i t_k t_j]] $[_{CP}$ dass $[_{VP}$ MAja singt $]]_k$.
I hope only that Maja sings
b. Ich_i $hoffe_j$ $[_{VP}$ t_i t_k t_j] $[_{CP}$ dass $[_{VP}$ nur $[_{VP}$ MAja singt $]]]_k$.

The restriction of a focus particle's scope by the CP node and the availability of two different adjunction sites in complex sentences also give us a simple explanation of the ambiguity of the sentences in (3) and (4), discussed by von Stechow (1991a) and Büring & Hartmann (2001). In the (a)-readings of the sentences, the focus particle has scope over the matrix verb, while in the (b)-readings, this is not the case.

(3) weil sie nur SPAnisch zu lernen versuchten
because they only Spanish to learn tried
a. The only thing they tried to learn is Spanish.
b. They tried to learn nothing but Spanish.[2]
(von Stechow 1991a: 810)

2. Von Stechow gives a different paraphrase for the second reading ("The only thing they tried to do was to learn Spanish"). This is obviously a mistake, as both von Stechow's paraphrases – contrary to what he says about them in the text – represent wide scope readings differing only in the size of the focus.

(4) weil ich nur GERda geküsst zu haben bereue
because I only Gerda kissed to *aux*$_p$ regret
a. The only person that I regret to have kissed is Gerda.
b. I regret to have kissed nobody but Gerda.
(Büring & Hartmann 2001: 252)

The explanation von Stechow gives for the observed ambiguity is that the focus particle and its focus, both originating from the embedded non-finite clause, can undergo Quantifier Raising together, yielding the wide scope reading. This analysis mirrors the commonly accepted analysis of the corresponding English data, first discussed by Taglicht (1984). However, as noted by Büring & Hartmann (2001), the ambiguity found in the German sentences can more straightforwardly be explained as a syntactic ambiguity: the focus particle can be adjoined to the matrix VP as well as to the VP of the embedded infinitival clause; cf. (5). The two variants do not differ in their surface word order, but result in a different scope of the particle.

(5) a. weil sie [$_{VP}$ nur [$_{VP}$ [$_{CP}$ *PRO* SPAnisch zu lernen]
because they only Spanish to learn
versuchten]]
tried
b. weil sie [$_{VP}$ [$_{CP}$ [$_{VP}$ nur [$_{VP}$ *PRO* SPAnisch zu lernen]]] versuchten]

If (3) is turned into a V2-clause, the two variants are clearly distinguished by means of prosodic phrase boundaries. A boundary immediately after the particle triggers the wide scope reading, while a boundary preceding *nur* triggers the narrow scope interpretation. These boundaries are (optionally) indicated by commas in the written language; cf. (6).

(6) a. Sie versuchten nur, SPAnisch zu lernen.
they tried only Spanish to learn
b. Sie versuchten, nur SPAnisch zu lernen.

Furthermore, it comes as no surprise that the ambiguity disappears as soon as the embedded CP is extraposed. In (7), the position of *nur* to the right of the matrix verb *versuchten* indicates that it belongs to the embedded clause, allowing the narrow scope reading only.

(7) weil sie versuchten, nur SPAnisch zu lernen
because they tried only Spanish to learn
(von Stechow 1991a: 810)

In analogy to CP, the property of restricting the scope of a focus particle has been ascribed to NP/DP (cf. Jacobs 1983; König 1991c; Krifka 1992a) and PP (cf. König 1991c). In (8), the focus particle is adjoined to an AP within a DP (cf.

Section 4.4.5). This DP restricts the scope of *nur*: the linguist in (8a) is proud of nothing but his hairstyle, and the rock band in (8b) is not better than mediocre, but the sentences do not say that the speaker did not see any other linguists or rock bands, respectively. To get the wide scope reading, the focus particle must precede the whole DP in both cases. König's (1991c) example in (9) shows that PPs also restrict the scope of focus particles. The sentence does not say that ten marks is the only amount of money you can get a very good meal for. What the particle contributes to the meaning is that ten marks is not much (for a good meal).

(8) a. Ich sah [$_{DP}$ einen nur auf seine FrisUR stolzen Linguisten] .
I saw a only of his hairstyle proud linguist

b. Ich sah [$_{DP}$ eine nur MITtelmäßige Rockband] .
I saw a only mediocre rock_band

(9) [$_{PP}$ Für nur ZEHN Mark] kannst du ein sehr gutes Essen bekommen.
for only ten marks can you a very good meal get
(König 1991c: 50)

Unfortunately, the data is not always that clear. In particular, focus particles adjoined to genitive complements of nouns seem to have wide scope readings in some cases. While in (10a) only the narrow scope reading is plausible ('It won't stop the rebels if only the leader dies.'), (10b) has a wide scope reading at least for some speakers ('The leader is the only one whose death could stop the rebels.'). The word order is perceived as archaic or marked, but marginally possible.

(10) a. Der Tod nur des /ANführers wird die Rebellen NICHT aufhalten.
the death only the$_{gen}$ leader$_{gen}$ *aux$_f$* the rebels not stop

b. Der Tod nur des ANführers kann die Rebellen aufhalten.
the death only the$_{gen}$ leader$_{gen}$ can the rebels stop

The status of such data is unclear, and we do not have a satisfying explanation to offer. It seems, however, that such an explanation would have to be given in connection with an account of the conditions under which a focus particle can adjoin to a DP in German. That these two issues, the possibility of wide scope readings and the adjunction sites of focus particles, are somehow related, is also demonstrated by the examples in (11). *Nur* in (11a) can have narrow ('Maja researches the lives of rock stars who are not better than mediocre.') or wide scope ('Maja only researches the lives of mediocre rock stars.').[3] The same holds for (11b); here, however, the narrow scope reading is extremely implausible, as *berühmt* ('famous') can hardly be interpreted as ranking low on a scale. In (11c), this implausible reading is enforced; the sentence does not have a wide scope reading. What is the difference between (11a)/(11b) and (11c)? In the latter sentence, *nur* is clearly within the genitive DP; it must be adjoined to the AP headed by *berühmten*. As the genitive complements in (11a) and (11b) lack overt determiners, *nur* can be adjoined to the AP or to the whole genitive DP. It is plausible that this syntactic ambiguity is the reason for the availability of the two readings and that a wide scope interpretation is only possible if the focus particle is adjoined to the genitive DP. A more detailed examination of these constructions must be left for further research.

(11) a. Maja erforscht das Leben nur MITtelmäßiger Rockstars.
Maja researches the life only mediocre$_{gen}$ rock_stars$_{gen}$
b. Maja erforscht das Leben nur BERÜHMter Rockstars.
Maja researches the life only famous$_{gen}$ rock_stars$_{gen}$
c. Maja erforscht das Leben der nur BERÜHMten Rockstars.
Maja researches the life the$_{gen}$ only famous$_{gen}$ rock_stars$_{gen}$

5.2 Relative scope of focus particles and other scope-bearing elements

In addition to the absolute scope of a focus particle discussed in the previous section, the relative scope of a particle and other scope-bearing elements[4] is another decisive factor for the interpretation of the respective sentences; cf. Jacobs (1983), König (1991c), and Pafel (2006), among others. Jacobs (1983), for instance, argues that the indefinite pronoun *jemandem* ('someone') is in the scope of the focus particle in (12a), but not in (12b), the reason being the reverse linear order of the two elements.

(12) a. Peter wollte sogar / auch / nur mit jemandem FLIRten.
Peter wanted even / also / only with someone to_flirt
b. Peter wollte mit jemandem sogar / auch / nur FLIRten.
Peter wanted with someone even / also / only to_flirt
(Jacobs 1983: 14)

3. The third possibility, an intermediate scope extending to the DP *das Leben nur mittelmäßiger Rockstars*, is removed from consideration.

4. The term *scope-bearing elements* rather than *quantifiers* is used in order to include elements such as negation and to exclude referential expressions, which are usually also analyzed as (generalized) quantifiers, but do not show the scope properties relevant here.

Although Jacobs' examples illustrate the relevant point, they are not ideally suited for the discussion of relative scope, as they are too complex and involve additional complications. On the one hand, it is not clear whether the modal auxiliary *wollen* ('to want') also enters into scope relations with other elements. While Jacobs (1983: 53) claims that this is the case, Pafel (1998, 2006) argues that non-epistemic modal auxiliaries do not belong to the group of scope-bearing elements. On the other hand, the indefinite *jemandem* cannot be accented, which makes the determination of the focus in Jacobs' examples difficult, particularly since no contexts are given. For an adequate analysis of scope phenomena in focus particle constructions, however, it is essential to keep the effects of focus and scope apart. To avoid these complications, we restrict our attention to simpler cases.

An important question is which elements could possibly show effects of relative scope when they co-occur with focus particles. One plausible candidate is negation, which will be looked at in Section 5.2.1. For the identification of other scope-bearing elements in German, we take the list put together by Pafel (1998, 2006) as the basis. Scope-bearing DPs and adverbials will be considered in Section 5.2.2. Section 5.2.3 will briefly deal with multiple occurrences of focus particles. The view taken here presupposes that focus particles are scope-bearing elements themselves. Consequently, effects of relative scope should be observable in constructions with more than one focus particle. Pafel (1998, 2006) includes *nur*, but not *auch* and *sogar*, in his list of scope-bearing elements, the reason being that *nur*, in contrast to the other particles, has an effect on the truth conditions (cf. Chapter 3). However, if presuppositions are also taken into account, it becomes clear that all three particles are scope-bearing elements and enter into scope relations in the same way. The only difference is that the semantic effects of these scope relations are relevant for different components of the meaning.

5.2.1 Negation

We will restrict our attention to the negator *nicht* ('not'), which has similar syntactic properties as focus particles (cf. Chapter 4 and Jacobs 1982, 1991). In the German middlefield, it can be analyzed as an adjunct to VP, c-commanded by the sentence adverbials (cf. Steube 2005, 2006). As will be shown below, the relative order of *nicht* and a focus particle is not fixed – focus particles can occur either before or after the negator. This gives rise to the expectation that the two variants differ in the relative scope of the operators. In addition, *nicht* may belong to the focus or to the background of a sentence. If it is in the scope of a focus particle, this should also be relevant for the derivation of the meaning.

Before we turn to some examples, a comment on the distinction between wide scope and narrow scope readings of the relevant operators is in order. It is not always easy to determine whether the first of two adjacent operators has wide scope or whether its scope is restricted to the second operator. Dimroth (2004: 143–144) argues for the latter possibility in the case of the combination *nicht nur* ('not only'), which she analyzes as a complex focus particle.[5] However, we do not see any good reasons for adopting such an analysis as long as the assumption that the first operator has wide scope allows for a compositional derivation of the correct meaning. In the following, we therefore assume that the individual operators have wide scope.

An example with *nicht* followed by *nur* is given in (13).[6] Here, the focus particle is in the scope of the negation; the whole material following *nicht*, i.e., the particle together with its domain,[7] is negated. As demonstrated in Chapter 3, a structure modified by *nur* presupposes the meaning of the corresponding structure without the particle, while the exclusion of alternatives characteristic of *nur* constitutes the assertion. From the fact that negation affects the assertion, but not the presupposition, it follows that (13) says that Maja read a book (= presupposition) and that she did something else (= negated assertion). If the focus particle was outside the scope of the negation, the book-reading itself would be negated. An analysis of *nicht nur* as a complex focus particle is conceivable; however, as discussed above, it has no advantages over an analysis with hierarchical scopes, and it obscures the compositionality of the meaning. In (14) and (15), the operators occur in the reverse order, i.e., *nur* precedes *nicht*. The examples show two things. First, relative scope again corresponds to the linear order of the operators. The focus particle has scope over the negation here. Second, while *nicht* is in the scope of *only* in both cases, it belongs to the domain of the particle only if it is focused. This is the case in (15), but not in (14).

(13) dass Maja$_i$ [$_{VP,[+F]}$ nicht [$_{VP}$ nur [$_{VP}$ t$_i$ ein BUCH gelesen hat]]]
that Maja not only a book read *aux$_p$*
nicht > nur

(14) Was hat Maja nicht erledigt? – Ich glaube, ...
('What has Maja not done? – I think ...')
dass sie$_i$ [$_{VP,[+F]}$ nur [$_{VP}$ nicht$_{[-F]}$ [$_{VP}$ t$_i$ die FENster geputzt
that she only not the windows cleaned
hat]]]
aux$_p$
= The only thing that Maja hasn't done is to clean the windows.

5. Dimroth refers to Koktova (1987), ignoring that Koktova actually argues for a wide scope analysis of *nicht* in this case.

6. 'X > Y' stands for 'X has scope over Y'.

7. We assume that the main verb (realized as a perfect participle) belongs to the focus and, thus, to the domain of the particle in the examples of the present subsection.

≠ The only thing that Maja has done is not to clean the windows.
nur > nicht

(15) Warum hat Maja ihren Job verloren? – Ich glaube, ...
('Why has Maja lost her job? – I think ...')

dass sie_i $[_{VP,[+F]}$ nur $[_{VP}$ $nicht_{[+F]}$ $[_{VP}$ t_i den CHEF gegrüßt
that she only not the boss greeted
hat]]]
aux_p
= The only thing that Maja has done is not to greet the boss.
≠ The only thing that Maja hasn't done is to greet the boss.
nur > nicht

Neither in (14) nor in (15) is the restrictive meaning component introduced by *nur* negated, indicating that *nur* has scope over the negation in both cases. As a consequence, the negation is relevant for spelling out the meaning contribution of the particle. Here, the different information-structural status of *nicht* in the two examples comes into play. As it is already part of the context question, the negation belongs to the background in (14); consequently, it is not part of the particle's domain. For the interpretation, alternatives to 'clean the windows' (with respect to the background 'what Maja hasn't done) are relevant, instead of alternatives to 'not clean the windows' (with respect to the background 'what Maja has done'). This is confirmed by the different adequacy of the two paraphrases. The relevant alternatives in (14) are non-negated; they could, for instance, include 'do the laundry' and 'go shopping'. In (15), on the other hand, the negation is focused and belongs to the domain of *nur*. The relevant alternative set contains alternatives to 'not greet the boss' (with respect to the background 'what Maja has done'), i.e., possible reasons for Maja to lose her job. In this case, the alternatives can be negated or non-negated, e.g., 'not do her work', 'oversleep frequently', and 'reveal trade secrets'.

The same patterns can be observed in sentences with *nicht* plus *auch*. If *nicht* precedes *auch*, it has scope over the particle; cf. (16). Due to the reverse distribution of assertion and presupposition in constructions with *auch*, the sentence says that Maja did not read the Zauberberg (= negated assertion), but that she did something else (= presupposition, unaffected by negation).[8] If *nicht* follows *auch*, as in (17) and (18), it is in the scope of the particle. Again, it only belongs to the particle's domain if it is focused. This is the case in (18), but not in (17).

8. It is unclear why (16) is less acceptable without the second additive particle *noch* ('else').

(16) dass Maja$_i$ [$_{VP,[+F]}$ nicht [$_{VP}$ auch (noch) [$_{VP}$ t$_i$ den ZAUberberg
that Maja not also else the Zauberberg
gelesen hat]]]
read *aux$_p$*
nicht > auch

(17) Was hat Maja außerdem nicht getan? – Ich glaube, ...
('What else has Maja not done? – I think ...')
dass sie$_i$ [$_{VP,[+F]}$ auch [$_{VP}$ nicht$_{[-F]}$ [$_{VP}$ t$_i$ den ZAUberberg gelesen
that she also not the Zauberberg read
hat]]]
aux$_p$
= What Maja hasn't done either is to read the Zauberberg.
auch > nicht

(18) Was hat sich Maja noch zu Schulden kommen lassen? – Ich glaube, ...
('What else has Maja done wrong? – I think ...')
dass sie$_i$ [$_{VP,[+F]}$ auch [$_{VP}$ nicht$_{[+F]}$ [$_{VP}$ t$_i$ den ZAUberberg gelesen
that she also not the Zauberberg read
hat]]]
aux$_p$
= What Maja has also done is not to read the Zauberberg.
auch > nicht

The focus particle *sogar* shows a different behavior, which, however, can be explained on independent grounds. On the one hand, it cannot occur in the scope of negation; cf. (19). Like the fact that *sogar* cannot be focused, this is arguably due to its property of expressing epistemic meaning (cf. Section 4.5.2). If metalinguistic corrections are removed from consideration, an attitude of a speaker cannot be negated.[9] The variant with the reverse relative scope of the operators, on the other hand, is expressed by the complex focus particle *nicht einmal* ('not even') instead of the expected combination *sogar nicht*; cf. (20). In contrast to the cases discussed so far, the meaning of (20b) cannot be derived compositionally with reference to the meanings of *nicht* and *einmal* ('once'). The sentence means what (20a) would be expected to mean if it was not ungrammatical, and the correct paraphrase indicates that the operator corresponding to *sogar* has scope over the negation.[10] The

9. Jacobs (1983: 211–213) argues that *sogar* is a positive polarity item, and that this property, rather than its epistemic meaning component, is the reason for its inability to occur in the scope of negation. However, this account fails to explain why *sogar* cannot be focused/accented.

10. Interestingly, the scope relations in the English counterpart of *nicht einmal*, *not even*, seem not to correspond to the linear order of the negator and the focus particle, either. See Karttunen & Peters (1979) and Wilkinson (1993, 1996) for proposals along these lines and Rooth (1985),

use of *sogar nicht* is blocked by the availability of the idiosyncratic lexicalization *nicht einmal*.

(19) *dass Maja$_i$ [$_{VP,[+F]}$ nicht [$_{VP}$ sogar [$_{VP}$ t$_i$ den ZAUberberg gelesen
that Maja not even the Zauberberg read
hat]]]
aux$_p$

(20) a. *dass Maja$_i$ [$_{VP,[+F]}$ sogar [$_{VP}$ nicht [$_{VP}$ t$_i$ den ZAUberberg gelesen
that Maja even not the Zauberberg read
hat]]]
aux$_p$

b. dass Maja$_i$ [$_{VP,[+F]}$ nicht einmal [$_{VP}$ t$_i$ den ZAUberberg gelesen
that Maja not once the Zauberberg read
hat]]
aux$_p$
= It is even the case that Maja hasn't read the Zauberberg.
≠ It is not the case that Maja has even read the Zauberberg.
sogar > nicht

To summarize the observations: Leaving aside the exceptional behavior of *sogar*, focus particles can both precede and follow the negator *nicht* in the middlefield, and the order of the two operators corresponds to their relative scope. The first operator has always scope over the second. We assume that focus particles and *nicht* are adjuncts to VP, and that both orders are base-generated, i.e., that there is no underlying order from which the other one is derived by movement. As expected, the information-structural status of a negation in the scope of a focus particle determines whether it belongs to the particle's domain. While defocused *nicht* following a focus particle is in the particle's scope, it is not part of its domain.

Another point that is relevant in the present context is that focused DPs can precede the negator *nicht* in the middlefield. For specific and generic indefinites, this is even obligatory (cf. Steube 2006). As shown by (21), these DPs nevertheless follow a focus particle with scope over the negation, and they belong to the domain of the particle.

(21) dass Maja$_i$ [$_{VP,[+F]}$ nur [$_{VP}$ [ein / das BUCH]$_j$ [$_{VP}$ nicht [$_{VP}$ t$_i$ t$_j$
that Maja only a / the book not
gelesen hat]]]]
read *aux$_p$*

Herburger (2000), and Rullmann (1997, 2003) for alternative proposals, assuming that *even* is lexically ambiguous. For a different analysis of *nicht einmal*, see Schwarz (2005).

5.2.2 DPs and adverbials

Typical scope-bearing DPs are DPs beginning with elements such as *jed-* ('every'), *all-* ('all'), *viel-* ('many'), and *einig-* ('some'); cf. Pafel (2006: 16). They can occur either before or after a focus particle, resulting in different interpretations. As opposed to the case of the negator *nicht*, we assume that the position preceding the focus particle is derived by movement of the DP across the particle. We will mainly consider the relative scope of focus particles and scope-bearing DPs in the middlefield and only take a brief look at structures involving movement of a scope-bearing DP to the prefield.

Even if we ignore the exact information structure of the sentences in (22) and merely assume that the main verb *gelesen* ('read') is defocused, there is a clear difference in meaning between the two variants.[11] (22a) says that Buddenbrooks was read by some students and that some other book was read by some students / by someone else.[12] It is not necessarily the case that there are students who read both Buddenbrooks and another book. Exactly this, however, is expressed by (22b). We will argue that this difference is due to the different relative scope of *einige Studenten* ('some students') and *auch* in the two sentences. Corresponding with the linear order of the relevant elements, the focus particle has scope over the scope-bearing DP in (22a), while it is the other way around in (22b).

(22) a. dass auch einige Studenten die BUDdenbrooks gelesen haben
that also some students the Buddenbrooks read aux_p
auch > einige Studenten
b. dass einige Studenten auch die BUDdenbrooks gelesen haben
einige Studenten > auch

Some authors, among them Koktova (1987) and Dimroth (2004), claim that the difference between such sentences can be reduced to a difference in focusing, i.e. in the domain of the focus particle.[13] There are at least two arguments showing that this cannot result in a correct description of the data. First, if we do not distinguish between the focus and the scope of an operator, the different behavior of scope-bearing DPs and proper names (or similar expressions) in constructions with focus particles cannot be accounted for (cf. Chapter 3). The sentences in (23) only differ in the type of the subject constituent, which is a proper name in (23a) and a scope-bearing DP in (23b). However, while (23a) can be paraphrased by (24a), (23b)

---

11. Similar examples are discussed by Jacobs (1983: 196–202).

12. The choice between these two alternatives depends on whether *einige Studenten* ('some students') is focused or not (see below).

13. Koktova (1987) uses a different terminology. In her paper, *scope* refers to what is called the domain of a focus particle here.

does not have the analogous paraphrase (24b). For (23b) to be true, it need not be the case that no student read any book apart from Buddenbrooks. It suffices if there are at least some students who read Buddenbrooks and no other book. The correct paraphrase for (23b) is thus (24c).

(23) a. dass Maja nur die BUDdenbrooks gelesen hat
that Maja only the Buddenbrooks read *aux*$_p$
b. dass einige Studenten nur die BUDdenbrooks gelesen haben
that some students only the Buddenbrooks read *aux*$_p$

(24) a. Buddenbrooks is the only book that was read by Maja.
b. Buddenbrooks is the only book that was read by some students.
c. For some students, Buddenbrooks is the only book they read.

Second, it can be shown that the property of being focused and the property of being in the scope of an operator are independent of each other. Elements in the scope of a focus particle may be focused or defocused, and the same holds for elements outside its scope. For clarification, we consider the possible focus-background partitions of the examples in (22). (22b), the variant with the scope-bearing DP *einige Studenten* ('some students') outside the scope of *auch*, is repeated in (25) with the sentence adverbial *wahrscheinlich* ('probably') added. The position of the DP *einige Studenten* relative to the sentence adverbial indicates that it belongs to the background in (25a) and to the focus in (25b). As it is outside the scope of *auch* in both cases, it does not belong to the particle's domain, even if it is focused.

(25) a. dass [einige Studenten]$_i$ wahrscheinlich [$_{VP,[+F]}$ auch [$_{VP}$ t$_i$ die
that some students probably also the
BUDdenbrooks gelesen$_{[-F]}$ haben]]
Buddenbrooks read *aux*$_p$
b. dass wahrscheinlich [$_{VP,[+F]}$ [einige Studenten]$_i$ auch [$_{VP}$ t$_i$ die
BUDdenbrooks gelesen$_{[-F]}$ haben]]

If *einige Studenten* is supposed to be in the scope of *auch*, it must follow the particle and, as a consequence, the sentence adverbial. Thus, there is only one possible word order in this case; cf. (26). Nevertheless, *einige Studenten* can be focused or defocused. If we take the theory presented in Chapter 4 as the basis, the variant where it is part of the focus, i.e., (26a), is the expected one: the DP is likely to carry a prenuclear accent and belongs to the particle's domain, and the sentence says that Buddenbrooks was read by some students, and that another book was read by someone else. If, on the other hand, *einige Studenten* is defocused, as indicated by the index [–F] in (26b), it is unaccented and does not belong to the domain of *auch*. In this case, the sentence says that Buddenbrooks was read by some students and that another book was also read by some students, but not necessarily by the same students.

(26) a. dass wahrscheinlich $[_{VP,[+F]}$ auch $[_{VP}$ einige Studenten die
that probably also some students the
BUDdenbrooks gelesen haben]]
Buddenbrooks read *aux$_p$*

b. dass wahrscheinlich $[_{VP,[+F]}$ auch $[_{VP}$ [einige Studenten $]_{[-F]}$ die
BUDdenbrooks gelesen haben]]

The requirement that the linear order of two scope-bearing elements must reflect their relative scope is stronger than the requirement that defocused constituents must leave the focus domain and adjoin to the left of the sentence adverbials. In addition to the defocused constituents that cannot or optionally do not scramble in German (cf. Section 4.4.2), defocused scope-bearing elements thus represent a second type of expressions that may intervene between a focus particle and its domain in the middlefield. This observation has already been made by Jacobs (1983: 83–86), who considers scope to constrain his *Principle of Maximal Closeness to the Focus (Prinzip der maximalen Fokusnähe).*[14]

The discussion of the examples in (22)–(26) has revealed two peculiarities we did not deal with in Chapter 4. First, scope-bearing elements outside the scope of a focus particle do not belong to the particle's domain, even if they are focused. This distinguishes them from non-scope-bearing elements, which always belong to the domain of the particle if they are focused and occur in the same minimal clause. Second, defocused scope-bearing elements occur in the c-command domain of a focus particle if the intended relative scope of the particle and the relevant element makes it necessary.

So far, we have assumed that the relative order of two scope-bearing elements – or, more precisely, the c-command relation between them – corresponds to their relative scope. In other words, we have assumed that the first (higher) of the elements has scope over the second (lower), but not the other way around. However, this is a simplification. The relative scope may deviate from the surface order if the first element can be reconstructed in a position below the second. This phenomenon, often called *scope inversion*, is also relevant for the scope of focus particles (cf. Jacobs 1983: 200; König 1991c: 47; Bayer 1999). We cannot give a comprehensive account of the necessary and sufficient conditions for the possibility of reconstruction. Factors that might play a role include the surface position of

14. "Die Partikel rückt im allgemeinen [...] genau so weit an ihren Fokus heran, wie es der intendierte semantische Bereich der Partikel und die Forderung, daß der Fokus innerhalb ihres syntaktischen Bereichs liegen muß, erlauben." (Jacobs 1983: 86) See also Reis (2005: 469–470).

the relevant constituent,[15] its base position, its syntactic function, its information-structural status and prosodic properties, and certain semantic characteristics of the elements the relative scope of which would be inverted by reconstruction.[16] In the examples in (27), a scope-bearing DP is located in the prefield. In (27a), reconstruction of the prefield element below the focus particle is possible, if not preferred. In (27b), on the other hand, the reconstruction reading is strongly dispreferred. This difference is due to the different type of the scope-bearing elements occupying the prefield in the two sentences.

(27) a. Alle Bücher von Thomas Mann hat nur MAja gelesen.
all books of Thomas Mann aux_p only Maja read
alle Bücher > nur
nur > alle Bücher

b. Einige Bücher von Thomas Mann hat nur MAja gelesen.
some books of Thomas Mann aux_p only Maja read
einige Bücher > nur
??nur > einige Bücher

The described effects of relative scope cannot only be observed with scope-bearing DPs, but also with certain types of adverbials (cf. Jacobs 1983: 85; König 1991c: 30, 46; Reis & Rosengren 1997: 270). According to Pafel (2006), scope-bearing adverbials include certain local and temporal adverbials such as *überall* ('everywhere'), *vielerorts* ('in many places'), and *jederzeit* ('everytime'), frequency adverbials such as *immer* ('always') and *oft* ('often'), mental attitude adverbials such as *absichtlich* ('intentionally') and *freiwillig* ('voluntarily'), and others. These adverbials can also occur either before or after a focus particle in the middlefield, the two possibilities corresponding to different relative scopes.[17] In (28a), *freiwillig* has scope over *nur*; in (28b), the scope of the two operators is reversed. In the latter example, the interpretation additionally depends on whether *freiwillig* is focused or not. Only if it is focused, it belongs to the domain of *nur*. If it is defocused, its placement to the right of the focus particle is made possible by the intended relative scope.

15. Prefield constituents are more likely to undergo reconstruction than middlefield elements. However, contrary to what is sometimes claimed, middlefield elements can also be reconstructed under certain circumstances.

16. For different approaches to this problem, see Frey (1993), Büring (1997a, b), and Pafel (1998, 2006). We will return to this issue in Section 5.3.

17. There is controversy in the literature as to whether adverbials have fixed base positions in the German middlefield and can undergo scrambling, or whether they are base-generated in different positions (cf. Frey & Pittner 1998; Frey 2000a, 2003; Haider & Rosengren 1998; Haider 2000; Schäfer 2005). This issue is ignored here.

(28) a. dass Maja freiwillig nur Tod in VENEdig gelesen hat
that Maja voluntarily only Death in Venice read aux_p
freiwillig > nur
b. dass Maja nur freiwillig Tod in VENEdig gelesen hat
nur > freiwillig

5.2.3 Multiple focus particles

Sentences with more than one focus particle represent a challenge for every theory of the grammar of focus particle constructions. On the one hand, there are various possibilities for the relation between the individual particles and their interaction (see below). On the other hand, many combinations of focus particles are ruled out by semantic restrictions. As the theoretical description of constructions with multiple focus particles is complicated and even the data itself is often unclear, most authors are rather vague about this issue or do not address it at all. Here, we also only (!) make a few general comments on sentences with more than one focus particle and then turn to the question of whether the relative scope of the particles shows the expected effects.

An overview of different types of constructions with multiple focus particles in English is provided by Krifka (1992a). Krifka's examples are given in (29);[18] similar sentences can be constructed in German.

(29) a. John, who is quite notorious as a party guest, did not only behave well at yesterday's party.
John even_i [only_j [drank WAter $]_{D_j}$ $]_{D_i}$.
b. At yesterday's party, people stayed with their first choice of drink. Bill only drank wine, Sue only drank beer, and
John even_i only_j drank [WAter $]_{D_{i,j}}$.
c. Most people drank water at some time during yesterday's party.
John even_i drank [ONly_j $]_{D_i}$ [water $]_{D_j}$.
d. Even_i [JOHN $]_{D_i}$ drank only_j [water $]_{D_j}$.
(Krifka 1992a: 21–24)

In (29a), the second focus particle is part of the domain of the first; in (29b), the two particles have the same domain. These cases are relatively easy to account for. In both sentences, the domain of the particle consists of the focused elements in its scope. The difference is that, in (29a), *only* is focused and thus belongs to the domain of *even*, while in (29b) it does not belong to the focus and is therefore excluded from the domain of *even*. According to Hoeksema & Zwarts (1991), the

18. The focus particles are co-indexed with their respective domains.

combination of *even* and *only* in cases like (29b) should be treated as a complex focus particle.[19] However, we suggest to pursue a compositional analysis for as long as possible, and Krifka (1992a: 30–32) shows that this is possible for the example under discussion.

Sentence (29c) is more problematic. Here, the second focus particle (*only*) alone forms the domain of the first (*even*) and carries the sentence accent. While the domain of *even* thus corresponds to the sentence focus and is accented, the domain of *only* is neither focused nor accented and must be identified by the context. This is the same problem as in the cases with contrastively focused focus particles discussed in Section 4.1.3. However, as both construction types have specific conditions of use and impose stringent restrictions on the context, the identification of the particle's domain does not cause any difficulties.

The most interesting case for the present discussion is (29d). Here, two focus particles have distinct, non-overlapping domains. Although Krifka does not give a context for this example, its meaning and information-structural relation to possible contexts is obvious: The sentence, or more precisely, the domain of the second focus particle, exemplifies the phenomenon of the so-called *second occurrence focus* (SOF; cf. Krifka 2004a; Dimroth 2004). In (30), a corresponding German example is given together with a suitable context.[20] SOF means that a focus particle together with its domain – *nur Doktor Faustus* in (30) – is repeated from a preceding sentence. The resulting sentence has a new focus (*Maja*), which carries the sentence accent and can also be associated with a focus particle. SOF thus has a special information-structural status: on the one hand, it is given information and belongs to the background part of the sentence; on the other hand, it forms the domain of a focus particle and should therefore have the properties of a focus.

(30) Henry hat nur Doktor Faustus gelesen, Phillip hat nur Doktor Faustus gelesen, und ich glaube, ...
('Henry only read Doctor Faustus, Phillip only read Doctor Faustus, and I think ...')

19. "If more than one focus adverb is associated with a focus expression, then we are dealing with a complex focus adverb, not a free syntactic combination." (Hoeksema & Zwarts 1991: 66)

20. While the majority of the constructions with more than one focus particle and non-overlapping domains involve SOF, there are also cases where all focus particles are associated with first occurrence foci; cf. (i).

(i) Alle Studenten haben die Buddenbrooks gelesen, aber ich glaube, ...
('All students read Buddenbrooks, but I think ...')

dass	nur	[	MAja	$]_D$	auch	[	den	ZAUberberg	$]_D$	gelesen	hat
that	only		Maja		also		the	Magic_Mountain		read	*aux*$_p$

dass sogar [MAja]$_D$ nur [Doktor Faustus]$_D$ gelesen hat.
that even Maja only Doctor Faustus read aux_p

That the domain of a focus particle is background information in cases like (30) has been considered as an argument against semantic theories of association with focus and in favor of pragmatic accounts (cf. Rooth 1992; von Fintel 1994).[21] The domain of the second focus particle cannot be determined with reference to the focus and/or the sentence accent of the relevant sentence. However, as shown by Krifka (2004a), the problem disappears if we take the information structure of the preceding sentence into account and analyze SOF as a type of anaphora. According to Krifka, the second occurrence expression (SOE; *nur Doktor Faustus gelesen* in our example) is anaphorically linked to an identical expression in the preceding discourse, the meaning of which is transferred to the SOE. Crucially, this meaning depends on the original focus-background partition of the expression in the first sentence and therefore reflects the association of the focus particle with a focused element. As a consequence, "we do not need any overt focus marking in the second occurrence utterance to identify this specific interpretation, as the interpretation is simply copied from the antecedent occurrence" (Krifka 2004a: 204).[22]

Finally, we turn to the scope relations between the focus particles. The observations about the relative scope of focus particles and other scope-bearing elements made so far give rise to the expectation that the relative scope of two particles should also depend on their c-command relation. The examples in (31) confirm this expectation. In (31a), *nur* has scope over *auch*; in (31b), it is the other way around.

(31) a. dass nur [MAja]$_D$ auch [Wälsungenblut]$_D$ gelesen hat
that only Maja also Wälsungenblut read aux_p
= Maja is the only person who also read Wälsungenblut.
nur > auch

b. dass auch [WÄLsungenblut]$_D$ nur [Maja]$_D$ gelesen hat
that also Wälsungenblut only Maja read aux_p
= Wälsungenblut, too, was only read by Maja.
auch > nur

21. See the discussion in Chapter 3 and Krifka (2004a).

22. A number of recent studies have shown that SOF is nevertheless prosodically marked, even though different means might be involved in the marking of first and second occurrence foci. See Bartels (2004), Rooth (2004), Jaeger (2004), and Beaver, Clark, Flemming, Jaeger & Wolters (2007) for English and Féry & Ishihara (2009) for German. For the question of how the results of these studies can be reconciled with Krifka's theory, see Krifka (2004b).

5.3 The (no) reconstruction argument against adjunction to XP

Büring & Hartmann (2001:259–263) make use of scope data to argue against the possibility of adjunction of focus particles to non-verbal projections. Their way of reasoning is as follows: The scope ambiguity observable in examples like (32a) shows that sentence-initial scope-bearing (object) DPs can be reconstructed in German. The sentence either says that the same mistake was made by everyone, or that everyone made some mistake, but not necessarily the same one. Although (32b) has a similar structure involving a topicalized object DP, it does not show the same ambiguity. The sentence says that Maria is the only person who is loved by everyone, not that everyone only loves Maria. This means that *nur* and the object DP *Maria* cannot be reconstructed together. Büring & Hartmann conclude that the particle does not form a constituent with the object DP: "Our argument, then, is that a mixed theory does not explain why the [focus particle] cannot reconstruct together with the DP in a configuration like [(32b)], even though we know that DP alone *in principle* can (as evidenced in [(32a)])." (Büring & Hartmann 2001:261)

(32) a. [Einen Fehler]$_i$ hat vermutlich jeder t$_i$ gemacht.
a/one mistake *aux$_p$* presumably everyone made
einen Fehler > jeder
jeder > einen Fehler
b. Nur Maria liebt jeder.
only Maria loves everyone
nur > jeder
*jeder > nur
(Büring & Hartmann 2001:260)

In the following, it will be shown that Büring & Hartmann's (2001) (no) reconstruction argument against adjunction to XP is problematic and that an alternative explanation can be given for the unavailability of the reconstruction reading in (32b) and comparable sentences. The first step is relatively simple. As shown by Fanselow (2004a) and Reis (2005), Büring & Hartmann's generalization that a prefield element cannot be reconstructed together with a preceding focus particle is incorrect;[23] cf. Reis' counterexample in (33)[24] and the comparable sentence in (34), which is based on an example by Fanselow (2003b).

23. See also Büring & Hartmann's (2001:260–261) Footnote 21, where the authors report a comment by an anonymous reviewer that points in the same direction.

24. Reis only gives the accentuation pattern in (33a) – a rising accent on the particle, another accent on *Maria*, and the falling sentence accent on the subject *keiner*. However, the variants in (33b) and (33c) are also possible.

(33) a. /NUR MARIA liebt KEIner.
only Maria loves no_one
b. /NUR Maria liebt KEIner.
c. Nur Ma/RIA liebt KEIner.
*nur > keiner
keiner > nur
(Reis 2005: 478)

(34) a. /NUR die BIbel hat NIEmand gelesen.
only the Bible aux_p no_one read
b. /NUR die Bibel hat NIEmand gelesen.
c. Nur die /BIbel hat NIEmand gelesen.
*nur > niemand
niemand > nur

Given the indicated accentuation patterns, reconstruction of the combination of focus particle and object DP is possible – and in fact obligatory – in both (33) and (34). In all intonational variants, the subject DP has scope over the focus particle: there is no one who only loves Maria or only read the Bible. As a consequence, Büring & Hartmann's (no) reconstruction argument loses its validity. Reconstruction data can no longer be considered as evidence against adjunction-to-XP structures. On the contrary, the examples in (33) and (34) show that adjunction of a focus particle to a DP in the prefield must be allowed if one wants to account for the observed reconstruction readings.

What remains to be explained is why reconstruction is possible in (33) and (34), but not in (32b). By comparing the examples, two factors can be identified that play a role here (cf. Reis 2005: 477–478). First, the scope-bearing subject DP is of a different type in (32b) and (33)/(34). While *jeder* ('everyone') corresponds to a universal quantifier, *keiner* and *niemand* ('no one') represent negated existential quantifiers. Second, a rising prenuclear accent somewhere within the preverbal material is a prerequisite for reconstruction. If the falling sentence accent is located in the prefield in (33) and (34), reconstruction is impossible; cf. (35). On the other hand, if we try to combine the intonational patterns of (33) and (34) with the sentence in (32b), the result is ungrammatical; cf. (36).

(35) a. Nur MARIA liebt keiner.
only Maria loves no_one
b. Nur die BIbel hat niemand gelesen.
only the Bible aux_p no_one read
nur > keiner/niemand
*keiner/niemand > nur

(36) a. */NUR MARIA liebt JEder.
only Maria loves everyone

b. */NUR Maria liebt JEder.
c. *Nur Ma/RIa liebt JEder.

Following Reis (2005), we assume that the bridge contour intonation (rising prenuclear accent in the prefield, falling sentence accent in the middlefield) is a necessary condition for the reconstruction of the prefield element in the sentences under discussion. This means that the cases showing the reconstruction reading involve contrastive topics. However, contrastive topics impose additional restrictions on the sentences in which they occur, and these restrictions play an important role here. At this point, the first of the two factors mentioned above – the type of the subject DP – comes into play. The impossibility of reconstruction in the cases with universally quantified subjects directly follows from Büring's (1997a, b) Condition of Disputability (COD; cf. Section 4.5). This condition says that a sentence with a contrastive topic can only be a partial answer to an (implicit) question, i.e., after uttering the sentence, there must still be disputable elements in the *topic value* of the sentence (a set of sets of propositions) – the so-called *residual topics*. In other words: "If a sentence *S* with a Topic accent is uttered given some Context CX, and there is no disputable Residual Topic the sentence establishes, the utterance of *S* in CX is infelicitous." (Büring 1997a: 180)

What does this mean for the examples given above? The reconstruction reading fulfills the COD in (33) and (34), but not in (32b). If the universal quantifier corresponding to the subject *jeder* gets wide scope in (32b), the sentence says that everyone loves nobody but Maria. As a consequence, there are no disputable propositions of the form *x loves y* left; nobody apart from Maria can be loved by anyone. Hence, the sentence is a complete rather than a partial answer and incompatible with the bridge contour intonation. The reconstruction reading has contradictory requirements: on the one hand, it calls for the bridge contour intonation; on the other hand, it is semantically incompatible with a contrastive topic.

In the cases where the subject corresponds to a negative existential quantifier, no such problem arises. This quantifier can get scope over the focus particle without reducing the number of disputable residual topics to zero. After uttering (33) and (34), there are still disputable propositions of the types *x loves y* and *x read y*, respectively. If this line of argument is correct, we expect reconstruction to be possible in cases where the subject corresponds neither to a universal nor to a negated existential quantifier. As long as reconstruction does not result in wide scope of a universal quantifier, the COD should not be violated. This prediction is borne out; cf. (37).[25]

25. We refrain from giving the different intonational variants here.

(37) a. /NUR die BIbel haben mindestens ZWEI Personen gelesen.
only the Bible aux_p at_least two people read
mindestens zwei Personen > nur

b. /NUR die BIbel haben die MEIsten gelesen.
only the Bible aux_p the most read
die meisten > nur

The above remarks on the reasons for the (un)availability of reconstruction readings in constructions with sentence-initial focus particles are only a first step towards a comprehensive account of the phenomenon. Many questions remain open. For instance, it is not clear why reconstruction requires the bridge contour intonation in the cases under discussion, and why the rising accent may be located on the particle itself or on its domain in the prefield. A related question is what the alternatives induced by the contrastive accent are – if focus particles are involved, this is no trivial question – and what the resulting topic values of the sentences actually look like. While it is intuitively clear that the reconstruction reading violates the COD in sentences with universally quantified subjects, but not in sentences with negative existential quantifiers as subjects, an explicit formal description of this intuition – one that refers to the semantic representation of *nur* – must still be found.

However, if it is true that *nur* corresponds to a universal quantifier (cf. Chapter 3), we can also explain our observations regarding the unavailability of the non-reconstruction readings in the examples given above. A consequence of Büring's proposal is that universal quantifiers may never have scope over negated existential quantifiers or other universal quantifiers, if one of the quantifiers involved is realized as a contrastive topic (cf. Büring 1997a: 191). This explains why the sentences in (36) are ungrammatical not only in the reconstruction reading, but also in the reading corresponding to the surface order of the focus particle and the subject quantifier: as we are dealing with two universal quantifiers, both possibilities of their relative scope are predicted to be incompatible with a contrastive topic. It is also explained why reconstruction is obligatory in (33) and (34): in the impossible reading with scope corresponding to the surface order of the quantifiers, the universal quantifier has scope over the negated existential quantifier. While Büring's account thus makes correct predictions for these cases as well, it is not clear how the unavailability of the non-reconstruction readings in (33), (34), and (36) can be connected with our non-technical understanding of the COD, i.e., the requirement that a sentence with a contrastive topic is only a partial answer to a question.

Another question we cannot answer yet is how to deal with sentences like (38), taken from Büring & Hartmann (2001). For the reasons presented above, the sentence-initial focus particle cannot be reconstructed here, but – in contrast to the examples considered so far – the immediately following element clearly can be. A promising direction for further research would be to investigate whether this problem can be solved by adopting a framework allowing for late adjunction (cf. Lebeaux 1988).

(38) Nur ein Bild von seiner$_i$ Frau besitzt jeder Mann$_i$.
only a picture of his wife possesses every man
(Büring & Hartmann 2001:261)

Although many problems remain unresolved, it should be clear that Büring & Hartmann's (2001) (no) reconstruction argument does not serve its original purpose. That sentence-initial focus particles can be reconstructed together with their domains indicates that they must be allowed to adjoin to non-verbal projections in the prefield. Hence, the impossibility of reconstruction in Büring & Hartmann's original examples must be explained on the basis of constraints other than a general ban on adjunction to XP. A plausible candidate for such an alternative explanation was presented above.

5.4 Summary and consequences

Chapters 3 and 4 described the relation between the focus-background partition of sentences on the one hand and focus particles and their domains on the other. It was said that the domain of a focus particle corresponds to the sentence focus, irrespective of the position of the focused elements, and that the particle establishes a characteristic relation between the focus and its relevant alternatives with respect to the background of the sentence. Initially, we only looked at examples where the focus particle has scope over the whole sentence. The examination of the factor scope in more complex cases in the present chapter showed that the above generalizations must be qualified. In addition to focus, scope plays an important role in the determination of a focus particle's meaning contribution, and the two factors must be carefully kept apart.

To put it in more concrete terms, it was shown that scope restricts both the focus and the background relevant for specifying the meaning of a focus particle. Focused elements outside the scope do not belong to the particle's domain, i.e., only those focused elements constitute the domain of a focus particle that are in its scope. Likewise, background elements outside the scope are not relevant for the particle's meaning contribution. As a consequence, the members of minimal pairs of sentences that only differ in the scope of a focus particle have different meanings, even if they have identical focus-background partitions. This proves that the scope of a particle and its domain are distinct properties and that it is impossible to reduce one of them to the other. The necessary qualification of the generalizations formulated in Chapters 3 and 4 is to say that they hold within the scope of a focus particle.

It was also shown what determines the scope of a focus particle in a given sentence. On the one hand, scope is restricted by certain syntactic nodes, including CP, DP, and PP. On the other hand, we observed effects of the relative scope of focus particles and other scope-bearing elements. Usually, the relative scope corresponds to the c-command relation between the relevant elements: the higher operator has scope over the lower. However, we must also take into account the possibility of reconstruction, resulting in a relative scope that does not correspond to the surface order of the operators. Given that reconstruction is possible, but not obligatory, in many cases, it is not surprising that sentences can be ambiguous with respect to the scope of a focus particle.

To sum up, the inclusion of scope in our considerations revealed a more complex picture of the relation between the domain of a focus particle, the focus of the respective sentence, and the c-command relations in the corresponding syntactic structure. In the previous chapter, it was demonstrated that the domain of a focus particle need not be identical to the element(s) that it c-commands. The discussion in the present chapter showed that the domain is not always identical to the focus of the sentence, either, as it may be restricted by the particle's scope. The scope, in turn, cannot be equated with the c-command domain of the particle. Restrictions imposed by absolute scope left out of consideration, non-scope-bearing elements belong to the scope of a focus particle even if the particle does not c-command them. In addition, relative scope can be reversed by reconstruction. Altogether, the following picture emerges: The c-command relations within a focus particle construction affect, but do not completely determine, both the scope of the particle and the location and size of the focus. Scope and focus, on the other hand, interact in determining the domain of the particle as well as the part of the background that is relevant for specifying the particle's meaning contribution.

CHAPTER 6

The prosody of sentences with stressed additive focus particles

This chapter examines constructions with the stressed variant of the focus particle *auch* from a prosodic point of view. In Section 4.5, we proposed an analysis based on Krifka's (1999) *Contrastive Topic Hypothesis*, claiming that the element associated with stressed *auch* – the AC[1] – is the contrastive topic of the respective sentence. Although Krifka is certainly right in assuming that the marking of the AC by means of the typical rising contrastive accent is optional, an empirical examination of the prosodic properties makes sense for two reasons. First, even if the prosodic marking is not obligatory, it should show up at least in parts of the data. The correctness of this expectation is checked in Section 6.2, which looks at a small corpus of utterances collected from movies and TV series. Second, the probability of the AC being marked by a contrastive accent should be higher in constructions with more than one candidate for the association, i.e., in sentences that are ambiguous with respect to the associated element. Prosody is expected to play a more important role if syntax does not provide sufficient cues for the interpretation. This suspected effect is made use of in several controlled speech production and perception experiments reported in Sections 6.3 to 6.6. The overall aim of the different empirical approaches presented in this chapter is to get a detailed picture of the prosodic characteristics of utterances containing stressed *auch*, and ultimately to derive evidence for or against the *Contrastive Topic Hypothesis* from the findings. The results and their consequences for the theory of stressed additive focus particles in German proposed above are discussed and summarized in Section 6.7.

6.1 Starting points and first observations

The prosodic realization of contrastive topics has been subject to much discussion in the linguistic literature. The respective constructions are often characterized as involving the so-called *bridge contour* (or *hat pattern*) intonation (cf.

1. As the domain of the focus particle corresponds to a single constituent in the cases to be discussed, it is referred to as the particle's AC (= associated constituent) in Chapters 6 and 7.

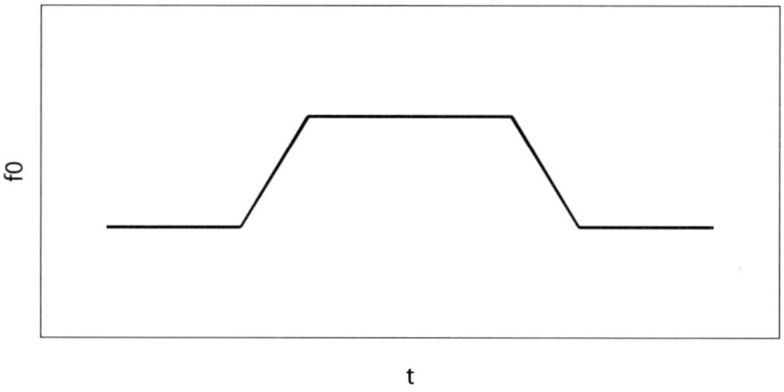

Figure 6.1 Schematic illustration of an f_0-contour typical of the so-called *bridge contour* intonation

Uhmann 1991; Féry 1993; Büring 1997b; Jacobs 1997; Molnár & Rosengren 1997; Mehlhorn 2001; Steube 2003; van Hoof 2003). This intonational pattern combines two pitch accents: a rising or falling-rising accent[2] on the contrastive topic, and a falling accent on the corresponding focus part. Together, the two accents give the f_0-contour the characteristic shape of a bridge or a hat; cf. the schematic illustration in Figure 6.1.

Frascarelli & Hinterhölzl (2007) claim that German contrastive topics are marked by L*H accents, which distinguish them from other types of topics, such as shifting topics (marked by LH* accents) and familiar/continuing topics (marked by L* accents or unaccented). This account, which associates the information-structural category contrastive topic with a particular accent type, is called into question by Mehlhorn (2001), Braun & Ladd (2003), and Braun (2005, 2006). On the basis of experimental results, these authors stress the importance of gradual phonetic parameters such as peak height, duration, or accent alignment for the prosodic marking of contrastive topics. Although different values of these parameters do not necessarily result in different accent labels, they may characterize a topical element as contrastive or non-contrastive.

Taking the results of the theoretical and empirical work on contrastive topics as a starting point, we can now turn to the prosody of constructions containing stressed *auch*, in particular to the marking of the involved ACs. Three issues are investigated throughout this chapter. First, are the ACs characterized by a specific prosodic realization? If so, does it resemble the described marking of contrastive

2. For the assumption that the first accent must be a fall-rise, see Jacobs (1997), who calls the resulting pattern *Wurzelkontur* ('root contour'). Most of the other authors assume that the fall preceding the rise is not obligatory. In the following discussion, we will concentrate on the rising f_0-movement.

topics, and does it call for a description in terms of categorical distinctions between accent types or in terms of gradual phonetic parameters? Second, what is the status of the optionality of the prosodic marking proposed by Krifka (1999)? Third, is the prosodic realization of ACs perceptively relevant; in other words, does it influence the interpretation of the respective utterances?

Some preliminary observations were made on the basis of utterances elicited in a speech production experiment that was carried out for an independent purpose. In this experiment, four female participants were asked to read short paragraphs aloud. The speakers' productions were digitally recorded. A later inspection of the materials revealed that four of the paragraphs included a sentence containing the focus particle *auch*. In all of these cases, the context and the syntactic structure of the sentences gave rise to the expectation that the stressed variant of the particle should be produced. The four sentences of interest are given in (1). The AC of *auch* is located in the prefield in all four sentences.[3] In three cases, the AC is the subject of the sentence; only in (1c) is it the direct object. If contextual information is removed from consideration, (1a) and (1b) are still unambiguous with respect to the association of the focus particle, as there is only one element to the left of *auch* that may serve as AC. In (1c) and (1d) on the other hand, there are two candidates for the association with the particle: in addition to the elements in brackets, *auch* could be associated with *das Paar* ('the couple') in (1c) and with *sie* ('them') in (1d).

(1) a. [Reitwege]$_D$ gäbe es bestimmt AUCH.
bridle_paths would_be there certainly also

b. Aber Pragmatik gefällt ihnen gut, und ...
('But pragmatics they like very much and ...')
[Typologie]$_D$ in der Regel AUCH.
typology as a rule also

c. [Ikea-Regale]$_D$ will das Paar AUCH nicht anschaffen.
Ikea_shelves wants the couple also not to_buy

d. [Das Geisteswissenschaftliche Zentrum]$_D$ beeindruckte sie AUCH.
the humanities center impressed them also

As each of the sentences was produced by four different speakers, a total of 16 utterances could be analyzed. It turned out that in one case, *auch* did not bear the nuclear accent. This utterance was excluded from further analysis. The accent

3. (1b) is an elliptical construction without a finite verb, but the parallelism to the immediately preceding sentence suggests that the sentence-initial AC is also in the prefield.

Table 6.1 Accents on the AC and on the focus particle in 15 utterances of a speech production experiment

AC		*auch*	
accent	frequency	accent	frequency
L*H	12	HL*	12
LH*	3	H*L	2
		H*	1
total	15	total	15

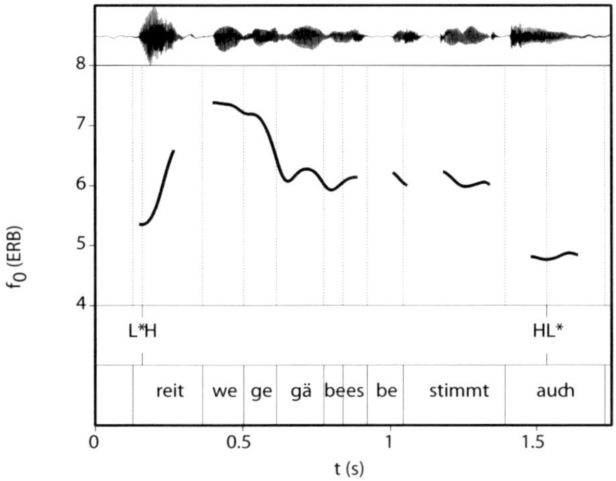

Figure 6.2 f_0-contour of an utterance of the sentence "*[Reitwege]*$_D$ *gäbe es bestimmt* AUCH." (cf. (1a)), produced by Speaker 1

realizations in the remaining 15 utterances are summarized in Table 6.1. The AC carried a rising pitch accent in all cases, which was classified as L*H in 12 utterances and as LH* in the remaining three. The most frequent pitch accent on the particle was HL* (12 times); other realizations were H*L, which occurred twice, and H*, which was found in one utterance. The intonational pattern with the highest frequency (L*H on the AC, HL* on *auch*), which was realized in 11 out of 15 cases, is exemplified in Figures 6.2 and 6.3. An example of an LH*-type accent on the AC is given in Figure 6.4.

The L*H and LH* accents on the ACs in the utterances displayed in Figures 6.3 and 6.4, respectively, had a very similar shape. The only difference lay in the location of the L- and H-tones. The local f_0-minimum of the L*H accent was located within the stressed syllable *gie*, and the f_0-peak was only reached in the post-stressed syllable. The f_0-minimum of the LH* accent, on the other hand, preceded the stressed syllable, which included the peak in this case.

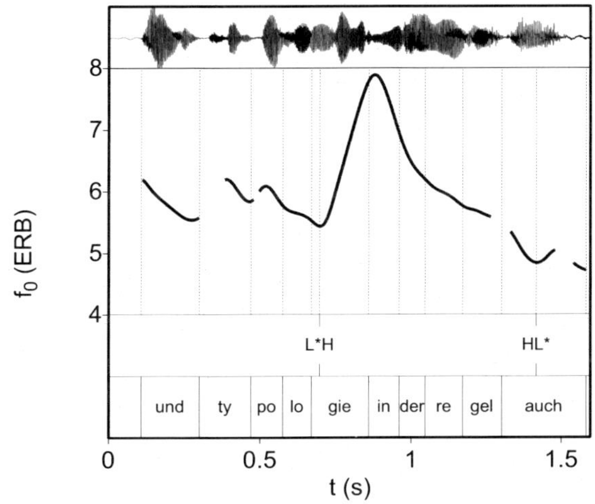

Figure 6.3 f_0-contour of an utterance of the sentence "*[Typologie]*$_D$ *in der Regel* AUCH." (cf. (1b)), produced by Speaker 3

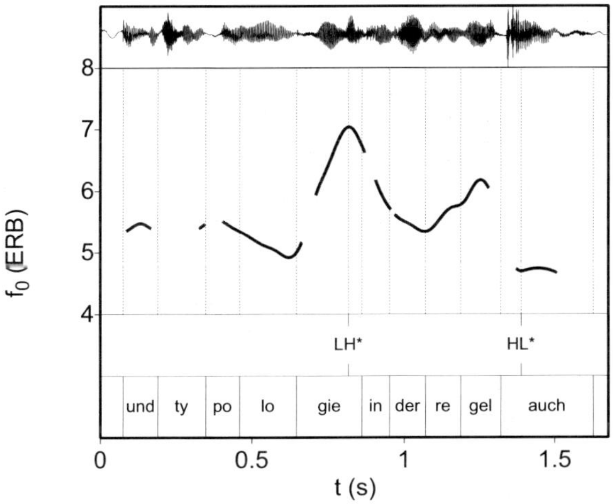

Figure 6.4 f_0-contour of an utterance of the sentence "*[Typologie]*$_D$ *in der Regel* AUCH." (cf. (1b)), produced by Speaker 1

The number of utterances was too small to allow any far-reaching conclusions. However, an important result was that, for the most part, the utterances involved a rising accent on the AC and a falling one (the nuclear accent) on the stressed focus particle and thus showed the bridge contour intonation described above. In order to be able to access a broader variety and greater quantity of data for analysis, a corpus study was carried out. This study will be presented in the following section.

6.2 Corpus study

The analyzed corpus consisted of utterances containing stressed *auch* taken from several movies and episodes of a TV series. Due to the nature of the material, the corpus study was limited to a qualitative analysis in terms of GToBI. As the utterances could not be controlled in any way, a more fine-grained quantitative prosodic analysis, aiming at factors such as peak height, duration, or alignment, was impossible. The syntactic as well as the phonetic properties of the sentences were too heterogeneous; among other things, they differed in length, sentence type, the position of the AC, and the choice of the lexical material (e.g., the use of pronouns vs. non-pronominal XPs). Many utterances were elliptical to a high degree, making a syntactic analysis difficult or impossible. In addition, the syllable structure varied greatly between the individual ACs, which – together with the fact that there was no control condition where the respective elements were not associated with the particle – had the consequence that the observed intonational patterns could not be directly compared between utterances.

In spite of these drawbacks, looking at corpus data proved to be a useful method for gaining a first impression of the phenomenon under investigation and the variety of prosodic realizations one must take into consideration. The provisional results were beneficial for designing experiments to examine the prosodic properties in greater detail. Furthermore, the quasi-natural speech data from movies and TV series can be considered as an important source of evidence, as it was not produced under laboratory conditions and therefore more or less reflects the natural use of constructions with stressed *auch* in spoken German.

6.2.1 The corpus

The corpus was built by extracting a total of 225 utterances containing stressed *auch* from 9 movies and 12 episodes of a TV series, which were either German productions or dubbed versions of American productions. A complete list of the sources is given in Appendix A.1. The relevant utterances were easily and accurately identified by using scripts or transcriptions obtained from the Internet.

The first step was to determine the ACs of *auch* through context. Next, the utterances were classified with respect to several syntactic properties such as the position and function of the AC and sentence type. All occurring pitch accents (on the AC, the focus particle, and other elements) were independently labeled by two annotators, using information from f_0-tracks. The annotation of the pitch accents was based on the slightly modified version of GToBI introduced in Section 2.4. The few utterances for which accents had initially been labeled differently by the two annotators were discussed separately; in all of these cases, agreement was achieved quickly. The results of the qualitative analyses will be presented in the following two subsections.

6.2.2 Syntactic description of the corpus material

Various clause types were represented in the corpus, with verb-second (V2) declaratives occurring most frequently (69.7%). 9.8% of the constructions were verb-first (V1) constructions (imperatives and polar interrogatives), and 4.9% were verb-final (VF) embedded argument and adjunct clauses. The remaining 15.6% of the constructions were classified as ellipses, the crucial criterion being the absence of a finite verb.

93.3% of the utterances contained one AC, while the remaining 6.7% (N = 15) contained two conjoined ACs, showing that the phenomenon of split domains (cf. Section 4.5.2) does exist in natural data. An example of the latter type is given in (2). As for their position, 47.1% of the ACs were located in the prefield, and 32% in the middlefield. Conjoined ACs were either distributed between prefield and middlefield (4.4%) or both located in the middlefield (0.9%). In the elliptical cases, the position(s) of the AC(s) could not be determined. There was a great variety of syntactic functions of the ACs: 72.8% subjects, 13.4% objects (7.6% direct objects, 3.1% indirect objects, 2.7% prepositional objects), 5.8% adverbials, and 1.3% predicatives. The 6.7% of the cases with conjoined ACs all involved the subject and an object as ACs.

(2) Wir brauchen dich, und [du]$_D$ brauchst [uns]$_D$ doch AUCH.
we need you and you need us *prt* also

6.2.3 Intonational analysis

6.2.3.1 *Accents on* auch

Before turning to the accent distribution on the ACs of stressed *auch*, we briefly consider the accents on the particle itself. In the constructions under discussion, *auch* was expected to carry the falling nuclear accent. For the most part, this prediction was borne out: *auch* was characterized by a falling pitch accent in the majority of cases (72.4% H*L, 18.2% HL*). In 5.8% of the utterances, the particle carried an H* accent. Here, the falling f_0-movement was not realized due to a high boundary tone that immediately followed. In the remaining cases, we found L*H (2.7%) and LH* (0.9%) accents on *auch*, the rising intonation expressing paralinguistic meaning components. The most frequent intonational patterns observed on the particle are illustrated in Section 6.2.3.2.

6.2.3.2 *Accents on the ACs of* auch

The annotation results for the ACs of stressed *auch* in the corpus are given in Table 6.2. The utterances with two conjoined ACs are left aside for the time being (resulting in a reduced N of 210); we will return to them in Section 6.2.3.5. Almost half of the ACs were unaccented or covert (indicated by Ø). In the remaining cases, they carried high or rising pitch accents, i.e., L*H, LH*, or H*. Figures 6.5–6.7 illustrate the observed accent types. In the utterance displayed in Figure 6.5, the AC *ein Auto* ('a car') was characterized by an L*H accent. The low target was located on the stressed syllable, and the peak was only reached on the next syllable but one, i.e., on the finite verb *hab* ('have'). In the utterance displayed in Figure 6.6, on the other hand, the AC *einen Sprachfehler* ('a speech defect') carried an LH* accent, the f_0-rise starting earlier and reaching the peak within the stressed syllable. Figure 6.7 shows the f_0-track of an utterance with an H* accent on the AC of *auch*. Here, the high target was not preceded by a distinctive rise.

Table 6.2 Corpus study – accents on the ACs

accent	frequency	
L*H	35	16.7%
LH*	54	25.7%
H*	21	10.0%
unacc.	96	45.7%
Ø	4	1.9%
total	210	100%

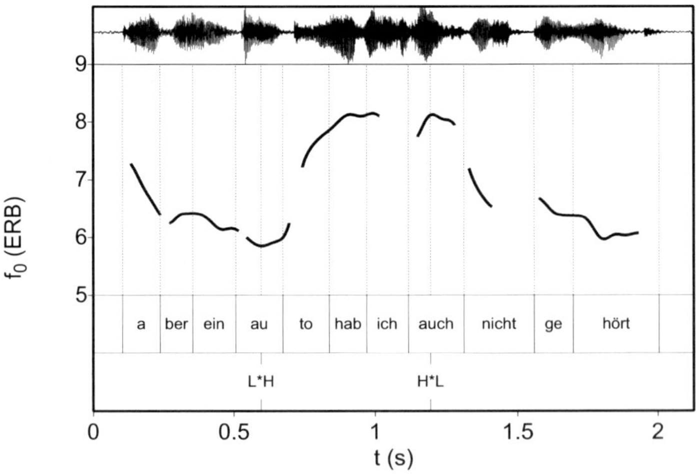

Figure 6.5 Corpus study – f_0-contour of an utterance of the sentence "*Aber [ein Auto]$_D$ hab ich* AUCH *nicht gehört.*" ('But a car I haven't heard either.')

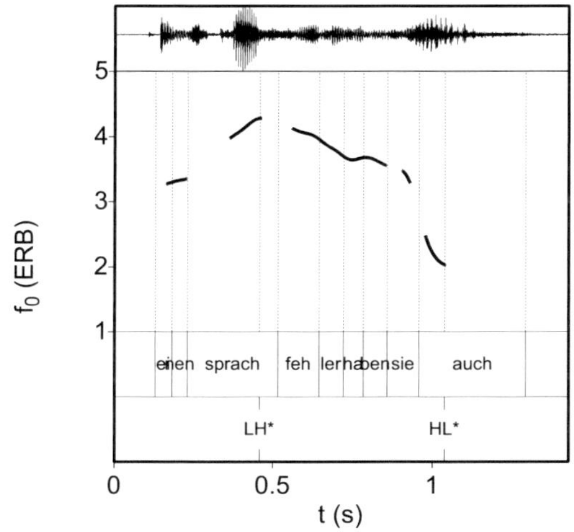

Figure 6.6 Corpus study – f_0-contour of an utterance of the sentence "*[Einen Sprachfehler]*$_D$ *haben sie* AUCH." ('You also have a speech defect.')

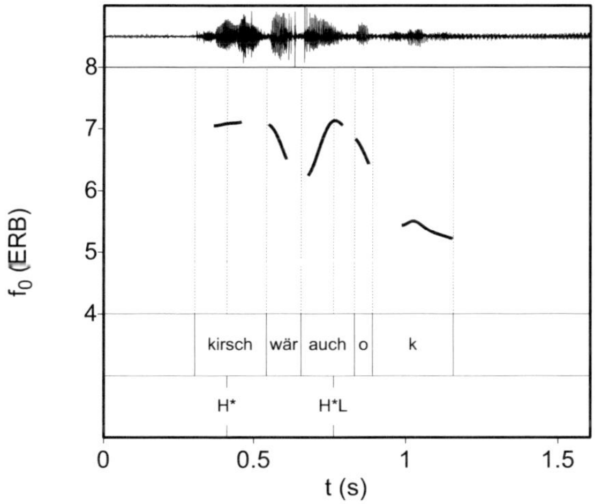

Figure 6.7 Corpus study – f_0-contour of an utterance of the sentence "*[Kirsch]*$_D$ *wär* AUCH *ok.*" ('Cherry would be ok, too.')

The heterogeneous picture of the different prosodic realizations of the ACs became somewhat more transparent when the ACs were subclassified according to their lexical properties. Table 6.3 shows that the accent distribution was highly dependent on the pronominal vs. non-pronominal status of the ACs. Altogether, 76.7% of the ACs were pronominal or covert, and 23.3% non-pronominal. All ACs not carrying an accent were either pronouns, as in the utterance given in (3), or

Table 6.3 Corpus study – accents on pronominal and non-pronominal ACs

accent	frequency			
	pron. ACs		non-pron. ACs	
L*H	17	10.6%	18	36.7%
LH*	29	18.0%	25	51.0%
H*	15	9.3%	6	12.3%
unacc.	96	59.6%	–	0%
Ø	4	2.5%	–	0%
total	161	100%	49	100%

not overtly realized at all, as in the one given in (4).[4] The reverse, however, did not hold: although the majority of the pronominal ACs were unaccented, there were also accented pronominal ACs. Non-pronominal ACs (full DPs, PPs, etc.) always carried an accent in the corpus.

(3) Bist [du]$_D$ AUCH bei Mr. Chomsky in Geschichte?
are you also at Mr. Chomsky in history_class

(4) Und was ist mit Monica? ('And what about Monica?')
[Ø]$_D$ Wird AUCH da sein.
aux$_f$ also there be

Table 6.4 contrasts the proportions of the three observed accent types on pronominal and non-pronominal ACs, leaving the unaccented pronominal ACs aside. LH* was the most frequent accent in both groups, followed by L*H. While similar proportions of the pronominal and non-pronominal ACs were characterized by LH* accents, the proportions of the other accents differed between the groups: H* was more frequent among the pronominal ACs, enlarging the proportion of high accents in this group. The reverse tendency – a higher percentage of L*H accents – could be observed for the non-pronominal ACs.

6.2.3.3 *Other accents*

In five utterances (2.4%), we found a pitch accent on a non-associated element. In all these cases, the actual AC of *auch* was unaccented. The relevant accents were classified as LH* (three cases), L*H (one case), or H* (one case). An example f_0-track of this rare utterance type is given in Figure 6.8.

4. These rare cases of covert ACs were grouped together with the pronominal ACs, the reason being that – as with pronouns – the entity they refer to must be identified by the context. For obvious reasons, covert elements cannot be accented.

Table 6.4 Corpus study – accents on pronominal and non-pronominal ACs (unaccented ACs excluded)

accent	frequency			
	pron. ACs		non-pron. ACs	
L*H	17	27.9%	18	36.7%
LH*	29	47.5%	25	51.0%
H*	15	24.6%	6	12.3%
total	61	100%	49	100%

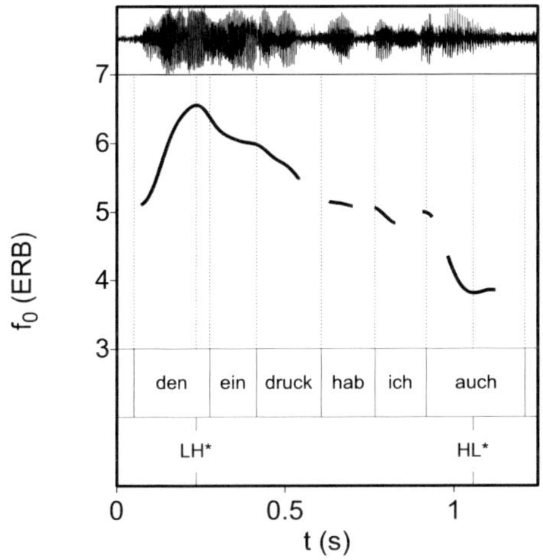

Figure 6.8 Corpus study – f_0-contour of an utterance of the sentence *"Den Eindruck hab [ich]*$_D$ AUCH." ('I have this impression, too.')

6.2.3.4 *Overall intonational patterns*

On the basis of the accent annotation, three groups of utterances differing in their overall intonational patterns could be identified: (i) utterances with only one pitch accent, namely, the nuclear accent on the focus particle; (ii) utterances with a high or rising prenuclear pitch accent on the AC and the nuclear accent on *auch*; and (iii) utterances with a high or rising prenuclear pitch accent on a non-associated element and the nuclear accent on *auch*.

The first group (95 utterances) involved, as already mentioned, exclusively pronominal and covert ACs. The majority of them (64.8%) were located in the middlefield; about half of the respective constructions were V1- or VF-clauses, the other half V2-clauses with (non-associated) pronouns, adverbials, etc. in the prefield. 32.6% of the unaccented ACs (including the four covert elements) were located in the prefield; the position of the remaining 12.6% could not be determined due to the elliptical nature of the constructions. The group with an accent both on the AC and on *auch* (110 utterances) could be characterized as follows: 55.5% of the cases involved pronominal ACs, of which 73.8% were located in the prefield and only 6.5% in the middlefield (19.7% elliptical constructions). Of the 44.5% non-pronominal ACs, 61.2% occurred in the prefield and 22.5% in the middlefield (16.3% elliptical constructions). Most of the utterances in this group were V2-constructions (75.5%), but V1- and VF-constructions were also represented. The five utterances of the third group (prenuclear accent on an element other than the AC) were V2-constructions. In all cases, the accented non-AC was located in the prefield, while the unaccented AC occupied a middlefield position.

6.2.3.5 *Accentuation in utterances with conjoined ACs*

The 15 utterances with two conjoined ACs have been left out of consideration so far for reasons of simplification. Most of the conjoined ACs were pronouns; 13 utterances contained two pronominal ACs, and the remaining two utterances contained one pronominal and one non-pronominal AC. Therefore, it was not surprising that we found a high proportion of unaccented ACs. The most frequent pattern (9 utterances) involved two unaccented ACs. In four cases, the first AC was accented, and the second was not; in one case it was the other way around. In only one utterance were both ACs accented. As for the accent type, we found L*H, LH*, and H* accents in similar proportions.

6.2.4 Discussion

With respect to the intonation of the utterances containing stressed *auch* in the corpus, we can make the following generalization: if the AC is accented, the expected bridge contour intonation can be observed. Although the initial hypothesis has thus been substantially confirmed, two qualifications are necessary. On the one hand, the prosodic marking of ACs is – as predicted by Krifka (1999) – not obligatory. Many of the (pronominal) ACs were unaccented. On the other hand, the accents found on the ACs in the corpus were not limited to L*H, which was not even the most frequent accent type. The high accent H* and the rising accent LH* were also represented in the material, the latter characterizing the largest proportion of the accented ACs. These two issues require some elaboration.

As mentioned above, there is a connection between the pronominal vs. non-pronominal status of the ACs and their accentuation status. This affects the issue of whether an AC is accented, as well the choice of the actual accent. Given that pronominal ACs are usually anaphoric in nature or refer to speaker or hearer(s), it is not surprising that they are frequently unaccented. If it is not grammatically ruled out, the pronominal ACs can even be dropped completely, as in (4) above. As noted in Section 4.5.3, the possibility of topic drop, which is the phenomenon instantiated by (4), is highly restricted in German. This explains the relative rareness of covert ACs in the corpus (only 4 utterances; cf. Table 6.2). In pro-drop languages such as Czech, on the other hand, pronominal ACs in subject function are standardly dropped; cf. the Czech equivalent of (4) in (5).[5]

(5)	(Ne)chodíš	taky	k	Chomskému	do	dějepisu?	[Cz.]
	(not)go	also	to	Mr._Chomsky	in	history_class	

Hence, association with stressed *auch* does not require a pronominal AC to be accented. This is in accord with Krifka's (1999) claim that the prosodic marking of constituents associated with stressed *auch* is not obligatory. However, the results in Table 6.3 suggest that the optionality of the prosodic marking is restricted to pronouns. All non-pronominal ACs do carry a high or rising pitch accent.[6]

Concerning the distribution of the different accent types among the pronominal and non-pronominal ACs (cf. Table 6.4), the most striking difference between the groups lies in the proportion of H* accents, which is about twice as high for the pronominal ACs as for the non-pronominal ones. As the proportion of LH* accents is similar in the groups, this difference must be compensated for by the percentage of L*H accents, which is considerably higher for the non-pronominal ACs. Two factors could be at work here, corresponding to two ways to subdivide the observed accents into complementary groups. On the one hand, the monotonal H* accent contrasts with the more complex bitonal accents LH* and L*H. As pronouns are often short, they may favor simple accents over complex ones, particularly at a high speech rate. Furthermore, the realization of an f_0-rise on short syllables might be more difficult, especially in the case of LH* accents on sentence-initial elements, where the rise is limited to the stressed syllable. As a result, we cannot exclude the possibility that underlying LH* accents – due to the phonetic properties and the position of the accented elements (i.e., the pronominal ACs) – are sometimes realized as H*. Another dividing line can be drawn between high (H*, LH*) and low accents (L*H), the proportion of the latter being higher among the non-pronominal ACs. In the literature, L*H is considered to have the highest contrastive potential (cf. Frascarelli & Hinterhölzl 2007). This goes together better with non-pronominal ACs, which can again be related to the fact that they are mostly non-anaphoric.

5. Thanks to Denisa Lenertová for this example.

6. The question is whether the relevant precondition for deaccentuation is indeed the pronominal status of the ACs. Alternatively, one could link the optionality of the prosodic marking directly to the property of being anaphoric or deictic. The latter view would predict, among other things, that anaphoric non-pronominal ACs may also be unaccented. Although this is a plausible assumption, the material in the corpus does not allow for a differentiation between the two possible explanations.

At the present stage of investigation, the given explanations for the differences in the accent distribution between the two groups of ACs can only be speculative. In addition, the results of the corpus study reflect tendencies rather than a strict correspondence between AC-form and intonation. As shown in Table 6.4, all three accent types are possible for pronominal as well as for non-pronominal ACs. This observation leads us to the question of which criteria are used for the choice between the possible AC-accents. A careful inspection of the contexts revealed no regularities or correlations that would explain the distribution in a straightforward way. Whether L*H, LH*, or H* was chosen, could not successfully be predicted on the basis of information-structural or semantic properties of the sentences. In other words, the choice of the AC-accent does not have any influence on the adequacy of an utterance containing stressed *auch* in different contexts, as long as a high or rising accent is used. However, influences of paralinguistic factors (such as emphatic meaning components) on the accent type cannot be excluded.

The above discussion has shown that ACs of stressed *auch* are often marked prosodically, but that there is no simple way to predict the specific prosodic realization. An additional complication is that a mapping in the opposite direction, i.e., from a high or rising prenuclear accent in a construction with stressed *auch* to the respective element's status of being associated with the particle, cannot be maintained either. This is obvious from the utterances that involved a prenuclear accent on a non-associated element, while the actual AC was unaccented. Three of the relevant sentences are given in (6).[7] In these cases, the sentence-initial element carried an LH* accent, although it was not associated with *auch*. The pronominal AC in the middlefield, on the other hand, was unaccented. The interpretation of the utterances indicated in (6) (with the element in brackets serving as the AC of *auch*) was only determined by the context. If the utterances are considered in isolation, they are also compatible with the (expected) interpretation where the sentence-initial element is associated with the particle. (7a), for instance, can have either of the two interpretations given in (7b) and (7c).

(6)	a.	Auf	DIESE	Frage	hätte	[ich]$_D$	AUCH	gern	'ne Antwort.
		to	this	question	would_have	I	also	like	an answer
	b.	DAS	würde	[mich]$_D$	jetzt	AUCH	interessieren.		
		that	would	me	now	also	interest		
	c.	DEN	Eindruck	hab	[ich]$_D$	AUCH.			
		this	impression	have	I	also			

(7)	a.	Auf	DIESE	Frage	hätte	ich	AUCH	gern	'ne Antwort.
		to	this	question	would_have	I	also	like	an answer

7. The prenuclear accents are also indicated by small capitals in these examples. An f_0-track for (6c) was given in Figure 6.8 above.

b. To this question, too, I would like to have an answer.
c. I, too, would like to have an answer to this question.

How can the accentuation exemplified in (6) be explained? To answer this question, we must clarify (i) why the actual AC is unaccented, (ii) why the non-associated element in initial position carries an accent, and (iii) why the utterances can nevertheless be interpreted correctly. Given that the AC is a pronoun in the cases under discussion, its deaccentuation does not come as a surprise. Interestingly, the AC refers to the speaker in all five utterances. As a consequence, it is highly accessible and can dispense with any prosodic marking. The question regarding the function of the prenuclear accent is more difficult to answer. In contrast to what is typically assumed to be characteristic of focus accents or (contrastive) topic accents (cf. Rooth 1985; Büring 1997b), the accents in the utterances in (6) do not necessarily evoke alternatives to the accented elements. For (6a) to be felicitously uttered, there must be other relevant people asking for an answer, but there need not be other relevant questions. Analogous conditions hold for (6b) and (6c). Instead, the accents signal paralinguistic meaning: the special intonation of the utterances expresses a negative judgement of the speaker, such as indignation or discontent. A more thorough investigation of this meaning component must be left for further research.

Why are the accented elements not interpreted as the ACs of stressed *auch* in these utterances? This question has already been partially answered. It is only by means of the context that the prosodically favored interpretation (accented element = AC) is overridden by a more plausible one with a different AC. (6a) is a response to a question asked immediately before, namely, *Wo sind deine anderen Kleider?* ('Where are your other clothes?'). As this question is the only one relevant in the given situation, there is no non-empty set of other questions it can sensibly be added to by means of *auch*. Consequently, the interpretation (7b) is ruled out, as it causes a presupposition failure. The reading given in (7c), on the other hand, is compatible with the context: the speaker says that she, in addition to the person who originally asked the question, is interested in knowing the answer. What is added, in other words, is not a question to a set of questions, but a person (the speaker) to a set of people (the people asking for an answer). This latter set is already established when the initial question is asked. To maintain consistency with the context, the hearer is thus forced to ignore the prosodic cues for association with *auch* and to choose the more plausible among the possible interpretations, i.e., (7c). The 'superfluous' accent on the sentence-initial element must be reinterpreted, giving rise to an paralinguistic meaning component.

Although the utterances with a prenuclear accent on a non-AC occurred only very rarely in the corpus, they are important for the understanding of the relation between association with *auch* and intonation. An accented element to the left of stressed *auch* cannot automatically be interpreted as associated with the particle. Instead, the context must be taken into consideration. It may neutralize the effects of the prosodic cues and enforce a different interpretation.

To summarize: It could be shown that ACs of stressed *auch* are often marked prosodically by high or rising pitch accents. However, the corpus study also revealed that there is no one-to-one mapping between association status and accentuation. First, not all ACs were accented in our material. While non-pronominal ACs without exception carried accents, pronominal ACs were unaccented in more than half of the cases. Second, there was no single accent type that corresponded to association with *auch*. Pronominal as well as non-pronominal ACs carried L*H, LH*, and H* accents. Third, the very same accents could be found on non-associated elements in utterances with stressed *auch*, conveying paralinguistic meaning.

The reported mismatches in the correspondence between form and function lead us to the question of whether prosody is relevant at all for the phenomenon under discussion. From the point of view of speech perception, this question was addressed by Experiments 2, 4, and 5, which will be presented below. Two controlled speech production experiments (Experiments 1 and 3) served to test whether prosodic properties beyond the categorical factor accent type are involved in the marking of constituents associated with stressed *auch*. As discussed above, the corpus data does not allow for an investigation of this question.

6.3 Experimental pilot study

A pilot study combining a speech production experiment with a speech perception experiment was carried out to examine the prosodic properties of constituents associated with stressed *auch* in greater detail. The idea behind this study was that the prosodic marking of the ACs can be expected primarily in cases where more than one constituent to the left of *auch* is able to associate with the focus particle. In (8), the subject *Maja* is the only candidate for association with *auch*. Therefore, it can be clearly identified even without any prosodic marking or contextual information. The sentences in (9), on the other hand, are potentially ambiguous: here, the particle can be associated with both the subject *Maja* and the direct object *den Bus* ('the bus').[8] This ambiguity should have an influence on the optionality of the prosodic marking, as prosody has the potential to disambiguate the utterances. (9a) and (9b) should have the two possible realizations indicated

8. There is probably a preference for association with the prefield element. We will return to this point below.

in (10a) and (10b), respectively, the actual choice depending on the intended interpretation.

(8) Maja hat wahrscheinlich AUCH gesungen.
Maja *aux*$_p$ probably also sung

(9) a. Maja hat den Bus wahrscheinlich AUCH verpasst.
Maja *aux*$_p$ the bus probably also missed
b. Den Bus hat Maja wahrscheinlich AUCH verpasst.
the bus *aux*$_p$ Maja probably also missed

(10) a. (i) /MAja hat den Bus wahrscheinlich AUCH verpasst.
Maja *aux*$_p$ the bus probably also missed
(ii) Maja hat den /BUs wahrscheinlich AUCH verpasst.
b. (i) Den /BUs hat Maja wahrscheinlich AUCH verpasst.
the bus *aux*$_p$ Maja probably also missed
(ii) Den Bus hat /MAja wahrscheinlich AUCH verpasst.

If the prosodic marking of the AC can be enforced or at least made more likely by using this type of construction in a controlled experiment, an extensive and fine-grained analysis of the involved parameters becomes possible. In contrast to the corpus study presented in Section 6.2, the design of the experimental study also allows direct comparisons between associated and non-associated constituents. In this way, additional factors that could have influenced the prosodic realization in the corpus data (ranging from effects of the lexical material and the syntactic structure to the possible involvement of paralinguistic meaning conveyed by prosody) can be reliably excluded or controlled.

In the production experiment (Experiment 1), speakers produced potentially ambiguous sentences containing the focus particle *auch*, similar to those in (9) above. The intended AC was varied by means of a preceding question context, which triggered one of two possible readings. The resulting utterances were analyzed with respect to the acoustic properties of the ACs in comparison to their non-associated counterparts in lexically identical sentences. In addition, the production data served as input for the subsequent perception experiment (Experiment 2). The participants were auditorily presented with the original utterances without context and had to disambiguate them in a sentence completion task. The findings of the acoustic analysis of the production material were related to the outcome of the perception experiment. As an improved version of this design was used for the experiments to be extensively dealt with in Sections 6.4 to 6.6, the present discussion of the methods and results is kept to a minimum.

6.3.1 Hypotheses

Experimental studies have shown that the prosodic marking of a constituent as a contrastive topic results, among other things, in a rising f_0-movement as well as in a lengthening of (parts of) this constituent (cf. Mehlhorn 2001; Braun & Ladd 2003; Braun 2005, 2006). To keep matters simple in the pilot study, only f_0-excursion and duration of the whole constituent were selected as the dependent variables to be examined. If elements associated with stressed *auch* are contrastive topics, as claimed by Krifka's (1999) *Contrastive Topic Hypothesis*, they should be marked by a clear f_0-rise, while the same constituents should show a much smaller f_0-rise or none at all if they are not associated with the particle. In addition, ACs should have a longer duration than their non-associated counterparts. As for the perception experiment, the reliability of the identification of the AC in a given utterance should depend on the strength of the prosodic marking. In other words, hearers should use the information conveyed by prosody for the interpretation. The hypotheses of both the production and the perception experiment are given in (11) and (12).

(11) **Hypothesis 1 (speech production):** Constituents associated with stressed *auch* show a greater f_0-rise and a longer duration than identical constituents in the same position, but not associated with the particle (comparison between utterances).

(12) **Hypothesis 2 (speech perception):** The interpretation of utterances containing stressed *auch* depends on their prosodic realization. The intended reading is more reliably recovered in utterances with a stronger marking of the AC (where 'stronger' is defined along the dimensions given in Hypothesis 1).

6.3.2 Experiment 1: Speech production

6.3.2.1 *Data elicitation*

Participants. Four female native speakers of German (aged 20 to 24) took part in the experiment. They were trained speakers, but did not have a background in linguistics and lacked any knowledge about the research question. The speakers were paid for their participation in the experiment.

Materials. Five pairs of sentences were constructed, each pair consisting of two sentences ambiguous with respect to the constituent associated with *auch*. One example pair is given in (13), the complete materials can be found in Appendix A.2. On condition that the particle was stressed, there were two potential ACs to the left of *auch* in each sentence (in (13): *Ingo* and *am Dienstag* 'on Tuesday'). One was located in the prefield, and the other in the middlefield immediately after the finite verb in the V2-position. The constituents potentially associated with *auch* were always the subject and a temporal adverbial, both being equally unmarked in the prefield and the middlefield. The two sentences of each pair only differed in the relative order of these elements. Both variants were included to be able to control possible preferences with respect to the position or syntactic function of the AC.

(13) a. Ingo ist am Dienstag wahrscheinlich auch in der Bibliothek
Ingo aux_p on Tuesday probably also in the library
gewesen.
been

b. Am Dienstag ist Ingo wahrscheinlich auch in der Bibliothek gewesen.

The individual items had a similar structure: The subjects were two-syllabic names with lexical stress on the first syllable, the temporal adverbials were three-syllabic PPs consisting of a one-syllabic preposition and a two-syllabic noun, with lexical stress on the first syllable of the noun. The two potential ACs were separated by the finite verb, which was the perfect auxiliary (*hat* or *ist*, depending on the main verb) in all cases. The first middlefield element was followed by a three-syllabic sentence adverbial (*wahrscheinlich* 'probably' or *vermutlich* 'presumably') and the focus particle *auch*. We included the sentence adverbial in order to avoid a stress clash between the second potential AC and the stressed particle, which might have obscured the results. The remainder of the sentence following *auch* had approximately the same number of syllables in all items.

For each pair of sentences two different contexts were constructed. They consisted of a wh-question followed by a specification. The function of the contexts was twofold: On the one hand, they primed the speakers to produce the stressed variant of *auch*, as all elements to the right of the particle were excluded from being possible ACs. On the other hand, the contexts determined whether the subject or the temporal adverbial had to be interpreted as the AC of the focus particle. Each of the two contexts was combined with both versions of the respective target sentence, resulting in four experimental conditions. The independent variables, their levels, and the experimental conditions are summarized in Table 6.5;[9] an example set of context – target item combinations is given in (14)–(17).

(14) *association with the subject in the prefield* (condition SUBJ-adv)

C: Weißt du, wer aus unserer Gruppe am Dienstag in der Bibliothek war? Ich habe nämlich nur Claudia dort gesehen. ('Do you know who of our group was in the library on Thursday? I saw only Claudia there.')

---

9. The condition names indicate the relative order of subject and temporal adverbial. The associated element is printed in capitals.

Table 6.5 Experiment 1 – independent variables and experimental conditions

independent variables		experimental condition
FUNCTION of the AC	POSITION of the AC	
subject	prefield	SUBJ-adv
subject	middlefield	adv-SUBJ
temp. adverbial	prefield	ADV-subj
temp. adverbial	middlefield	subj-ADV

T: Ingo ist am Dienstag wahrscheinlich auch in der Bibliothek
Ingo *aux*$_p$ on Tuesday probably also in the library
gewesen.
been

(15) *association with the subject in the middlefield* (condition adv-SUBJ)

C: Weißt du, wer aus unserer Gruppe am Dienstag in der Bibliothek war? Ich habe nämlich nur Claudia dort gesehen. ('Do you know who of our group was in the library on Thursday? I saw only Claudia there.')

T: Am Dienstag ist Ingo wahrscheinlich auch in der Bibliothek
on Tuesday *aux*$_p$ Ingo probably also in the library
gewesen.
been

(16) *association with the adverbial in the prefield* (condition ADV-subj)

C: Weißt du, wann Ingo letzte Woche in der Bibliothek war? Ich habe ihn nämlich nur am Donnerstag dort gesehen. ('Do you know when Ingo was in the library last week? I only saw him there on Thursday.')

T: Am Dienstag ist Ingo wahrscheinlich auch in der Bibliothek
on Tuesday *aux*$_p$ Ingo probably also in the library
gewesen.
been

(17) *association with the adverbial in the middlefield* (condition subj-ADV)

C: Weißt du, wann Ingo letzte Woche in der Bibliothek war? Ich habe ihn nämlich nur am Donnerstag dort gesehen. ('Do you know when Ingo was in the library last week? I only saw him there on Thursday.')

T: Ingo ist am Dienstag wahrscheinlich auch in der Bibliothek
Ingo *aux*$_p$ on Tuesday probably also in the library
gewesen.
been

The combination of the two target sentence variants with the two contexts for all five lexicalizations resulted in a total of 20 target utterances to be produced by each speaker. An additional set of items was constructed for use as practice items.

Furthermore, five filler sentences without focus particles were constructed, each of which was again embedded in two different question contexts. Depending on the context, either the prefield element or a constituent in the middlefield of the filler sentence was contrastively focused. The resulting 10 combinations of a context and a filler sentence were only included for use in the perception experiment, i.e., they did not serve as filler items in the production experiment. As in the case of the critical items, an additional practice item set was constructed. An example filler set is given in (18) and (19).

(18) C: Weißt du, ob Wilhelm am Wochenende im Schwimmbad gewesen ist? ('Do you know whether Wilhelm was at the swimming pool at the weekend?')

T: Peter	ist	am	Wochenende	im	Schwimmbad	gewesen.
Peter	*aux*$_p$	on_the	weekend	at_the	swimming_pool	been

(19) C: Weißt du, ob Peter am Wochenende im Kino gewesen ist? ('Do you know whether Peter was at the cinema at the weekend?')

T: Peter	ist	am	Wochenende	im	Schwimmbad	gewesen.
Peter	*aux*$_p$	on_the	weekend	at_the	swimming_pool	been

Procedure. All question contexts were recorded with a professional speaker in a separate session. The speech production experiment took place in a sound-proof booth at the Max Planck Institute for Human Cognitive and Brain Sciences, Leipzig. The participants' task was (i) to read through a context – target item combination silently, which was presented on a card, (ii) to listen to an acoustic presentation of the context, and (iii) to immediately produce the target sentence. This procedure was chosen to elicit utterances that are as natural as possible, in spite of the fact that the exact wording of the target utterances had to be determined in advance. The speakers were allowed to repeat their productions when they were not satisfied with the result, i.e., when they believed their own utterance to sound unnatural or inappropriate as a response in the given context. Every time a speaker made use of this possibility, the context utterance was replayed. Only the final production was considered in the analysis. The target utterances were digitally recorded using a DAT recorder with a sampling rate of 44.1 kHz (16 bit).

The items in this production experiment were not randomized. Instead, they were presented to the participants block-wise, and separately for each experimental condition. Every block of items was preceded by one practice item. After the four blocks of critical items, two blocks of filler utterances for the perception experiment were recorded. Between the blocks, the speakers had short breaks. Each speaker had to produce a total of 36 utterances; the entire experiment took about 45 minutes.

6.3.2.2 *Data analysis*

Data selection. The critical utterances were extracted using CoolEdit and superficially inspected. The software Praat[10] was employed for all subsequent analysis steps. All 80 critical utterances were included in the analysis.

Annotation and measurements. Syllable boundaries were annotated for the two relevant constituents in each utterance using information from waveform and spectrogram. On the basis of this annotation, the duration of the two potential ACs could be automatically determined. Fundamental frequency was extracted for the whole utterances making use of Praat's autocorrelation algorithm with a time step setting of 1 ms. It was necessary to manually correct artifacts produced by the algorithm, such as f_0-halving or f_0-doubling. Lastly, the size of the f_0-excursion was determined for the elements potentially associated with *auch* by measuring the f_0-maximum and the f_0-minimum within these constituents and computing the difference between them. In order to account for the fact that the perception of fundamental frequency is not linear (cf. Hermes & van Gestel 1991, among others), all measured f_0-values were transformed from the Hz-scale into the ERB-scale (equivalent rectangular bandwidth) using the formula given in (20), where f_{ERB} is the frequency in number of ERBs and f_{Hz} is the frequency in Hz.[11]

(20) $$f_{\mathrm{ERB}} = 16.7\,\lg\left(1 + \frac{f_{\mathrm{Hz}}}{165.4}\right)$$

6.3.2.3 *Qualitative results*

A superficial inspection of the f_0-tracks revealed that the utterances of the individual speakers in each experimental condition showed a high degree of consistency. In 14 out of 16 cases (four speakers in four conditions), all five utterances had the same contour shape. In the remaining two cases, we found four utterances with consistent contour shapes and one utterance considerably differing from the others. For the qualitative analysis, these two utterances were excluded from further

10. See http://www.praat.org.

11. This formula is taken from Hermes & van Gestel (1991:97). The authors attribute it to Greenwood (1961, 1990). In the literature, several different formulas for Hz-ERB transformations can be found; cf. the formula of Glasberg & Moore (1990) and Moore (1997) given in (i) and the formula used by Praat given in (ii).

(i) $$f_{\mathrm{ERB}} = 21.4\,\lg(4.37\,f_{\mathrm{Hz}} + 1)$$

(ii) $$f_{\mathrm{ERB}} = 11,17\,\ln\left(\frac{f_{\mathrm{Hz}} + 312}{f_{\mathrm{Hz}} + 14680}\right) + 43$$

However, the differences between the formulas can be neglected. In all cases, the non-linear nature of pitch perception is accounted for.

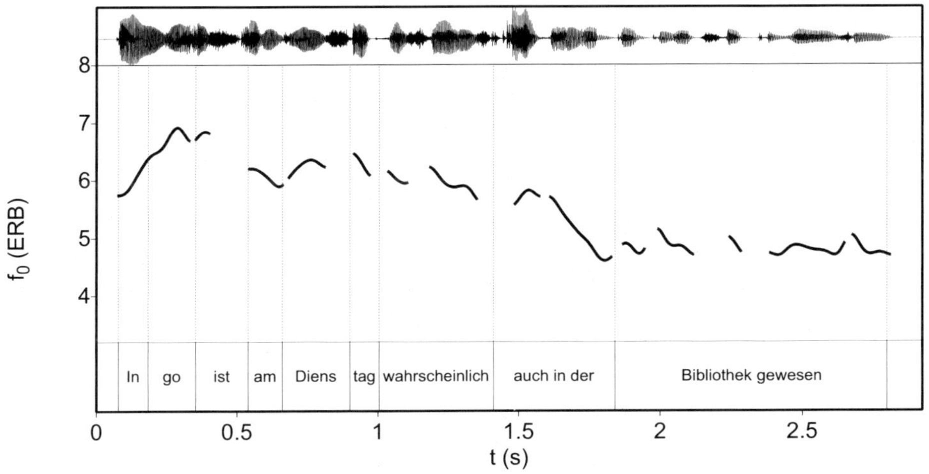

Figure 6.9 Experiment 1 – f_0-contour of an utterance of the sentence *"Ingo ist am Dienstag wahrscheinlich auch in der Bibliothek gewesen."* (cf. (14)), condition SUBJ-adv, produced by Speaker 1

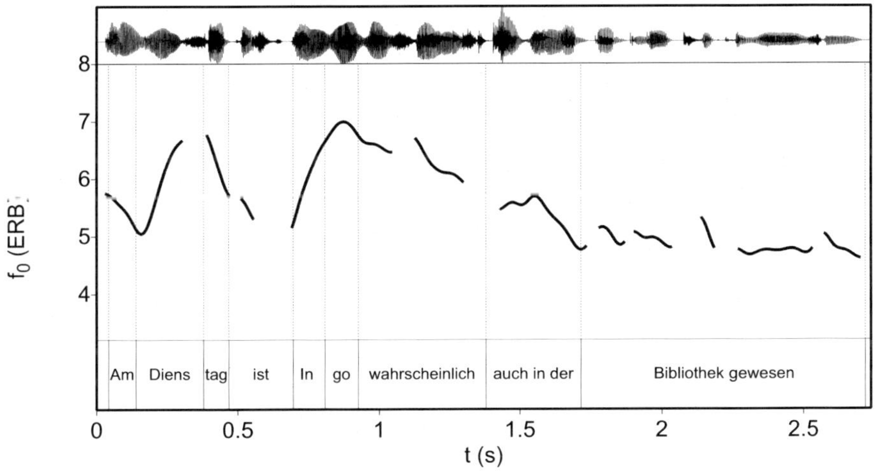

Figure 6.10 Experiment 1 – f_0-contour of an utterance of the sentence *"Am Dienstag ist Ingo wahrscheinlich auch in der Bibliothek gewesen."* (cf. (15)), condition adv-SUBJ, produced by Speaker 1

consideration. Crucially, all utterances were included in the quantitative analysis to be presented below. Example f_0-tracks of Speaker 1 in all four conditions are given in Figures 6.9–6.12. These contours can be regarded as prototypical of the majority of utterances in the individual conditions.

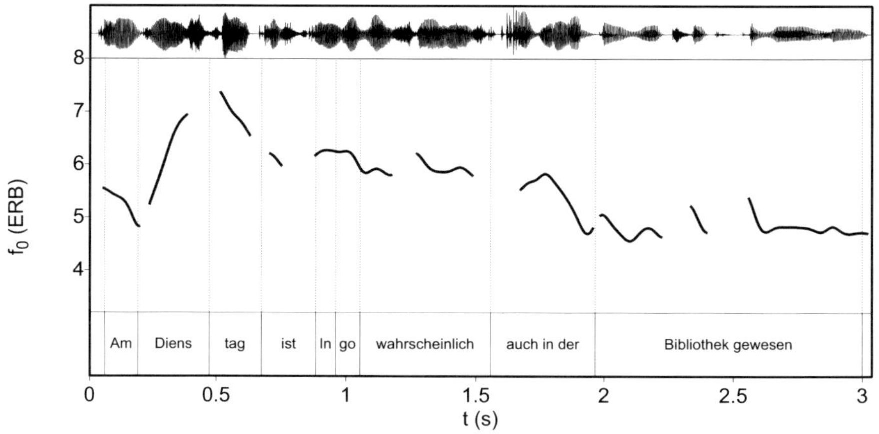

Figure 6.11 Experiment 1 – f_0-contour of an utterance of the sentence *"Am Dienstag ist Ingo wahrscheinlich auch in der Bibliothek gewesen."* (cf. (16)), condition ADV-subj, produced by Speaker 1

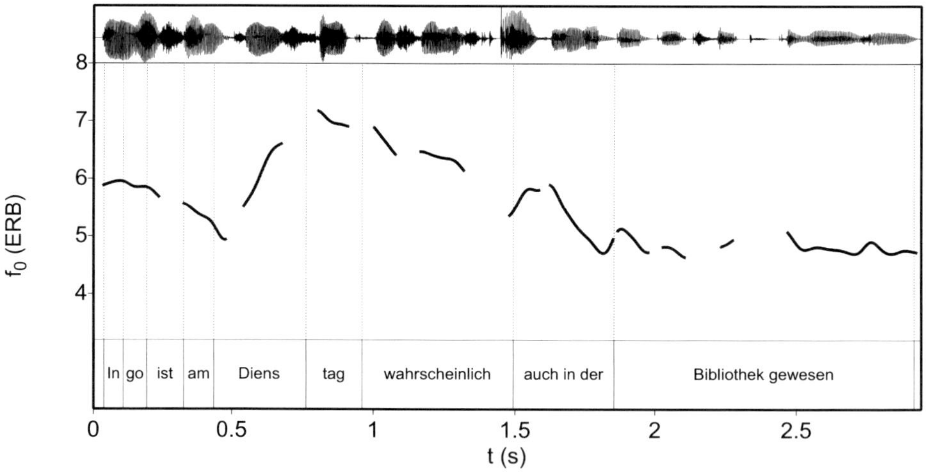

Figure 6.12 Experiment 1 – f_0-contour of an utterance of the sentence *"Ingo ist am Dienstag wahrscheinlich auch in der Bibliothek gewesen."* (cf. (17)), condition subj-ADV, produced by Speaker 1

For condition SUBJ-adv, we expected a clear f_0-rise on the associated subject in the prefield and a comparatively smaller rise, if any, on the non-associated adverbial in the middlefield. The contours of Speakers 1 and 2 corresponded to the expected pattern. Speaker 3 chose a different strategy to mark the AC: she produced a high peak on the accented syllable followed by a steep fall. The contours of

Speaker 4 only partially fulfilled our expectations: in addition to a clear rise on the AC, there was also a comparable rise on the non-associated middlefield element.

For condition adv-SUBJ, a clear rise on the associated subject in the middlefield and a smaller rise on the prefield adverbial were expected. Again, only Speakers 1 and 2 produced contours completely fulfilling the expectations. The contours of Speaker 3 showed a rise of approximately the same size on the subject and the adverbial. Speaker 4 consistently produced an intonational pattern that behaved in a manner completely opposite to what the hypothesis predicted: the rise on the non-associated adverbial was much greater than the rise on the associated subject, the resulting contours thus resembling those of condition ADV-subj.[12]

For condition ADV-subj, we expected a clear f_0-rise on the associated prefield adverbial and only a small rise, if any, on the middlefield subject. The contours of all four speakers fulfilled these expectations. For condition subj-ADV, a clear rise on the associated adverbial in the middlefield and a comparatively smaller rise on the subject in the middlefield were expected. While the contours of Speakers 1, 2, and 3 corresponded to the expected pattern, the contours of Speaker 4 had approximately the same rise on both relevant constituents.

The results of the qualitative analysis substantially confirmed our expectations. While the ACs of stressed *auch* were marked by a clear f_0-rise, the non-associated constituents showed a smaller rise or a rather flat contour shape. In condition adv-SUBJ alone was the difference not as obvious. Here, the non-associated adverbial in the prefield was also frequently characterized by a pronounced rise, as can be seen in Figure 6.10 above. In general, non-associated constituents showed a greater f_0-excursion if they were positioned in the prefield, but only a minimal excursion, if any, if located in the middlefield. This is in line with results of a study by Braun & Ladd (2003),[13] who found a prenuclear rise on sentence-initial constituents in German in both contrastive and non-contrastive conditions.

The ACs in most utterances showed an f_0-rise with its peak delayed into the post-stressed syllable. In the GToBI-notation, this corresponds to the typical rising contrastive accent L*H. The non-associated constituents did not show a uniform intonational pattern. The stressed focus particle consistently carried the falling focus accent (the nuclear accent) H*L, which became more salient through a directly preceding short f_0-rise; cf. the f_0-movement on the sentence adverbial *wahrscheinlich* ('probably') and on *auch* in Figures 6.9–6.12. This phenomenon has also been described by Mehlhorn (2001). The part of the contour after the nuclear accent on the focus particle remained relatively flat. In sum, one can say that the majority of

12. The perception experiment revealed that the utterances of Speaker 4 in condition adv-SUBJ were indeed interpreted as fitting the opposite context; cf. Section 6.3.3.2.

13. See also Braun (2005, 2006).

the utterances elicited in Experiment 1 showed the intonational pattern typical of bridge contours.

6.3.2.4 *Quantitative results*

In order to statistically validate the results with respect to Hypothesis 1 (cf. (11) above), we compared f_0-excursion (*df_0*) and duration (*dur*) of the potential ACs between utterances. The comparisons were made between associated and non-associated, but lexically identical constituents in identical positions. In other words, we compared (i) prefield subjects between conditions SUBJ-adv and subj-ADV, (ii) middlefield subjects between conditions adv-SUBJ and ADV-subj, (iii) prefield adverbials between conditions ADV-subj and adv-SUBJ, and (iv) middlefield adverbials between conditions subj-ADV and SUBJ-adv. No comparisons were made between lexically different constituents in different positions (e.g., between the two potential ACs within a given utterance) or between different speakers, as various intervening factors (effects imposed by the lexical material or the speakers' f_0-range, among others) were not or could not be controlled.

Table 6.6 summarizes the results of the comparisons with respect to the dependent variables *df_0* and *dur*. As the statistical method, paired t-tests were chosen. Due to the fact that multiple t-tests had to be carried out (8 in total), the α-level was adjusted to .00625 (Bonferroni adjustment).

Of the 160 computed values for *df_0* (two constituents in 80 critical utterances), 149 had a positive sign, i.e., even the non-associated constituents mostly showed a (small) f_0-rise. The remaining 11 values with a negative sign indicating an f_0-fall exclusively belonged to non-associated elements. The means of the f_0-excursions, displayed in the upper part of Table 6.6, corresponded to our expectation and

Table 6.6 Experiment 1 – f_0-excursion (*df_0*) and constituent duration (*dur*) compared between utterances; separate comparisons for prefield subjects (condition SUBJ-adv vs. condition subj-ADV), middlefield subjects (adv-SUBJ vs. ADV-subj), prefield adverbials (ADV-subj vs. adv-SUBJ), and middlefield adverbials (subj-ADV vs. SUBJ-adv); quantitative results and paired t-tests (one-tailed), N = 20, α = .00625 (Bonferroni adjustment, 8 t-tests)

variable	constituent	assoc.	non-ass.	sign.?	T	p
df_0 (ERB)	pref. subj.	1.36	0.68	✓	–3.29	<.003
	middlef. subj.	1.16	0.38	✓	–4.17	<.001
	pref. adv.	2.21	1.46	✓	4.61	<.001
	middlef. adv.	1.88	0.66	✓	7.10	<.001
dur (ms)	pref. subj.	276	228	✓	–3.38	<.002
	middlef. subj.	236	217	n.s.	–1.85	.041
	pref. adv.	589	520	✓	4.34	<.001
	middlef. adv.	535	439	✓	5.55	<.001

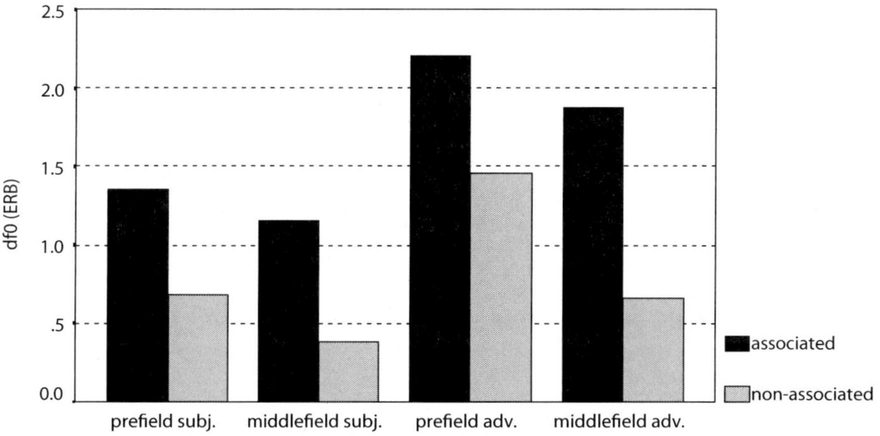

Figure 6.13 Experiment 1 – f_0-excursion (df_0) compared between utterances; separate comparisons for prefield subjects (condition SUBJ-adv vs. condition subj-ADV), middlefield subjects (adv-SUBJ vs. ADV-subj), prefield adverbials (ADV-subj vs. adv-SUBJ), and middlefield adverbials (subj-ADV vs. SUBJ-adv); N = 20

confirmed the conclusions drawn from the qualitative analysis: the f_0-rise on constituents associated with stressed *auch* was greater than the rise on the corresponding non-associated elements in lexically identical utterances. This is illustrated in Figure 6.13. The differences were significant for all four comparisons.

At first sight, it was somewhat surprising to find that in condition adv-SUBJ, the mean f_0-rise on the non associated adverbial in the prefield (1.46 ERB) was greater than the mean rise on the associated subject in the middlefield (1.16 ERB). This unexpected result can be partially attributed to the utterances of Speaker 4, who produced contours that differed significantly from the expectations in this condition (see above). However, the intonational patterns of the remaining speakers were also less clear in this experimental condition than in the other ones.

The means of the constituent durations, displayed in the lower part of Table 6.6, also confirmed Hypothesis 1, for the most part. As expected, the duration of ACs of stressed *auch* was longer than the duration of their non-associated counterparts in lexically identical utterances (cf. also Figure 6.14). However, at the adjusted α-level of .00625, the differences became significant in only three of the four comparisons; associated (236 ms) and non-associated subjects (217 ms) in the middlefield did not differ significantly in their duration. Again, this can at least partly be attributed to the unexpected productions of Speaker 4 in condition adv-SUBJ. If the utterances of Speaker 4 are excluded, the difference in duration between associated and non-associated middlefield subjects becomes significant (paired t-test, one-tailed, N = 15, *dur*(associated) = 247 ms, *dur*(non-associated) = 214 ms, $T = -3.14$, $p < .004$).

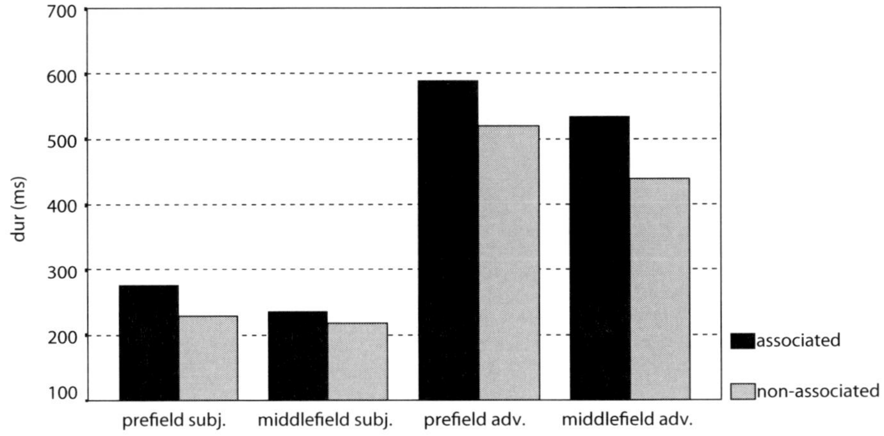

Figure 6.14 Experiment 1 – constituent duration (*dur*) compared between utterances; separate comparisons for prefield subjects (condition SUBJ-adv vs. condition subj-ADV), middlefield subjects (adv-SUBJ vs. ADV-subj), prefield adverbials (ADV-subj vs. adv-SUBJ), and middlefield adverbials (subj-ADV vs. SUBJ-adv); N = 20

6.3.2.5 *Discussion*

In the examined utterances, the constituents associated with stressed *auch* were marked by at least two distinct prosodic parameters: they showed a significantly greater f_0-rise and – with the exception of middlefield subjects – a significantly longer duration than corresponding constituents that were not associated with the focus particle. Although the results of Experiment 1 are only preliminary in nature, two conclusions can be drawn. First, speakers indicate the intended AC of *auch* in potentially ambiguous sentences by prosodic means. The perception experiment to be reported in the next subsection will show to what extent hearers make use of this source of information for disambiguation. A related question is whether a potential preference for associating stressed *auch* with constituents in a certain syntactic position (presumably the prefield) can be neutralized by the prosody of the respective utterance. Second, the observed intonational patterns suggest that the ACs are marked by the rising pitch accent L*H, which is assumed to be typical of contrastive topics (cf. Section 6.1). This is in line with the expectations formulated above.

6.3.3 Experiment 2: Speech perception

6.3.3.1 *Method*

Participants. 24 participants (aged 19 to 28, with a mean of 22.8; 21 females and 3 males) took part in the experiment. They were native speakers of German and lacked any knowledge about the topic being examined. They received a small financial reimbursement for their participation in the experiment.

Materials. The 80 recorded critical utterances from Experiment 1 served as stimuli for the perception experiment. In order to relate the prosodic realization of a given utterance to its interpretation by hearers, all utterances were classified with respect to whether their f_0-contours corresponded to the expectations for the respective contexts. Three categories were used: Utterances with a pronounced f_0-rise on the AC, where the other relevant constituent had a smaller rise or none at all, were classified as having expected contours. Utterances showing the reverse pattern, i.e., a noticeable rise on the non-associated constituent, were classified as behaving in a manner opposite to expectations. The remaining category was used for utterances showing an f_0-rise of approximately the same size on both relevant constituents. These were classified as having ambiguous contours.[14] The distribution of the critical utterances over the three categories is given in Table 6.7, confirming again that the majority of utterances were in accord with our hypothesis.

For each of the five sets of critical utterances (cf. Section 6.3.2.1), two continuations were constructed, each of them corresponding to one of the possible interpretations. The continuations for the items in (14)–(17) above are given in (21). The critical utterances in (14)–(17) can only be continued with (21a) if *auch* is interpreted as being associated with the temporal adverbial, while (21b) is an acceptable continuation only if the subject is considered to be the AC of the particle. Similar continuations were constructed for the filler items.

(21) a. ... und nicht nur am Donnerstag.
... and not only on Thursday
b. ... und nicht nur Claudia.
... and not only Claudia

Table 6.7 Experiment 2 – classification of the stimulus utterances

category	frequency	
expected f_0-contour	59	74%
opposite f_0-contour	7	9%
ambiguous f_0-contour	14	17%
total	80	100%

14. We are aware that this way of classifying is not objective enough, as no clear criterion was used for assigning the utterances to the categories. However, the classification did not depend on the experimenter's auditory impression, but on the visual inspection of the f_0-tracks. See Sections 6.5 and 6.6 for different approaches to the question under discussion.

Procedure. The perception experiment was based on a completion task. The participants were auditorily (via headphones) presented with the target utterances without context; the two possible continuations were given next to each other on a computer screen, their left-right order being randomized. After listening to an utterance, the participants had to select the continuation they considered to be more appropriate. The choice indicated which constituent was interpreted as being associated with *auch* in the respective utterances. In other words, by deciding between the two continuations, the participants reconstructed the original context of the target utterance.

After careful instruction and a short practice session consisting of four items, the participants worked through a web-based presentation in a self-paced manner. There was no time limit for the decisions, and the participants were allowed to listen to the utterances as many times as they needed. The 80 critical and 40 filler items were pseudo-randomized and divided into four blocks of 30 items each. Between the blocks, the participants could take short breaks. The entire perception experiment took about 20 minutes.

6.3.3.2 *Results and discussion*

For each target utterance, it was determined how frequently it was interpreted in agreement with its original context. Altogether, there were 73.5% matches and 26.5% mismatches among the 1920 decisions. With respect to the design of the perception experiment, Hypothesis 2 (cf. (12) above) can be put in the more concrete form given in (22) and (23). Together, these two hypotheses predict a decisive role of intonation for the interpretation.

(22) **Hypothesis 2a:** The results of the decision task reflect the classification of the items: items with expected f_0-contours are matched properly with respect to their original contexts, items with contours that are opposite to the expectations are mismatched, and items with ambiguous contours are matched and mismatched with a frequency equivalent to that of random choices.

(23) **Hypothesis 2b:** Utterances with expected f_0-contours are matched properly with respect to their original context regardless of the syntactic position (prefield vs. middlefield) and function (subject vs. adverbial) of the AC.

With respect to the classification of the utterances according to their f_0-contours, the individual speakers differed considerably; cf. Table 6.8 and Figure 6.15. While the utterances of Speakers 1 and 2 for the most part showed the expected pattern, Speaker 3 produced a larger number of ambiguous contours, and of the last speaker's contours, fewer than half corresponded to the expectations. Consequently, we expected different results in the matching task for the utterances of the individual speakers.

Table 6.8 Experiment 2 – classification of the stimuli, compared across speakers

category	speaker			
	Speaker 1	Speaker 2	Speaker 3	Speaker 4
opposite f_0	0%	5%	0%	30%
ambiguous f_0	5%	10%	30%	25%
expected f_0	95%	85%	70%	45%

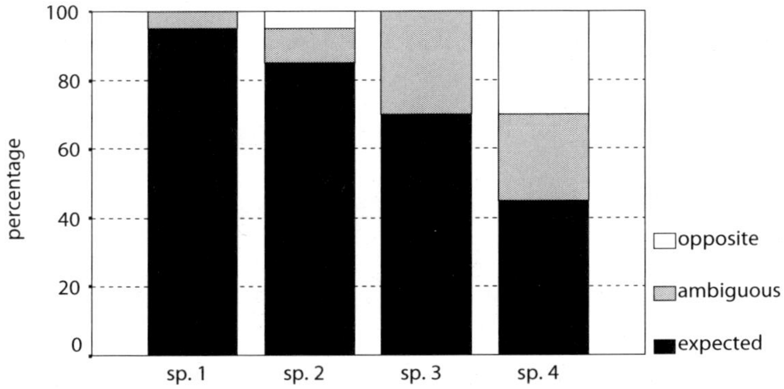

Figure 6.15 Experiment 2 – classification of the stimuli, compared across speakers

In fact, the matching percentages differed significantly across speakers (χ^2-test: $\chi^2 = 100.67$, $df = 3$, $p < .001$), as shown in Table 6.9 and Figure 6.16. Speaker 4, who produced the smallest number of utterances with f_0-contours expected for the given contexts, also received the worst matching results (only 56.3% matches). The utterances of Speaker 4 in condition adv-SUBJ, which were consistently produced with an intonational pattern opposite to the hypothesis (cf. Section 6.3.2.3), received the intended interpretation in only 19.2% of the cases.

More importantly, the percentages of matches differed significantly across the three categories of utterances (χ^2-test: $\chi^2 = 443.35$, $df = 2$, $p < .001$); cf. Table 6.10 and Figure 6.17. This confirms Hypothesis 2a (cf. (22) above): Utterances with expected f_0-contours showed the best matching results; they were interpreted in accordance with their original context in more than 85% of the cases. Utterances having contours that differed significantly from expectations showed the reverse pattern; in the majority of cases, their interpretation did not correspond to the reading induced by the original context. The items categorized as having ambiguous f_0-contours had results equivalent to matches being made at random.

As for Hypothesis 2b (cf. (23) above), we compared the percentage of properly matched items across the four experimental conditions only for the utterances

Table 6.9 Experiment 2 – matching percentage, compared across speakers

response	speaker			
	Speaker 1	Speaker 2	Speaker 3	Speaker 4
mismatch	19.0%	20.0%	23.1%	43.7%
match	81.0%	80.0%	76.9%	56.3%

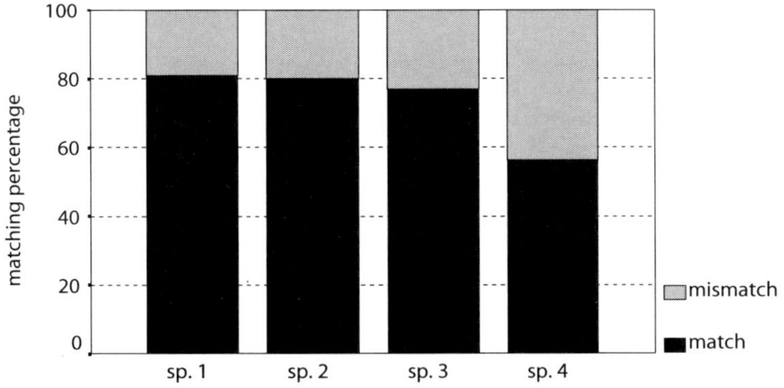

Figure 6.16 Experiment 2 – matching percentage, compared across speakers

Table 6.10 Experiment 2 – matching percentage, compared across categories of utterances

response	category of utterances		
	expected f_0	opposite f_0	ambiguous f_0
mismatch	14.8%	81.5%	48.2%
match	85.2%	18.5%	51.8%

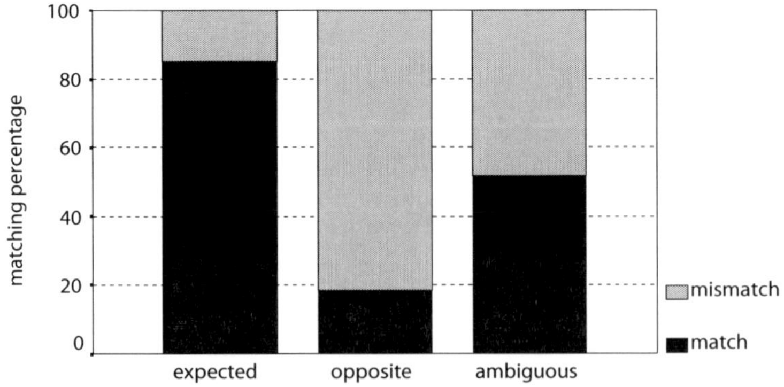

Figure 6.17 Experiment 2 – matching percentage, compared across categories of utterances

Table 6.11 Experiment 2 – matching percentage of the utterances with expected f_0-contours, compared across experimental conditions

response	experimental condition			
	SUBJ-adv	adv-SUBJ	ADV-subj	subj-ADV
mismatch	10.6%	16.0%	15.4%	18.3%
match	89.4%	84.0%	84.6%	81.7%

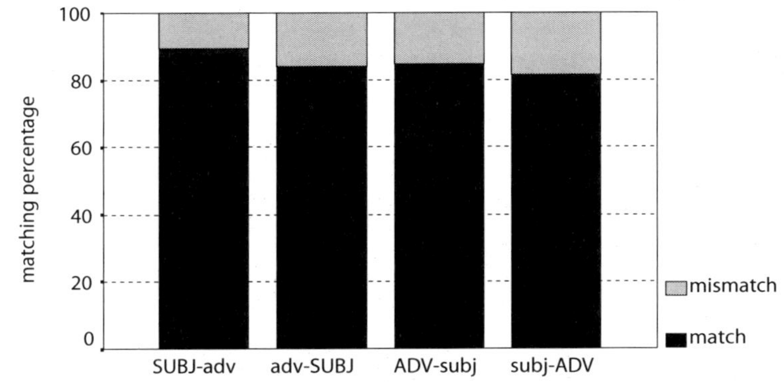

Figure 6.18 Experiment 2 – matching percentage of the utterances with expected f_0-contours, compared across experimental conditions

with expected f_0-contours. The examination of the results of individual participants did not reveal any special strategies with respect to the different conditions, so the overall results displayed in Table 6.11 and Figure 6.18 can be considered to reflect the behavior of the entire group of participants. Although the utterances of condition SUBJ-adv had slightly better results, all other conditions showed matching percentages higher than 80%, which we consider as a confirmation of our hypothesis: intonation played a crucial role for the interpretation of the utterances and was able to override potential preferences for a syntactic position or function.

6.3.4 General discussion

The results of the pilot study confirmed the hypothesis that the prosodic marking of constituents associated with stressed *auch* plays a decisive role in both the production and the perception of potentially ambiguous constructions. In the production experiment, speakers disambiguated the utterances by a prosodic marking characteristic of contrastive topics. This rising contrastive accent on the ACs was used by the hearers in the perception experiment to interpret the utterances. In this respect, the prosodic properties of constituents associated with stressed *auch* observed in our study were in line with Krifka's (1999) account.

While the pilot study presented above provided some preliminary insights into the production and perception of constructions containing the stressed focus particle *auch*, it was unsatisfactory in many respects. One major drawback was the nature of the stimulus materials. It turned out to be disadvantageous for the analysis that the proper names serving as subjects in the critical sentences were two-syllabic words with lexical stress on the first syllable and that they started with the stressed vowel, which was short in four out of five cases. Particularly in the subject-initial conditions (SUBJ-adv and subj-ADV), these factors resulted in the course of the f_0-contour on this constituent being hard to determine. The f_0-tracks showed many artifacts in the area of the utterance-initial glottal stop, and the f_0-excursion was extremely compressed. As the subject constituents differed considerably in structure from the temporal adverbials (which were three-syllabic PPs with lexical stress on the second syllable), the contour shapes on the two potential ACs could not be directly compared. It was not clear to what extent the observed qualitative differences must be attributed to the different lexical structure instead of the experimental manipulations.

In the quantitative analysis, this problem was avoided by comparing only lexically identical constituents between utterances of different experimental conditions. However, a comparison of the two potential ACs within utterances would be also desirable in order to get further insights into the prosodic marking of the elements associated with *auch*. With the used materials, such an analysis was impossible. In addition to the differences in the number of syllables and the stress position, properties such as syllable structure, vowel length, and vowel quality were in no way controlled. Consequently, it was impossible to compare duration and f_0-parameters directly within a given utterance.

Another drawback of our pilot study was that the stimuli were not randomized in the production experiment. On the one hand, the separate presentation for each condition might have been the reason for the high consistency of the f_0-contours. Speakers were not distracted by filler items or items from different experimental conditions, and could use the same prosodic pattern for a sequence of items immediately following each other. On the other hand, this procedure to some extent calls into question the meaningfulness of the results. The utterances of Speaker 4 in condition adv-SUBJ, for instance, all showed a prosodic pattern exactly opposite to our expectations, the f_0-rise on the non-associated adverbial in the prefield being considerably greater than the rise on the associated subject in the middlefield. In the perception experiment, *auch* was almost always interpreted as associated with the adverbial in these utterances; the interpretation thus corresponded to the prosodic realization, but not to the original context. Presumably, the speaker did no longer pay attention to the contexts for producing the utterances, but repeatedly used a prosodic pattern that she had transferred from one of the other conditions. This, however, undermines the idea behind the experiment, as the prosodic realization is supposed to depend on the context, rather than on other factors created by the experimental design.

A related aspect, which might also have played a role, are order effects. Due to the missing randomization, certain conditions were necessarily dealt with after others. It is conceivable that the speakers changed their strategies in the course of the experiment, as they became more accustomed to the task. Paying less attention to the context is one possibility of such a change in behavior. Together, the described factors may have led to the recorded utterances being (i) not as natural as they could have been within the limits of a laboratory experiment and (ii) too homogeneous to reflect the prosodic parameters relevant in natural speech production.

The disadvantages in the design of the production experiment also had some negative consequences for the perception experiment. As the two elements potentially associated with *auch* could not be compared within a given utterance, there was no reliable and objective criterion for the unambiguity of the prosodic marking. As for f_0-excursion, we had to confine ourselves to visually inspecting the contours in order to determine whether they corresponded to the hypothesis or not. Constituent duration could not be considered at all for the analysis of the perception data.

To summarize: On the on hand, the results of the pilot study are promising insofar as they suggest that ACs of stressed *auch* are indeed prosodically marked as contrastive topics in potentially ambiguous utterances. On the other hand, the mentioned drawbacks of the production and perception experiments call for a more sophisticated and elaborate study with an improved experimental design. Relevant aspects to be taken into consideration include the use of more controlled stimulus materials, the randomization of the items and the employment of fillers in the production experiment, and the analysis of several additional prosodic parameters such as f_0-peak and accent alignment. Three experiments that examined the production and perception of utterances containing stressed *auch* in greater detail will be presented in Sections 6.4 to 6.6.

6.4 Experiment 3: Stressed *auch* in speech production

The speech production experiment to be presented in this section was very similar in structure to Experiment 1. Again, the prosodic characteristics of constituents associated with stressed *auch* were examined in potentially ambiguous utterances. The most important changes related to the stimulus materials and the procedure (cf. Section 6.4.2 below), as well as to the number of parameters considered in the prosodic analysis (cf. Section 6.4.1).

6.4.1 Hypotheses

In Experiment 1, it was shown (i) that ACs of stressed *auch* are marked by a greater f_0-rise and a longer duration than their non-associated counterparts and (ii) that non-associated elements in the prefield or at the beginning of the middlefield also frequently show an f_0-rise, which is, however, comparatively smaller. In Experiment 3, the prosodic parameters distinguishing associated and non-associated constituents were subjected to a more fine-grained analysis involving the examination of three groups of prosodic variables: f_0-variables, duration variables, and alignment variables.

In the first group, the analysis of the f_0-rise was supplemented by the analysis of the f_0-minimum immediately preceding the rise and the f_0-peak marking the end of the rise. The extended f_0-excursion on the ACs found in Experiment 1 could be caused by a lowering of the minimum, by a raising of the peak, or by a combination of both factors. The question arose as to which of these possibilities is made use of in speech production. With respect to duration variables, the analysis was broadened in a similar way. It was not immediately obvious whether the observed lengthening of ACs was due exclusively to the lengthening of their stressed syllables, or whether preceding and following unstressed syllables were also lengthened. For this reason, several different duration variables were determined in the new version of the experiment. Alignment variables were not considered at all in Experiment 1. However, experimental results concerning the nature of topic accents in German (cf. Braun & Ladd 2003; Braun 2005, 2006; Mücke, Grice, Becker, Hermes & Baumann 2006) suggest that accent alignment plays an important role in the marking of contrastive topics. Therefore, the examination of alignment variables was included in Experiment 3, hypothesizing that constituents associated with *auch* should show a later alignment than their non-associated counterparts.

The hypotheses that served as the basis for Experiment 3 are given in (24) and (25). While Hypothesis 3 is an extension of Hypothesis 1 from Experiment 1 (cf. (11) above), Hypothesis 4 refers to the comparisons between associated and non-associated constituents within utterances, which became possible because of the improved stimulus materials.

(24) **Hypothesis 3:** Constituents associated with stressed *auch* show a greater f_0-rise (caused by a lower f_0-minimum or a higher f_0-peak or both), a longer duration (caused by lengthening of the stressed syllable or larger domains), and a later accent alignment than identical constituents in the same position, but not associated with the particle (comparison between utterances).

(25) **Hypothesis 4:** Constituents associated with stressed *auch* show a greater f_0-rise (caused by a lower f_0-minimum or a higher f_0-peak or both), a longer

duration (caused by lengthening of the stressed syllable or larger domains), and a later accent alignment than non-associated constituents in the same sentence (located in the prefield or at the beginning of the middlefield) that have the potential to serve as ACs of the particle (comparison within utterances).

6.4.2 Data elicitation

Participants. Seven female speakers aged 20 to 26 participated in the experiment. They were all native speakers of German who had no background in linguistics and who were unaware of the purpose of the experiment, particularly of our intentions for analysis.[15] None of the speakers had participated in the pilot study (Experiments 1 and 2) presented above. The speakers were paid for their participation.

The selection of the speakers for Experiment 3 was made on the basis of their speech production in a short test session. Candidates had to read aloud five sentences after an auditory presentation of a context. These test items did not show any similarities in structure and content to the items used in the actual experiment, but had – if produced in an appropriate way – a complex prosodic structure. The relevant phenomena characterizing the test sentences included ellipses, parallel constructions, and contrastive statements, all of them sharing the property that the correct prosodic realization crucially depends on the given context. Speakers were selected if they read fluently, naturally, and without strong dialect features, and if they were able to produce the utterances with an adequate, i.e., context-dependent, prosody instead of ignoring the context and following a default prosodic strategy.

Materials. The stimulus materials of Experiment 3 were similar in structure to those of Experiment 1. Again, five pairs of sentences ambiguous with respect to the AC of *auch* were constructed, the potential ACs always being the subject and a temporal adverbial. This time, however, the materials were more properly controlled: Both the subjects and the adverbials were three-syllabic constituents with lexical stress on the second syllable. The subjects were proper names or designations of origin such as *Wiener* ('Viennese'), preceded by the masculine definite article *der* ('the'). The temporal adverbials were PPs consisting of a one-syllabic preposition and a two-syllabic noun denoting a month, a season, or a time (of day). The two sentences of each pair differed only in the relative order of the potential ACs. Altogether, the critical sentences consisted of the following elements: the first potential AC, the perfect auxiliary, the second potential AC, a sentence adverbial, the focus particle *auch*, and the remainder of the VP including the main verb in the form of

15. But see the paragraph on data selection in Section 6.4.3.

a participle. The main verbs were chosen in such a way that the perfect auxiliary separating the potential ACs was always *hat*. The sentence adverbial, which was again included to avoid stress clashes, was *wahrscheinlich* ('probably') in all cases. An example sentence pair is given in (26). All sentences had an identical number of syllables before the focus particle and approximately the same number of syllables after it.

(26) a. Der Rudi hat im Juni wahrscheinlich auch einen Vortrag
the Rudi aux_p in June probably also a talk
gehalten.
given
b. Im Juni hat der Rudi wahrscheinlich auch einen Vortrag gehalten.

Within each sentence, the two potential ACs of *auch* were kept as parallel as possible with respect to their phonetic properties. The stressed and the post-stressed syllable of the subject and the adverbial were characterized by an identical syllable structure, vowel length, and vowel height. The last factor was controlled in order to avoid possible influences of intrinsic f_0, as described by Lehiste (1970) and Ladd & Silverman (1984). With the exception of one case (*Günther – Winter* 'winter'), the vowels of the stressed and post-stressed syllables were the same in the subject and the adverbial.

In Experiment 3, the target sentences were also embedded in contexts triggering one of the two possible interpretations. The independent variables and experimental conditions were the same as in Experiment 1; cf. the overview in Table 6.5 above. An example item set is given in (27)–(30); the complete materials can be found in Appendix A.4.

(27) *association with the subject in the prefield* (condition SUBJ-adv)
C: Kannst du mir verraten, wer von den Doktoranden im Juni einen Vortrag gehalten hat? Ich habe gehört, dass sich damals nur der Martin bereit erklärt hat. ('Can you tell me who of the PhD students gave a talk in June? I heard that at that time only Martin agreed to do it.')
T: Der Rudi hat im Juni wahrscheinlich auch einen Vortrag
the Rudi aux_p in June probably also a talk
gehalten.
given

(28) *association with the subject in the middlefield* (condition adv-SUBJ)
C: Kannst du mir verraten, wer von den Doktoranden im Juni einen Vortrag gehalten hat? Ich habe gehört, dass sich damals nur der Martin bereit erklärt hat. ('Can you tell me who of the PhD students gave a talk in June? I heard that at that time only Martin agreed to do it.')

T: Im Juni hat der Rudi wahrscheinlich auch einen Vortrag
in June aux_p the Rudi probably also a talk
gehalten.
given

(29) *association with the adverbial in the prefield* (condition ADV-subj)

C: Kannst du mir verraten, wann der Rudi in diesem Semester Vorträge gehalten hat? Ich weiß nur von dem Termin im Mai. ('Can you tell me when Rudi gave talks in this term? I only know of the one in May.')

T: Im Juni hat der Rudi wahrscheinlich auch einen Vortrag
in June aux_p the Rudi probably also a talk
gehalten.
given

(30) *association with the adverbial in the middlefield* (condition subj-ADV)

C: Kannst du mir verraten, wann der Rudi in diesem Semester Vorträge gehalten hat? Ich weiß nur von dem Termin im Mai. ('Can you tell me when Rudi gave talks in this term? I only know of the one in May.')

T: Der Rudi hat im Juni wahrscheinlich auch einen Vortrag
the Rudi aux_p in June probably also a talk
gehalten.
given

The 20 critical items (five lexicalizations in four experimental conditions) were supplemented by 20 filler items belonging to two different types. For the first type, the fillers of Experiment 1, exemplified in (18) and (19) above, were used again. Definite articles were inserted before the proper names serving as subjects to make the fillers more similar to the critical items. Examples of the second type of fillers are given in (31) and (32). Here, the negated target sentences were not disambiguated by the preceding context, but only by the part of the sentence beginning with *aber/sondern* ('but'). The difference between the two variants, which required distinct prosodic realizations, lay in the domain of negation: while *nicht* ('not') negates the subject *der Helmut* in (31), it negates the directional adverbial *ins Museum* ('to the museum') in (32). Additional items of all types were constructed for use as practice items.

(31) C: Der Helmut ist am Dienstag ins Museum gegangen, oder? ('Helmut went to the museum on Tuesday, didn't he?')

T: Der Helmut ist am Dienstag nicht ins Museum gegangen,
the Helmut aux_p on Tuesday not to_the museum gone
aber die Gabi.
but the Gabi

(32) C: Der Helmut ist am Dienstag ins Museum gegangen, oder? ('Helmut went to the museum on Tuesday, didn't he?')

T:	Der	Helmut	ist	am	Dienstag	nicht	ins	Museum gegangen,
	the	Helmut	*aux*$_p$	on	Tuesday	not	to_the	museum gone
	sondern	ins	Theater.					
	but	to_the	theater					

Procedure. The experimental procedure was essentially the same as in Experiment 1. Recordings took place in a sound-proof booth at the Max Planck Institute for Human Cognitive and Brain Sciences, Leipzig. The speakers had to read through a visually presented context – target item combination silently, listen to the auditory presentation of the context (which had been recorded with a professional speaker), and produce the target sentence. Repeated productions (with the context replayed each time) were allowed when the speakers believed their utterances to be unnatural or inappropriate. In case of repetitions, only the last production was considered in the analysis. The target utterances were digitally recorded using a DAT recorder with a sampling rate of 44.1 kHz (16 bit).

As opposed to Experiment 1, the 20 critical items were interspersed with the 20 filler items described above. The resulting set of 40 items was pseudo-randomized for each participant using CMix.[16] A short practice session consisting of five items served to familiarize the speakers with the task. In the course of the actual experiment, the participants were allowed to take several short breaks. Some of the items were repeated at the end, as they had been produced with pauses, hesitations, or slips of the tongue that were not noticed by the speakers themselves. These additional trials took place after another short break, during which the respective items were, like the earlier set, pseudo-randomized and interspersed with fillers. The total duration of the experiment was about 45 minutes. Afterwards, the participants were asked to describe what they thought to be the purpose of the experiment to make sure that the randomization was successful in disguising the research intention.

6.4.3 Data analysis

Data selection. The utterances of one speaker were excluded from the analysis because the questioning at the end of the experiment revealed that the critical sentences containing stressed *auch* had attracted her attention. Although she could not discover the precise question investigated in the experiment, the speaker suspected the *auch*-sentences to be the object of research, which is why she could not be considered an unbiased participant. The utterances of the remaining six

16. The relevant randomization parameters required that two items of one lexicalization were separated by at least four other items and that two items of the same experimental condition were separated by at least one other item.

speakers were extracted using CoolEdit and superficially inspected. Of these 120 utterances, 13 had to be excluded for various reasons: In seven cases, the unstressed variant of *auch* was produced.[17] The characteristics of four utterances suggested that the utterance planning was not successful. Clearly, the speakers changed their prosodic strategy in the middle of the utterance, which resulted in an unnatural and inappropriate production. Two more utterances had to be excluded because of a defective recording and a long hesitation of the speaker, respectively. Altogether, 107 utterances could be included in the analysis.

Annotation and measurements. In a first step, syllable boundaries and the onsets of the stressed vowels were annotated for the two potential ACs in each utterance using information from waveforms and spectrograms. On the basis of this temporal annotation, the three groups of dependent variables (f_0-variables, duration variables, alignment variables) were determined. To facilitate a qualitative intonational analysis, we also annotated the accents on the potential ACs as well as on the focus particle in all utterances on the basis of the slightly modified version of the GToBI-system introduced in Section 2.4.

For the extraction of f_0, Praat's autocorrelation algorithm was used (time step setting: 1ms). After manually correcting artifacts (f_0-halving or -doubling), we linearly interpolated missing values and smoothed the f_0-tracks with a bandwidth of 10 Hz. For the calculation of mean contours, f_0 was measured at each quarter of a syllable on the two potential ACs and the finite auxiliary intervening between them and at 13 points in the rest of the utterance, the total number of measuring points thus being 41. As in Experiment 1, all measured f_0 values were transformed into the ERB-scale (cf. Section 6.3.2.2 above).

The f_0-contours of each speaker in each condition were checked for consistency by visual inspection. Although the items had been presented in a pseudo-randomized order, we found extremely consistent contours within the individual conditions for all speakers. To illustrate this, the five contours of Speaker 1 in condition subj-ADV are given in Figure 6.19. In the next step, we computed mean contours for the individual speakers in all conditions by averaging time and f_0-values at each of the 41 measuring points. These mean contours were checked for consistency within each experimental condition. Leaving aside differences in f_0-register, the contours of the six speakers were very similar and consistent within all conditions. Again, the contours of condition subj-ADV are given for illustration; cf. Figure 6.20. Lastly, we computed a mean contour for each experimental

17. These utterances were characterized by a single accented element – the AC of *auch* – which preceded the focus particle and carried the nuclear accent H*L. As described in Chapter 4, utterances of this type belong to a different usage pattern of focus particles. However, as answers to the context questions used in the experiment, they were not entirely adequate.

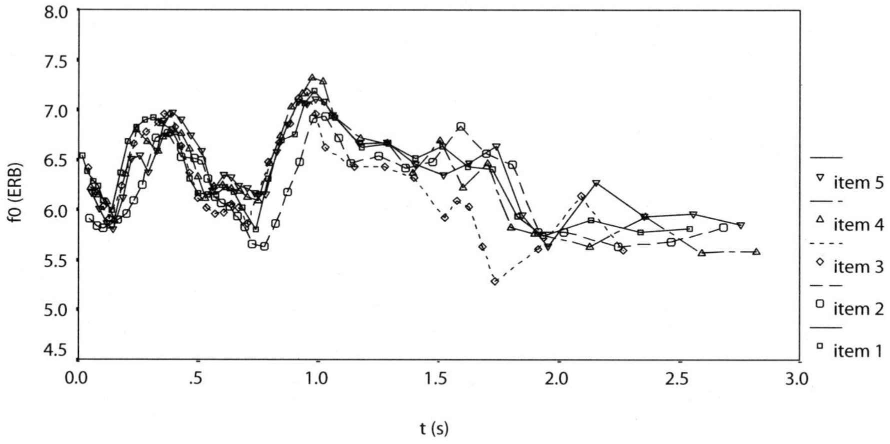

Figure 6.19 Experiment 3 – f_0-contours of Speaker 1 in condition subj-ADV

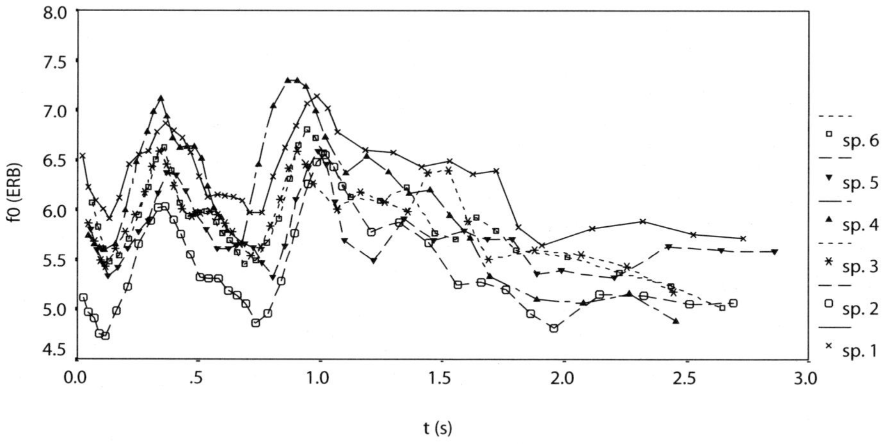

Figure 6.20 Experiment 3 – mean f_0-contours of all speakers in condition subj-ADV

condition by averaging the time and f_0-values of the utterances of all speakers. These contours will be discussed in Section 6.4.4.

In almost all utterances, both potential ACs (the subject and the temporal adverbial) showed a positive f_0-excursion. For the statistical comparisons, the following dependent f_0-variables were determined for both relevant constituents in all utterances: *f_0-min* – the f_0-value of the local minimum preceding the rise; *f_0-max* – the f_0-value of the local maximum representing the endpoint of the rise; and *df_0* – the size of the f_0-excursion, i.e., the difference between *f_0-max* and *f_0-min*. In one case, a potential AC showed an f_0-fall instead of a rise. For this constituent, *df_0*

Table 6.12 Experiment 3 – dependent variables determined for both potential ACs in all utterances

variable type	variable	unit	description
f_0-variables	f_0*-min*	ERB	f_0 of local minimum
	f_0*-max*	ERB	f_0 of local maximum
	df_0	ERB	size of f_0-excursion
duration variables	*dur-*s_1	ms	duration of 1st syllable
	dur-s_2	ms	duration of 2nd syllable
	dur-s_3	ms	duration of 3rd syllable
	dur-s_{23}	ms	duration of 2nd and 3rd syllable
	dur-s_{123}	ms	duration of whole constituent
alignment variables	*al-min*	ms	alignment of local minimum
	al-max	ms	alignment of local maximum

was calculated by subtracting f_0*-max* from f_0*-min*, resulting in a negative value for the f_0-excursion.

With regard to the duration parameter, several dependent variables were determined in order to be able to compare different domains with respect to their durational properties. First, the variables *dur-*s_1, *dur-*s_2, and *dur-*s_3 (the duration of the first, second, and third syllable of the potential ACs, respectively) were automatically extracted from the temporal annotation. Second, *dur-*s_{23} (the duration of the noun or proper name of the potential ACs, i.e., the duration of the constituent without the preposition or definite article) was determined by calculating the sum of *dur-*s_2 and *dur-*s_3, and *dur-*s_{123} (the duration of the whole constituent) was calculated by adding up the durations of all three syllables.

Two alignment variables were determined: *al-min* (the alignment of the f_0-minimum) and *al-max* (the alignment of the f_0-maximum). For both alignment variables, the onset of the stressed vowel (second syllable) served as the segmental reference point. As most of the f_0-minima were located in the first syllable of the potential ACs, the values of *al-min* were mostly negative. The values of *al-max*, on the other hand, were exclusively positive, as the f_0-peaks followed the onset of the stressed vowel in all cases. The dependent variables examined in Experiment 3 are summarized in Table 6.12.

6.4.4 Qualitative results

An inspection of the accents on the focus particle itself revealed that in almost all cases, the falling nuclear accent H*L was realized. Only two of the 107 utterances showed an HL* accent on *auch*. The part of the f_0-contour following the accent on the particle remained rather flat.

Table 6.13 Experiment 3 – accents on associated prefield and middlefield constituents

accent	frequency					
	prefield		middlefield		total	
L*H	46	83.6%	41	78.8%	87	81.3%
LH*	9	16.4%	10	19.2%	19	17.8%
H*	–	0%	1	1.9%	1	0.9%
total	55	100%	52	100%	107	100%

Table 6.14 Experiment 3 – accents on non-associated prefield and middlefield constituents

accent	frequency					
	prefield		middlefield		total	
L*H	24	46.2%	8	14.5%	32	29.9%
LH*	17	32.7%	4	7.3%	21	19.6%
H*	1	1.9%	4	7.3%	5	4.7%
unacc.	10	19.2%	39	70.9%	49	45.8%
total	52	100%	55	100%	107	100%

The accent distribution on the ACs is displayed in Table 6.13. Constituents associated with stressed *auch* were always accented by the speakers in the production experiment. With the exception of one case, they carried rising pitch accents (L*H or LH*), L*H being by far the most frequent. The positioning of the AC in the prefield or middlefield did not have any influence on the accent realization: ACs in both positions showed approximately the same distribution.

The non-associated constituents showed a less uniform picture with clear differences between prefield and middlefield; cf. Table 6.14. Non-associated prefield elements were accented in more than 80% of the cases, L*H and LH* being the most frequent accents realized. In the remaining fifth of the utterances, the non-associated constituent was unaccented. Of the non-associated elements located in the middlefield, on the other hand, less than a third were accented. Here, three types of accents occurred: L*H, LH*, and H*.

Not only the accent distribution among associated and non-associated constituents, but also the resulting accent combinations within the utterances might be of interest. The frequencies of all observed patterns are listed in Tables 6.15 and 6.16 for prefield and middlefield association, respectively. As for the cases where *auch* was associated with the prefield element, combinations of a rising accent on the AC and no accent on the non-AC were most frequent, followed by a pattern with L*H accents on both relevant constituents. Most of the cases with middlefield association were characterized by an L*H accent on the AC, preceded by an L*H, LH*, or no accent on the non-associated prefield element. A combination of two L*H accents was the most frequent pattern.

Table 6.15 Experiment 3 – accent combinations in utterances with prefield association (conditions SUBJ-adv and ADV-subj)

accent		frequency	
assoc. pref.	n.-ass. middlef.		
L*H	–	30	54.5%
LH*	–	9	16.4%
L*H	L*H	8	14.5%
L*H	H*	4	7.3%
L*H	LH*	4	7.3%
total		55	100%

Table 6.16 Experiment 3 – accent combinations in utterances with middlefield association (conditions adv-SUBJ and subj-ADV)

accent		frequency	
n.-ass. pref.	assoc. middlef.		
L*H	L*H	19	36.5%
LH*	L*H	14	26.9%
–	L*H	7	13.5%
L*H	LH*	4	7.7%
–	LH*	3	5.8%
LH*	LH*	3	5.8%
H*	L*H	1	1.9%
L*H	H*	1	1.9%
total		52	100%

To facilitate a consistent labeling, the distinction between L*H and LH* accents in the qualitative analysis was again based on the position of the f_0-peak. If it lay within the stressed syllable, we annotated LH*, while if it was only reached in the post-stressed syllable, L*H was chosen. However, the accentual status of the constituents did not affect the overall contour shape. The consistency check reported in Section 6.4.3 revealed that the f_0-contours were highly similar within the individual experimental conditions, independently of the actual accent labels assigned to the potential ACs. It was this high consistency that we took as justification for computing a mean contour for each condition. These contours are given in Figures 6.21 and 6.22: Figure 6.21 displays the mean contours for the conditions with the AC being located in the prefield, i.e., SUBJ-adv and ADV-subj, while Figure 6.22 shows the contours of the conditions with middlefield association, i.e., adv-SUBJ and subj-ADV.

While the mean contours of conditions with the same association position were almost identical, there were obvious differences between the conditions with prefield and middlefield association. Most clearly, the contours differed in the area

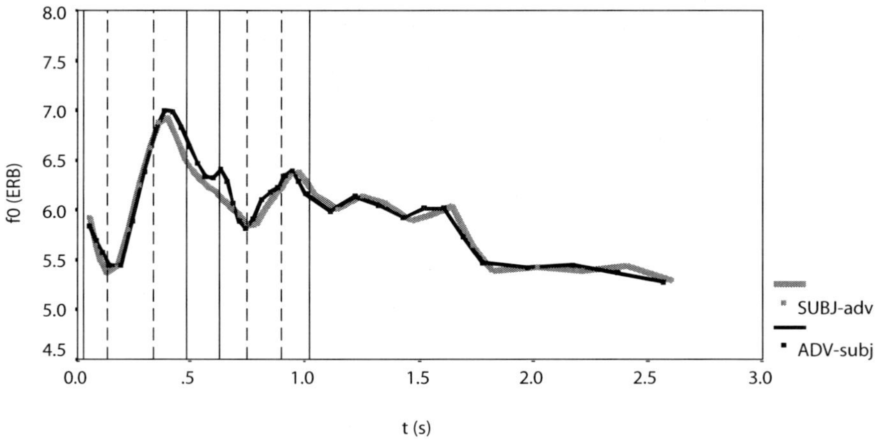

Figure 6.21 Experiment 3 – mean f_0-contours of conditions SUBJ-adv and ADV-subj (all speakers); continuous vertical lines indicate constituent boundaries; dotted vertical lines indicate syllable boundaries within constituents

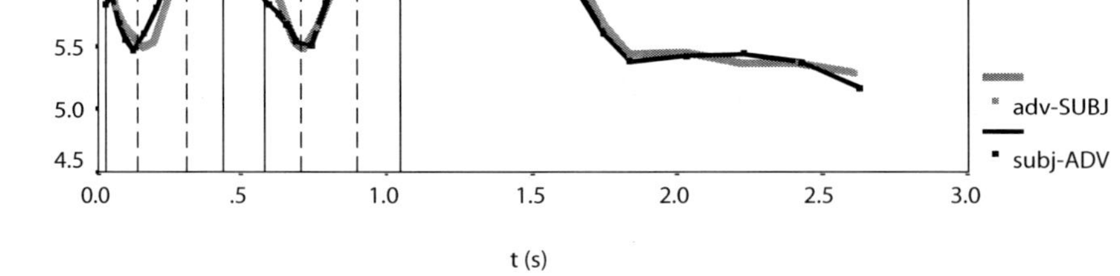

Figure 6.22 Experiment 3 – mean f_0-contours of conditions subj-ADV and adv-SUBJ (all speakers); continuous vertical lines indicate constituent boundaries; dotted vertical lines indicate syllable boundaries within constituents

of the non-associated constituents: non-ACs located in the prefield showed a much greater f_0-excursion than non-ACs in the middlefield. This reflects the results from the accent annotation; cf. Table 6.14 above. Non-ACs in the middlefield were unaccented more frequently than non-ACs in the prefield. The part of the f_0-contour following the second potential AC was similar for all four experimental conditions.

6.4.5 Quantitative results

6.4.5.1 *Comparison of associated and non-associated constituents between lexically identical utterances*

With respect to the dependent variables given in Table 6.12 above, comparisons were made between associated and non-associated, but lexically identical, constituents in identical positions. These comparisons were based on minimal pairs of utterances, the two utterances of each pair differing only in the discourse context used in the production task. Only 96 of the 107 utterances could be included in the analysis, the reason being that in case one utterance of a minimal pair was discarded (cf. Section 6.4.3), the other had to be excluded as well. This left us 48 minimal pairs for analysis.

The mean contours as well as the means of the individual dependent variables suggested that the prosodic realization of the utterances was independent of the syntactic function (subject vs. temporal adverbial) of the potential ACs: the conditions with identical association positions were characterized by similar prosodic properties. For this reason, the data was pooled for the quantitative analysis, i.e., no difference was made between subjects and adverbials in the statistical comparisons. However, separate comparisons were made for prefield and middlefield constituents, as the qualitative analysis had revealed clear differences between the two association positions. As in Experiment 1, we used the statistical method of paired t-tests. The overall results are given in Table 6.17, the significance tests being based on an adjusted α-level of .0042 (Bonferroni adjustment, 12 t-tests).

With respect to the f_0-variables, the results of Experiment 1 could be replicated and extended. Constituents associated with stressed *auch* showed a significantly lower f_0-minimum preceding the rise and a significantly higher f_0-maximum representing the endpoint of the rise than their counterparts in lexically identical utterances. The combination of both factors resulted in a significantly greater f_0-excursion for ACs. This is illustrated in Figure 6.23.

As for duration, we expected ACs of stressed *auch* to be longer than their counterparts not associated with the particle. However, it was not clear from the outset what the domain of the hypothesized lengthening under association would be. In the literature, different statements can be found. On the one hand, there is good evidence (i) that the domain of accentual lengthening is larger than the stressed vowel (cf. Crystal & House 1988; Turk & Sawusch 1997 and references therein; Turk & White 1999; Braun 2005; the investigated languages being English and German) and (ii) that the domain is of a linguistic nature instead of corresponding, e.g., to a fixed extent of time (cf. Turk & Sawusch 1997; Turk & White 1999). The results of the studies referred to suggest that accentual lengthening applies

Table 6.17 Experiment 3 – f_0-, duration, and alignment variables compared between utterances; separate comparisons for prefield elements (conditions SUBJ-adv, ADV-subj vs. conditions subj-ADV, adv-SUBJ) and middlefield elements (adv-SUBJ, subj-ADV vs. ADV-subj, SUBJ-adv); quantitative results and paired t-tests (one-tailed), N = 48, α = .0042 (Bonferroni adjustment, 12 t-tests)

variable	position	assoc.	non-ass.	sign.?	T	p
f_0-*min* (ERB)	prefield	5.30	5.42	✓	3.38	<.001
	middlefield	5.42	5.74	✓	–8.47	<.001
f_0-*max* (ERB)	prefield	7.13	6.75	✓	–5.67	<.001
	middlefield	6.93	6.44	✓	7.63	<.001
df_0 (ERB)	prefield	1.83	1.33	✓	–6.77	<.001
	middlefield	1.51	0.70	✓	13.10	<.001
dur-s_{23} (ms)	prefield	346	300	✓	–5.24	<.001
	middlefield	340	281	✓	9.10	<.001
al-min (ms)	prefield	–47	–41	n.s.	0.95	.345
	middlefield	–48	–44	n.s.	–0.58	.562
al-max (ms)	prefield	193	173	✓	–2.95	<.003
	middlefield	185	139	✓	5.11	<.001

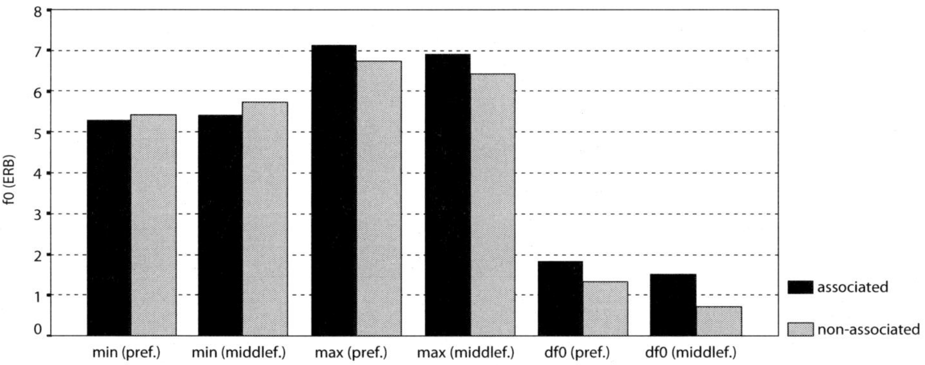

Figure 6.23 Experiment 3 – f_0-variables compared between utterances; separate comparisons for prefield elements (conditions SUBJ-adv, ADV-subj vs. conditions subj-ADV, adv-SUBJ) and middlefield elements (adv-SUBJ, subj-ADV vs. ADV-subj, SUBJ-adv); N = 48

to a linguistic unit that has at least the size of a syllable.[18] On the other hand, it is less clear how far durational effects of accentuation may extend. Sluijter & van Heuven (1995) consider the domain of lengthening in Dutch to be the word, as

18. Here, 'linguistic unit' refers to the Prosodic Hierarchy as defined by Nespor & Vogel (1986) and Hayes (1989), among others.

in their data, word-initial and word-final unstressed syllables are also lengthened. Because Turk & Sawusch (1997) do not find any effect on word-initial unstressed syllables in English, the authors conclude "that the domain of accentual lengthening is a unit which begins with a pitch accented syllable and includes at least one syllable to its right within a word" (Turk & Sawusch 1997:36). This conclusion is slightly modified by Turk & White (1999), who assume pitch accents (to the left) and word boundaries (in both directions) only to result in an attenuation of lengthening effects, but not in their complete blocking. In addition to relatively strong rightward effects, the authors find small leftward effects within a word. Still, there is no evidence for leftward effects of accentual lengthening across word boundaries.

To determine the domain of lengthening in our data, we analyzed the durations of all three syllables of the relevant constituents independently. In addition, the duration of the whole constituent and the duration of the constituent minus the first syllable (corresponding to the article or preposition) were analyzed. The results are given in Table 6.18 (10 paired t-tests; Bonferroni adjustment: $\alpha = .005$). The table shows that all examined units were longer in ACs than in their non-associated counterparts. The differences were significant for all variables except *dur-s*$_1$ (the duration of the first syllable), suggesting that the domain of lengthening was the content word of the constituents (the stressed syllable and the following unstressed syllable) in our data. This is consistent with the results of Sluijter & van Heuven (1995), Turk & Sawusch (1997), and Turk & White (1999) discussed above. As both the second and third syllable of the potential ACs showed a

Table 6.18 Experiment 3 – duration variables compared between utterances; separate comparisons for prefield elements (conditions SUBJ-adv, ADV-subj vs. conditions subj-ADV, adv-SUBJ) and middlefield elements (adv-SUBJ, subj-ADV vs. ADV-subj, SUBJ-adv); quantitative results and paired t-tests (one-tailed), $N = 48$, $\alpha = .005$ (Bonferroni adjustment, 10 t-tests)

variable	position	assoc.	non-ass.	sign.?	T	p
dur-s$_1$ (ms)	prefield	107	106	n.s.	–0.20	.846
	middlefield	119	117	n.s.	0.44	.659
dur-s$_2$ (ms)	prefield	195	171	✓	–4.16	<.001
	middlefield	192	153	✓	8.08	<.001
dur-s$_3$ (ms)	prefield	151	129	✓	–5.08	<.001
	middlefield	147	128	✓	5.07	<.001
dur-s$_{23}$ (ms)	prefield	346	300	✓	–5.24	<.001
	middlefield	340	281	✓	9.10	<.001
dur-s$_{123}$ (ms)	prefield	453	406	✓	–4.77	<.001
	middlefield	459	398	✓	7.34	<.001

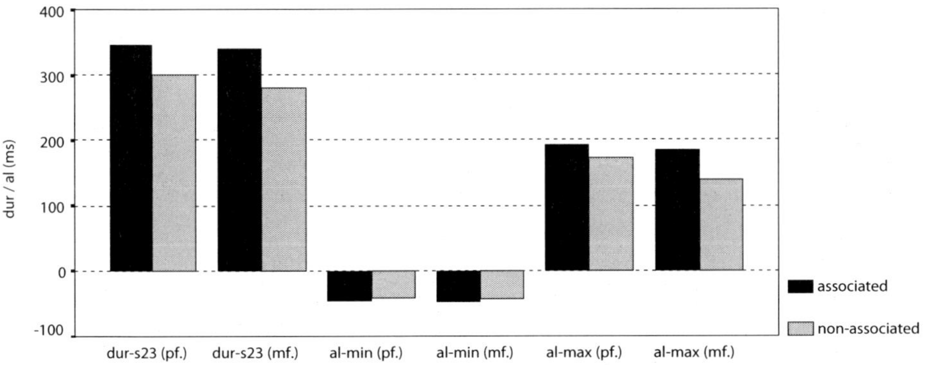

Figure 6.24 Experiment 3 – duration and alignment variables compared between utterances; separate comparisons for prefield elements (conditions SUBJ-adv, ADV-subj vs. conditions subj-ADV, adv-SUBJ) and middlefield elements (adv-SUBJ, subj-ADV vs. ADV-subj, SUBJ-adv); N = 48

significant lengthening effect under association with *auch*, the variable *dur-*s_{23} was used for the overall statistics (cf. Table 6.17) and the subsequent comparisons to be reported below.

With respect to the alignment variables, the comparison between utterances yielded the following results: The alignment of the local f_0-minimum preceding the rise did not differ significantly between associated and non-associated constituents. The f_0-peak, on the other hand, was aligned significantly later in ACs compared to their non-associated counterparts. The results of the comparisons concerning the duration and alignment variables are illustrated in Figure 6.24.

To sum up the statistical comparisons between utterances, constituents associated with stressed *auch* had a significantly lower f_0-minimum, higher f_0-maximum, greater f_0-rise, longer duration, and later peak alignment than the respective non-associated elements in lexically identical utterances.

6.4.5.2 *Comparison of associated and non-associated constituents within utterances*

In the next step, the two potential ACs were compared within each utterance. Naturally, the compared elements were not lexically identical; however, as described in Section 6.4.2 above, effects caused by the lexical material were minimized by matching the phonetic properties of the relevant constituents as much as possible. A sufficient standardization could not be achieved for the pre-stressed syllable (corresponding to prepositions in the case of the temporal adverbials and to definite articles in the case of the subject constituents). As the local f_0-minimum was located in this syllable in most cases, the variables f_0*-min* and *al-min* were

Table 6.19 Experiment 3 – f_0-, duration, and alignment variables compared between associated and non-associated constituents in utterances with the AC in the prefield (conditions SUBJ-adv and ADV-subj); quantitative results and paired t-tests (one-tailed), N = 55, α = .0063 (Bonferroni adjustment, 8 t-tests)

variable	association/position		sign.?	T	p
	assoc. pref.	n.-ass. middlef.			
f_0-*max* (ERB)	7.19	6.45	✓	9.52	<.001
df_0 (ERB)	1.92	0.70	✓	14.01	<.001
dur-s_{23} (ms)	352	277	✓	8.80	<.001
al-max (ms)	196	137	✓	6.49	<.001

Table 6.20 Experiment 3 – f_0-, duration, and alignment variables compared between associated and non-associated constituents in utterances with the AC in the middlefield (conditions subj-ADV and adv-SUBJ); quantitative results and paired t-tests (one-tailed), N = 52, α = .0063 (Bonferroni adjustment, 8 t-tests)

variable	association/position		sign.?	T	p
	n.-assoc. pref.	assoc. middlef.			
f_0-*max* (ERB)	6.71	6.91	✓	–3.65	<.001
df_0 (ERB)	1.33	1.52	✓	–2.95	<.003
dur-s_{23} (ms)	300	343	✓	–4.96	<.001
al-max (ms)	173	185	n.s.	–1.70	.049

not compared within utterances, thus leaving f_0-*max*, df_0, *dur*-s_{23}, and *al-max* for analysis.[19]

All 107 utterances could be used for the comparison within utterances. As the observed intonational patterns for prefield association (associated prefield constituent; non-associated middlefield constituent) and middlefield association (non-associated prefield constituent; associated middlefield constituent) differed considerably (cf. Figures 6.21 and 6.22 above), independent comparisons were made for the two association positions. The results of the paired t-tests are shown in Table 6.19 and Table 6.20 for prefield and middlefield association, respectively (8 paired t-tests, Bonferroni adjustment: α = .0063).

The comparison of the f_0-variables (f_0-*max* and df_0) within utterances complemented the comparison between utterances: constituents associated with stressed *auch* were characterized by a significantly higher f_0-maximum and greater f_0-rise

19. We are aware that, strictly speaking, df_0 should also have been excluded from the comparison within utterances, as it partly depended on f_0-*min*. However, as the observed differences could not have been caused by the intrinsic f_0 of the vowel in the first syllable alone, we nevertheless included this variable.

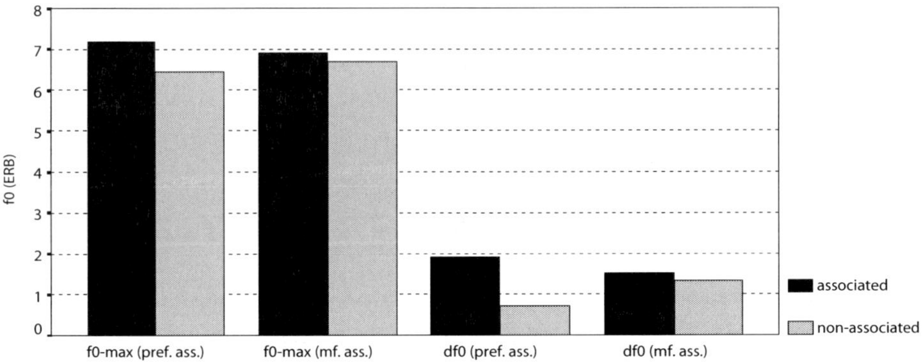

Figure 6.25 Experiment 3 – f_0-variables compared between associated and non-associated constituents within utterances; separate comparisons for utterances with prefield association (conditions SUBJ-adv and ADV-subj, N = 55) and utterances with middlefield association (conditions subj-ADV and adv-SUBJ, N = 52)

than other potentially associated elements in the same utterance. The results also confirmed what was suggested by the mean contours given in Figures 6.21 and 6.22 above: the difference between associated and non-associated constituents was more pronounced when the AC was located in the prefield. However, although the effect was smaller for middlefield association, it was still significant. The comparison of the f_0-variables is visualized in Figure 6.25.

The comparison of the duration and alignment variables revealed a similar picture. ACs of *auch* showed a longer duration and a later peak alignment than their non-associated counterparts in the same utterance. The differences were significant in all cases but one: although the mean values for peak alignment under middlefield association also diverged in the expected direction, the effect was not significant at the adjusted α-level of .0063. The overall picture, shown in Figure 6.26, resembled that of the f_0-variables: the differences in prosodic marking between AC and non-AC were greater under prefield association than under middlefield association.

6.4.5.3 *Comparison between prefield association and middlefield association*

The differences between associated and non-associated constituents with respect to f_0-*max*, df_0, *dur*-s_{23}, and *al-max* were also compared between cases with prefield association and cases with middlefield association. The goal was to show that there were indeed statistically significant differences in the clearness of the prosodic marking between the two order variants, as suggested by Figures 6.21 and 6.22 as well as by the results of the comparisons within utterances. For the reason given above, the variables f_0-*min* and *al-min* were not taken into account.

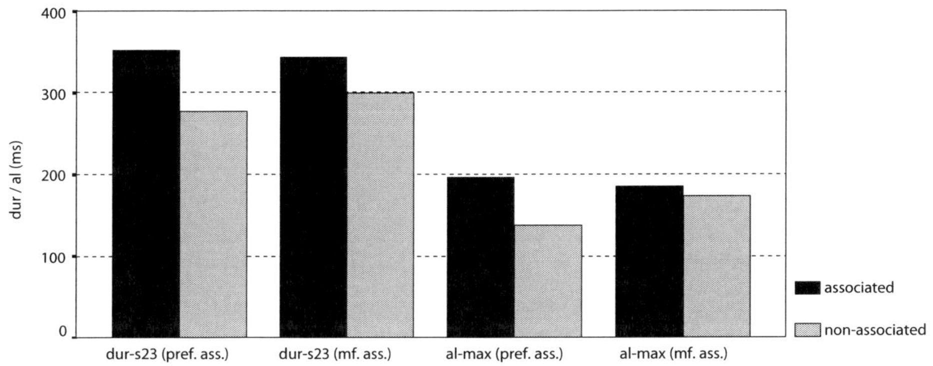

Figure 6.26 Experiment 3 – duration and alignment variables compared between associated and non-associated constituents within utterances; separate comparisons for utterances with prefield association (conditions SUBJ-adv and ADV-subj, N = 55) and utterances with middlefield association (conditions subj-ADV and adv-SUBJ, N = 52)

Four derived variables were determined for each utterance by subtracting the relevant value of the non-associated element from the value of the respective AC; cf. (33). The resulting variables thus represented the clearness of the prosodic marking expressed by the individual parameters. The calculation of these derived variables was based on differences between the values of associated and non-associated constituents instead of ratios between the values; the reason for this was that two of the four variables (*df*$_0$ and *al-max*) are not compatible with measurements on a ratio scale, as they do not have a meaningful zero value.

(33) *diff-f*$_0$*-max* = *f*$_0$*-max*(associated) – *f*$_0$*-max*(non-associated)
diff-df$_0$ = *df*$_0$(associated) – *df*$_0$(non-associated)
diff-dur-s$_{23}$ = *dur-s*$_{23}$(associated) – *dur-s*$_{23}$(non-associated)
diff-al-max = *al-max*(associated) – *al-max*(non-associated)

The values of each derived variable were compared between cases with prefield association (conditions ADV-subj and SUBJ-adv) and cases with middlefield association (conditions adv-SUBJ and subj-ADV) by means of t-tests for unrelated measures. The α-level was adjusted to .013 (Bonferroni adjustment, 4 t-tests). The results of the comparisons are given in Table 6.21. They confirmed our expectations: the differences between associated and non-associated elements were significantly greater if the AC was located in the prefield. This was true for all four examined prosodic parameters. In Figure 6.27, the results of the comparison between prefield and middlefield association are illustrated graphically.

Table 6.21 Experiment 3 – differences between associated and non-associated constituents with respect to *f_0-max*, *df_0*, *dur-s_{23}*, and *al-max*, compared between utterances with prefield association (conditions SUBJ-adv and ADV-subj) and utterances with middlefield association (conditions subj-ADV and adv-SUBJ); quantitative results and t-tests (two-tailed), $N_1 = 55$, $N_2 = 52$, $\alpha = .013$ (Bonferroni adjustment, 4 t-tests)

variable	association position		sign.?	T	df	p
	prefield ass.	middlef. ass.				
diff-f_0-max (ERB)	0.74	0.20	✓	5.79	94.62	<.001
diff-df_0 (ERB)	1.22	0.19	✓	9.46	99	<.001
diff-dur-s_{23} (ms)	75	42	✓	2.69	105	<.009
diff-al-max (ms)	59	12	✓	4.18	98.82	<.001

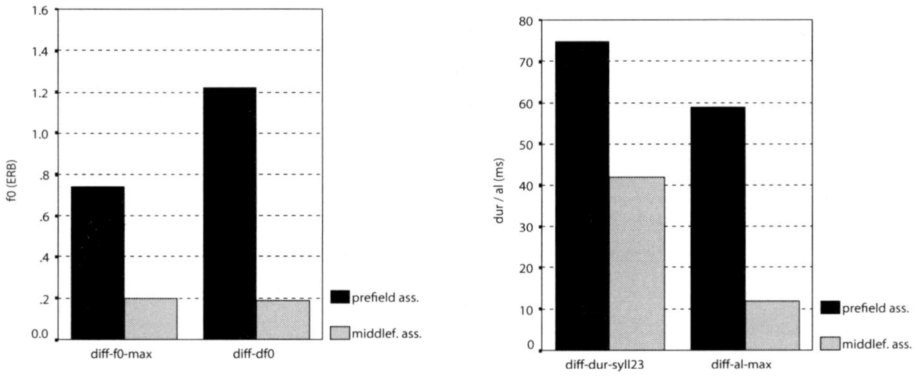

Figure 6.27 Experiment 3 – differences between associated and non-associated constituents with respect to *f_0-max*, *df_0* (left panel) and *dur-s_{23}*, *al-max* (right panel), compared between utterances with prefield association (conditions SUBJ-adv and ADV-subj, N = 55) and utterances with middlefield association (conditions subj-ADV and adv-SUBJ, N = 52)

6.4.5.4 *Summary*

In our data, constituents associated with the stressed variant of the focus particle *auch* were characterized by a lower f_0-minimum and a higher f_0-maximum, resulting in a greater f_0-rise, as well as a longer duration of the stressed and post-stressed syllable and a later peak alignment than corresponding non-associated elements in lexically identical utterances. Furthermore, significant differences with respect to f_0-peak and -rise, duration, and peak alignment (the last-named only in cases with prefield association) could also be observed between the two potential ACs of *auch* within one utterance. It was shown that the differences between associated and non-associated elements were greater when the AC was located in the prefield, but far more subtle when it followed the finite verb.

6.4.6 Discussion

Experiment 3 essentially replicated the qualitative results of the pilot study (Experiment 1). Speakers marked constituents associated with stressed *auch* in an extremely consistent way by rising pitch accents. Occurring in more than 80% of the cases, L*H was by far the most frequent accent type realized. Together with the falling nuclear accent H*L observed on the focus particle itself, this indicates the significance of the bridge contour intonation for the constructions examined.

Nevertheless, the results showed that there was no one-to-one correspondence between a constituent's status of being associated with stressed *auch* and a certain pitch accent type, thus confirming the outcome of the corpus study presented in Section 6.2. On the one hand, the ACs were not characterized by a specific pitch accent. In addition to L*H, at least one other accent – namely, LH* – served to mark ACs in a relevant proportion of the utterances. On the other hand, the picture was complicated by additional accents on non-associated elements. In more than half of the utterances, non-ACs were also marked by high or rising pitch accents, among which L*H was again the most frequent one. As noted above, non-ACs were much more likely to be accented when they were located in the prefield. In many cases, the AC and a non-associated element even carried the same accent. The pattern with an L*H accent on both the AC and the non-AC, for instance, occurred in 14.5% of the prefield association cases and 36.5% of the middlefield association cases, thus being characteristic of a large part of the data. It follows that the AC of *auch* often cannot be identified on the basis of the accent distribution alone.

This problem prompts the question of whether prosodic factors are involved in the marking of ACs that are not captured by the categorical distinctions of the GToBI-system. Overcoming the limitations on the prosodic analysis posed by the nature of the stimulus materials in Experiment 1, this question could now be addressed in much greater detail. The answer is positive: it was shown that several continuous prosodic parameters – at least f_0-minimum, -maximum, and -peak, duration and peak alignment – contribute to the marking of ACs. The observed differences between associated and non-associated elements (compared both between and within utterances) generally did not result in different accent categories. Nevertheless, we expect them to have a crucial impact on the interpretation of the utterances.

Another important outcome of Experiment 3 concerns the influence of the syntactic function and position of the AC on the prosodic realization. The former factor is irrelevant: subjects and temporal adverbials, which were carefully controlled with respect to their phonetic properties at the segmental level, showed almost identical contour shapes if position and association status were kept constant. AC-placement in the prefield vs. middlefield, on the other hand, proved to be of crucial impact on the way the AC is prosodically realized. Utterances with prefield association were characterized by clear prosodic differences in all four examined parameters (f_0-peak, f_0-rise, duration, and peak alignment) between associated and non-associated elements. For middlefield association, the differences were much smaller, but – with the exception of peak alignment – still significant. The finding that the prosodic marking of associated middlefield elements was only slightly stronger than the marking of the corresponding non-associated prefield constituents was not unexpected, given that f_0-excursions normally decline from left to right in the contour. Additional prenuclear pitch accents not related to focus marking could frequently be found in the prefield; in the middlefield, they were less frequent and characterized by smaller f_0-excursions. Therefore, an accent on a middlefield AC should be perceptually salient even if it is preceded by an accent of almost equal strength on the non-associated prefield element, thus facilitating a correct identification of the AC.[20]

The predictions with respect to the interpretation of the utterances under discussion were tested in two perception experiments (based on natural and manipulated stimulus materials; cf. Sections 6.5 and 6.6, respectively), which were similar in structure to Experiment 2 (cf. Section 6.3.3 above). As the parallel phonetic structure of the two potential ACs allowed their comparison within a given utterance, we were in a much better position to relate prosodic properties to interpretation than in Experiment 2. The clearness of the prosodic marking needed no longer be expressed in more or less arbitrary categories, but could be operationally defined on the basis of the differences in f_0-peak, f_0-rise, duration, and peak alignment between the two candidates.

6.5 Experiment 4: The perception of utterances containing stressed *auch* (natural speech data)

In Experiment 4, as in Experiment 2, the participants were auditorily presented with the utterances elicited in the production experiment and had to choose one of two possible continuations, the choice indicating which constituent they interpreted as being associated with *auch*. This time, the results of the perception task could be more directly related to the prosodic structure of the utterances, the relevant aspects of which were determined by comparing the potential ACs of each utterance with respect to f_0-peak, f_0-rise, duration, and peak alignment.

20. For the so-called *Gussenhoven-Rietveld effect* relevant in this context, see Gussenhoven & Rietveld (1988) and Ladd, Verhoeven & Jacobs (1994).

6.5.1 Hypotheses

The main question examined was to what extent hearers make use of prosodic information for identifying the AC of stressed *auch*. On the basis of the more fine-grained results of the production experiment, Hypothesis 2 (cf. (12) above) could be reformulated in two different ways, referring to the qualitative analysis in terms of the GToBI-annotation (Hypothesis 5) and to the quantitative phonetic analysis (Hypothesis 6).

(34) **Hypothesis 5:** The results of the perception task depend on the types of pitch accents realized on the two potential ACs: utterances with a 'contrastive' accent (L*H) on the AC and a 'non-contrastive' accent (LH* or H*) or no accent at all on the non-AC are matched properly with their original contexts, while utterances showing the reverse pattern are mismatched, and utterances with the same accent type realized on both potential ACs are matched and mismatched at random.

(35) **Hypothesis 6:** The percentage of correct responses for a given utterance in the perception task is positively correlated to the difference between AC and non-AC for each of the four prosodic variables f_0*-max*, df_0, $dur\text{-}s_{23}$, and *al-max* (e.g., the higher the difference in f_0-peak between AC and non-AC, the better the matching results for the respective utterance).

As it had not shown any significant differences in the production experiment, the variable *al-min* was not taken into consideration; f_0*-min* was not looked at as its effect on the marking was already captured by the interplay of f_0*-max* and df_0.

6.5.2 Method

Participants. 32 participants (aged 20 to 38, with a mean of 24.8; 18 females and 14 males), all of whom were native speakers of German and had no knowledge of the problem under examination, took part in the experiment. They received a financial reimbursement for their participation. None of them had participated in any of the other project experiments.

Materials. The original utterances of five speakers from Experiment 3 served as stimuli for Experiment 4. We excluded all utterances that had not been included in the qualitative analysis because of being defective or unacceptable (cf. Section 6.4.3 above). To keep the experiment to a reasonable length, we also excluded all utterances of Speaker 2 (the speaker with the smallest number of usable utterances). This left us 91 critical utterances for the perception experiment, which were supplemented by 69 filler utterances randomly selected from all six speakers.

Table 6.22 Experiment 4 – classification of the stimulus utterances with respect to their accent distribution

category	description	number of utterances	
		prefield ass.	**middlefield ass.**
A	AC accented (L*H or LH*), non-AC unaccented	35	7
B	both elements accented, AC bearing L*H, non-AC (L)H*	7	11
C	both elements accented, bearing the same accent (L*H or LH*)	7	20
D	both elements accented, AC bearing LH*, non-AC L*H	0	4
total		49	42

In preparation for the analysis, all critical utterances were evaluated with respect to the accent distribution and the prosodic variables examined in the quantitative comparisons within utterances. As for the accents on the two potential ACs, each utterance was assigned to one of four groups, the relevant criterion being the relation between the AC-accent and the accent on the non-associated element. Group A consisted of the utterances with an accented AC (bearing an L*H or LH* accent) and an unaccented non-AC. In group B, all utterances were included where both potential ACs were accented, and the actual AC carried a contrastive L*H accent, while the non-AC was marked by a non-contrastive (L)H* accent. Utterances characterized by the same accent (again, L*H or LH*) on both candidates for association were assigned to group C, and the remaining cases – utterances with a non-contrastive accent (LH*) on the AC and a contrastive accent (L*H) on the non-AC – to group D. Among the original utterances from the production experiment, there were no cases with an unaccented AC and an accented non-AC. An overview of the four categories and the number of utterances per category is given in Table 6.22.

We had already determined a measure for the clearness of the prosodic marking in a given utterance by calculating the differences between the associated and the non-associated element with respect to the phonetic variables f_0*-max*, df_0, *dur-*s_{23}, and *al-max* (cf. the comparison between prefield and middlefield association in Section 6.4.5.3 above). For each of the variables, the resulting values were transformed to a scale ranging from 0 (corresponding to the smallest difference between AC and non-AC) to 1 (corresponding to the biggest difference). The values between the extremes were mapped proportionally onto real numbers between 0 and 1. In this way, each utterance was characterized by four derived parameters (called *p-*f_0*-max*, *p-*df_0, *p-dur-*s_{23}, and *p-al-max*), which could be related to the percentage of correct responses in the perception experiment.

For each target utterance (critical as well as filler items), two possible continuations were constructed, either of them being compatible with only one of the two interpretations. As an illustration, the continuations for the target utterances in (27)–(30) are given in (36). For the second filler type (cf. (32) above), the continuations were identical to the last part of the target utterances (starting with *aber* or *sondern*), which was cut off the recorded utterances for their use in the perception experiment.

(36)	a.	...	und	nicht	nur	im	Mai.
		...	and	not	only	in	May
	b.	...	und	nicht	nur	der	Martin.
		...	and	not	only	the	Martin

Procedure. The procedure of Experiment 4 was almost identical to that of Experiment 2: the participants listened to a target utterance and had to select one of the two continuations, which were presented on a computer screen, their left-right order being randomized. From the participants' choices, it was reconstructed which element they interpreted as being associated with *auch*.

After familiarizing themselves with the task in a practice session consisting of five items, the participants worked through the full set of 160 items, which were pseudo-randomized and divided into four blocks of 40 items each. The participants were allowed to listen to the utterances as many times as they liked, and they were encouraged to take short breaks between the blocks; the entire experiment took about 30 minutes.

6.5.3 Results and discussion

For each critical utterance, the correct and incorrect responses (i.e., responses corresponding to and conflicting with the original context) were counted. Of the total of 2912 responses, 72.4% were correct and 27.6% incorrect. The percentage of matching answers differed significantly between cases with prefield association and cases with middlefield association: ACs positioned in the prefield were correctly identified in 84.5% of the cases, while utterances with middlefield ACs got only 58.3% correct responses (χ^2-test: $\chi^2 = 258.16$, df $= 1$, $p < .001$). However, this does not mean that there is a strong general preference for prefield association. As the original utterances from the perception experiment served as stimuli, the prosodic properties of the materials could not be balanced at all. This problem could be overcome by using manipulated stimulus materials in Experiment 5 (cf. Section 6.6). On the other hand, the percentage of correct responses did not depend on the syntactic function of the AC: subject ACs were correctly identified in

Table 6.23 Experiment 4 – percentage of correct responses, compared across categories of utterances

category	description	% correct responses	
		prefield ass.	middlefield ass.
A	AC accented (L*H or LH*), non-AC unaccented	87.4%	71.0%
B	both elements accented, AC bearing L*H, non-AC (L)H*	78.6%	56.8%
C	both elements accented, bearing the same accent (L*H or LH*)	75.9%	53.1%
D	both elements accented, AC bearing LH*, non-AC L*H	–	66.4%

72.9% and adverbial ACs in 72.0% of the cases. This difference is not significant (χ^2-test: $\chi^2 = 0.30$, df = 1, p = .582).

The percentage of correct responses was determined for each of the four categories of utterances formed on the basis of the accent distribution. We expected different proportions of matching answers across the four groups (cf. Hypothesis 5): Utterances of group A should be assigned the intended interpretation most frequently. The results for group B should be worse, but still better than those for the utterances of group C, which should be matched and mismatched at random. Group D was expected to receive the worst matching results (even less accurately than if matches were made at random).

The results are given in Table 6.23. Again, cases with prefield and middlefield association were treated separately. For both association positions, the percentage of correct responses differed significantly between the categories of utterances (χ^2-tests; prefield association: $\chi^2 = 25.93$, df = 2, p < .001; middlefield association: $\chi^2 = 25.65$, df = 3, p < .001). As expected, utterances of group A (accented AC, unaccented non-AC) were assigned the intended interpretation more frequently than utterances of the other groups. However, our expectations were not confirmed within the categories of utterances with an accent on both potential ACs. As for prefield association, the results for group C (same accent on both elements) were clearly better than if they had been selected at random. As for middlefield association, on the other hand, there was not even a decrease in the percentage of correct responses from group B to group D: groups B and C had random results, while the utterances of group D were interpreted correctly in almost two-thirds of the cases. Hence, the difference between L*H and (L)H* accents was not a decisive factor for resolving the ambiguity in the interpretation process. More generally, the accent distribution in terms of GToBI was not able to explain the participants' interpretational choices.

Table 6.24 Experiment 4 – correlation between the percentage of correct responses and *p-f_0-max*, *p-df_0*, *p-dur-s_{23}*, and *p-al-max* for utterances with prefield association (conditions SUBJ-adv and ADV-subj, N = 49) and utterances with middlefield association (conditions adv-SUBJ and subj-ADV, N = 42)

parameter	prefield association			middlef. association		
	r	sign.?	p	r	sign.?	p
p-f_0-max	.502	✓	< .001	.525	✓	< .001
p-df_0	.626	✓	< .001	.385	✓	< .007
p-dur-s_{23}	.253	✓	< .001	.387	✓	< .007
p-al-max	.223	n.s.	.062	–.092	n.s.	.281

Crucially, both for prefield and middlefield association, the proportion of correct responses depended on the clearness of the prosodic marking as reflected by three of the four parameters assigned to each utterance (cf. Section 6.5.2). In Table 6.24, the correlations between the individual parameters (*p-f_0-max*, *p-df_0*, *p-dur-s_{23}*, and *p-al-max*) and the percentage of correct responses in the perception experiment are given. The percentage of correct responses was positively correlated with *p-f_0-max*, *p-df_0*, and *p-dur-s_{23}* to various degrees, but not with *p-al-max*. However, as the individual parameters were not independently varied, we cannot conclude that peak alignment was perceptually irrelevant. Rather, possible effects of alignment were outweighed by effects of the other parameters. In addition, the proportion of the contribution might have differed between the parameters with significant effects, particularly since the parameters themselves are most likely interrelated.[21] Such an interrelation is reasonable to assume between peak height and the size of the f_0-rise. Though less plausible, it is also possible that an interrelation exists between the f_0-parameters and duration.

A simple scenario would be that the three parameters for which significant correlations were found were equally strong perceptual cues for association with *auch* in our data. Figures 6.28 and 6.29 illustrate the correlations between the percentage of correct responses and the sum of *p-f_0-max*, *p-df_0*, and *p-dur-s_{23}* for prefield and middlefield association, respectively. Both correlations were statistically significant (prefield association: $r = .555$, $p < .001$; middlefield association: $r = .557$, $p < .001$). A more detailed examination of the interaction between the individual parameters and perception lies beyond the scope of this study, as it requires the independent variation of the prosodic factors (cf. Braun 2004a, 2005, 2006; Bartels & Kingston 1994). Crucially, the clearness of the prosodic marking of an utterance

21. Hypothetically, a parameter showing a significant correlation with the percentage of correct responses could be perceptually irrelevant. The correlation could result from its interrelation with another, perceptually relevant parameter.

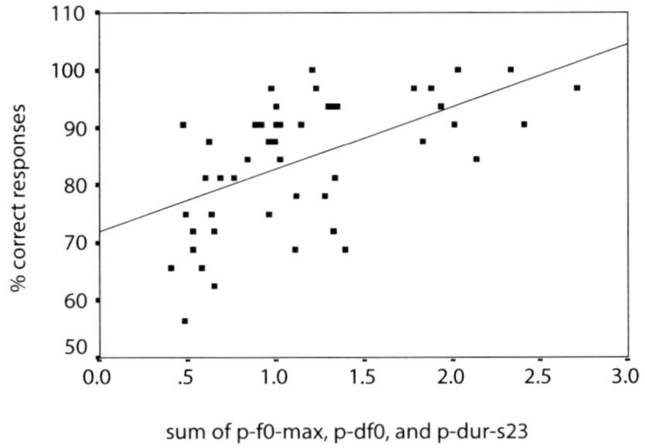

Figure 6.28 Experiment 4 – correlation between the percentage of correct responses and the sum of *p-*f_0*-max*, *p-d*f_0, and *p-dur-*s_{23} for utterances with prefield association (conditions SUBJ-adv and ADV-subj, N = 49)

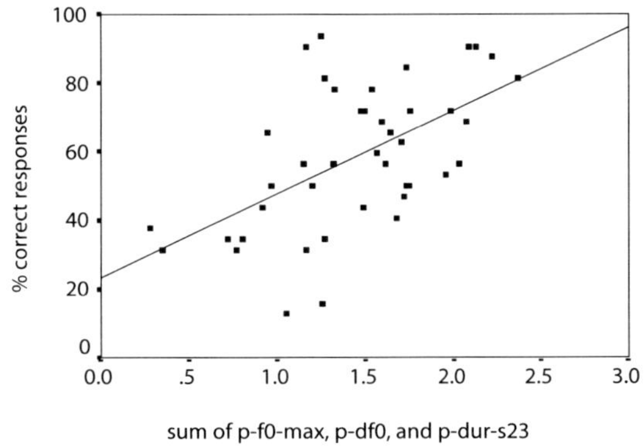

Figure 6.29 Experiment 4 – correlation between the percentage of correct responses and the sum of *p-*f_0*-max*, *p-d*f_0, and *p-dur-*s_{23} for utterances with middlefield association (conditions adv-SUBJ and subj-ADV, N = 42)

was positively correlated with the proportion of correct responses it received in the perception study.

Of the two hypotheses given in (34) and (35) above, only the second could thus be confirmed. The identification of the AC of stressed *auch* was governed by the comparison of the candidates with respect to the continuous phonetic variables. The distribution of the observed pitch accent types, on the other hand, did not facilitate a reliable prediction of the participants' interpretive decisions. Interestingly, the only relevant phonetic variable that is at least to some extent reflected in the accent labels, namely, peak alignment, did not correlate with the percentage of correct responses, while the cues that showed a significant correlation (peak height, f_0-rise, and duration) are not captured by GToBI at all. Consequently, the categorical GToBI-labels are not an adequate way to characterize the relevant prosodic parameters involved in the marking of ACs of stressed *auch* or – more generally – in the marking of contrastive topics.[22]

Two questions could not be answered by means of Experiment 4. First, what was the source of the different proportions of correct responses for prefield and middlefield association? More specifically, were they due to the unbalanced stimulus materials or other effects of the experimental design, or is there a general tendency to associate stressed *auch* with the prefield constituent? Second, is it possible to establish perceptual categories on the basis of the prosodic variables examined in the production experiment? This would be desirable, as the GToBI-accents have proved to be unsuitable categories for the AC/non-AC distinction. In the next section, these questions will be addressed by means of a perception experiment based on manipulated stimulus materials.

6.6 Experiment 5: The perception of utterances containing stressed *auch* (manipulated speech data)

In Experiment 5, the participants were repeatedly presented with 11 versions of one stimulus utterance, manipulated with respect to the prosodic realization of the two potential ACs. The stimuli ranged from a clear case of prefield association (Stimulus 1) to a clear case of middlefield association (Stimulus 11), the remaining versions being regularly distributed between the two extremes. Again, the participants' interpretation of the utterances was determined by means of a completion task.

6.6.1 Hypotheses

The goal of Experiment 5 was to give a more precise answer to the question of how the prosodic realization influences the interpretation of the utterances under discussion. Given the important role that prosody was shown to play, the tendency for prefield association found in Experiment 4 should disappear in an experiment based on balanced stimulus materials. The two possible interpretations being categorically distinct, we furthermore expected an s-shaped response curve for the intermediate stimuli (cf. Gussenhoven 2006; Schneider, Lintfert, Dogil & Möbius 2006). The two specific hypotheses for Experiment 5 are given in (37) and (38).

22. For results pointing in the same direction, see Braun (2004a, b, 2005, 2006).

(37) **Hypothesis 7:** The two extreme stimulus versions show the clearest interpretation preferences: Stimulus 1 receives the highest percentage of decisions for prefield association and Stimulus 11 receives the highest percentage of decisions for middlefield association. The percentage of expected decisions is similarly high for both extremes, i.e., there is no bias towards one of the two association positions.

(38) **Hypothesis 8:** The results for all 11 stimuli form an s-shaped curve typical of categorical perception, i.e., there is an abrupt change in interpretation (somewhere on the way from Stimulus 1 to Stimulus 11) in spite of the gradual change of the manipulation parameters.

6.6.2 Method

Participants. 44 native speakers of German (aged 19 to 34, with a mean of 24.0; 28 females and 16 males) participated in the experiment. They had no knowledge about the problem under examination, and none had participated in any of the other project experiments. They were paid for their participation.

Materials. Experiment 5 was based on 11 manipulated and resynthesized versions of one recorded utterance. The relevant sentence, which was taken from the stimulus materials of Experiment 3, is given in (39). We systematically and jointly manipulated f_0*-min*, f_0*-max*, *dur-*s_{23}, and *al-max* on both potential ACs. The variation of f_0*-min* and f_0*-max* was automatically accompanied by a variation of df_0; *al-min* was not manipulated as it did not show any significant effects in the production study.

(39) Der Wiener hat um sieben wahrscheinlich auch einen Anruf
the Viennese *aux*$_p$ at seven probably also a call
bekommen.
received

The 11 stimulus versions were produced in the following way. First, a trained female speaker was instructed to produce (39) with a neutral intonation and a similar prominence on both potential ACs. Second, the prosodic parameters for manipulation were determined. For the two extreme versions (the clear cases of prefield and middlefield association), the parameters were based on some prototypical utterances from the production study (Experiment 3) that had received good results in Experiment 4. For the f_0-variables, the prototypical values were expressed as a percentage relative to the mean f_0 of the utterances. The values of *dur-*s_{23} were expressed as proportions of the total durations of the utterances, and for alignment, the absolute values were used. On the basis of these prototypical

Table 6.25 Experiment 5 – manipulation parameters

stimulus	prefield constituent				middlefield constituent			
version	*f_0-min* (ERB)	*f_0-max* (ERB)	*dur-s_{23}* (ms)	*al-max* (ms)	*f_0-min* (ERB)	*f_0-max* (ERB)	*dur-s_{23}* (ms)	*al-max* (ms)
1	4.69	6.91	379	215	5.55	5.99	270	90
2	4.74	6.83	368.1	206	5.50	6.03	280.9	98.2
3	4.79	6.76	357.2	197	5.45	6.08	291.8	106.4
...	...	...	...	...	...	...	...	...
11	5.19	6.14	270	125	5.03	6.41	379	172

values and the values of the recorded source utterance of (39), the target values for the manipulation of the two extremes were determined. The target values for the 9 intermediate stimulus versions represented equal steps on the scale between the two extremes. This is illustrated in Table 6.25. For the prefield constituent, the values of *f_0-min* increased between Stimulus 1 and Stimulus 11, while the values of *f_0-max*, *dur-s_{23}*, and *al-max* decreased. For the middlefield constituent, it was the other way around.

In a final step, the 11 versions were resynthesized using Praat's PSOLA-algorithm: The f_0-contour of the recorded utterance was stylized, i.e., reduced to the perceptually relevant f_0-targets, resulting in a so-called *close-copy* (cf. Hermes 2006).[23] Next, 11 versions with manipulated duration were resynthesized. In each of these versions, the f_0- and alignment values were adjusted, followed by the resynthesis of the final versions. In this way, accent alignment was not affected by the manipulation of duration, i.e., the absolute alignment values were retained in the manipulated stimuli.[24] In spite of the fact that the utterances had to be resynthesized twice, the final stimuli still sounded natural. Uninformed hearers did not recognize them as being manipulated.

The f_0-tracks of all 11 target utterances are plotted in Figure 6.30. As the manipulations were based on idealizations of the production data, the range of variation was greater for the prefield constituent than for the middlefield constituent. The f_0-tracks of the two extremes thus resembled the mean contours for prefield and middlefield association given in Figures 6.21 and 6.22 above. The manipulation of peak alignment – although present – is not clearly visible for the

23. Stylization was necessary, as the alternative technique, the rescaling of every single point in the f_0-contour, is not applicable to the manipulation of two different f_0-parameters (*f_0-min* and *f_0-max*) and the manipulation of alignment. Experimental results reported by Ladd & Morton (1997) suggest that stylization has no influence on the responses in perception experiments.

24. For discussion, see Atterer & Ladd (2003).

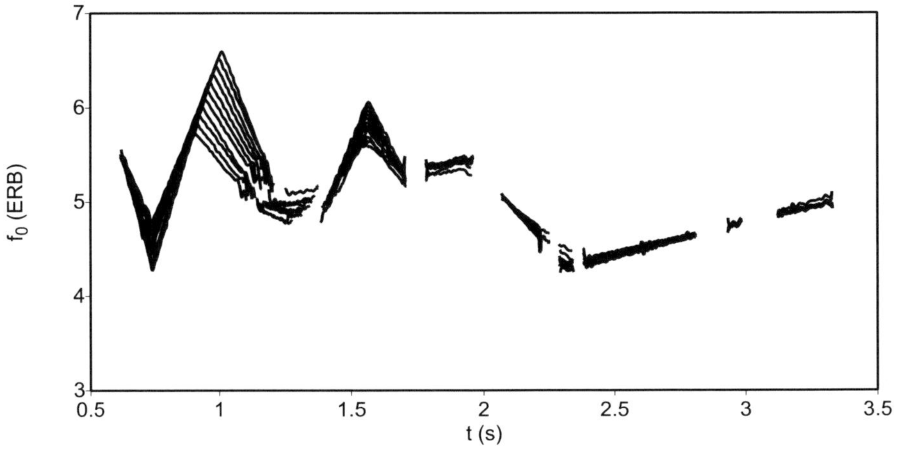

Figure 6.30 Experiment 5 – f_0-contours of the 11 stimulus versions

middlefield constituent in Figure 6.30, as the lengthening in the prefield shifted the contours with early alignment on the middlefield constituent to the right, resulting in approximately the same absolute positions for the middlefield peaks.

Most of the filler utterances of the first type from the production study (Experiment 3) served as filler items for Experiment 5. We used utterances of all 6 speakers, including the training items. The possible continuations presented in the perception task were the same as in Experiment 4.

Procedure. Experiment 5 was based on the same task and mode of presentation as Experiments 2 and 4: the participants had to select one of two visually presented continuations (with randomized left-right order) to an auditorily presented stimulus utterance. The 11 stimulus versions were repeatedly presented: each participant judged each of the versions 6 times, resulting in a total of 66 critical items. These were interspersed with another 66 filler items and pseudo-randomized for each participant.

Two critical items were always separated by one filler to prevent the participants from making direct comparisons between the different versions of the utterance. The participants were informed that they would have to judge many instances of the same sentence and instructed to decide afresh each time. The actual experiment was preceded by a short practice session consisting of 6 items. During the experiment, the participants could take short breaks whenever they wanted. At the end, they were asked to describe the strategy they used for their decisions as well as possible difficulties with the task. The entire experiment took about 30 minutes.

6.6.3 Results and discussion

In Figure 6.31, the percentage of decisions for prefield association is given for all 11 stimulus versions. The extreme versions clearly differed in the percentage of expected judgements: Stimulus 1 was interpreted as involving prefield association in 82.2% of the cases, while Stimulus 11 was assigned the expected interpretation (i.e., middlefield association) in only 71.2% of the cases. Furthermore, the curve between the two extremes was linear rather than s-shaped.

However, a manual inspection of the individual participants' patterns revealed that there were two groups of participants with different behaviors. For one-third of the participants (N = 15), the decisions were independent of the prosodic variation in the stimulus materials. All 11 versions received about the same percentage of choices for prefield and middlefield association; the respective decision curves did not show a downward trend. Three of the 15 participants even consequently chose the same interpretation in all cases (two of them always selected prefield association and one middlefield association). In the following, we will refer to the participants insensitive to the prosodic variation as group A. The remaining participants (N = 29) used prosody as a cue for their decisions; we will refer to them as group B. The patterns for the two groups of participants are given separately in Figure 6.32.

The participants of group A used strategies that are unclear to us; it is likely that some of them randomly selected the continuations. This is not surprising given that many participants reported to have had difficulties with the task. They could not hear any differences between the critical stimuli. On the other hand, the percentage of correct responses was very high for the filler items (above 90% for almost all participants). As the participants of group A obviously did not pay attention to the prosody of the critical items, the discussion of the reasons for their behavior will not be pursued any further.

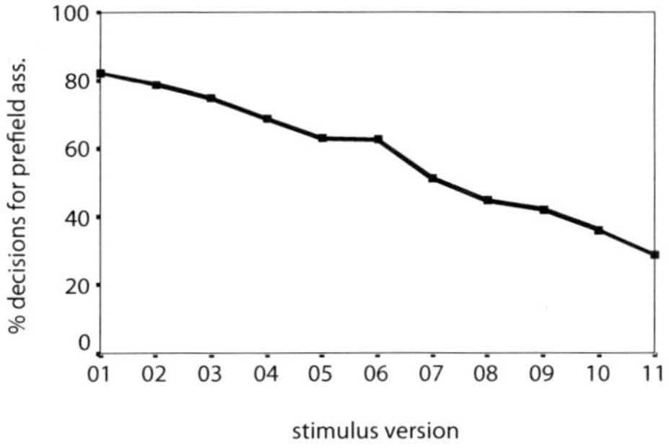

Figure 6.31 Experiment 5 – percentage of decisions for prefield association, compared across the 11 stimulus versions; all participants (N = 44)

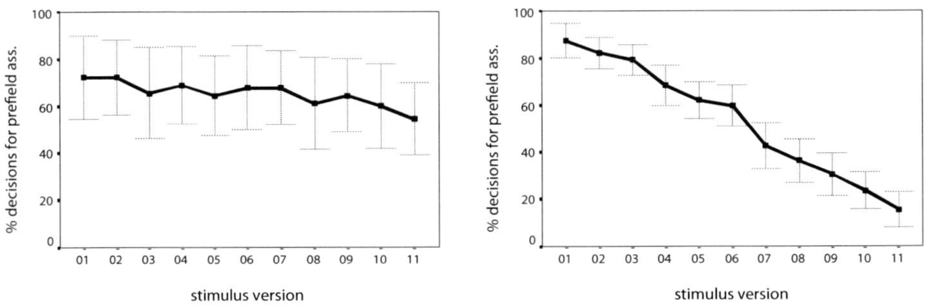

Figure 6.32 Experiment 5 – percentage of decisions for prefield association, compared across the 11 stimulus versions, and 95% confidence intervals; participants of group A (N = 15, left panel) and group B (N = 29, right panel)

The results of group B showed a completely different pattern. Here, Stimuli 1 and 11 were assigned the expected interpretations in 87.4% and 84.5% of the cases, respectively. Both extremes were thus interpreted in accordance with the expectations in a similarly high proportion of the cases. Hypothesis 7 could be confirmed for the majority of the participants: if prosody was used as a cue for interpretation, there were no signs of a preference for a certain association position.

However, if the prosodic marking of the potential ACs was ignored, the two interpretations had different probabilities for being chosen. Most of the participants of group A preferred prefield association over middlefield association. Altogether, the continuation corresponding to association of *auch* with the prefield element was selected in 65% of the cases by group A. In comparison, the participants of group B chose prefield association in 53% of the trials. If prosodic cues could not be used for the interpretation, the participants fell back upon a default strategy in many cases, associating stressed *auch* with the sentence-initial element.

These results shed new light on the outcome of Experiment 4. There, a tendency for the participants to choose prefield association could also be observed. Many utterances originally produced in middlefield association contexts were assigned prefield association interpretations, but not vice versa, resulting in a considerably lower matching percentage for utterances with the intended AC in the middlefield. Due to the unbalanced stimulus materials – the original utterances elicited in Experiment 3 were used – it was impossible to classify the participants of Experiment 4 according to their strategies for selecting the continuations. However, if we assume that the same two strategies were used as in Experiment 5, the results have a straightforward explanation. If a subgroup of the participants interpreted the utterances on the basis of their prosodic properties, while others ignored prosody and preferentially decided in favor of prefield association, it comes as no surprise that the combined matching results for the utterances with intended middlefield association were only slightly above chance level.[25] As in Experiment 5, the overall interrelation between prosodic marking and interpretation (cf. Figures 6.28 and 6.29) was thus most likely weakened by the participants insensitive to the prosodic variation in the stimulus materials.

Unexpectedly, the results of group B did not show an s-shaped curve typical of categorical perception, refuting Hypothesis 8. Instead, there was a rather linear relationship between the number of decisions for a particular association position and the prosodic parameters of the 11 stimulus versions.[26] The participants obviously did not assign the gradually differing stimuli to distinct perceptual categories. This is all the more surprising as, from a semantic point of view, the two interpretations are clearly categorically distinct. The stimulus sentence is repeated in (40). The two interpretations differ in their semantic content; more specifically, in their presuppositions (cf. Section 3.2.4). While (40a) presupposes other people who received a call at 7 o'clock, a presupposition of (40b) is that the Viennese fellow received another call at a different time. The sentence must be interpreted in one of the two ways – there are no 'intermediate' interpretations between (40a) and (40b).

(40) a. [Der Wiener $]_D$ hat um sieben wahrscheinlich auch einen
the Viennese *aux*$_p$ at seven probably also a
Anruf bekommen.
call received

b. Der Wiener hat [um sieben $]_D$ wahrscheinlich auch einen Anruf bekommen.

Why does this categoricalness in interpretation not correspond to categorical perception? We cannot give a satisfactory answer to this question. What might have played a role is that the task the participants were confronted with in Experiment 5 differed from the task in typical experiments attempting to establish categorical perception. The relevant experimental paradigm was originally developed for the investigation of phenomena concerning segmental phonemes, such as the perception of plosives (cf. Liberman, Harris, Hoffman & Griffith 1957; Repp 1984), but has also been applied to prosodic phenomena (cf. Kohler 1990; Ladd & Morton 1997; Schneider, Lintfert, Dogil & Möbius 2006). In the respective experiments, one or more segmental properties (e.g., voice onset time or formant transitions) or prosodic parameters (e.g., f_0-range or accent alignment) are varied on a single

25. The expected criterion for the decisions, i.e., prosody, could be obscured much better in Experiment 4 than in Experiment 5, where the participants were aware that they were judging many lexically identical utterances.

26. The observed linear dependency did not result from variation between the participants.

element. The participants are asked to assign the realizations to different categories (*identification task*).[27] In our case, on the other hand, the interpretation did not depend on the phonetic properties of a single element, but on the relation between the simultaneously varied properties of two elements (the potential ACs). In other words, a constituent was not assigned the status of being associated with stressed *auch* after considering only its own prosodic properties. Instead, an element was selected from the set of potential ACs on the basis of a comparison between the candidates: the constituent with the 'strongest' perceived marking was chosen. It is conceivable that the more complex nature of the decision-making involved in interpreting ambiguous constructions with stressed *auch* was responsible for the fact that the results showed no signs of categorical perception. A more thorough examination of this issue is necessary, but must be left for further research.[28]

Altogether, the results of the first two perception studies (Experiments 2 and 4) could be confirmed by Experiment 5: most participants based the interpretation of ambiguous utterances containing stressed *auch* on the prosodic variation in the speech data. In particular, the choice of the AC depended on several continuous phonetic parameters such as f_0-rise and duration, the constituent with the 'more contrastive' prosodic marking among the candidates being the preferred element for association with *auch*. What was the relation between the participants' judgements and the pitch accents on the potential ACs in the materials of Experiment 5? With respect to the location of the f_0-peak, the 11 stimulus versions showed the following variation: On the constituents with the earliest peak alignment (the clear cases of non-ACs), the peak was reached at the beginning of the post-stressed syllable. In all other versions up to the opposite end of the continuum, it was reached even later. Thus, all potential ACs in the manipulated stimuli had f_0-peaks delayed into the post-stressed syllable, and the respective pitch accents were of the type L*H. This means that the accent distribution in the stimulus materials provided no information at all that could be used for the identification of the ACs. If the disambiguation of the utterances was based on accent type alone, the proportions of prefield and middlefield answers should not differ between the individual stimulus versions. The actual results – clear interpretive preferences for the extreme stimuli and gradually changing proportions between the extremes – are not compatible

27. The categorical perception paradigm involves a second task (the so-called *discrimination task*), where the participants report whether they perceive the members of a pair of stimuli to be identical or different. If the perception of the property under consideration is categorical, the participants have much better discriminatory abilities in the area of the category boundary than within the categories. As the identification task of Experiment 5 did not reveal a clear category boundary between the two interpretations, no discrimination experiment was carried out.

28. Another question is whether the perception of contrastiveness in contexts with only one contrastive/non-contrastive accent is categorical in German.

with this prediction and confirm once more that hearers use non-categorical phonetic properties rather than categorical information about accent types for the identification of constituents associated with stressed *auch*.

6.7 General discussion and summary

In this chapter, the prosodic marking of constituents associated with the stressed variant of the focus particle *auch* was examined by means of a corpus study and several speech production and perception experiments. The different methodical approaches with their specific data types facilitated an investigation of the phenomenon from various perspectives, yielding related results and conclusions. The most general outcome is the following. All of the empirical approaches substantially confirmed the predictions derived from Krifka's (1999) *Contrastive Topic Hypothesis*: ACs of stressed *auch* are often, although not always, characterized by prosodic properties typical of contrastive topics, and this prosodic marking is relevant for the interpretation of the utterances.

The corpus study and the speech production experiments showed that ACs of stressed *auch*, if accented, carry high or rising pitch accents, i.e., L*H, LH*, and H*. As the nuclear accent on the focus particle itself is a falling accent (H*L or HL*) in the vast majority of cases, the overall intonational pattern is that of a bridge contour. The actual accent distribution differed between corpus study and laboratory experiments. The pronominal ACs in the corpus were frequently unaccented. Non-pronominal ACs (in the corpus and in the experimental data), on the other hand, always carried an accent, indicating that the optionality of the prosodic marking assumed by Krifka is restricted to pronominal elements. Furthermore, the proportion of L*H accents was higher in the experimental than in the corpus data; for LH* and H* accents, it was the other way around.[29] These differences in the accent distribution can be attributed to the lexical properties of the ACs (the corpus contained a high percentage of pronominal ACs; the ACs in the experimental materials were exclusively non-pronominal) as well as to the fact that the sentences used in the experimental studies were ambiguous, i.e., they contained two potential ACs to the left of *auch*. The latter did not hold for most of the corpus utterances.

The two speech production studies (Experiments 1 and 3) showed that ACs of stressed *auch* are characterized by several additional prosodic properties, expressed in terms of gradual phonetic variables. More specifically, ACs have a lower f_0-minimum, higher f_0-maximum and greater f_0-rise, as well as a longer duration

29. H* accents on ACs are negligible in the experimentally elicited utterances.

and a later peak alignment than comparable non-associated elements. In the literature, these characteristics have been claimed to be typical of the marking of contrastive topics in German. The perception studies (Experiments 2, 4, and 5) confirmed that the prosodic marking of ACs found in the production data was indeed used by the hearers for the interpretation of the utterances. At least in the absence of contextual information, the hearers' judgements are mainly based on prosodic cues.

The question arises of how the relation between an element's status of being associated with stressed *auch* and its prosodic properties can be adequately modeled. What must be explicated for the phenomenon under discussion, in other words, is the nature of the correspondence between form and function. The empirical results suggest that there are two conceivable ways to tackle this problem. The prosodic marking characterizing ACs of stressed *auch* could be described either in terms of discrete phonological categories or in terms of gradual phonetic parameters.

The first possibility was explored in the corpus study and the qualitative analysis of Experiment 3, the relevant phonological categories being the pitch accent types defined in the GToBI-system. Neither the examination of the accent distribution among the ACs of *auch* nor the comparison with the accents on non-associated elements yielded promising results – it could be shown that there is no one-to-one correspondence between association with *auch* and a particular accent type. In the corpus, a large proportion of the ACs was not accented at all, and the accented ACs in the experimental and corpus data were characterized by several different accent types. Furthermore, the accents found on the ACs could also be observed on non-associated elements, in both the experimentally elicited utterances and the corpus data.[30] As for the experimental data, the reason was most likely structural: the sentences contained much non-pronominal material to the left of *auch*, encouraging additional accents not related to focus or topic marking.[31] The rare cases of accents on non-ACs in the corpus, on the other hand, conveyed paralinguistic meaning.

The conclusion drawn from these mismatches between form and function is that ACs of stressed *auch* cannot be identified on the basis of the accent distribution in a given utterance. As shown by Experiments 2, 4, and 5, however, hearers are able to successfully determine the intended AC in ambiguous constructions

30. Often, the AC of *auch* and a non-associated element even carried the same accent in one utterance.

31. That the accentuation of non-ACs in these utterances had structural rather than discourse-pragmatic or other reasons is supported by the fact that it was much more likely to occur in the prefield than in the middlefield.

using prosodic information. Thus, a description of the prosodic properties involved in the marking of ACs in terms of accent types misses the point. This conclusion is corroborated by the results of Experiment 4, showing that accentual information, in particular the distinction between L*H and LH* accents, is not the decisive factor for the interpretation of utterances containing stressed *auch*. The participants showed matching results with better success than if they had chosen randomly even for utterances where the AC and its non-associated counterpart were characterized by the same accent.

Another outcome of the corpus study and the speech production experiments is that the different pitch accents carried by the ACs of *auch* do not correspond to different semantic or information-structural categories. This is in accord with the fact that the criteria for annotating a certain accent in the GToBI-system are sometimes rather arbitrary. With respect to the distinction between L*H and LH*, the annotation was mainly based on the position of the f_0-peak. If it was reached within the stressed syllable, we annotated LH*, otherwise L*H was chosen. However, the data did not really support this classification: instead of a clear-cut categorical distinction, there was a gradual transition in peak alignment between the two accents. In many cases, the peak was located close to the offset of the stressed syllable, either shortly before or after the syllable boundary. The respective LH* and L*H accents were perceptually almost equivalent.

This brings us to the second possibility envisaged above, namely, to describe the prosodic properties of constituents associated with stressed *auch* in terms of continuous phonetic parameters. From the point of view of speech production (cf. Experiments 1 and 3), this method characterizes the relevant differences between ACs and non-ACs more adequately than a description in terms of accent types. Moreover, the speech perception studies (Experiments 2, 4, and 5) confirmed that the way the participants interpret a given utterance can be much better predicted if phonetic variables such as f_0-peak, f_0-rise, or duration are taken into account. Prosodic variation with respect to these parameters is not captured by the GToBI-annotation at all. In particular, Experiment 5 showed that the participants can have clear interpretive preferences even when the potential ACs are characterized by the same pitch accent. This cannot be explained without reference to (the comparison of) non-categorical prosodic properties.

The findings described above are important for our understanding of the relation between prosody and semantics / information structure. It was shown that the variation of continuous phonetic parameters not only affects paralinguistic aspects of utterances but can also be a decisive factor for truth-conditionally or information-structurally relevant meaning components. As the prosodic properties discussed here are non-categorical, a description in terms of pitch accent types is not an adequate method. Although these issues have been brought forward before (cf. Braun & Ladd 2003; Braun 2004a, b, 2005, 2006; Calhoun 2003, 2004), a theoretical model of the relation between prosody and meaning accounting for the status of gradual phonetic parameters is still to be developed.

It was also shown that the interdependence of prosodic structure and meaning cannot be seen independently of other factors such as syntactic structure or (linguistic) context. In the production and interpretation of utterances containing stressed *auch*, these factors play an important role. As for speech production, the syntactic position of the ACs influences the size of the prosodic differences between ACs and non-associated elements. The results of Experiment 3 showed clear differences between ACs and non-ACs for prefield association, but only small differences for middlefield association. The speech perception experiments (in particular Experiment 5), on the other hand, revealed that hearers use a default strategy based on word order if they cannot access prosodic information for the identification of the AC. In the absence of prosodic cues, *auch* is more likely associated with the prefield element. The influence of the context is twofold as well. It can override preferences for association with a particular element based on the prosodic structure (as in the corpus study), and it can encourage a clear prosodic marking of the ACs (as in the speech production studies).

To sum up the most important results of this chapter in one sentence, the prosodic marking of constituents associated with stressed *auch* found in the corpus study and the experimental studies is consistent with Krifka's (1999) *Contrastive Topic Hypothesis*, but the relation between (prosodic) form and function is not as straightforward as expected, and poses problems for common views on the interface between prosody and semantics / information structure.

CHAPTER 7

Focus particles and contrast

In the previous chapter, ACs of stressed additive focus particles were examined from a prosodic point of view. Complementing these investigations, the current chapter takes a closer look at the prosodic realization of ACs of unstressed focus particles. Again, the research interest concerns the relation between focus particles and information structure. More specifically, the question under consideration is whether focus particles are always associated with contrastive foci, as claimed by Altmann (1976a, b) and Foolen (1993), among others. The modular theory of the grammar and information structure of focus particle constructions proposed in Chapter 4 makes a different prediction: focus particles should be able to associate with both contrastive and non-contrastive (i.e., new information) foci. An empirical approach to this problem will yield insights into the way focus particles interact with the focus-background partition of the sentences in which they occur.

This chapter is structured as follows. Section 7.1 revisits the two views on the relation between focus particles and information structure introduced in Section 4.2.3 above and compares them with respect to their predictions about the prosodic properties of ACs of unstressed focus particles. Section 7.2 constitutes a short digression on the prosodic peculiarities of contrast marking in German and other languages, concentrating on contrast in the canonical position of the sentence focus (i.e., in the middlefield in German). A speech production experiment examining the prosody of the relevant focus particle constructions is described in Section 7.3. Section 7.4 presents an additional experiment on the perception of contrast, based on the utterances investigated in the production study. The final section summarizes the results and their theoretical implications and names open questions.

7.1 Focus particles, the focus-background partition, and contrast

The usage pattern of focus particles investigated in the previous chapter – an obligatorily accented particle linearly following its AC – is to some extent exceptional. In the standard case, the AC is accented, rather than the focus particle itself, and the linear order is reversed.[1] The consensus in the literature is that the AC of the particle corresponds to the sentence focus in these cases, which in turn must be marked by the nuclear accent on the focus exponent. However, the question of how association with focus is established in grammar has been the subject of controversy. As described in Section 4.2.3, focus particles are regarded either as focus-inducing elements that create a focus structure themselves or as focus sensitive operators that interact with an independently given focus-background partition.[2]

The former point of view is characteristic of relational theories of focus, such as Taglicht (1984), Jacobs (1983, 1986, 1988), Altmann (1993), Foolen (1993), Drubig (1994), and Bayer (1996). A common assumption in these works is that focus particles induce contrastive focus (cf. Altmann 1976a: 18–21; Altmann 1976b; Foolen 1993: 143–144), i.e., that the AC is contrasted with some contextually given or derivable alternative. The second conception of the relation between focus particles and information structure, represented by Büring & Hartmann (2001), Dimroth & Klein (1996), and Dimroth (2004), among others, is based on the assumption that the focus-background partition in a given sentence is independent of the presence of an operator. Focus particles are considered to be sensitive to this information-structural property of sentences. A prediction of these theories, as well as of the modular account presented in Chapter 4, is that focus particles can associate with both contrastive and new information foci.[3]

The question of whether focus particles always co-occur with a contrastive focus or whether they can associate with contrastive as well as non-contrastive foci can be reformulated as a prosodic question that is empirically testable: Does the AC of an unstressed focus particle always carry a contrastive pitch accent? Before we present experiments attempting to answer this question, it is necessary to

1. This does not mean that the former pattern is necessarily less frequent. By means of a corpus study, Nederstigt (2003: Chapter 4) shows that the stressed variant of *auch* is actually more frequent than its unstressed counterpart. However, as discussed in detail above, this pattern is restricted to additive particles in their non-scalar readings. As a consequence, most focus particles only occur in an unstressed form.

2. Independently of whether focus particles are considered to *induce* focus or not, it is commonly acknowledged that they often *indicate* the focus of a sentence (cf., for instance Ladd 1983a). In other words, focus particles can serve as cues to the location of the focus, in particular if prosodic information is not available (e.g., in written language). This property is a consequence of the restrictions governing the placement of focus particles relative to the focus (cf. Chapter 4), and it is made use of in a number of psycholinguistic studies (cf. Ni, Crain & Shankweiler 1996; Clifton, Bock & Radó 2000; Sedivy 2002; Heim & Alter 2006, 2007; Stolterfoht 2005; Stolterfoht & Bader 2004; Stolterfoht, Friederici, Alter & Steube 2007).

3. See also Umbach (2004).

provide a few remarks on the prosodic realization of contrast in the position of the regular sentence focus.

7.2 Prosodic correlates of contrastive focus

Contrastive focus has received much attention in the prosodic literature. However, there is disagreement as to whether contrastive and non-contrastive nuclear accents have a different prosodic realization, and what prosodic features are relevant for signalling contrast. Before we turn to the German data, we briefly review some results of studies on contrast in other languages.

Bolinger (1961) claims that, unlike contrastive stress (stress in a position where it would not occur under new information focus), contrastive accent does not show a unique behavior in English: "Contrastive accent is not phonetically definable." (Bolinger 1961: 96) Pierrehumbert & Hirschberg (1990), on the other hand, assume a categorical difference in the marking of new and contrastive information. While the former is said to be characterized by H* accents, LH* accents are considered to be adequate for the latter. In their perception study on contrastive accents in English, Bartels & Kingston (1994) find that a continuous phonetic parameter – namely, peak height – is the most important cue for contrastiveness. Mehlhorn (2002) observes categorical differences in accent type as well as gradual phonetic differences between contrastive and non-contrastive accents in Russian. In her data, contrastive information is indicated by rising-falling accents, which show a greater f_0-excursion than comparable new information accents, combined with a significant lengthening of the accented syllable. In addition, Mehlhorn (2002) finds a global feature relevant for the marking of contrast: the f_0-contour before and after the contrastive accent is considerably flattened. In particular, prenuclear accents show a smaller f_0-excursion than in utterances without a contrastive element. Krahmer & Swerts (2001) claim that there is no specific contrastive accent in Dutch. According to their view, contrast is detected by the comparison of an element with its prosodic context, the relevant cues being f_0 and intensity.

The same diversity of findings as in the works cited above can be found in the literature on German. Fuchs (1976) identifies certain cues for contrastiveness, such as a higher intensity and a greater f_0-excursion, but claims that these features are neither necessary nor sufficient conditions for contrast. The author's conclusion is that contrastive accents do not substantially differ from non-contrastive ones. This result is questioned by the findings of Bannert (1985), who analyzes contrastive and non-contrastive utterances elicited by means of a dialog reading task. Bannert identifies the following characteristics of contrastive accents in German: (i) a greater f_0-excursion, caused by a lower f_0-minimum and a higher f_0-maximum; (ii) a longer duration of the accented syllable; (iii) the use of a different accent type, namely, a rising-falling accent instead of the falling accent typical of non-contrastive focus;[4] and (iv) a compression of the f_0-excursion of prenuclear accents.

Similar results are reported by Alter, Mleinek, Rohe, Steube & Umbach (2001),[5] who also find categorical as well as non-categorical differences between non-contrastive and contrastive accents. In their data (experimentally elicited productions of sentences embedded in contrast-inducing and non-contrast-inducing contexts), new information focus is characterized by falling accents integrated into the global falling contour, whereas contrastive focus is indicated by local f_0-rises. Because the direction of the f_0-movement of contrastive accents is opposite to the declination, they stand out clearly and are more marked than new information accents.[6] In terms of GToBI, the difference is one between H*L (new information focus) and LH* accents (contrastive focus); the former, but not the latter, are often downstepped. As for the gradual phonetic parameters, it is claimed that contrastive accents show a much greater f_0-excursion. On the other hand, Alter et al. do not find any evidence for a lengthening of the accented syllable in the contrast condition. Another result of this study is that utterances involving contrastive and new information focus do not differ in the distribution of prosodic boundaries, as shown by the investigation of final lengthening, pause insertion, and boundary tones.

Three recent empirical studies also deal with the prosodic realization of contrast in German. Analyzing read dialogs, Toepel & Alter (2004)[7] confirm the relevance of peak height for the marking of contrast, but come to a different conclusion concerning the accent types characteristic of new and contrastive information. The observed accents – LH* (new information focus) and LH*L- (contrastive focus) – are most likely due to the specific form of the stimulus materials used in the experiment, which might have introduced additional factors influencing the intonation. Baumann, Grice & Steindamm (2006) substantially replicate the

4. Dietrich (1990), on the other hand, claims that contrast can be marked by rising as well as falling accents in German.

5. See also Alter (2002b).

6. "Ein Kontrastakzent ist hervorgehobener als ein normaler Satzakzent. Die Markierung von Kontrast/Korrektur erfolgt dabei über einen lokalen F0-Anstieg. Bei Neuinformationsfokus ist der Satzakzent dagegen in eine globale fallende Kontur eingebettet. Der Satzakzent ist bei NIF [new information focus] in die globale F0-Deklination, in eine stetig fallende F0-Kontur eingepasst und bleibt damit für den F0-Parameter unmarkiert. Der Kontrastakzent dagegen durchbricht die F0-Deklination und scheint dadurch markierter zu sein als ein durch NIF induzierter Satzakzent." (Alter, Mleinek, Rohe, Steube & Umbach 2001:64)

7. See also Toepel, Pannekamp & Alter (2007).

results of Alter, Mleinek, Rohe, Steube & Umbach (2001). While their data (read question answer pairs) shows significant differences between contrastive and (narrow) new information focus in f_0-maximum and f_0-excursion, duration does not differentiate between the two types of focus. In addition, it is reported that, unlike new information accents, contrastive accents are never downstepped and tend to have late f_0-peaks. By means of a corpus study, Becker, Schröder & Barry (2006) confirm that contrastive information is often characterized by LH* accents.

There is only one study that explicitly deals with the intonation of utterances containing focus particles in German. Based on the results of a corpus analysis, Müller (1999)[8] claims that the AC of a focus particle usually carries the falling H*L accent or its downstepped counterpart !H*L, which signal new information. In addition, Müller finds L*HL accents[9] on the ACs in some cases, which – according to the author – signal unexpectedness of the information or contrast.

To summarize this overview, there is no general agreement about the prosodic realization of contrast in the regular focus position. While a few authors assume that non-contrastive and contrastive accents differ neither phonologically nor phonetically, most others maintain that contrastive focus is indeed characterized by several specific prosodic features. On the basis of empirical results, a variety of properties have been claimed to be involved in the marking of contrast in German. The most promising candidates include (i) the use of rising(-falling) instead of falling pitch accents, (ii) an extended f_0-excursion on contrastive accents, caused by a lower f_0-minimum or a higher f_0-maximum or both, (iii) the inadequacy of downstep, and (iv) the compression of the f_0-movement on prenuclear accents. Contradictory evidence is reported with respect to the duration parameter: while Bannert (1985) reports a considerable lengthening of the accented syllable in the case of contrastive focus, no such effect is present in the data of Alter, Mleinek, Rohe, Steube & Umbach (2001) and Baumann, Grice & Steindamm (2006). Intensity has not yet been sufficiently investigated.

7.3 Experiment 6: Focus particles and contrast in speech production

The findings assembled in the previous section served as background for a speech production study, which examined the prosodic realization of the ACs of unstressed focus particles in German. The question under consideration was whether a focus particle alone is sufficient to induce a contrastive prosody. For this reading experiment, simple sentences with focus particles were embedded in

8. See also Müller (1998).

9. The labeling system used by Müller is based on Féry (1993).

contextsinducing a contrastive or non-contrastive interpretation of the element bearing the nuclear accent. In addition, two control conditions employing similar sentences without focus particles (embedded in comparable contexts) were included to be able to investigate the effects of the context and the presence or absence of a focus particle independently. The resulting productions were compared with respect to several categorical and gradual prosodic features. The main hypothesis, derived from the modular theory of the interaction between focus particles and information structure proposed in Chapter 4, was that the prosodic realization depends on the nature of the context, but not on the occurrence of a particle.

7.3.1 Experimental conditions and hypotheses

The two independent variables with their levels and the resulting four experimental conditions are summarized in Table 7.1. The two control conditions without focus particles (NFP-NC and NFP-C) served to identify the prosodic differences between new information focus and contrastive focus in our specific type of material and under the experimental setup to be described below. Given the empirical findings discussed in Section 7.2, we expected considerable prosodic differences between these conditions. In a second step, the utterances of the two critical conditions with focus particles (FP-NC and FP-C) were compared to the control conditions. If the context, but not the presence/absence of a focus particle influences the prosody of the utterances, the conditions with comparable contexts should show a similar behavior: condition FP-NC should be realized like NFP-NC, and condition FP-C like NFP-C. In other words, the difference between conditions FP-NC and FP-C should be similar to the difference between conditions NFP-NC and NFP-C. These hypotheses are summarized in (1) and (2).

(1) **Hypothesis 1 (control conditions):** The prosody of the utterances without focus particles (conditions NFP-NC and NFP-C) depends on the nature of the context (contrast-inducing vs. non-contrast-inducing). The utterances of condition NFP-C show (i) a different type of nuclear accent (rising(-falling) instead of falling accents) and fewer downsteps, (ii) a greater f_0-excursion on

Table 7.1 Experiment 6 – independent variables and experimental conditions

independent variables		experimental condition
PARTICLE	CONTEXT	
not present	non-contrastive	NFP-NC
not present	contrastive	NFP-C
present	non-contrastive	FP-NC
present	contrastive	FP-C

the nuclear accent and a smaller f_0-excursion on prenuclear accents, and possibly (iii) a longer duration and greater intensity of the elements bearing the nuclear accent than the utterances of condition NFP-NC.

(2) **Hypothesis 2 (conditions with focus particles):** The insertion of a focus particle does not have a significant effect on the prosodic properties of the utterances on its own nor does it show an interaction with the type of context. Conditions NFP-NC and FP-NC are realized alike, and the same holds for conditions NFP-C and FP-C. The prosodic difference between conditions FP-NC and FP-C is the same as between conditions NFP-NC and NFP-C (cf. Hypothesis 1).

Hypothesis 2 stands in direct contradiction to the predictions that can be derived from the claims made by Altmann (1976a, b) and Foolen (1993). If focus particles induce contrastive focus themselves, then the utterances of condition FP-NC should prosodically behave like those of conditions NFP-C and FP-C, i.e., the nuclear accents in condition FP-NC should have the properties of contrastive accents. The utterances of condition NFP-NC, where neither the context nor a focus particle has the potential to induce contrast, should prosodically differ from all other conditions. The contradicting predictions are summarized in (3).

(3) a. prediction by Dimroth (2004), among others, and the theory presented in Chapter 4:

NFP-NC = FP-NC ≠ NFP-C = FP-C

b. prediction by Altmann (1976a, b) and Foolen (1993), among others:

NFP-NC ≠ FP-NC = NFP-C = FP-C

7.3.2 Data elicitation

Participants. Four female native speakers of German (aged 20 to 26) participated in the experiment. They lacked any knowledge about the research question and were paid for their participation.

Materials. Six sets of sentences with similar structures were constructed, each set consisting of three versions of a sentence. An example set, indicating the assignment of the versions to the experimental conditions, is given in (4); the complete materials can be found in Appendix A.6.

(4) a. Am Freitag ist nur Sabine gekommen. (conditions FP-NC / FP-C)
on Friday *aux*$_p$ only Sabine come

b. Am Freitag ist dann Sabine gekommen. (condition NFP-NC)
on Friday *aux*$_p$ then Sabine come

c. Am Freitag ist die Sabine gekommen. (condition NFP-C)
on Friday aux_p the Sabine come

The target sentences for the two critical conditions with focus particles were identical; cf. (4a). They consisted of a three-syllabic PP (a temporal, local, or directional adverbial) in the prefield, the perfect auxiliary (*ist* or *hat*), the focus particle, the AC of the focus particle, which was always a three-syllabic proper name serving as the subject of the sentence, and the three-syllabic perfect participle. Although the subject was located in the middlefield, the word order of the sentences is relatively unmarked (cf. Pittner 1999). The critical sentences of all sets had the same number of syllables and the same lexical stress positions. In three sets, the focus particle used was *nur*, while in the remaining three sets it was *auch*. The choice of the focus particle was not included in the analysis as an independent variable, as the use of different particles only served to make the sentences less similar as regards content, so that the participants were less likely to see through the experimental design. We did not use *sogar* as it has two syllables and would have made it impossible to keep the sentences parallel with respect to the number of syllables.

The intended ACs of the focus particles had similar phonological properties in the individual lexicalizations. In addition to the number of syllables and stress position (penultimate stress), they were controlled with respect to the syllable structure and vowel length of the stressed syllable (always open syllables with long vowels). The post-stressed syllables were also open syllables in all cases. It was not possible to fully control the vowel height of the stressed syllable; the vowels used are [i:] and [e:]. However, this had no negative effect, as prosodic comparisons were only made between the items of one set (see below).

For the critical sentences of condition NFP-NC (cf. (4b) above), the focus particle was replaced by the temporal adverbial *dann* ('then') in all lexicalizations. The focus particle was not simply omitted, as this would have changed the number of syllables of the sentences. In addition, *dann* typically occurs in narrative discourses and thus makes a contrastive reading of the sentence unlikely. For the sentences of condition NFP-C (cf. (4c)), the focus particle was replaced by the definite article *die*, which is compatible with a contrastive interpretation of the construction.

For all critical sentences, short paragraphs providing plausible contexts were constructed. The individual paragraphs were about the same length (4 to 7 sentences) and described everyday situations in an anecdotal manner. The critical sentence was always the one before the last; the final sentence served to prevent possible effects of the end of the utterance (e.g., creaky voice). The function of the contexts was to determine the information structure of the target sentences and the location of the nuclear accent, as well as to induce a non-contrastive (conditions NFP-NC and FP-NC) or contrastive (conditions NFP-C and FP-C) interpretation of the focus constituent. The contrastive reading resulted from the fact that the respective paragraphs described misconceptions or misunderstandings and their corrections by the persons involved. The four contexts for the set of target sentences in (4) are given in (5)–(8).[10] Given the information structuring induced by the contexts, the nuclear accent had to be located on the subject constituent in all target sentences. The accent position was thus kept constant and did not provide any information concerning the type of accent. Depending on the context, the nuclear accents indicated narrow new information or contrastive focus on the subject.

(5) condition FP-NC
Das Institut für Germanistik hat letzte Woche neue Bücherregale bekommen. Da dem Institut nur wenig Geld zur Verfügung steht, hatten sich einige Studenten bereiterklärt, beim Aufbauen zu helfen. An den meisten Tagen waren Ina und Gabriel da und haben die Handwerker kräftig unterstützt. **Am Freitag ist nur Sabine gekommen.** Das war aber nicht schlimm, denn es gab ohnehin nicht mehr viel zu tun.
('The department of German got new bookshelves last week. As the department is short of money, some students had volunteered to put together the shelves. On most of the days, Ina and Gabriel were present and supported the workers. On Friday, only Sabine came. But that didn't matter, as most of the work had already been done.')

(6) condition FP-C
Drei Schüler der Klasse 10a haben sich in der letzten Ferienwoche etwas Geld verdient, indem sie hin und wieder im BMW-Werk Maschinen reinigten. Leider ist die Anwesenheitsliste von Freitag verlorengegangen. Die Sekretärin sagte dem Abteilungsleiter, dass an diesem Tag alle drei Schüler gearbeitet haben. Das stimmt aber nicht. **Am Freitag ist nur Sabine gekommen.** Alle anderen hatten bereits keine Lust mehr.
('Three pupils of class 10a earned some money in the last week of the school vacation by now and then cleaning machines in the BMW factory. Unfortunately, Friday's attendance list went missing. The secretary told the head of department that all three pupils had worked on that day. But she was wrong. On Friday, only Sabine came. The others weren't in the mood for working any longer.')

(7) condition NFP-NC
Letzte Woche hatte Tom jeden Tag Besuch. Am Montag sind Martin und Friedrich zum Essen gekommen. Am nächsten Tag hat ihm Claudia ihre Urlaubsfotos von den kanarischen Inseln gezeigt. Von Mittwoch bis Donnerstag war seine Mutter da, denn sie hatte Urlaub und wollte mal wieder etwas

10. The target sentences are emphasized here for an easier orientation. In the materials presented to the participants, of course no such emphasis was present.

mit ihrem Sohn unternehmen. **Am Freitag ist dann Sabine gekommen.** Sie hat ihr neugeborenes Kind mitgebracht.
('Last week, Tom had visitors every day. On Monday, Martin and Friedrich came for dinner. On the next day, Claudia showed him her photographs from the Canaries. From Wednesday to Thursday, his mother was there, as she had vacation and wanted to spend some time with her son. Then, on Friday, Sabine came. She brought her newborn baby with her.')

(8) condition NFP-C
Die ganze Familie wollte Weihnachten zusammen feiern, und in der Woche vor Heiligabend ist einer nach dem anderen zu Hause in Regensburg eingetrudelt. Am Freitag gab es eine Überraschung. Andreas hatte uns gesagt, dass an diesem Tag Franziska anreisen würde. Er hat aber alles durcheinandergebracht. **Am Freitag ist die Sabine gekommen.** Franziska musste nämlich noch arbeiten.
('The whole family wanted to spend Christmas together, and in the week before Christmas Eve, one by one arrived at home in Regensburg. On Friday, there was a big surprise. Andreas had told us that Franziska would arrive on that day. But he had completely mixed it up. On Friday, Sabine came. Franziska still had to work.')

At this point, it must be noted that the information-structural differences between the critical sentences in conditions NFP-NC and FP-NC on the one hand and those in conditions NFP-C and FP-C on the other did not only concern the status of the subject. In the non-contrastive conditions, the sentence-initial adverbial could be interpreted as a contrastive topic, contrasting with other adverbials of the same type in the preceding context. Together with the focused subject, it possibly formed a bridge contour. In the contrastive conditions, on the other hand, the adverbial was a background element repeated from one of the preceding sentences. We will return to this potential drawback of the materials in the discussion of the results.

In addition to determining the information structure, the context paragraphs served to mask the target sentences, which – due to their high similarity – would otherwise have been easily detectable for the participants. Braun (2005, 2006), who used a similar method for the investigation of (contrastive and non-contrastive) topics in German, reports that the materials fulfill this function very well: the speakers concentrate on the content of the paragraphs and do not realize the occurrence of identical sentences in different conditions. In this way, it becomes possible to employ a within-subjects design in which the speakers produce all four sentences of each set, thus facilitating a fine-grained prosodic analysis without taking the risk that the participants will become aware of the experimental manipulations.

In addition to the 24 critical items (4 experimental conditions, 6 lexicalizations), 24 paragraphs of about the same length and with comparable contents were constructed for use as fillers, half of them being the critical items of another experiment.

Procedure. The 48 paragraphs were pseudo-randomized for each participant using the software CMix.[11] The paragraphs were separately printed on cards and presented to the participants one at a time. The recording sessions took place in a sound-proof booth at the linguistics department of the University of Leipzig. The speakers were instructed to read through each paragraph silently before reading it aloud. Apart from the request to speak as naturally as possible, they were not given any further instructions. The speakers were allowed to repeat items when they were not satisfied with their results, e.g., when they had made slips of the tongue. In these cases, the entire paragraph was reread. Additional items were repeated at the end of the session, as they had been produced with defects (hesitations, slips of the tongue, reading mistakes) that remained unnoticed by the speakers themselves. These items were, like the earlier set, pseudo-randomized and interspersed with fillers. Only the final production of each item was considered in the analysis. The target utterances were digitally recorded using a DAT recorder with a sampling rate of 44.1 kHz (16 bit). The participants were allowed to take short breaks during the recording session; the entire experiment took about 45 minutes. After the recordings, the participants were asked to describe what they thought to be the purpose of the experiment.

7.3.3 Data analysis

Data selection. The questioning of the participants revealed that none of them had noticed the critical sentences or understood the purpose of the experiment. The critical utterances were extracted using CoolEdit and superficially inspected. As there were no defective recordings, all utterances were used for the analysis. For all subsequent analysis steps, the software Praat[12] was used.

Annotation and measurements. As predicted, the subjects of the critical sentences – referred to below as the target words – carried the nuclear accent in all elicited utterances. These accents were annotated using the slightly modified version of GToBI introduced in Section 2.4. In addition, the adverbials located in the

11. Two critical items were always separated by a filler, and two items of the same set were always separated by at least six other (critical or filler) items to prevent the participants from noticing the similar target sentences within the sets. In addition, two critical items of the same experimental condition were always separated by at least four other items.

12. See http://www.praat.org.

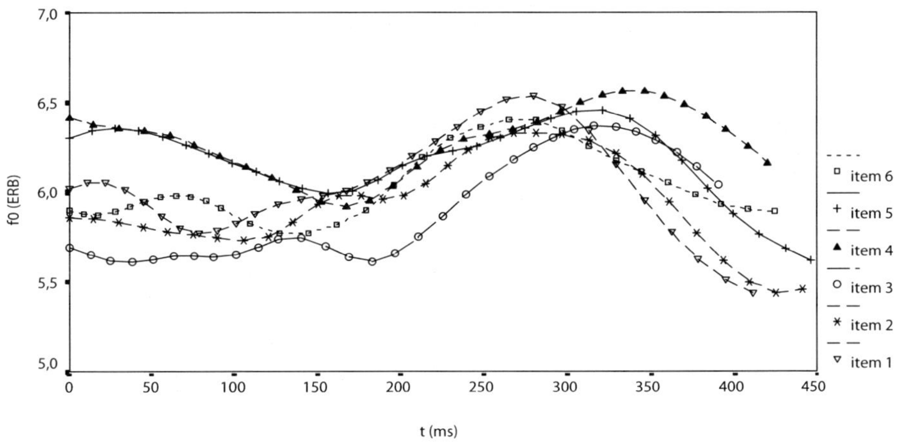

Figure 7.1 Experiment 6 – f_0-contours of Speaker 2 in condition FP-C (target words)

prefield carried prenuclear accents in all cases. The syllable boundaries of the target words were determined; they served as the basis for the phonetic measurements to be described below.

Praat's autocorrelation algorithm with a time step setting of 1ms was used for the extraction of f_0. We manually corrected artifacts (f_0-halving or -doubling), linearly interpolated missing values and smoothed the resulting contours with a bandwidth of 10 Hz. f_0 was measured at 10 measuring points per syllable on the target words, and the f_0-values were transformed into the ERB-scale (cf. Section 6.3.2.2). The f_0-movements on the target words were checked for consistency within the experimental conditions. It turned out that the six contours of each speaker were not always consistent (see the discussion of the qualitative results below). In particular, we observed rising as well as falling f_0-movements corresponding to different accent types. The contours of Speaker 2 in condition FP-C, which showed a relatively high degree of consistency, are given in Figure 7.1 for illustration.

For the quantitative analysis, we determined several dependent phonetic variables. As for the f_0-variables, we measured f_0*-min* (the f_0-minimum) and f_0*-max* (the f_0-maximum) on the target words and calculated the f_0-excursion (df_0) by subtracting f_0*-min* from f_0*-max*, irrespective of whether the f_0-maximum followed the f_0-minimum or the other way around.[13] The only duration variable determined was the duration of the stressed and post-stressed syllable of the target word

13. It might be an unwarranted simplification to collapse these two cases. However, if they were treated separately, the comparison between rising and falling accents with respect to f_0-excursion (see below) would no longer be possible.

Table 7.2 Experiment 6 – dependent variables determined for the target words and the elements bearing prenuclear accents in all utterances

variable type	variable	unit	description
f_0-variables	f_0-*min*	ERB	f_0 of local minimum (target word)
	f_0-*max*	ERB	f_0 of local maximum (target word)
	df_0	ERB	size of f_0-excursion (target word)
	f_0-min_p	ERB	f_0 of local minimum (prenuclear)
	f_0-max_p	ERB	f_0 of local maximum (prenuclear)
	df_{0p}	ERB	size of f_0-excursion (prenuclear)
duration variable	*dur*-s_{23}	ms	duration of 2nd and 3rd syllable (target word)
intensity variables	*int-syll*	–	relative intensity of stressed syllable (target word)
	int-const	–	relative intensity of target word

(*dur*-s_{23}). In Experiment 3, this variable had turned out to be the most meaningful one among the possible duration variables (cf. Section 6.4.5 above). Furthermore, we determined two intensity variables, namely, the relative intensity of the syllable carrying the nuclear accent (*int-syll*) and the relative intensity of the whole target word (*int-const*). These intensity variables were relative insofar as they were determined by dividing the respective intensity values by the mean intensity of the whole utterance. This was done to exclude effects of factors such as the speaker's distance from the microphone, which may have varied during the session.[14]

We also determined f_0-minimum, f_0-maximum, and f_0-excursion for the prefield constituents in order to be able to examine the phonetic properties of the prenuclear accents. The respective variables were f_0-min_p, f_0-max_p, and df_{0p}. Alignment variables were not considered as the different accent types observed do not allow meaningful comparisons with respect to alignment. The dependent variables examined in Experiment 6 are summarized in Table 7.2.

7.3.4 Results: Control conditions

First, the two control conditions were compared to each other. The results served as the basis for the investigation of the data with focus particles (cf. Section 7.3.5 below).

7.3.4.1 *Qualitative results*

The distribution of the types of nuclear accents (located on the penultimate syllable of the target word) in the non-contrastive control condition (NFP-NC) is given

14. The resulting values of *int-syll* and *int-const* thus represented ratios; a value of 1.03, for instance, meant that the relevant syllable/constituent had an intensity that was 3% above the average intensity of the utterance.

Table 7.3 Experiment 6 – nuclear accents on the target words in condition NFP-NC (N = 24)

accent	frequency	
H*L	16	66.7%
HL*	6	25.0%
LH*	2	8.3%
total	24	100%

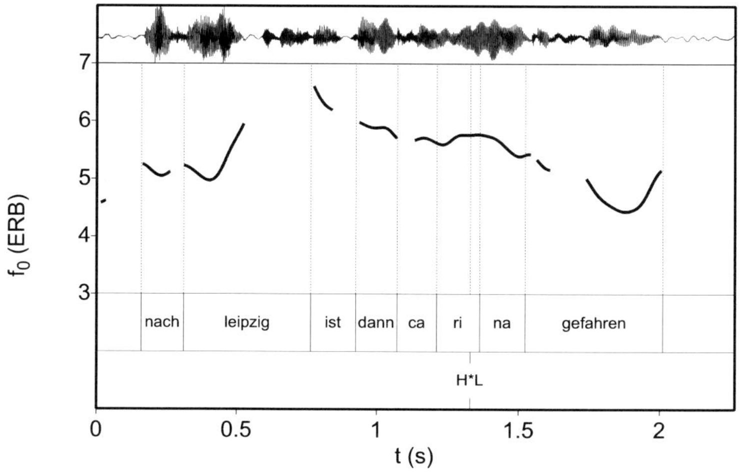

Figure 7.2 Experiment 6 – f_0-contour of an utterance of the sentence "*Nach Leipzig ist dann Carina gefahren.*" ('Then, Carina went to Leipzig.'), condition NFP-NC, produced by Speaker 2

in Table 7.3. As expected, the nuclear accents were realized as falling accents (H*L or HL*) in the majority of cases. Only two utterances were characterized by a rising nuclear accent (LH*); these utterances were produced by the same speaker (Speaker 3). The other speakers showed extremely consistent realizations of HL* (Speaker 4) and H*L accents (Speakers 1 and 2). The most frequent accent type (H*L) is illustrated by the f_0-track in Figure 7.2. In most cases (22 out of 24, i.e., 91.7%), the H-tone of the nuclear accent was downstepped relative to the H-tone of a prenuclear accent.[15] The overall f_0-contours of the utterances were thus characterized by an initial rise and a more or less continuous f_0-fall stretching

15. For reasons of clarity, downstepped accents were not counted as separate categories in the analysis of the accent distributions. Instead, downstep was looked at independently. Of the two non-downstepped accents in condition NFP-NC, one was rising, the other one falling.

Table 7.4 Experiment 6 – nuclear accents on the target words in condition NFP-C (N = 24)

accent	frequency	
H*L	6	25.0%
HL*	2	8.3%
L*H	4	16.7%
LH*	12	50.0%
total	24	100%

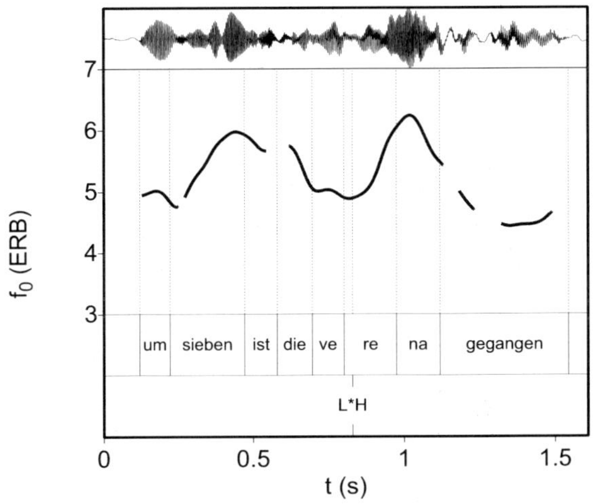

Figure 7.3 Experiment 6 – f_0-contour of an utterance of the sentence "*Um sieben ist die Verena gegangen.*" ('At seven, Verena went away.'), condition NFP-C, produced by Speaker 2

over the remaining utterance. The falling nuclear accents were integrated into the declination and did not stand out in any way.

The contrastive control condition (NFP-C) showed a more complex picture; cf. Table 7.4. In one-third of the utterances, the nuclear accents were similar to those observed in condition NFP-NC, i.e., we found falling accents with a preference for H*L. The remaining two-thirds of the utterances had a clearly different prosodic realization: they were characterized by rising nuclear accents, either LH* or L*H. An example f_0-track of the latter type is given in Figure 7.3. In this experimental condition, downstep of the nuclear accent could only be observed in half of the cases (12 out of 24 utterances). Most of the falling accents as well as some of the rising ones were downstepped, but the majority of the rising accents had H-tones characterized by an f_0 as high as or higher than that of the H-tones in the prenuclear accents. As can be seen in Figure 7.3, the f_0-movement of these accents stood out clearly from the falling declination line.

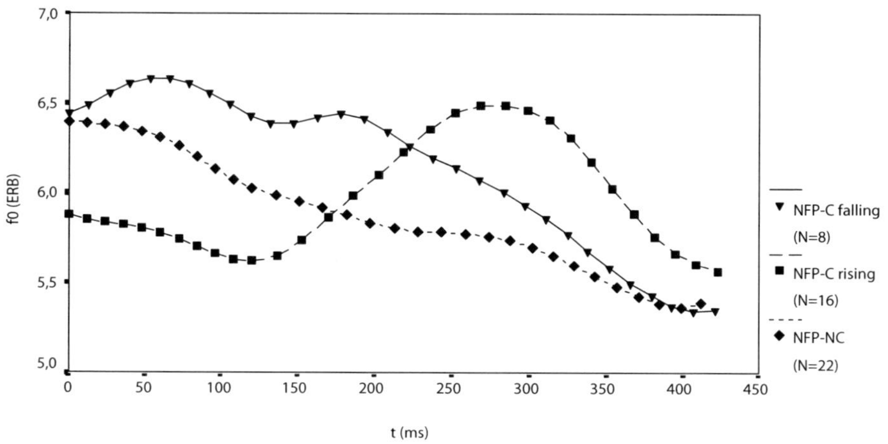

Figure 7.4 Experiment 6 – mean f_0-contours on the target words in the control conditions (NFP-NC and NFP-C)

A separate examination of the individual speakers' productions revealed that the strategy for the prosodic realization in condition NFP-C was highly speaker-dependent. While Speaker 1 mostly made use of H*L accents, Speakers 2 and 3 consistently produced rising accents. Speaker 4 was inconsistent in the use of rising and falling accents. A comparison of the accent distribution between the two control conditions yielded the following picture: Only two of the four speakers – namely, Speakers 2 and 3 – made consistent differences in accent type between the non-contrastive and the contrastive condition. They produced falling accents in the former and rising ones in the latter. The remaining two speakers used similar intonational means in the two conditions (Speaker 1) or produced inconsistent realizations in the contrastive condition (Speaker 4).

The f_0-contours of the individual utterances mainly differed in the direction of the f_0-movement on the nuclear accent. The distinction between rising and falling nuclear accents clearly affected the overall contour shape. The categorical distinctions within these groups (L*H vs. LH* in the group of rising accents and H*L vs. HL* in the group of falling accents), on the other hand, did not influence the contour shape in a substantial way. Mean contours representing the f_0-movement on the target words in the two control conditions are given in Figure 7.4.[16] For the mean contour of the non-contrastive condition (NFP-NC), the two utterances with rising accents were removed from consideration, resulting in a reduced N of 22.[17]

16. As in Experiment 3, the mean contours were computed by averaging time and f_0-values at all measuring points.

17. However, all utterances were included in the quantitative analysis (see below).

As for the contrastive condition (NFP-C), separate contours were computed for the utterances with rising (N = 16) and falling (N = 8) nuclear accents.

7.3.4.2 *Quantitative results*

With respect to the dependent variables given in Table 7.2 above, statistical comparisons were made between the members of minimal pairs of utterances, i.e., between lexically almost identical utterances read by the same speaker, differing only in the elements substituted for the focus particles (i.e., *dann* and *die*) and in the context story they were originally embedded in. The members of 24 minimal pairs (6 lexicalizations, 4 speakers) were compared by means of paired t-tests with an adjusted α-level of .0056 (Bonferroni adjustment, 9 t-tests). As a focus particle was not present in either of the two control conditions, the only independent variable considered was the (non-contrastive vs. contrastive) nature of the context (factor CONTEXT). The mean values for the 9 dependent variables and the results of the statistical comparisons are given in Table 7.5.

In the contrastive condition, the subject constituents were characterized by a significantly higher peak than in the non-contrastive condition. However, there were no significant differences between the two conditions with respect to f_0-minimum and f_0-excursion on the target words. While there was no effect of the context on the f_0-minimum of the prenuclear accents, contrastive utterances showed a significantly lower prenuclear f_0-peak and f_0-excursion than their non-contrastive counterparts. The f_0-differences are illustrated in Figure 7.5.

As for duration, we also found a difference in the expected direction. In contrastive utterances, on average, the two relevant syllables were 10ms longer than in non-contrastive ones. However, at the adjusted α-level of .0056, this difference was

Table 7.5 Experiment 6 – f_0-, duration, and intensity variables compared between the non-contrastive control condition (NFP-NC) and the contrastive control condition (NFP-C); quantitative results and paired t-tests (one-tailed, except for f_0-*min* and f_0-min_p), N = 24, α = .0056 (Bonferroni adjustment, 9 t-tests)

variable	non-contr.	contr.	sign.?	T	p
f_0-*min* (ERB)	5.46	5.55	n.s.	1.29	.209
f_0-*max* (ERB)	6.32	6.55	✓	2.87	<.005
df_0 (ERB)	0.86	1.00	n.s.	1.32	.100
dur-s_{23} (ms)	288	298	n.s.	1.74	.048
int-syll	0.99	1.03	✓	6.47	<.001
int-const	1.00	1.03	✓	5.80	<.001
f_0-min_p (ERB)	5.47	5.47	n.s.	–0.07	.949
f_0-max_p (ERB)	7.31	6.93	✓	–3.60	<.001
df_{0p} (ERB)	1.84	1.46	✓	–3.70	<.001

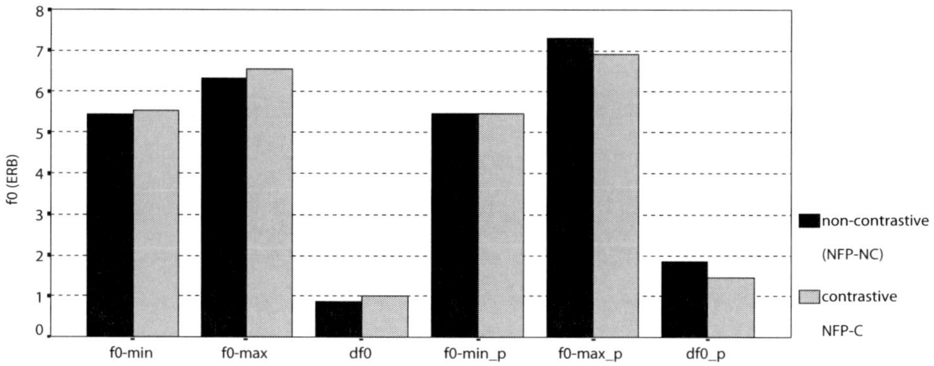

Figure 7.5 Experiment 6 – f_0-variables compared between the non-contrastive control condition (NFP-NC) and the contrastive control condition (NFP-C); N = 24

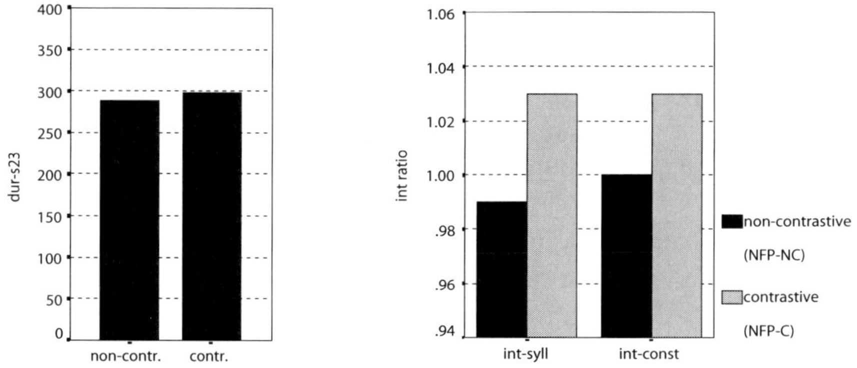

Figure 7.6 Experiment 6 – duration (left panel) and intensity variables (right panel) compared between the non-contrastive control condition (NFP-NC) and the contrastive control condition (NFP-C); N = 24

not significant. With respect to the two intensity variables, significant differences could be observed. The syllable carrying the nuclear accent as well as the whole target word had a greater intensity in the contrastive than in the non-contrastive condition. The differences were small, but highly consistent across the items.[18] The results of the comparison concerning the duration and intensity variables are illustrated in Figure 7.6.

18. The small effect size was partly due to the fact that relative intensities were used.

7.3.5 Results: Conditions with focus particles

7.3.5.1 *Qualitative results*

The accent distribution in the non-contrastive condition with focus particles (condition FP-NC) was very similar to that of the non-contrastive control condition (NFP-NC); cf. Table 7.6. We mostly found falling nuclear accents with a slight preference for H*L. The two instances of rising accents (LH*) were again produced by Speaker 3. Speaker 4 consistently produced HL* accents; the remaining two speakers mainly realized the nuclear accents as H*L. An example contour involving the latter accent is given in Figure 7.7. In condition FP-NC, the H-tone of the nuclear accent was downstepped relative to a prenuclear H-tone in 23 out of 24 cases (95.8%). The resulting overall contour shape of the majority of utterances thus strongly resembled the one that was most frequently observed in condition NFP-NC: a prenuclear rise followed by a slowly falling contour without any remarkable deviating f_0-movements.

Table 7.6 Experiment 6 – nuclear accents on the target words in condition FP-NC (N = 24)

accent	frequency	
H*L	13	54.2%
HL*	9	37.5%
LH*	2	8.3%
total	24	100%

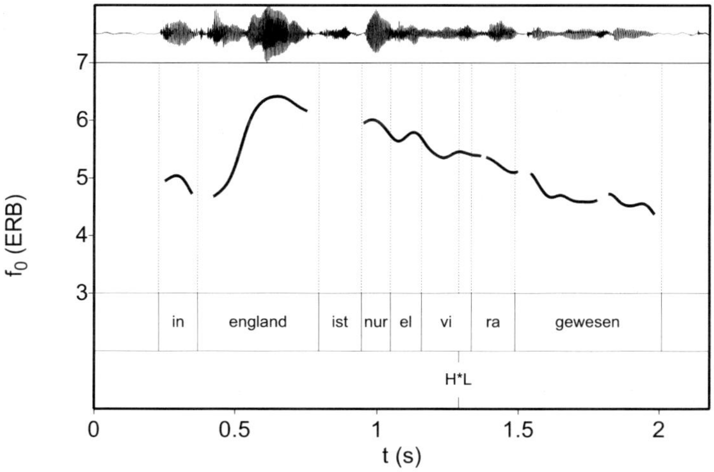

Figure 7.7 Experiment 6 – f_0-contour of an utterance of the sentence "*In England ist nur Elvira gewesen.*" ('Only Elvira went to England.'), condition FP-NC, produced by Speaker 2

The utterances produced in contrastive contexts (condition FP-C) showed a different accent distribution, resembling that from the contrastive control condition (NFP-C); cf. Table 7.7. Half of the utterances were characterized by falling nuclear accents (H*L or HL*, the former being more frequent), the other half by rising ones (L*H or LH*). An example of an L*H accent on the subject constituent is given in Figure 7.8. As in condition NFP-C, about half of the nuclear accents (13 out of 24 cases, 54.2%) were downstepped relative to a prenuclear H-tone, and again, it was mainly the falling accents that were affected by downstep. The rising accents, on the other hand, had H-tones that clearly stood out from the falling f_0-movement. As in the control conditions, downstep was thus clearly less frequent in contrast-inducing contexts.

The diversity of accent types observed in condition FP-C led us again to look at the individual speakers' productions separately. As in condition NFP-C, we found that speakers followed different prosodic strategies in producing the utterances. Speaker 1 consequently realized H*L accents; Speakers 2 and 3 both produced

Table 7.7 Experiment 6 – nuclear accents on the target words in condition FP-C (N = 24)

accent	frequency	
H*L	8	33.3%
HL*	4	16.7%
L*H	5	20.8%
LH*	7	29.2%
total	24	100%

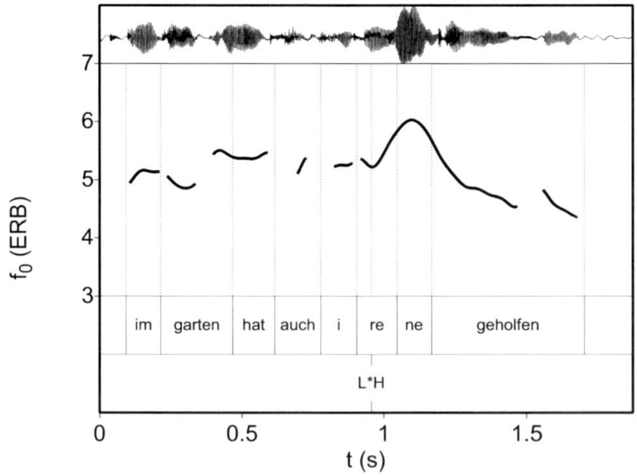

Figure 7.8 Experiment 6 – f_0-contour of an utterance of the sentence *"Im Garten hat auch Irene geholfen."* ('Irene helped in the garden, too.'), condition FP-C, produced by Speaker 2

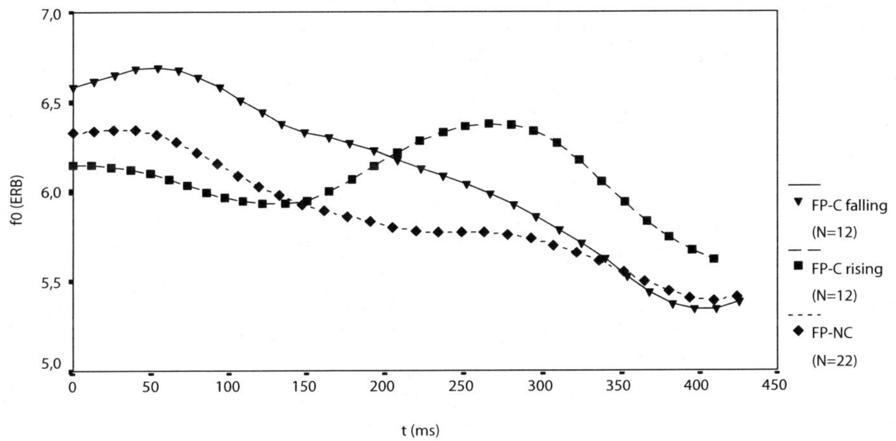

Figure 7.9 Experiment 6 – mean f_0-contours on the target words in the conditions with focus particles (FP-NC and FP-C)

rising accents, but differed in their preferred accent type: L*H (Speaker 2) or LH* (Speaker 3). The utterances of Speaker 4 were characterized by falling nuclear accents (H*L and HL*).

A comparison between conditions FP-NC and FP-C revealed that, as in the control conditions, only two of the four speakers made consistent differences in accent type between the utterances embedded in non-contrastive and contrastive contexts. These were the same speakers who made intonational differences between conditions NFP-NC and NFP-C (Speakers 2 and 3). The remaining two speakers produced similar patterns in the contrastive and the non-contrastive condition.

Figure 7.9 shows the mean contours representing the f_0-movement on the target words in the two experimental conditions with focus particles. The differences in the direction of the f_0-excursion are clearly visible. For the mean contour of condition FP-NC, the two utterances with rising accents were excluded, resulting in a reduced N of 22; as for condition FP-C, separate contours were computed for the utterances with rising and falling accents (N = 12 in both groups).[19] Again, the distinction between H*L and HL* in the group of falling accents and the distinction between L*H and LH* in the group of rising accents were irrelevant for the overall contour shape, which is why these differentiations are ignored here.

We also compared all four experimental conditions with respect to accent distribution and downstep. From what was said above, it should be clear that corresponding utterances with and without focus particles showed a very similar

19. As in the control conditions, all utterances were included in the quantitative analysis (see below).

picture in the qualitative analysis, if they were produced in contexts of the same type. If the speakers produced different intonational patterns at all, the (contrast-inducing or non-contrast-inducing) context rather than the presence or absence of a focus particle was crucial for the realization of the nuclear accent.

The correspondence between the two non-contrastive conditions NFP-NC and FP-NC and between the two contrastive conditions NFP-C and FP-C became particularly obvious when the accent distributions were compared for each speaker individually; cf. Table 7.8. With few exceptions, Speakers 1 and 4 produced falling accents in all conditions. The intonation of their utterances was thus neither affected by the context nor by the presence/absence of a focus particle. Speakers 2 and 3, on the other hand, produced clearly different intonational patterns in the contrastive and non-contrastive conditions, but did not differentiate between the utterances that contained a focus particle and those that did not.

Similar results were found with respect to the occurrence of downstep. The percentage of downstepped nuclear accents across the four experimental conditions is illustrated in Figure 7.10. The non-contrastive conditions NFP-NC and FP-NC showed downstep in almost all cases, while in the contrastive conditions NFP-C and FP-C, downstep could only be found in about half of the utterances.[20] Thus, the occurrence of downstep also depended on the nature of the context, but not on the presence or absence of a focus particle.

Table 7.8 Experiment 6 – nuclear accents on the target words, compared across experimental conditions

speaker	Speaker 1				Speaker 2			
accent	H*L	HL*	L*H	LH*	H*L	HL*	L*H	LH*
NFP-NC	6	–	–	–	6	–	–	–
NFP-C	5	–	–	1	–	–	4	2
FP-NC	4	2	–	–	5	1	–	–
FP-C	6	–	–	–	–	–	5	1
speaker	**Speaker 3**				**Speaker 4**			
accent	H*L	HL*	L*H	LH*	H*L	HL*	L*H	LH*
NFP-NC	4	–	–	2	–	6	–	–
NFP-C	–	–	–	6	1	2	–	3
FP-NC	4	–	–	2	–	6	–	–
FP-C	–	–	–	6	2	4	–	–

20. As noted above, the downstepped nuclear accents in the contrastive conditions mainly belonged to the group of falling accents, which corresponded to the typical accentuation pattern of the non-contrastive conditions.

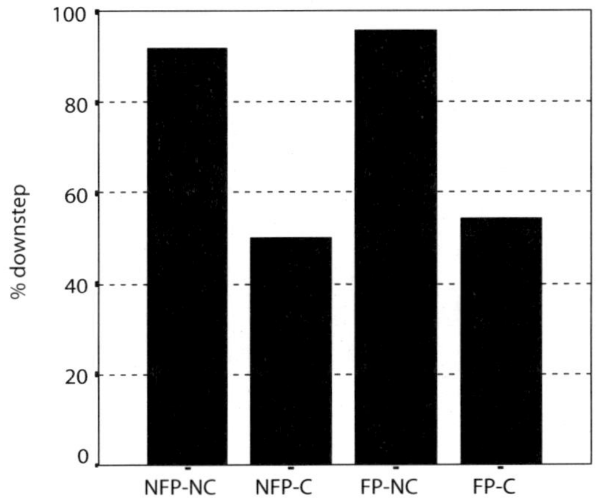

Figure 7.10 Experiment 6 – percentage of downstepped nuclear accents on the target words, compared across experimental conditions (N = 24 in each condition)

7.3.5.2 *Quantitative results*

To compare the prosodic properties of the elicited utterances in all four experimental conditions quantitatively, we performed a number of ANOVAs. As each speaker had produced all critical sentences, it was possible to employ a repeated-measures design with the nature of the context (factor CONTEXT; contrast-inducing vs. non-contrast-inducing) and the presence of a focus particle (factor PARTICLE; present vs. not present) as the two independent variables.[21] For dependent variables, we chose the variables that had shown significant differences in the comparison of the control conditions, i.e., the variables that had turned out to be relevant for the marking of contrast in the position of the regular focus accent: the f_0-maximum of the nuclear accent (f_0-*max*), the two intensity variables (*int-syll* and *int-const*), and the f_0-maximum (f_0-max_p) and f_0-excursion (df_{0p}) of the prenuclear accent.[22]

The mean values for f_0-*max* in the individual experimental conditions are given in Table 7.9 and illustrated in Figure 7.11. We found a significant main effect of the factor CONTEXT: f_0-*max* was significantly higher in the utterances embedded in contrast-inducing contexts ($F = 14.87$, $p < .002$). There was no main effect of the factor PARTICLE ($F = 1.08$, $p = .310$) and no interaction between the two factors

21. See also Table 7.1 above.

22. As the duration variable *dur*-s_{23} had at least shown a trend in the expected direction, an ANOVA was carried out for this variable, too. However, we found no significant main effects of the independent variables on duration and no interaction.

Table 7.9 Experiment 6 – f_0-*max*, compared across experimental conditions; mean values in ERB (N = 24 in each condition)

	non-contr. ...-NC	contrastive ...-C
without FP NFP-...	6.32	6.55
with FP FP-...	6.22	6.48

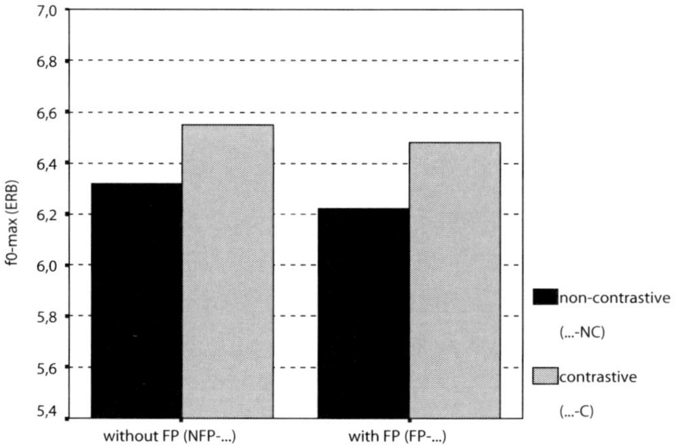

Figure 7.11 Experiment 6 – f_0-*max*, compared across experimental conditions (N = 24 in each condition)

(F = 0.06, p = .814). Post hoc contrast tests revealed a similar picture: Conditions NFP-NC and NFP-C differed significantly (F = 8.22, p < .01), and so did conditions FP-NC and FP-C (F = 8.28, p < .01), indicating an influence of CONTEXT on f_0-*max*. On the other hand, there was no significant difference between conditions NFP-NC and FP-NC (F = 0.65, p = .428) or between conditions NFP-C and FP-C (F = 0.98, p = .333), suggesting that f_0-*max* did not depend on the presence of a focus particle.

The results for the intensity variables are given in Table 7.10 and Figure 7.12. For *int-syll* as well as for *int-const* we found a significant main effect of CONTEXT (*int-syll*: F = 43.20, p < .001; *int-const*: F = 40.46, p < .001), but no main effect of PARTICLE (*int-syll*: F = 0.88, p = .359; *int-const*: F = 3.78, p = .064) and no interaction (*int-syll*: F = 3.11, p = .091; *int-const*: F = 0.88, p = .362). The target words had a higher intensity in utterances produced in contrast-inducing contexts. Post hoc contrast tests revealed significant differences between conditions NFP-NC and NFP-C (*int-syll*: F = 41.87, p < .001; *int-const*: F = 33.66,

Table 7.10 Experiment 6 – intensity variables *int-syll*/*int-const*, compared across experimental conditions; mean values (N = 24 in each condition)

	non-contr. ...-NC	contrastive ...-C
without FP NFP-...	0.99 / 1.00	1.03 / 1.03
with FP FP-...	0.99 / 1.00	1.02 / 1.02

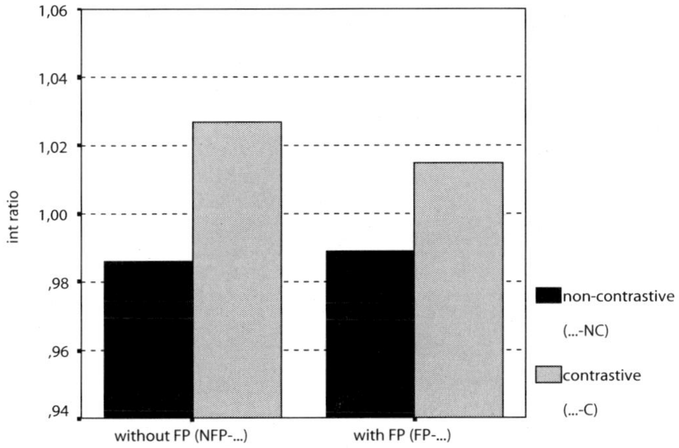

Figure 7.12 Experiment 6 – *int-syll*, compared across experimental conditions (N = 24 in each condition)

p < .001) and between conditions FP-NC and FP-C (*int-syll*: F = 15.21, p < .002; *int-const*: F = 20.17, p < .001), but not between conditions NFP-NC and FP-NC (*int-syll*: F = 0.29, p = .595; *int-const*: F = 0.643, p = .431) or between conditions NFP-C and FP-C (*int-syll*: F = 2.52, p = .126; *int-const*: F = 2.86, p = .105). The intensity of the element bearing the nuclear accent was clearly also influenced by the type of the context, but not by the presence or absence of a focus particle in the utterance.

As shown by the mean values in Table 7.11 (cf. also Figure 7.13), the prenuclear f_0-maximum was smaller in contrast-inducing contexts than in non-contrast-inducing ones. While this main effect of CONTEXT was statistically significant (F = 23.39, p < .001), there was neither a main effect for PARTICLE (F = 0.06, p = .812) nor an interaction between the two factors (F = 1.46, p = .240). The post hoc contrast tests did not yield clear results this time: Although there were significant differences between conditions NFP-NC and NFP-C (F = 12.99, p < .002), conditions FP-NC and FP-C did not differ significantly in the peak of the prenuclear accent (F = 3.73, p = .066). Again, there was no significant difference between

Table 7.11 Experiment 6 – f_0-max_p, compared across experimental conditions; mean values in ERB (N = 24 in each condition)

	non-contr. ...-NC	contrastive ...-C
without FP NFP-...	7.31	6.93
with FP FP-...	7.23	7.04

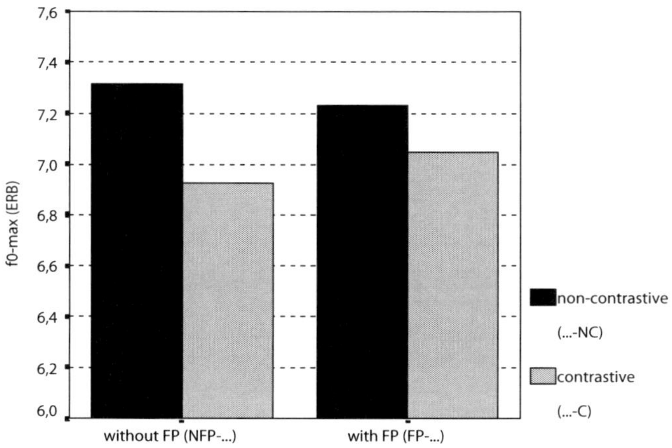

Figure 7.13 Experiment 6 – f_0-max_p, compared across experimental conditions (N = 24 in each condition)

conditions NFP-NC and FP-NC ($F = 0.43$, $p = .521$) or between conditions NFP-C and FP-C ($F = 1.56$, $p = .224$).

The results for the f_0-excursion of the prenuclear accents are given in Table 7.12 and Figure 7.14. There was a main effect of CONTEXT ($F = 27.70$, $p < .001$) – the prenuclear f_0-excursion was significantly smaller in utterances produced in contrastive contexts. As in the cases of the other variables, there was no significant main effect for PARTICLE ($F = 0.13$, $p = .719$) and no significant interaction between the two factors ($F = 0.78$, $p = .338$). The post hoc contrast tests confirmed these results: Conditions NFP-NC and NFP-C differed significantly ($F = 13.71$, $p <.002$), and so did conditions FP-NC and FP-C ($F = 4.89$, $p < .04$). On the other hand, there was neither a significant difference between conditions NFP-NC and FP-NC ($F = 0.63$, $p = .437$) nor between conditions NFP-C and FP-C ($F = 0.26$, $p = .612$).

Table 7.12 Experiment 6 – df_{0P}, compared across experimental conditions; mean values in ERB (N = 24 in each condition)

	non-contr. ...-NC	contrastive ...-C
without FP NFP-...	1.84	1.46
with FP FP-...	1.74	1.51

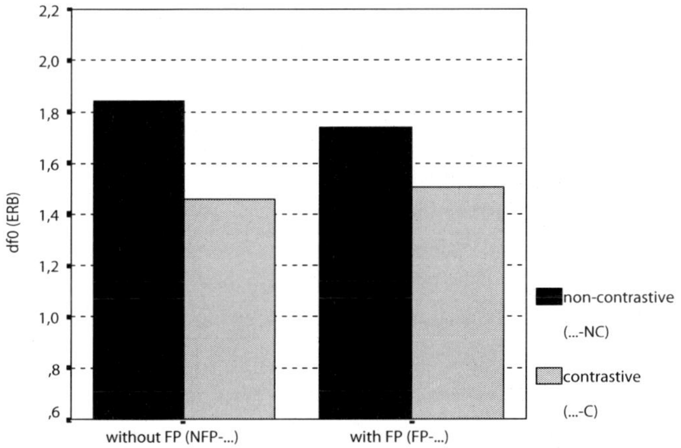

Figure 7.14 Experiment 6 – df_{0P}, compared across experimental conditions (N = 24 in each condition)

7.3.6 Discussion

The purpose of Experiment 6 was to determine whether focus particles are always associated with contrastive foci. To answer this question, we had to look at the prosodic realization of contrast in the position of the regular sentence focus first. We will discuss the latter issue in Section 7.3.6.1, before we will return to our original research question in Section 7.3.6.2.

7.3.6.1 *The prosodic marking of contrast in focus position*

In the utterances of the two control conditions without focus particles (NFP-NC and NFP-C), we found both qualitative (phonological) and quantitative (phonetic) differences between new information focus and contrastive focus. In this subsection, the results are summarized and evaluated with respect to the findings reported in the literature and the predictions formulated in Hypothesis 1 above.

Nuclear accents of utterances produced in non-contrastive contexts were falling pitch accents (H*L or HL*), which were integrated in the f_0-declination. They were typically downstepped. In contrast-inducing contexts, on the other hand, nuclear accents were realized as rising pitch accents (L*H or LH*) in a high proportion of the cases, but the falling accents typical of the non-contrastive condition could also be observed. Downstep was much less frequent here. Thus, we found clear categorical differences between nuclear accents corresponding to new information and contrastive nuclear accents.

While the individual speakers' productions in the non-contrastive control condition were relatively consistent, there was a higher variability of prosodic realizations in the contrast condition. The speakers either used the same prosodic pattern as in the non-contrastive contexts, or they produced a clearly distinct pattern involving rising instead of falling accents. There are two possible sources of this variability. It is possible that there are indeed different ways to realize contrastive focus prosodically, i.e., that speakers have the choice between the two prosodic patterns. However, the observed variability could also be an artifact of the experimental design. It may be that the speakers simply did not consistently produce contrastive accents, either because they did not notice the intended contrast in the context paragraphs or because they used a 'narrative prosody' neutralizing contrastive accents.

We can only speculate about the reason for the inconsistent prosodic realizations in the contrast condition, but the second of the mentioned possibilities is more plausible. From the point of view of linguistic economy, it is unlikely that an information-structural category such as contrast can be expressed by two entirely different prosodic patterns, one of which is also typical of the opposite category (new information focus). In addition, the observed variability in the prosodic realization was mainly a variability between speakers. With the exception of Speaker 4, the individual speakers were relatively consistent in their productions across the items. Thus, it is plausible that two speakers consequently produced the intended differences between contrastive and non-contrastive utterances, whereas the other two speakers did not use or only insufficiently used the context information for the determination of the appropriate prosodic structure. This issue will be looked at from the point of view of speech perception in Section 7.4.

In addition to the differences in accent type and the occurrence of downstep, we observed significant quantitative differences between the contrastive and the non-contrastive control condition. Contrastive nuclear accents showed higher f_0-maxima, and the accented elements were characterized by a higher intensity. Their duration, however, was not significantly longer than the duration of elements bearing non-contrastive nuclear accents. Another relevant feature of the examined contrastive utterances was that, compared to their non-contrastive counterparts, the prenuclear accents were compressed, i.e., they showed a lower f_0-maximum and f_0-excursion. Through this flattening of the initial part of the f_0-contour, the contrastive nuclear accent became even more salient and outstanding. Importantly, the observed differences between the two control conditions were statistically significant even though the 'non-contrastive' realizations in contrastive contexts were included in the analysis.

In Section 7.3.2, it was noted that the sentences of the contrastive and non-contrastive conditions did not only differ in the information-structural status of the target word. In particular, it can be argued that the sentence-initial adverbial was a contrastive topic in the non-contrastive conditions, but a background element in the contrastive conditions, and that this was relevant for the prosody of the elicited utterances. There are at least two conceivable effects of this difference on the outcome of the production experiment. First, it may have been decisive for the prosodic differences observed on the sentence-initial adverbials themselves. As contrastive topics, the adverbials are predicted to show a greater f_0-maximum and f_0-excursion than as background elements. In the latter case, one might even expect them to be completely deaccented. That we nevertheless found prenuclear accents in all utterances is probably due to the fact that the adverbials were non-pronominal, full PPs rather than proadverbs.

Second, the information-structural status and resulting prosodic properties of the adverbials may have influenced the realization of the target words, i.e., the subjects bearing the nuclear accent. A greater prominence of the sentence-initial element could have led to a reduced prominence on the target word, and vice versa. This may have affected the gradual phonetic properties of the target words. In particular, it is likely to have affected their intensity, as intensity was measured rel ative to the mean intensity of the respective utterances. However, the differences in the type of the nuclear accent (falling vs. rising) between the non-contrastive and contrastive conditions cannot be put down to differences concerning the sentence-initial elements. The nuclear accent type depended on the information-structural properties of the target word only, and the target word was characterized by new information focus in the non-contrastive condition and by contrastive focus in the contrastive condition.

To sum up: With regard to the prosodic realization of the constituent bearing the nuclear accent, our study substantially confirmed the results of Bannert (1985), Alter, Mleinek, Rohe, Steube & Umbach (2001), and Baumann, Grice & Steindamm (2006). To the factors investigated by these authors, we added intensity, showing that this parameter is also relevant for the marking of contrast in German. Hypothesis 1 could partly be confirmed: The nature of the context (contrast-inducing vs. non-contrast-inducing) influenced the prosody of the examined utterances. However, in contrast to our original intention, the prosodic differences resulted not only from the variation of the information-structural properties of the elements bearing the nuclear accent, but also from the differences in the status of the sentence-initial adverbials. We now return to the question of whether the presence of a FP has an additional effect on the prosodic realization.

7.3.6.2 *The relation between focus particles and information structure*

The qualitative and the quantitative comparison between all four conditions showed that the utterances with focus particles prosodically behaved like the corresponding utterances without particles. There were clear differences between the non-contrastive (NFP-NC and FP-NC) and the contrastive conditions (NFP-C and FP-C), i.e., the (non-)contrastivity of an utterance, determined by the content of the respective context paragraph, crucially influenced its prosodic properties. On the other hand, we did not find differences between the conditions with (FP-NC and FP-C) and without focus particles (NFP-NC and NFP-C), nor did we find an interaction between the nature of the context and the presence/absence of a focus particle. This suggests that the occurrence of a focus particle was irrelevant for prosody. In particular, condition FP-C corresponded to the contrastive control condition NFP-C, and condition FP-NC corresponded to the non-contrastive control condition NFP-NC, but not to the contrastive conditions NFP-C and FP-C. The presence of a focus particle was clearly not sufficient for the realization of a contrastive focus accent, confirming Hypothesis 2.

As with the control conditions, we found a higher variability in the prosodic realization in the contrastive condition FP-C than in the non-contrastive condition FP-NC. While the utterances of the latter were almost always characterized by falling focus accents, the critical contrastive condition showed the division into utterances with falling and utterances with rising nuclear accents familiar from the contrastive control condition. Again, this was mainly a variability between speakers, and only the two speakers that did not consistently produce rising accents in condition NFP-C did the same in condition FP-C. As argued above, the different realizations are likely to be caused by the experimental design. We consider the rising accents to represent the appropriate prosodic pattern in the contrastive conditions. Importantly, the observed prosodic variability does not reduce the meaningfulness of the results with respect to our research question, as it occurred in the contrastive control condition (NFP-C) as well as in the critical contrastive condition with focus particles (FP-C). In spite of the fact that the results in the contrastive conditions partly contradicted our expectations, it could be shown that the contrastive conditions prosodically differed from the non-contrastive ones and that there was no difference in prosody between the corresponding conditions with and without focus particles.

The results of Experiment 6 provided evidence for the claim that focus particles can associate with both new information foci and contrastive foci. The type of focus is determined by the information-structural function of the utterance in the discourse, which was controlled by the context paragraphs in our experiment.

Consequently, focus particles do not induce a certain type of focus, but interact with an independently given focus-background partition. Our findings thus support the modular perspective on the relation between focus particles and information structure argued for by Dimroth (2004), among others.

7.4 Experiment 7: Contrast in speech perception

The utterances elicited in Experiment 6 were used as stimuli in a speech perception experiment that tested whether the proposed prosodic correlates of contrastive focus give rise to a contrastive interpretation. The participants were auditorily presented with the utterances and had to indicate whether they perceived them as non-contrastive or contrastive. These judgements were related to the intended information structure of the utterances (determined by the original contexts used in the production study) and to their categorical prosodic properties. In this way, we also addressed the question of whether both of the two distinct prosodic patterns observed in the contrastive conditions of Experiment 6 express contrast or whether only the cases with rising nuclear accents create a contrastive impression, as suggested above.

7.4.1 Hypotheses

We expected the participants in the perception experiment to be sensitive to the prosodic variation in the stimuli. By and large, the utterances that were originally embedded in contrast-inducing contexts (conditions NFP-C and FP-C) should be interpreted as contrastive more frequently than the utterances originally embedded in non-contrastive contexts (conditions NFP-NC and FP-NC). However, as shown above, not all utterances produced in contrastive contexts were characterized by the prosodic properties that were claimed to be typical of the marking of contrast in German. If we are right in assuming that some utterances were produced with a non-contrastive prosody even when the context called for a contrastive accent, these utterances should be interpreted as not involving contrast, i.e., like the utterances that come from non-contrastive contexts. The two hypotheses of Experiment 7 are given in (9) and (10).

(9) **Hypothesis 3:** Utterances embedded in contrast-inducing contexts receive contrastive interpretations more frequently than utterances produced in non-contrast-inducing contexts.

(10) **Hypothesis 4:** Utterances with rising nuclear accents receive contrastive interpretations more frequently than utterances with falling nuclear accents.

Under the assumption that contrast in the position of the regular sentence focus is marked by rising nuclear accents, while non-contrastive utterances are characterized by falling accents, the type of the nuclear accent of an utterance (Hypothesis 4) should facilitate a better prediction of the utterance's preferred interpretation than the type of its context in the production experiment (Hypothesis 3).

7.4.2 Method

Participants. 40 participants (aged 20 to 35, with a mean age of 24.1), of whom 33 were female and 7 male, took part in Experiment 7. All of them were native speakers of German and lacked any knowledge about the purpose of the study. They received a small financial reimbursement for their participation.

Materials. All 96 elicited utterances from Experiment 6 (4 conditions, 6 lexicalizations, 4 speakers) were used as stimuli for Experiment 7. The focus particles (*auch*, *nur*), as well as the words substituting them in the control conditions (*dann*, *die*), were cut from the utterances to avoid a possible influence on the interpretation. As these words were short and unaccented in the original utterances, their removal did not cause an unnatural prosody. As a result, the four sentences of each lexicalization did not differ in their wording in the perception task, and the only information participants could use for their decisions was of a prosodic nature. We did not use any fillers in Experiment 7.

Procedure. Before the actual experiment, the participants were made familiar with the notion of contrast. With an example sentence embedded in contexts comparable to those in (7) and (8) above (presented in written form), the two relevant information-structural usages (non-contrastive vs. contrastive) were introduced. By comparing the corresponding discourse functions, it was demonstrated that a single sentence can be used for both purposes; however, the participants' attention was not explicitly drawn to the role of prosody in differentiating between the two usages. The participants were instructed to listen to the stimulus utterances one after another and to choose which of the two usages they found more plausible, without being aware of the actual discourse context.

For the perception experiment, we used a web-based presentation, which the participants worked through at their own pace. The stimulus utterances were presented via headphones, and the participants could listen to them repeatedly; there was no time limit. After listening to an utterance, the participants had to select either *kein Kontrast* ('no contrast') or *Kontrast* ('contrast') on the screen, before they continued with the next item. To avoid confusion, the left-right order of the two possible choices was not randomized. A short practice session consisting of four items served to familiarize the participants with the task. The 96 critical items were pseudo-randomized for each participant. The participants were allowed to take short breaks whenever they wanted; the experiment took about 15 minutes.

7.4.3 Results and discussion

For each stimulus utterance, the number of responses for non-contrast and contrast was determined. Altogether, the participants chose the two possible discourse functions with a similar frequency (non-contrast: 50.8%; contrast: 49.2%).[23] The distribution of the judgements was related to the type of the original context (testing Hypothesis 3) and to the intonation of the individual stimulus utterances (testing Hypothesis 4).

The results for intended contrast/non-contrast, based on the type of context used in the production experiment, are given in Table 7.13 and illustrated in Figure 7.15. As expected, utterances that were originally embedded in contrast-inducing contexts (conditions NFP-C and FP-C) were more frequently interpreted

Table 7.13 Experiment 7 – percentage of contrastive and non-contrastive interpretations, compared across context types

response	**context type**	
	non-contrastive	**contrastive**
non-contrastive	59.5%	42.0%
contrastive	40.5%	58.0%

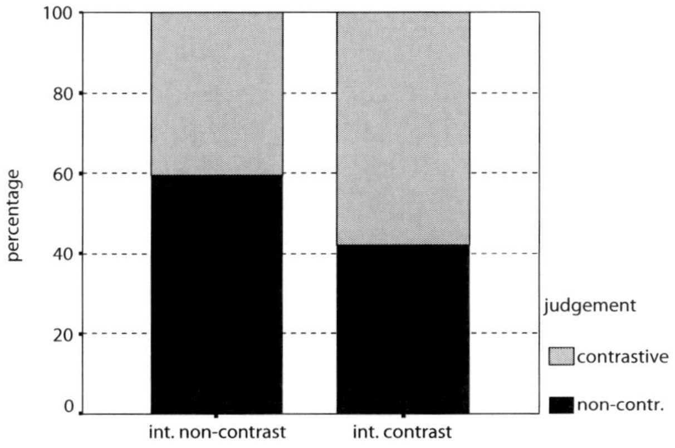

Figure 7.15 Experiment 7 – percentage of contrastive and non-contrastive interpretations, compared across context types

23. The total number of judgements was 3840.

as being contrastive than utterances embedded in non-contrast-inducing contexts (conditions NFP-NC and FP-NC). This difference was statistically significant (χ^2-test: $\chi^2 = 118.33$, df = 1, $p < .001$). These results confirmed Hypothesis 3: the interpretation of the utterances depended on the contexts they were originally embedded in. Thus, the information structure of the utterances must have been reflected in their prosody, and this information was used by the hearers to interpret the utterances.

We also compared the proportions of the two possible judgements between the utterances that originally contained a focus particle (conditions FP-NC and FP-C) and those that did not (conditions NFP-NC and NFP-C). The somewhat unexpected result was that the focus particle utterances were assigned less contrastive interpretations (41.8%) than the utterances that did not have a focus particle in the production experiment (56.7%), the difference also being significant (χ^2-test: $\chi^2 = 85.82$, df = 1, $p < .001$). At first sight, this result seems to contradict Altmann's (1976a, b) and Foolen's (1993) hypothesis that focus particle utterances always involve contrast, as well as our hypothesis that the information structure of an utterance is independent of the presence or absence of a focus particle. However, as noted above, the speakers in the production study did not always use the expected contrastive prosody in the utterances of the contrastive conditions, as the contexts did not reliably evoke contrast. The unexpected non-contrastive realizations (downstepped falling instead of rising nuclear accents) of utterances with intended contrast were more frequent in the condition with focus particles (FP-C) than in the condition without particles (NFP-C). Although we do not have a straightforward explanation of this fact (it can only be speculated that the reason lay in the stimulus materials, i.e., in the quality of the context paragraphs), it certainly had an effect on the information-structural interpretation of the utterances and thus contributed to the described distribution of judgements in the perception study.

There is another fact that indicates that the correspondence of an utterance with our hypotheses about the prosodic realization of contrast is a better predictor of its interpretation in the perception task than the type of the original context: as mentioned in Section 7.3.6.1, the prosodic variability observed in the conditions with contrast-inducing contexts was mainly a variability between speakers. While Speakers 2 and 3 produced consistent differences between the utterances intended to be contrastive and non-contrastive, Speakers 1 and 4 did not use or only inconsistently used prosody to differentiate between the conditions. A separate consideration of the utterances of each speaker and their interpretation revealed that the utterances of Speakers 2 and 3 were interpreted as being contrastive more frequently than the utterances of the remaining two speakers; cf. Table 7.14. This corresponds to our hypothesis that Speakers 2 and 3 predominantly used a contrastive prosody in the conditions with intended contrast, while Speakers 1 and 4 did not.

Table 7.14 Experiment 7 – percentage of contrastive and non-contrastive interpretations, compared across speakers

response	**speaker**			
	Speaker 1	**Speaker 2**	**Speaker 3**	**Speaker 4**
non-contrastive	60.8%	41.4%	45.0%	55.8%
contrastive	39.2%	58.6%	55.0%	44.2%

Table 7.15 Experiment 7 – percentage of contrastive and non-contrastive interpretations, compared across types of nuclear accents (falling vs. rising)

response	**nuclear accent type**	
	falling	**rising**
non-contrastive	60.3%	34.0%
contrastive	39.7%	66.0%

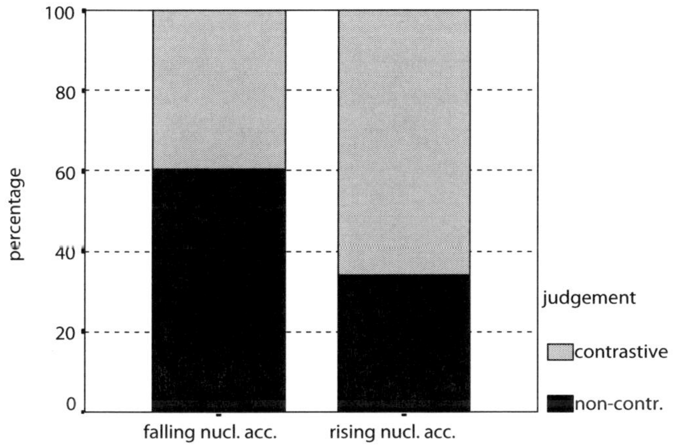

Figure 7.16 Experiment 7 – percentage of contrastive and non-contrastive interpretations, compared across types of nuclear accents (falling vs. rising)

Addressing the question of the relation between an utterance's intonation and its interpretation directly, we compared the utterances with rising and falling nuclear accents with respect to the proportions of contrastive and non-contrastive interpretations in the perception experiment; cf. Table 7.15 and Figure 7.16. Utterances with rising nuclear accents were significantly more often interpreted as involving contrast than utterances with falling nuclear accents (χ^2-test: $\chi^2 = 242.86$, $df = 1$, $p < .001$). Hypothesis 4 could therefore also be confirmed.

More importantly, the direction of the f_0-movement on the nuclear accent facilitates a better prediction of the interpretation than the type of the original context of a given utterance: the percentage of contrastive interpretations was higher for the utterances with rising nuclear accents (66.0%) than for the utterances originally embedded in contrast-inducing contexts (58.0%). Once more, this suggests that only a subgroup of the utterances from the contrastive conditions – those with rising nuclear accents – were actually characterized by a contrastive intonation. On the other hand, the percentage of contrastive judgements was about the same for the utterances with falling nuclear accents and the utterances produced in non-contrast-inducing contexts (39.7% and 40.5%, respectively). This was expected given that there was much less variation in the realization of the utterances in the non-contrastive conditions – the majority of them were characterized by falling nuclear accents.

In the analysis of the speech perception data, we have so far only distinguished between rising and falling nuclear accents. The assumption was that rising accents are typical of contrastive focus, while non-contrastive (new information) focus is characterized by falling nuclear accents (cf. Section 7.2). However, it might be useful to look separately at the individual pitch accent types identified in the production study (H*L, HL*, L*H, LH*) to see whether they had an influence on the interpretation that goes beyond the effect of being rising or falling. The relevant results are given in Table 7.16 and Figure 7.17. As expected, the rising accents did not differ significantly in their interpretations (χ^2-test: $\chi^2 = 1.32$, df $= 1$, p $= .251$). L*H and LH* were interpreted as contrastive in a similar proportion of the cases. Both accents are adequate for the marking of contrast in the position of the regular sentence focus in German. Although the interpretations of the two falling accents H*L and HL* were also comparable, the small difference between them turned out to be statistically significant (χ^2-test: $\chi^2 = 12.35$, df $= 1$, p $< .001$). H*L received a contrastive interpretation more frequently than HL*. Still, both accents are more adequate for non-contrastive than for contrastive utterances.

The results discussed above suggest that the prosodic variability observed in the experimental conditions with intended contrast did not result from the availability of different strategies for the marking of contrast in German, but from the fact that not all speakers realized the utterances of the contrastive conditions with a contrastive prosody. To test this hypothesis, we compared the interpretation the presumably non-contrastive realizations in the contrastive conditions to the interpretation of the contrastive realizations in the same conditions and the non-contrastive realizations in the non-contrastive conditions. The proportions of contrastive/non-contrastive judgements for the three groups of utterances are given in Table 7.17; cf. also Figure 7.18. The first group (N = 44) included the utterances of conditions NFP-NC and FP-NC, but without the four utterances of Speaker 3 that were characterized by a rising nuclear accent. The second group (N = 20)

Table 7.16 Experiment 7 – percentage of contrastive and non-contrastive interpretations, compared across nuclear accents

response	nuclear accent			
	H*L	HL*	L*H	LH*
non-contrastive	57.3%	64.5%	30.6%	33.9%
contrastive	42.7%	35.5%	69.4%	66.1%

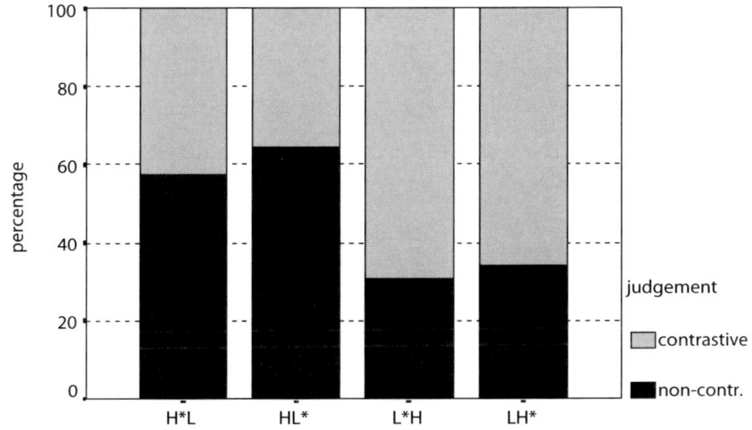

Figure 7.17 Experiment 7 – percentage of contrastive and non-contrastive interpretations, compared across nuclear accents

consisted of those utterances of the contrastive conditions NFP-C and FP-C that were produced with falling nuclear accents, i.e., that showed an intonation typical of non-contrastive utterances. The remaining utterances of the contrastive conditions (N = 28), i.e., those with rising nuclear accents typical of contrast, were combined in the third group.

It turned out that the presumably non-contrastive realizations in the contrastive conditions were interpreted as being contrastive in a similarly low percentage of the cases as the utterances from the non-contrastive conditions. While the difference between the second and the third group in Table 7.17 was statistically significant (χ^2-test: $\chi^2 = 124.94$, df = 1, $p < .001$), that between the first and the second group was not (χ^2-test: $\chi^2 = 3.72$, df = 1, $p = .054$). We consider this result as a confirmation of our hypothesis that only one intonational pattern is adequate for the marking of contrast in the position of the sentence focus in German, namely, the one involving a rising pitch accent on the focus exponent.

To sum up: Although the differences in the distribution of the judgements were not exceptionally high – many participants reported difficulties with judging

Table 7.17 Experiment 7 – percentage of contrastive and non-contrastive interpretations; utterances of the contrastive conditions with falling nuclear accents (middle) compared to the utterances of the non-contrastive conditions with falling accents (left) and to the utterances of the contrastive conditions with rising accents (right)

response	group of utterances		
	non-contr./fall.	contr./fall.	contr./rising
non-contrastive	60.9%	56.9%	31.3%
contrastive	39.1%	43.1%	68.7%

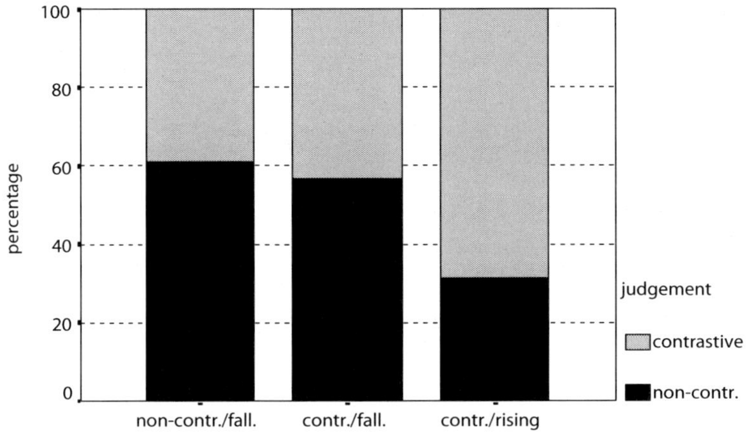

Figure 7.18 Experiment 7 – percentage of contrastive and non-contrastive interpretations; utterances of the contrastive conditions with falling nuclear accents (middle) compared to the utterances of the non-contrastive conditions with falling accents (left) and to the utterances of the contrastive conditions with rising accents (right)

the utterances out of context – both Hypothesis 3 and Hypothesis 4 could be confirmed. Utterances originally embedded in contrastive contexts showed a higher percentage of contrastive interpretations than utterances extracted from non-contrastive contexts, and utterances with rising nuclear accents received a higher percentage of contrastive judgements than utterances with falling nuclear accents. In addition, it was shown that the second criterion is a better predictor of the preferred interpretation. The participants' judgements in the perception task crucially depended on the direction of the f_0-movement on the nuclear syllable, and the deviating realizations with falling accents in the contrastive conditions must be attributed to the insufficient potential of the context paragraphs in the production study to reliably evoke contrast. It might be interesting to look at the relation between the judgements in the perception task and the continuous prosodic parameters involved in contrast marking, for instance using the gating paradigm (cf. Grosjean 1996; Grosjean & Hirt 1996). Such research, however, requires the analysis of more speech data and lies beyond the scope of the present study.

7.5 General discussion and summary

The aim of this chapter was to determine whether focus particles always have contrastively focused ACs in German, as claimed by Altmann (1976a, b) and Foolen (1993), or whether they can associate with both contrastive and new information foci, as predicted by the modular theory presented in Chapter 4 as well as by Dimroth (2004), among others. This question was addressed by empirically investigating the prosodic properties of constructions with unstressed focus particles preceding their AC in the middlefield.

Initially, specific claims from the literature concerning the prosodic marking of contrast were tested with utterances not containing any focus particles. It could be shown that contrast in the position of the regular sentence focus is characterized by at least the following properties: (i) the use of rising (L*H and LH*) instead of falling (H*L and HL*) nuclear accents, (ii) the prevention of downstep of the nuclear accent, (iii) a higher f_0-peak and a greater intensity on the nuclear syllable, and (iv) a reduced f_0-peak and f_0-excursion on prenuclear accents compared to non-contrastive utterances. Thus, utterances produced in contrast-inducing contexts differ from comparable utterances embedded in non-contrast-inducing contexts in several categorical and gradual prosodic properties. It was then demonstrated that the same prosodic differences can be observed in utterances with unstressed focus particles in the middlefield. In these cases, the AC of the particle coincides with the sentence focus (cf. Chapter 4) and carries the nuclear accent. Still – as in the cases without focus particles – the discourse context of the utterance determines whether or not it is realized with a contrastive prosody. The occurrence of a focus particle alone is not sufficient for a contrastive realization. Moreover, as the comparison between the utterances with and without focus particles showed, the presence or absence of a particle is completely irrelevant for the prosody of the utterances.

Qualifying the results described above, it must be said that a relevant proportion of the utterances produced in contrast-inducing contexts did not show the prosodic properties claimed to be typical of contrast in German. As this was true both for the utterances with focus particles and those without, it did not directly affect the meaningfulness of the results for the main research question. However, as the cause of the unexpected realizations was not immediately clear, a speech perception study using the utterances elicited in the production experiment as stimuli was carried out. It turned out that the utterances from the contrastive conditions characterized by a 'non-contrastive' intonation were indeed interpreted like the (prosodically rather homogeneous) utterances from the non-contrastive conditions, i.e., for the most part as being non-contrastive. This led us to the conclusion that the utterances under discussion are not entirely appropriate in discourse contexts calling for a contrastive realization. Most likely, the unexpected realizations are an artifact of the experimental design.

Altogether, the findings presented in this chapter show that it is not the case that focus particles can only associate with contrastively focused elements in German. The AC of a focus particle can also be a new information focus marked by a falling nuclear accent. The actual type of focus is not determined by the particle, but by the information-structural properties of the sentence, which in turn crucially depend on the discourse context and the function of the utterance in the discourse. These results strongly support the view that focus particles do not induce (a certain type of) focus themselves, but interact with or are sensitive to an independently given focus-background partition.

The two experiments leave open three (sets of) questions that call for further research. The first concerns the appropriateness of the experimental design. As described above, the employed method of a reading experiment based on short paragraphs containing the critical sentences serves as a much better way to mask the research interest than, for instance, the use of question-answer pairs (cf. Braun 2005, 2006). The problem with this method, however, is that it did not reliably evoke contrast in our case. Some of the speakers also used a 'narrative prosody' for utterances embedded in contexts that were intended to give rise to a contrastive interpretation. Although this does not directly affect our conclusions, it indicates the significance of dealing with unwanted effects of the experimental design in reading studies. In order to confirm our findings with different methods, it would be interesting to see whether it is possible to reproduce the results with spontaneous speech, corpus data, or data elicited using an interactive game task (cf. Ito & Speer 2006; Schafer, Speer & Warren 2004; Schafer, Speer, Warren & White 2000).

The second issue relates to the nature and type of the prosodic parameters relevant for contrast marking. As in the experiments on the prosodic realization of ACs of stressed *auch* reported in Chapter 6, the marking of contrast in the canonical focus position was shown to involve not only categorical (accent type, downstep) but also gradual means (f_0, intensity). The question is how these types of features act in combination and how their interaction can be captured theoretically. Unlike phonological categories such as accent types, gradual phonetic parameters cannot easily be mapped onto semantic or information-structural categories. Nevertheless, they have proven to be crucial means of prosodic marking (cf. also Braun 2005, 2006; Calhoun 2003, 2004; Niebuhr 2007), and the theoretical modeling of their meaning contribution is an important issue for further research. A more specific goal is to gain a better understanding of the individual phonetic parameters and their effects on the interpretation. In addition to the question of why duration does not show stable differences between contrastive and non-contrastive utterances,[24] it might be interesting to ask whether there are additional parameters contributing to the marking of contrast, and to which extent speakers differ in their use of the available prosodic means (cf. Baumann, Grice & Steindamm 2006). In particular to answer the last-named question, it is necessary to analyze data of more speakers.

The last issue concerns the grammatical status of contrastive focus. While our data supports the basic distinction between non-contrastive and contrastive focus, it is not clear whether the classification of focus types must be further refined (cf. Molnár 2006). One possibility is that the corrective focus elicited in our experiment is only a subtype of contrastive focus, which prosodically differs from new information focus, but also from other types of contrastive focus, such as identificational focus.

24. In our experiments we only looked at the duration of the target words, i.e., the accented elements. However, it is also conceivable that contrast affects the duration of the whole utterance.

CHAPTER 8

Conclusion

The present study dealt with the syntax, information structure, and prosody of focus particle constructions in German. Its main goal was to explicate the interaction of the particles with information structure, in particular with the focus-background partition, and the effects of this interaction at the individual levels of grammar. The theoretical literature has mainly addressed isolated issues of the syntactic and semantic analysis of focus particles in German and other languages. However, a comprehensive description of their grammatical properties can only be successful if the perspective is broadened and the relations among the levels of grammar themselves and their relation to information structure are taken into account. The results presented in this study are the first step in the direction of a general theory of focus particles that explains their characteristics on the basis of the properties of the interface between information structure and grammar. The theoretical considerations were complemented by several empirical investigations concerning the prosody of focus particle constructions. This aspect, which has rarely been dealt with in the literature, allows additional conclusions to be drawn about the grammar of focus particles.

In the introduction, several research questions to be addressed in this study were identified. They belong to four main groups and are repeated here for convenience:

- What is an adequate syntactic representation of sentences containing focus particles? What categorial status do focus particles have, and how are they integrated into the syntactic structure? Are there any restrictions on the type of a focus particle's sister constituent?
- How can the relation between a focus particle and the associated elements be modeled? What are the syntactic preconditions of the association, and what information-structural prerequisites and/or effects does it have?
- Constructions with the stressed variant of the focus particle *auch* or comparable particles present a problem for most theories of the grammar of focus particle constructions. How can these constructions be accounted for?
- What prosodic properties do sentences with focus particles have, and what does the prosody of the constructions tell us about their information-structural characteristics? What is the relation between focus particles and contrast?

Without repeating details of the argumentation, the following list briefly summarizes the main answers to these questions that were given in the present study:

- Focus particles are phrasal categories that adjoin to VP (or AP) in the standard case. Their position is in accord with the information-structural partition of the German clause: focus particles c-command the syntactically determined focus domain in the middlefield, and they are c-commanded by the sentence adverbials and the designated positions of background elements. In addition, focus particles can adjoin to contrastively focused XPs of any kind.
- The domain of a focus particle consists of all focused elements in its scope. The scope of a focus particle is restricted by certain syntactic nodes, such as CP, DP, and PP, and it depends on the particle's relation to other scope-bearing elements in the clause. In the default case, a focus particle c-commands its domain, and – as background elements preferentially leave the focus domain – it c-commands only its domain. Exceptions to this generalization (parts of the domain not c-commanded by the particle and background elements in their base positions in the focus domain) can be put down to independent movement requirements or movement restrictions.
- Focus particles are sensitive to the information structure of the sentences in which they occur. Their meaning contribution depends on the focus; however, they do not induce the focus-background partition, but interact with an independently given one. Focus particles can associate with contrastive as well as with new information foci.
- Focus particle constructions show complex interactions between the sentence focus, the c-command relations in the sentence, and the scope of the particle: C-command affects, but does not completely determine, both the scope of the particle and the focus. Scope and focus, in turn, interact in determining the domain of the particle and the background relevant for specifying the particle's meaning contribution.
- Constructions with stressed additive focus particles do not require a separate treatment; they can be derived from the same underlying structure as constructions with unstressed focus particles. The domain of a stressed additive focus particle is a contrastive topic, which is why it has to leave the focus domain via movement to the left periphery. The special characteristics of this usage pattern – the accent on the particle and the reverse order of the particle and its domain – follow from its special information structure.
- In accordance with their information-structural status, the domains of unstressed focus particles can be marked by non-contrastive or contrastive accents. The domains of stressed additive focus particles often, but not always, show the prosodic marking typical of contrastive topics in German. Contrast marking involves both categorical and gradual prosodic means.

In the individual chapters of this study, several problems and open questions were pointed out. Instead of repeating them here, we will outline three possible directions for further research. First, the influence of information structure on the syntactic realization of sentences in German requires a more thorough investigation. While the idea that syntax depends to some extent on information structure has gained widespread acceptance, the precise nature of this connection has not been fully understood. Focus particle constructions are a particularly well-suited subject of investigations in this area, as they make visible many properties and processes of the interface between information structure and syntax that are otherwise not as clearly observable.

A second important topic for future research is the connection between semantics and information structure on the one hand and prosody on the other. It has been shown that both categorical properties (accent type and downstep) and non-categorical parameters (f_0, duration, alignment, and intensity) are involved in the prosodic marking of elements associated with stressed and unstressed focus particles. However, an adequate theoretical model describing the status the two types of prosodic means and their relation to meaning is still to be developed.

Third, it is necessary to compare the grammatical behavior of German focus particles to that of their equivalents in other languages in more detail. The grammatical realization of information-structural categories differs considerably across languages, and focus particles are expected to react to the differing conditions in a specific way. A comparative approach would help to explore the nature of focus particles and their relation to grammar at a more abstract level.

The proposed extensions of the research serve to continue what has been striven for in the present study: the integration of focus particle constructions into a general and modular theory of grammar and information structure.

Appendix

A.1 Sources of the spoken language corpus analyzed in Section 6.2

Table A.1 provides the sources of the utterances analyzed in Section 6.2 and the number of utterances taken from each source.[1]

A.2 Materials of Experiment 1

A.2.1 Critical items

(1) C_1: Weißt du, wer aus unserer Gruppe am Dienstag in der Bibliothek war? Ich habe nämlich nur Claudia dort gesehen. ('Do you know who of our group was in the library on Thursday? I saw only Claudia there.')

C_2: Weißt du, wann Ingo letzte Woche in der Bibliothek war? Ich habe ihn nämlich nur am Donnerstag dort gesehen. ('Do you know when Ingo was in the library last week? I only saw him there on Thursday.')

T_1: Ingo ist am Dienstag wahrscheinlich auch in der Bibliothek gewesen.
Ingo aux_p on Tuesday probably also in the library been

T_2: Am Dienstag ist Ingo wahrscheinlich auch in der Bibliothek gewesen.
on Tuesday aux_p Ingo probably also in the library been

(2) C_1: Kannst du mir sagen, wer von den Praktikanten am Abend mit dem Chef gesprochen hat? Sind nur Maria und Christian bei ihm gewesen? ('Can you tell me who of the trainees talked to the boss in the evening? Did only Maria and Christian meet him?')

C_2: Kannst du mir sagen, wann Anna gestern mit dem Chef geredet hat? Ist sie nur am Vormittag bei ihm gewesen? ('Can you tell me when Anna talked to the boss yesterday? Did she meet him only in the morning?')

T_1: Anna hat am Abend vermutlich auch mit dem Chef gesprochen.
Anna aux_p in_the evening presumably also to the boss talked

T_2: Am Abend hat Anna vermutlich auch mit dem Chef gesprochen.
In_the evening aux_p Anna presumably also to the boss talked

1. The choice of the movies and TV series was not determined by our personal taste but by the availability of electronic screenplays or transcripts, which proved to be very helpful in finding instances of the special construction type looked at.

Table A.1 Sources of the spoken language corpus analyzed in Section 6.2

movie or TV series	no. of utt.
Bin ich schön? (Germany 1998, directed by Doris Dörrie)	13
Buffy – Im Bann der Dämonen (Buffy the Vampire Slayer) Season 1 (USA 1997)	
Episode 1: Welcome to the Hellmouth	6
Episode 2: The Harvest	8
Episode 3: The Witch	6
Episode 4: Teacher's Pet	9
Episode 5: Never Kill a Boy on the First Date	13
Episode 6: The Pack	7
Episode 7: Angel	10
Episode 8: I, Robot – You, Jane	8
Episode 9: The Puppet Show	7
Episode 10: Nightmares	3
Episode 11: Invisible Girl	8
Episode 12: Prophecy Girl	6
Eine Sommernachts-Sexkomödie (A Midsummer Night's Sex Comedy; USA 1982, directed by Woody Allen)	19
Gloomy Sunday – Ein Lied von Liebe und Tod (Germany 1999, directed by Rolf Schübel)	20
Jackie Brown (USA 1997, directed by Quentin Tarantino)	10
Kleine Haie (Germany 1992, directed by Sönke Wortmann)	14
Lügen & Geheimnisse (Secrets & Lies; France/UK 1996, directed by Mike Leigh)	22
Das merkwürdige Verhalten geschlechtsreifer Großstädter zur Paarungszeit (Germany 1998, directed by Marc Rothemund)	16
Schlaraffenland (Germany 1999, directed by Friedemann Fromm)	10
Winterschläfer (Germany 1997, directed by Tom Tykwer)	10
total	225

(3) C_1: Weißt du, wer aus dem Sprachkurs im Sommer in Italien war? Ich dachte, dass es sich letztendlich nur Sabine und Manfred leisten konnten. ('Do you know who of the language course went to Italy in summer? I thought that at last only Sabine and Manfred could afford it.')

C_2: Weißt du, wann Udo letztes Jahr in Italien war? Er wollte doch nur Weihnachten dort verbringen. ('Do you know when Udo went to Italy last year? He wanted to spend only Christmas there, didn't he?')

T_1: Udo ist im Sommer wahrscheinlich auch nach Italien gefahren.
Udo *aux*$_p$ in summer probably also to Italy gone

T_2: Im Sommer ist Udo wahrscheinlich auch nach Italien gefahren.
in summer *aux*$_p$ Udo probably also to Italy gone

(4) C_1: Kannst du mir verraten, wer von den Doktoranden im Juni einen Vortrag gehalten hat? Ich habe gehört, dass sich damals nur Martin bereit erklärt hat. ('Can

you tell me who of the PhD students gave a talk in June? I heard that at that time only Martin agreed to do it.')

C_2: Kannst du mir verraten, wann Ulla in diesem Semester Vorträge gehalten hat? Ich weiß nur von dem Termin im Mai. ('Can you tell me when Ulla gave talks in this term? I only know of the one in May.')

T_1: Ulla hat im Juni vermutlich auch einen Vortrag gehalten.
Ulla *aux*$_p$ in June presumably also a talk given

T_2: Im Juni hat Ulla vermutlich auch einen Vortrag gehalten.
in June *aux*$_p$ Ulla presumably also a talk given

(5) C_1: Weißt du, wer aus der Redaktion am Sonntag im Kino gewesen ist? Ich habe nämlich nur einen Bericht von Friedrich bekommen. ('Do you know who of the editorial staff went to the cinema on Sunday? I only received a report from Friedrich.')

C_2: Weißt du, wann Emma letzte Woche im Kino gewesen ist? Mir hat sie nur von der Vorstellung am Freitag erzählt. ('Do you know when Emma went to the cinema last week? She only told me about Friday's showing.')

T_1: Emma ist am Sonntag wahrscheinlich auch ins Kino gegangen.
Emma *aux*$_p$ on Sunday probably also to_the cinema gone

T_2: Am Sonntag ist Emma wahrscheinlich auch ins Kino gegangen.
on Sunday *aux*$_p$ Emma probably also to_the cinema gone

A.2.2 Filler items

(6) C_1: Weißt du, ob Wilhelm am Wochenende im Schwimmbad gewesen ist? ('Do you know whether Wilhelm was at the swimming pool at the weekend?')

C_2: Weißt du, ob Peter am Wochenende im Kino gewesen ist? ('Do you know whether Peter was at the cinema at the weekend?')

T: Peter ist am Wochenende im Schwimmbad gewesen.
Peter *aux*$_p$ at_the weekend at_the swimming_pool been

(7) C_1: Sag mal, hat Wolfgang in den Ferien den Rasen gemäht? ('Tell me, did Wolfgang mow the lawn during the holidays?')

C_2: Sag mal, hat Johannes in den Ferien den Zaun gestrichen? ('Tell me, did Johannes paint the fence during the holidays?')

T: Johannes hat in den Ferien den Rasen gemäht.
Johannes *aux*$_p$ during the holidays the lawn mown

(8) C_1: Weißt du, ob Petra zu Weihnachten Plätzchen gebacken hat? ('Do you know whether Petra made cookies for Christmas?')

C_2: Weißt du, ob Julia zu Weihnachten Stollen gebacken hat? ('Do you know whether Julia made stollen for Christmas?')

T: Julia hat zu Weihnachten Plätzchen gebacken.
Julia *aux*$_p$ for Christmas cookies made

(9) C_1: Sag mal, ist Martina am Neujahrstag nach New York geflogen? ('Tell me, did Martina fly to New York on New Year's Day?')

C_2: Sag mal, ist Paula am Neujahrstag nach San Francisco geflogen? ('Tell me, did Paula fly to San Francisco on New Year's Day?')

T: Paula ist am Neujahrstag nach New York geflogen.
Paula *aux*$_p$ on New_Year's_Day to New York flown

(10) C_1: Weißt du, ob Helmut im November die Krankenkasse gewechselt hat? ('Do you know whether Helmut changed his health insurance company in November?')
C_2: Weißt du, ob Klaus im November die Bank gewechselt hat? ('Do you know whether Klaus changed his bank in November?')
T: Klaus hat im November die Krankenkasse gewechselt.
Klaus *aux*$_p$ in November the health_insurance_company changed

A.3 Materials of Experiment 2

(11) continuations for (1)
a. ... und nicht nur am Donnerstag.
... and not only on Thursday
b. ... und nicht nur Claudia.
... and not only Claudia

(12) continuations for (2)
a. ... und nicht nur am Vormittag.
... and not only in_the morning
b. ... und nicht nur Maria und Christian.
... and not only Maria and Christian

(13) continuations for (3)
a. ... und nicht nur an Weihnachten.
... and not only at Christmas
b. ... und nicht nur Sabine und Manfred.
... and not only Sabine and Manfred

(14) continuations for (4)
a. ... und nicht nur im Mai.
... and not only in May
b. ... und nicht nur Martin.
... and not only Martin

(15) continuations for (5)
a. ... und nicht nur am Freitag.
... and not only on Friday
b. ... und nicht nur Friedrich.
... and not only Friedrich

(16) continuations for (6)
a. ... und nicht Wilhelm.
... and not Wilhelm
b. ... und nicht im Kino.
... and not at_the cinema

(17) continuations for (7)

a. ... und nicht Wolfgang.
... and not Wolfgang

b. ... und nicht den Zaun gestrichen.
... and not the fence painted

(18) continuations for (8)

a. ... und nicht Petra.
... and not Petra

b. ... und nicht Stollen.
... and not stollen

(19) continuations for (9)

a. ... und nicht Martina.
... and not Martina

b. ... und nicht nach San Francisco.
... and not to San Francisco

(20) continuations for (10)

a. ... und nicht Helmut.
... and not Helmut

b. ... und nicht die Bank.
... and not the bank

A.4 Materials of Experiment 3

A.4.1 Critical items

(21) C_1: Kannst du mir verraten, wer von den Doktoranden im Juni einen Vortrag gehalten hat? Ich habe gehört, dass sich damals nur der Martin bereit erklärt hat. ('Can you tell me who of the PhD students gave a talk in June? I heard that at that time only Martin agreed to do it.')

C_2: Kannst du mir verraten, wann der Rudi in diesem Semester Vorträge gehalten hat? Ich weiß nur von dem Termin im Mai. ('Can you tell me when Rudi gave talks in this term? I only know of the one in May.')

T_1: Der Rudi hat im Juni wahrscheinlich auch einen Vortrag gehalten.
the Rudi *aux*$_p$ in June probably also a talk given

T_2: Im Juni hat der Rudi wahrscheinlich auch einen Vortrag gehalten.
in June *aux*$_p$ the Rudi probably also a talk given

(22) C_1: Weißt du, wer von den Gästen aus Österreich um sieben einen Anruf erhalten hat? War das nur der Salzburger? ('Do you know who of the guests from Austria received a call at seven o'clock? Was that only the one from Salzburg?')

C_2: Weißt du, wann der Gast aus Wien einen Anruf erhalten hat? Hat ihn nur um fünf jemand angerufen? ('Do you know when the guest from Vienna received a call? Was it only at five o'clock that someone called him?')

T$_1$: Der Wiener hat um sieben wahrscheinlich auch einen Anruf
the Viennese aux_p at seven probably also a call
bekommen.
received

T$_2$: Um sieben hat der Wiener wahrscheinlich auch einen Anruf
at seven aux_p the Viennese probably also a call
bekommen.
received

(23) C$_1$: Kannst du mir sagen, wer von den Praktikanten am Abend mit der Chefin gesprochen hat? Sind nur Maria und Christian bei ihr gewesen? ('Can you tell me who of the trainees talked to the boss in the evening? Did only Maria and Christian meet her?')

C$_2$: Kannst du mir sagen, wann der Arend gestern mit der Chefin geredet hat? Ist er nur am Vormittag bei ihr gewesen? ('Can you tell me when Arend talked to the boss yesterday? Did he meet her only in the morning?')

T$_1$: Der Arend hat am Abend wahrscheinlich auch mit der Chefin
the Arend aux_p in_the evening probably also to the boss
gesprochen.
talked

T$_2$: Am Abend hat der Arend wahrscheinlich auch mit der Chefin
in_the evening aux_p the Arend probably also to the boss
gesprochen.
talked

(24) C$_1$: Weißt du, wer aus unserer Abteilung im Winter Urlaub gemacht hat? Ich dachte, dass letztendlich nur Sabine und Manfred freigenommen haben. ('Do you know who of our department went on holiday in winter? I thought that at last only Sabine and Manfred had a holiday.')

C$_2$: Weißt du, wann der Günther letztes Jahr Urlaub gemacht hat? Er wollte doch nur im Sommer ein paar Tage freinehmen. ('Do you know when Günther went on holiday last year? He only wanted to take some days off in summer, didn't he?')

T$_1$: Der Günther hat im Winter wahrscheinlich auch Urlaub gemacht.
the Günther aux_p in winter probably also holidays made

T$_2$: Im Winter hat der Günther wahrscheinlich auch Urlaub gemacht.
in winter aux_p the Günther probably also holidays made

(25) C$_1$: Weißt du, welche von den Kanarienvögeln im Juli geimpft wurden? Sind das nur Hansi und Charly gewesen? ('Do you know which of the canaries were vaccinated in July? Was that only Hansi and Charly?')

C$_2$: Weißt du, wann der Bubi letztes Jahr vom Tierarzt geimpft wurde? Ist das nur im Januar gewesen? ('Do you know when Bubi was vaccinated by the veterinarian last year? Was that only in January?')

T$_1$: Der Bubi hat im Juli wahrscheinlich auch eine Impfung bekommen.
the Bubi aux_p in July probably also a vaccination got

T$_2$: Im Juli hat der Bubi wahrscheinlich auch eine Impfung bekommen.
in July aux_p the Bubi probably also a vaccination got

A.4.2 Filler items

(26) C_1: Weißt du, ob der Wilhelm am Wochenende im Schwimmbad gewesen ist? ('Do you know whether Wilhelm was at the swimming pool at the weekend?')

C_2: Weißt du, ob der Peter am Wochenende im Kino gewesen ist? ('Do you know whether Peter was at the cinema at the weekend?')

T: Der Peter ist am Wochenende im Schwimmbad gewesen.
the Peter aux_p at_the weekend at_the swimming_pool been

(27) C_1: Sag mal, hat der Wolfgang in den Ferien den Rasen gemäht? ('Tell me, did Wolfgang mow the lawn during the holidays?')

C_2: Sag mal, hat der Johannes in den Ferien den Zaun gestrichen? ('Tell me, did Johannes paint the fence during the holidays?')

T: Der Johannes hat in den Ferien den Rasen gemäht.
the Johannes aux_p during the holidays the lawn mown

(28) C_1: Weißt du, ob die Petra zu Weihnachten Plätzchen gebacken hat? ('Do you know whether Petra made cookies for Christmas')

C_2: Weißt du, ob die Julia zu Weihnachten Stollen gebacken hat? ('Do you know whether Julia made stollen for Christmas')

T: Die Julia hat zu Weihnachten Plätzchen gebacken.
the Julia aux_p for Christmas cookies made

(29) C_1: Sag mal, ist die Martina am Neujahrstag nach New York geflogen? ('Tell me, did Martina fly to New York on New Year's Day?')

C_2: Sag mal, ist die Paula am Neujahrstag nach San Francisco geflogen? ('Tell me, did Paula fly to San Francisco on New Year's Day?')

T: Die Paula ist am Neujahrstag nach New York geflogen.
the Paula aux_p on New_Year's_Day to New York flown

(30) C_1: Weißt du, ob der Helmut im November die Krankenkasse gewechselt hat? ('Do you know whether Helmut changed his health insurance company in November?')

C_2: Weißt du, ob der Klaus im November die Bank gewechselt hat? ('Do you know whether Klaus changed his bank in November?')

T: Der Klaus hat im November die Krankenkasse gewechselt.
the Klaus aux_p in November the health_insurance_company changed

(31) C: Der Helmut ist am Dienstag ins Museum gegangen, oder? ('Helmut went to the museum on Tuesday, didn't he?')

T_1: Der Helmut ist am Dienstag nicht ins Museum gegangen, aber die
the Helmut aux_p on Tuesday not to_the museum gone but the
Gabi.
Gabi

T_2: Der Helmut ist am Dienstag nicht ins Museum gegangen, sondern
the Helmut aux_p on Tuesday not to_the museum gone but
ins Theater.
to_the theater

(32) C: Die Britta wird nächste Woche mit dem Zug fahren, oder? ('Britta will go by bus next week, won't she?')

T_1: Die Britta wird nächste Woche nicht mit dem Zug fahren, aber die
the Britta aux_f next week not by the train go but the
Ulrike.
Ulrike

T_2: Die Britta wird nächste Woche nicht mit dem Zug fahren, sondern mit
the Britta aux_f next week not by the train go but by
dem Bus.
the bus

(33) C: Der Monteur ist vorgestern zu spät gekommen, oder? ('The engineer was late the day before yesterday, wasn't he?')

T_1: Der Monteur ist vorgestern nicht zu spät gekommen,
the engineer aux_p the_day_before_yesterday not too late come
aber der Elektriker.
but the electrician

T_2: Der Monteur ist vorgestern nicht zu spät gekommen,
the engineer aux_p the_day_before_yesterday not too late come
sondern zu früh.
but too early

(34) C: Morgen will die Claudia zum Finanzamt gehen, oder? ('Tomorrow, Claudia wants to go to the tax office, doesn't she?')

T_1: Morgen will die Claudia nicht zum Finanzamt gehen, aber am
tomorrow wants the Claudia not to_the tax_office to_go but on
Freitag.
Friday

T_2: Morgen will die Claudia nicht zum Finanzamt gehen, sondern
tomorrow wants the Claudia not to_the tax_office to_go but
zum Steuerberater.
to_the tax_consulter

(35) C: Im September hat der Leiter mit der Baufirma verhandelt, oder? ('In September, the manager negotiated with the building firm, didn't he?')

T_1: Im September hat der Leiter nicht mit der Baufirma
in September aux_p the manager not with the building_firm
verhandelt, aber im Oktober.
negotiated but in October

T_2: Im September hat der Leiter nicht mit der Baufirma
in September aux_p the manager not with the building_firm
verhandelt, sondern mit dem Architekten.
negotiated but with the architect

A.5 Materials of Experiment 4

(36) continuations for (21)

a. ... und nicht nur im Mai.
   ... and not only in May

b. ... und nicht nur der Martin.
   ... and not only the Martin

(37) continuations for (22)

a. ... und nicht nur um fünf.
   ... and not only at five

b. ... und nicht nur der Salzburger.
   ... and not only the one_from_Salzburg

(38) continuations for (23)

a. ... und nicht nur am Vormittag.
   ... and not only in_the morning

b. ... und nicht nur Maria und Christian.
   ... and not only Maria and Christian

(39) continuations for (24)

a. ... und nicht nur im Sommer.
   ... and not only in summer

b. ... und nicht nur Sabine und Manfred.
   ... and not only Sabine and Manfred

(40) continuations for (25)

a. ... und nicht nur im Januar.
   ... and not only in January

b. ... und nicht nur Hansi und Charly.
   ... and not only Hansi and Charly

(41) continuations for (26)

a. ... und nicht der Wilhelm.
   ... and not the Wilhelm

b. ... und nicht im Kino.
   ... and not at_the cinema

(42) continuations for (27)

a. ... und nicht der Wolfgang.
   ... and not the Wolfgang

b. ... und nicht den Zaun gestrichen.
   ... and not the fence painted

(43) continuations for (28)

a. ... und nicht die Petra.
   ... and not the Petra

b. ... und nicht Stollen.
   ... and not stollen

(44) continuations for (29)

a. ... und nicht die Martina.
... and not the Martina

b. ... und nicht nach San Francisco.
... and not to San Francisco

(45) continuations for (30)

a. ... und nicht der Helmut.
... and not the Helmut

b. ... und nicht die Bank.
... and not the bank

For (31)–(35), the continuations were identical to the last part of the target utterances (starting with *aber* or *sondern*), which was not included in the auditory presentation.

A.6 Materials of Experiment 6

(46) Am Freitag ist nur / dann / die Sabine gekommen.
on Friday aux_p only / then / the Sabine come

C_1: condition FP-NC
Das Institut für Germanistik hat letzte Woche neue Bücherregale bekommen. Da dem Institut nur wenig Geld zur Verfügung steht, hatten sich einige Studenten bereiterklärt, beim Aufbauen zu helfen. An den meisten Tagen waren Ina und Gabriel da und haben die Handwerker kräftig unterstützt. *Am Freitag ist nur Sabine gekommen.* Das war aber nicht schlimm, denn es gab ohnehin nicht mehr viel zu tun.

C_2: condition FP-C
Drei Schüler der Klasse 10a haben sich in der letzten Ferienwoche etwas Geld verdient, indem sie hin und wieder im BMW-Werk Maschinen reinigten. Leider ist die Anwesenheitsliste von Freitag verlorengegangen. Die Sekretärin sagte dem Abteilungsleiter, dass an diesem Tag alle drei Schüler gearbeitet haben. Das stimmt aber nicht. *Am Freitag ist nur Sabine gekommen.* Alle anderen hatten bereits keine Lust mehr.

C_3: condition NFP-NC
Letzte Woche hatte Tom jeden Tag Besuch. Am Montag sind Martin und Friedrich zum Essen gekommen. Am nächsten Tag hat ihm Claudia ihre Urlaubsfotos von den kanarischen Inseln gezeigt. Von Mittwoch bis Donnerstag war seine Mutter da, denn sie hatte Urlaub und wollte mal wieder etwas mit ihrem Sohn unternehmen. *Am Freitag ist dann Sabine gekommen.* Sie hat ihr neugeborenes Kind mitgebracht.

C_4: condition NFP-C
Die ganze Familie wollte Weihnachten zusammen feiern, und in der Woche vor Heiligabend ist einer nach dem anderen zu Hause in Regensburg eingetrudelt. Am Freitag gab es eine Überraschung. Andreas hatte uns gesagt, dass an diesem Tag Franziska anreisen würde. Er hat aber alles durcheinandergebracht. *Am Freitag ist die Sabine gekommen.* Franziska musste nämlich noch arbeiten.

(47) Nach Leipzig ist nur / dann / die Carina gefahren.
to Leipzig *aux*$_p$ only / then / the Carina gone

C_1: condition FP-NC

Im Mai veranstalteten die sächsischen Universitäten einen Tag der offenen Tür, an dem zukünftige Studenten die Institute besichtigen konnten. Auch aus der Klasse 12b des Goethe-Gymnasiums in Torgau haben einige Schüler dieses Angebot wahrgenommen. Fabian und Yvonne sind in Chemnitz gewesen, und Conny und Petra waren zusammen in Dresden. *Nach Leipzig ist nur Carina gefahren.* Die Uni dort ist anscheinend nicht sehr beliebt.

C_2: condition FP-C

Weil die Computerfirma Helmbrecht aus Grimma ein relativ kleines Unternehmen ist, schickt sie ihre fünf Mitarbeiter regelmäßig zur Weiterbildung in Partnerunternehmen in größeren Städten. Neulich war der Chef ziemlich verwirrt. Er dachte, dass im Mai alle Mitarbeiter bei Prosoft in Leipzig waren, aber da irrte er sich. *Nach Leipzig ist nur Carina gefahren.* Die anderen waren bei einer Firma in Halle.

C_3: condition NFP-NC

Die Kulturredaktion der Thüringer Landeszeitung muss bei den Reisekosten ihrer Mitarbeiter sparen. Zu den beiden deutschen Buchmessen konnte deshalb nur noch jeweils ein Mitarbeiter entsandt werden. Die Messe in Frankfurt hat Jochen übernommen, denn er wollte auf dem Rückweg seine Schwester in Fulda besuchen. *Nach Leipzig ist dann Carina gefahren.* Sie wollte unbedingt sehen, wie sich die Stadt in den letzten Jahren verändert hat.

C_4: condition NFP-C

Drei Studenten der Musikhochschule in Weimar haben im Oktober verschiedene Wirkungsstätten Bachs besucht, um Nachforschungen für eine Projektarbeit anzustellen. Auf der Nachbesprechung im November war die betreuende Professorin sehr verärgert. Sie dachte, dass Ulrike im Leipziger Bach-Archiv gewesen ist, aber das stellte sich als falsch heraus. *Nach Leipzig ist die Carina gefahren.* Ulrike war in Arnstadt, wo Bach zuerst tätig war.

(48) In England ist nur / dann / die Elvira gewesen.
in England *aux*$_p$ only / then / the Elvira been

C_1: condition FP-NC

Die Göttinger Anglistikstudenten müssen mindestens ein Semester im englischsprachigen Ausland verbringen. Im letzten Jahr waren die Universitäten in den USA besonders begehrt. Gleich 5 Studenten haben das Sommersemester dort verbracht. Christian und Robert waren in Australien und haben sich den typischen Akzent angewöhnt. *In England ist nur Elvira gewesen.* Wahrscheinlich schreckt viele das schlechte englische Wetter ab.

C_2: condition FP-C

Nachdem alle fünf Mitbewohner unserer Wohngemeinschaft aus den Sommerferien zurückgekehrt waren, zeigten wir uns gegenseitig die Urlaubsfotos. Es war ein ziemlich lustiger Abend. Christoph war total erstaunt. Er hatte nämlich gedacht, dass Elvira und Heinrich zusammen in England waren, aber davon war nie die Rede. *In England ist nur Elvira gewesen.* Heinrich hat seine Cousine in Belgien besucht.

C_3: condition NFP-NC
Um einen neuen Reiseführer über Großbritannien zu erstellen, hat der kleine Verlag "Reisebuch" einige Mitarbeiter nacheinander in die verschiedene Teile des Landes geschickt, damit sie dort Informationen sammeln und Fotos machen können. Zuerst war Manfred zwei Wochen in Schottland, und danach ist Helga nach Wales geflogen. *In England ist dann Elvira gewesen.* Ines hat zuletzt noch Nordirland besucht.

C_4: condition NFP-C
Die meisten Mitarbeiter in unserem Team haben schon Auslandserfahrungen gemacht, die für die Arbeit sehr nützlich sind. Als der Chef gestern jemanden mit guten Englischkenntnissen für ein Interview suchte, war er sehr verwundert. Er hatte geglaubt, dass Anja ein Jahr in England verbracht hat, aber sie sagte, dass das nicht stimmt. *In England ist die Elvira gewesen.* Anja lebte eine Weile im Süden Frankreichs.

(49) Im Juli hat auch / dann / die Regina bestanden.
in July auxp also / then / the Regina passed

C_1: condition FP-NC
Die Theologiestudenten in Mannheim müssen in Bibelkunde einen Leistungsschein erwerben. Die Klausur fand im Mai statt, und im Juli gab es eine Wiederholungsklausur für alle, die beim ersten mal durchgefallen waren. Die Klausur im Mai war allerdings ziemlich einfach, so dass bereits die meisten Studenten erfolgreich waren. *Im Juli hat auch Regina bestanden.* Sie hatte die Mindestpunktzahl beim ersten Mal knapp unterschritten.

C_2: condition FP-C
Das Sprachenzentrum hat im Juli und im August jeweils einen Latein-Intensivkurs angeboten, da einige Studenten schnellstmöglich das Latinum machen mussten. Bei der Auswertung der Abschlussprüfungen ist der Leiterin ein Fehler unterlaufen. Auf der Liste stand, dass aus dem ersten Kurs nur Paula und Joachim bestanden haben. Das war aber falsch. *Im Juli hat auch Regina bestanden.* Zum Glück wurde der Fehler noch rechtzeitig bemerkt.

C_3: condition NFP-NC
Die drei Enkel von Herrn Müller haben im Sommer den Führerschein gemacht. Alles hat wunderbar geklappt. Die Theorieausbildung absolvierten sie zusammen, aber die praktische Fahrprüfung mussten sie zeitversetzt ablegen, da am Anfang noch nicht alle 18 waren. Matthias und Paul haben die Prüfung bereits Anfang Mai erfolgreich abgelegt. *Im Juli hat dann Regina bestanden.* Anschließend gab es eine große Feier.

C_4: condition NFP-C
Alle Mädchen, die beim Roten Kreuz in Magdeburg ein freiwilliges soziales Jahr absolvieren, müssen am Anfang einen Erste-Hilfe-Lehrgang besuchen und eine Prüfung ablegen. Jeden Monat wird ein solcher Lehrgang angeboten. Im Juli hat nur ein Mädchen die Prüfung bestanden, und der Ausbilder dachte, dass das Simone war. Er hatte aber etwas verwechselt. *Im Juli hat die Regina bestanden.* Simone wollte sich erst im August prüfen lassen.

(50) Um sieben ist auch / dann / die Verena gegangen.
at seven *aux*$_p$ also / then / the Verena gone

C_1: condition FP-NC
Im dem kleinen Café, das Martina gehört, war am Freitagnachmittag nicht viel los. Die drei Angestellten hatten so gut wie nichts zu tun und langweilten sich. Als gegen fünf immer noch nicht mehr Gäste gekommen waren und es wirklich nichts mehr zu erledigen gab, hat Martina schließlich Gabi und Renate nach Hause geschickt. *Um sieben ist auch Verena gegangen.* Martina ist gut alleine zurechtgekommen.

C_2: condition FP-C
Die chirurgische Station der Helios-Klinik hat momentan zu wenig Personal, so dass die Schwestern häufig Überstunden machen müssen. Obwohl am Mittwoch wieder einige länger arbeiteten, gab es Ärger mit der Oberschwester. Diese hat nämlich gedacht, dass zum regulären Schichtwechsel um sieben nur Katharina gegangen ist, aber das stimmte nicht. *Um sieben ist auch Verena gegangen.* Sie hatte nur nicht bescheidgesagt.

C_3: condition NFP-NC
Der Studentenrat ist für seine ausufernden Sitzungen bekannt. Letzte Woche Montag war es wieder einmal besonders schlimm. Die Versammlung begann um eins, und um 5 war immer noch kein Ende abzusehen. Kurz vor sechs haben Manuel und Christina die Sitzung verlassen, weil sie an dem Abend noch ins Kino gehen wollten. *Um sieben ist dann Verena gegangen.* Die übrigen Mitglieder haben noch bis um acht weiterdiskutiert.

C_4: condition NFP-C
Steffen hat bei der letzten Versammlung seiner Greenpeace-Ortsgruppe das Protokoll geschrieben. Es war schwieriger, als er gedacht hätte, denn die Sitzung war ziemlich turbulent. Diana machte ihn am nächsten Tag auf einen Fehler im Protokoll aufmerksam. Steffen hatte geschrieben, dass Ute um sieben wütend das Zimmer verlassen hat, aber das hat er verwechselt. *Um sieben ist die Verena gegangen.* Ute ist bis zum Schluss geblieben.

(51) Im Garten hat auch / dann / die Irene geholfen.
in_the garden *aux*$_p$ also / then / the Irene helped

C_1: condition FP-NC
Im April haben wir endlich unser Haus, den Garten und die Garage auf Vordermann gebracht. So ein Frühjahrsputz war dringend nötig, und eigentlich hat es sogar Spaß gemacht. Die Kinder haben fleißig mitgeholfen und waren richtig stolz auf ihre Leistung. Benni und Max haben uns beim Putzen von Haus und Garage unterstützt. *Im Garten hat auch Irene geholfen.* Sie hat zwei Stunden lang Unkraut gejätet.

C_2: condition FP-C
Familie Schöning hat letzte Woche Dienstag bei der Gärtnerei Brandt eine Großladung Blumen für den Balkon und den Schrebergarten bestellt. Die Kinder sollten dem Vater beim Einpflanzen helfen, aber niemand hatte so richtig Lust dazu. Am Abend war die Mutter ziemlich sauer. Sie dachte, dass im Garten nur Maria mitgemacht hat. Aber sie hatte Unrecht. *Im Garten hat auch Irene geholfen.* Nur Florian war lieber schwimmen gegangen.

C_3: condition NFP-NC
Zum 50. Geburtstag unseres Vaters haben wir eine große Gartenparty veranstaltet. Natürlich gab es viel zu tun, so dass wir ein paar unserer Freundinnen baten, uns zu helfen. Bereits am Vormittag kamen Brigitte und Monika, die mit uns das Essen vorbereitet haben. Wir machten verschiedene Salate und setzten eine Bowle an. *Im Garten hat dann Irene geholfen.* Sie brachte Girlanden und eine Lichterkette mit.

C_4: condition NFP-C
Die alten Maiers bewirtschaften ihre Schweinezucht und den Gemüsegarten immer noch selbst. Nur in den Sommerferien kommen meist die beiden Enkel und helfen mit. Als diese letztes Jahr am Ende der Ferien wieder nach Hause kamen, war die Mutter ziemlich überrascht. Sie hatte gedacht, dass Peter im Garten gearbeitet hat, aber da wurde sie eines Besseren belehrt. *Im Garten hat die Irene geholfen.* Peter wollte lieber die Schweine füttern.

Bibliography

Abraham, Werner. 1991. Discourse particles in German: How does their illocutive force come about? In *Discourse Particles*, Werner Abraham, ed., 203–252. Amsterdam, Philadelphia: Benjamins.

Abraham, Werner. 1997. The base structure of the German clause under discourse functional weight: Contentful functional categories vs. derivative functional categories. In *German: Syntactic Problems – Problematic Syntax*. Werner Abraham and Elly van Gelderen, eds., 11–42. Tübingen: Niemeyer.

Abraham, Werner. 2003. The syntactic link between Thema and Rhema: The syntax-discourse interface. In *Optionality in Syntax and Discourse Structure – Aspects of Word Order Variation in (West-) Germanic and Other Indo-European Languages. Folia Linguistica XXXVII*, Werner Abraham and László Molnárfi, eds., 13–34. Berlin, New York: Mouton de Gruyter.

Abraham, Werner. 2007. Topic, focus, and default vs. contrastive accent. Typological differences with respect to discourse prominence. In *On Information Structure, Meaning and Form. Generalizations across languages*, Susanne Winkler and Kerstin Schwabe, eds., 183–203. Amsterdam, Philadelphia: Benjamins.

Abraham, Werner and Molnárfi, László. 2002. German clause structure under discourse functional weight. Focus and antifocus. In *Issues in Formal German(ic) Typology*, Werner Abraham and C. Jan-Wouter Zwart, eds., 3–43. Amsterdam, Philadelphia: Benjamins.

Aloni, Maria, Beaver, David I. and Clark, Brady Z. 1999. Focus and Topic Sensitive Operators. In *Proceedings of the 12th Amsterdam Colloquium*, Paul Dekker, ed., 61–66. Amsterdam: ILLC Publications.

Alter, Kai. 2002a. *Prosodie zwischen Sprachproduktion und -perzeption*. Habilitation Thesis, University of Leipzig.

Alter, Kai. 2002b. Realisierung und Verarbeitung von KORREKTUR-Konstruktionen. Zum Zusammenhang von Bedeutung und Intonation. In *Sprachtheoretische Grundlagen der Kognitionswissenschaft: Sprachliches und nichtsprachliches Wissen. Linguistische Arbeitsberichte 79*, Anita Steube, ed., 255–274. Leipzig.

Alter, Kai. 2002c. Suprasegmentale Merkmale und Prosodie. In *Arbeitsbuch Linguistik*, Horst M. Müller, ed., 148–169. Paderborn, München, Wien, Zürich: Schöningh.

Alter, Kai, Mleinek, Ina, Rohe, Tobias, Steube, Anita & Umbach, Carla. 2001. Kontrastprosodie in Sprachproduktion und -perzeption. In *Kontrast – lexikalisch, semantisch, intonatorisch. Linguistische Arbeitsberichte 77*, Anita Steube and Carla Umbach, eds., 59–79. Leipzig.

Altmann, Hans. 1976a. *Die Gradpartikeln im Deutschen. Untersuchungen zu ihrer Syntax, Semantik und Pragmatik*. Tübingen: Niemeyer.

Altmann, Hans. 1976b. Gradpartikeln und Topikalisierung. In *Grammatik. Akten des 10. Linguistischen Kolloquiums, Tübingen 1975. Volume 2*, Kurt Braunmüller and Wilfried Kürschner, eds., 233–243. Tübingen: Niemeyer.

Altmann, Hans. 1978. *Gradpartikelprobleme. Zur Beschreibung von gerade, genau, eben, ausgerechnet, vor allem, insbesondere, zumindest, wenigstens.* Tübingen: Narr.

Altmann, Hans. 1993. Fokus-Hintergrund-Gliederung und Satzmodus. In *Wortstellung und Informationsstruktur*, Marga Reis, ed., 1–37. Tübingen: Niemeyer.

Anderson, Stephen, R. 1972. How to get *even*. *Language* 48: 893–906.

Atlas, Jay David. 1991. Topic/Comment, Presupposition, Logical Form and Focus Stress Implicatures: The Case of Focal Particles *only* and *also*. *Journal of Semantics* 8: 127–147.

Atlas, Jay David. 1993. The Importance of Being 'Only': Testing the Neo-Gricean Versus Neo-Entailment Paradigms. *Journal of Semantics* 10: 301–318.

Atlas, Jay David. 1996. 'Only' Noun Phrases, Pseudo-Negative Generalized Quantifiers, Negative Polarity Items, and Monotonicity. *Journal of Semantics* 13: 265–328.

Atterer, Michaela and Ladd, D. Robert. 2003. On the phonetics and phonology of "segmental anchoring" of F0: evidence from German. *Journal of Phonetics* 32: 177–197.

Bannert, Robert. 1985. Fokus, Kontrast und Phrasenintonation im Deutschen. *Zeitschrift für Dialektologie und Linguistik* 52: 289–305.

Bartels, Christine. 2004. Comments on Asher and Krifka: Acoustic Correlates of 'Second Occurrence' Focus: Towards an Experimental Investigation. In *Context-Dependence in the Analysis of Linguistic Meaning*, Hans Kamp and Barbara H. Partee, eds., 345–361. Amsterdam: Elsevier.

Bartels, Christine and Kingston, John. 1994. Salient Pitch Cues in the Perception of Contrastive Focus. In *Focus & Natural Language Processing. Volume 1: Intonation and Syntax*, Peter Bosch and Rob van der Sandt, eds., 1–10. Heidelberg: IBM.

Baumann, Stefan, Grice, Martine and Steindamm, Susanne. 2006. Prosodic Marking of Focus Domains – Categorical or Gradient?. In *Proceedings of Speech Prosody 2006*, Rüdiger Hoffmann and Hansjörg Mixdorff, eds., Dresden: TUDpress.

Bayer, Josef. 1996. *Directionality and Logical Form. On the Scope of Focusing Particles and Wh-in-situ.* Dordrecht: Kluwer.

Bayer, Josef. 1999. Bound Focus or How can Association with Focus be Achieved without Going Semantically Astray?. In *The Grammar of Focus*, Georges Rebuschi and Laurice Tuller, eds., 55–82. Amsterdam, Philadelphia: Benjamins.

Bayer, Josef and Grosu, Alexander. 2000. Feature Checking meets the Criterion Approach: Three ways of saying *only* in Romance and Germanic. In *Comparative Studies in Romanian Syntax*, Virginia Motapanyane, ed., 49–81. Amsterdam: North-Holland.

Beaver, David I. 2004. Five *Only* Pieces. *Theoretical Linguistics* 30: 45–64.

Beaver, David I. and Clark, Brady Z. 2002a. Monotonicity and Focus Sensitivity. In *Proceedings of SALT*, Brendan Jackson, ed., 40–58. Cornell: CLC Publications.

Beaver, David I. and Clark, Brady Z. 2002b. The Proper Treatments of Focus Sensitivity. In *Proceedings of WCCFL XXI*, Chris Potts and Line Mikkelson, eds., 15–28. Somerville: Cascadilla Press.

Beaver, David I. and Clark,Z. 2003. *Always* and *Only*: Why not all Focus Sensitive Operators are Alike. *Natural Language Semantics* 11: 323–362.

Beaver, David I., Clark, Brady Z., Flemming, Edward, Jaeger, T. Florian and Wolters, Maria. 2007. When Semantics Meets Phonetics: Acoustical Studies of Second-Ocurrence Focus. *Language* 83: 251–282.

Bech, Gunnar. 1955. *Studien über das deutsche Verbum infinitum. Volume 1.* Kopenhagen: Munksgaard.

Bech, Gunnar. 1957. *Studien über das deutsche Verbum infinitum. Volume 2.* Kopenhagen: Munksgaard.

Becker, Stephanie, Schröder, Marc and Barry, William J. 2006. Rule-based Prosody Prediction for German Text-to-Speech Synthesis. In *Proceedings of Speech Prosody 2006*, Rüdiger Hoffmann and Hansjörg Mixdorff, eds. Dresden: TUDpress.

Beckman, Mary E. and Pierrehumbert, Janet. 1986. Intonational Structure in Japanese and English. *Phonology Yearbook* 3: 255–309.

Bergsma, Wenda. 2006. (Un)Stressed *ook* in Child Dutch. In *Semantics in Acquisition*, Veerle van Geenhoven, ed., 329–348. Dordrecht: Springer.

Bhatt, Rakesh Mohan. 1999. *Verb Movement and the Syntax of Kashmiri*. Dordrecht: Kluwer.

Bierwisch, Manfred. 1988. On the Grammar of Local Prepositions. In *Syntax, Semantik und Lexikon. Rudolf Růžička zum 65. Geburtstag*, Manfred Bierwisch, Wolfgang Motsch and Ilse Zimmermann, eds., 1–65. Berlin: Akademie-Verlag.

Bierwisch, Manfred. 1989. The Semantics of Gradation. In *Dimensional Adjectives. Grammatical Structure and Conceptual Interpretation*, Manfred Bierwisch and Ewald Lang, eds., 71–261. Berlin, Heidelberg: Springer.

Bierwisch, Manfred and Schreuder, Robert. 1992. From concepts to lexical items. *Cognition* 42: 23–60.

Bolinger, Dwight L. 1958. A Theory of Pitch Accent in English. *Word* 14: 109–149.

Bolinger, Dwight L. 1961. Contrastive Accent and Contrastive Stress. *Language* 37: 83–96.

Bos, Johan. 1994. Focusing Particles & Ellipsis Resolution. In *Focus & Natural Language Processing. Volume 2: Semantics*, Peter Bosch and Rob van der Sandt, eds., 247–255. Heidelberg: IBM.

Bouma, Gosse, Hendriks, Petra and Hoeksema, Jack. 2007. Focus Particles Inside Prepositional Phrases: A Comparison of Dutch, English, and German. *Journal of Comparative Germanic Linguistics* 10: 1–24.

Brandt, Margareta, Reis, Marga, Rosengren, Inger and Zimmermann, Ilse. 1992. In *Satztyp, Satzmodus und Illokution Satz und Illokution. Volume 1*, Inger Rosengren, ed., 1–90. Tübingen: Niemeyer.

Braun, Bettina. 2004a. Answers to the Perception of Thematic Contrast and Questions Regarding the Perception of Thematic "Non-Contrast". In *Proceedings of Speech Prosody 2004, Nara*.

Braun, Bettina. 2004b. Phonetics and Phonology of Contrast Marking in German: Issues for the Prosody-Semantics Interface. In *KONVENS 2004 – Beiträge zur 7. Konferenz zur Verarbeitung natürlicher Sprache*, Ernst Buchberger, ed. Wien: Österreichische Gesellschaft für Artificial Intelligence.

Braun, Bettina. 2005. *Production and Perception of Thematic Contrast in German*. Oxford, Bern, Berlin, Bruxelles, Frankfurt am Main, New York, Wien: Peter Lang.

Braun, Bettina. 2006. Phonetics and Phonology of Thematic Contrast in German. *Language and Speech* 49: 451–493.

Braun, Bettina and Ladd, D. Robert. 2003. Prosodic Correlates of Contrastive and Non-Contrastive Themes in German. In *Proceedings of Eurospeech 2003, Geneva*, 789–792.

Braußе, Ursula. 2000. Die Partikel *allein*. Klassifizierungs- und Bedeutungsprobleme. *Linguistik Online* 6.

Breindl, Eva. 1989. *Präpositionalobjekte und Präpositionalobjektsätze im Deutschen*. Tübingen: Niemeyer.

Bruce, Gösta. 1977. *Swedish word accents in sentence perspective*. Lund: Gleerup.

Büring, Daniel. 1997a. The Great Scope Inversion Conspiracy. *Linguistics and Philosophy* 20: 175–194.

Büring, Daniel. 1997b. *The Meaning of Topic and Focus. The 59th Street Bridge Accent*. London, New York: Routledge.

Büring, Daniel and Hartmann, Katharina. 1995. All Right!. In *On Extraction and Extraposition in German*, Uli Lutz and Jürgen Pafel, eds., 179–211. Amsterdam, Philadelphia: Benjamins.

Büring, Daniel and Hartmann, Katharina. 2001. The Syntax and Semantics of Focus-Sensitive Particles in German. *Natural Language & Linguistic Theory* 19: 229–281.

Calhoun, Sasha. 2003. The nature of theme and rheme accents. In *Proceedings of the Linguistics Postgraduate Conference 2003, Edinburgh*.

Calhoun, Sasha. 2004. Phonetic dimensions of intonational categories: The case of L+H* and H*. In *Proceedings of Speech Prosody 2004, Nara*.

Carston, Robyn. 2004a. Explicature and semantics. In *Semantics: A Reader*, Steven Davis and Brendan S. Gillon, eds., 817–845. Oxford: Oxford University Press.

Carston, Robyn. 2004b. Relevance theory and the saying/implicating distinction. In *The Handbook of Pragmatics*, Laurence R. Horn and Gregory Ward, eds., 633–656. Oxford: Blackwell.

Carston, Robyn. 2004c. Truth-conditional content and conversational implicature. In *The Semantics/Pragmatics Distinction*, Claudia Bianchi, ed., 65–100. Stanford: CSLI Publications.

Chomsky, Noam. 1976. Conditions on Rules of Grammar. *Linguistic Analysis* 2: 303–351.

Chomsky, Noam. 1991. Some Notes on Economy of Derivation and Representation. In *Principles and Parameters in Comparative Grammar*, Robert Freidin, ed., 417–454. Cambridge: MIT Press.

Cinque, Guglielmo. 1993. A Null Theory of Phrase and Compound Stress. *Linguistic Inquiry* 24: 239–297.

Cinque, Guglielmo. 1999. *Adverbs and Functional Heads. A Cross-Linguistic Perspective*. Oxford: Oxford University Press.

Clifton, Charles, Bock, Jeannine and Radó, Janina. 2000. Effects of the Focus Particle *Only* and Intrinsic Contrast on Comprehension of Reduced Relative Clauses. In *Reading as a Perceptual Process*, Alan Kennedy, Ralph Radach, Dieter Heller and Joël Pynte, eds., 591–619. Amsterdam: Elsevier.

Crystal, Thomas H. and House, Arthur S. 1988. Segmental durations in connected-speech signals: Syllabic stress. *Journal of the Acoustical Society of America* 83: 1574–1585.

den Besten, Hans. 1977. On the Interaction of Root Transformation and Lexical Deletive Rules, manuscript, University of Amsterdam.

den Besten, Hans. 1983. On the Interaction of Root Transformation and Lexical Deletive Rules. In *On the Formal Syntax of the Westgermania*, Werner Abraham, ed., 47–138. Amsterdam, Philadelphia: Benjamins.

Diesing, Molly. 1988. Bare plural subjects and the stage/individual contrast. In *Genericity in Natural Language. Proceedings of the 1988 Tübingen Conference*, Manfred Krifka, ed., 107–154. University of Tübingen.

Dietrich, Rainer. 1990. Zu Form und Bedeutung der Kontrastintonation im Deutschen. *Linguistische Berichte* 129: 415–430.

Dimroth, Christine. 2004. *Fokuspartikeln und Informationsgliederung im Deutschen*. Tübingen: Stauffenburg.

Dimroth, Christine and Klein, Wolfgang. 1996. Fokuspartikeln in Lernervarietäten. Ein Analyserahmen und einige Beispiele. *Zeitschrift für Literaturwissenschaft und Linguistik* 104: 73–114.

Drach, Erich. 1937. *Grundgedanken der Deutschen Satzlehre*. Frankfurt am Main: Diesterweg.

Dretske, Fred I. 1972. Contrastive Statements. *The Philosophical Review* 81: 411–437.

Drubig, Hans Bernhard. 1994. *Island Constraints and the Syntactic Nature of Focus and Association with Focus. Arbeitsberichte des Sonderforschungsbereichs 340, 51.* Heidelberg: IBM.

Erdmann, Oskar. 1886. *Grundzüge der deutschen Syntax. Erste Abteilung. Gebrauch der Wortklassen. Die Formationen des Verbums in einfachen Sätzen und in Satzverbindungen.* Stuttgart: Cotta.

Ernst, Thomas. 2002. *The Syntax of Adjuncts*. Cambridge: Cambridge University Press.

Ernst, Thomas. 2003. Semantic features and the distribution of adverbs. In *Modifying Adjuncts*, Ewald Lang, Claudia Maienborn and Fabricius-Hansen, Catherine, eds., 307–334. Berlin, New York: Mouton de Gruyter.

Erteschik-Shir, Nomi. 2006. On the architecture of topic and focus. In *The Architecture of Focus*, Valéria Molnár and Susanne Winkler, eds., 33–57. Berlin, New York: Mouton de Gruyter.

Fanselow, Gisbert. 1991. *Minimale Syntax. Groninger Arbeiten zur germanistischen Linguistik 32.* Groningen: Rijksuniversiteit Groningen.

Fanselow, Gisbert. 2003a. Free Constituent Order: A Minimalist Interface Account. In *Optionality in Syntax and Discourse Structure – Aspects of Word Order Variation in (West-) Germanic and Other Indo-European Languages. Folia Linguistica XXXVII*, Werner Abraham and László Molnárfi, eds., 191–231. Berlin, New York: Mouton de Gruyter.

Fanselow, Gisbert. 2003b. Surprising Specifiers and Cyclic Spellout. In *Proceedings of Generative Linguistics in Poland 5: Morphosyntactic Investigations*, Piotr Banski and Adam Przepiorkowski, eds., 29–46. Warszawa: Polish Academy of Sciences.

Fanselow, Gisbert. 2004a. Cyclic Phonology-Syntax-Interaction: Movement to First Position in German. In *Interdisciplinary Studies on Information Structure 1*, Shinichiro Ishihara, Michaela Schmitz and Anne Schwarz, eds., 1–42. Potsdam: Universitätsverlag Potsdam.

Fanselow, Gisbert. 2004b. Münchhausen-style head movement and the analysis of verb second. In *Three papers on German verb movement. Linguistics in Potsdam 22*, Ralf Vogel, ed., 9–49. Potsdam.

Féry, Caroline. 1993. *German Intonational Patterns*. Tübingen: Niemeyer.

Féry, Caroline. 2006. Postponed *auch*: Where does its accent come from?. In *Between 40 and 60 Puzzles for Krifka: A web festschrift for Manfred Krifka*, Hans-Martin Gärtner, Sigrid Beck, Regine Eckardt, Renate Musan and Barbara Stiebels, eds. Zentrum für Allgemeine Sprachwissenschaft, Typologie und Universalienforschung (ZAS), Berlin (http://www.zas.gwz-berlin.de/40-60-puzzles-for-krifka).

Féry, Caroline. to appear. Prosody and information structure of the German particles *selbst*, *wieder* and *auch*. In *Prosody Matters: Essays in Honor of Elisabeth O. Selkirk*, Toni Borowsky, Shigeto Kawahara, Takahito Shinya and Mariko Sugahara, eds. London: Equinox Press.

Féry, Caroline and Ishihara, Shinichiro. 2009. The Phonology of Second Occurrence Focus. *Journal of Linguistics* 45: 285–313.

Féry, Caroline and Krifka, Manfred. 2008. Information Structure: Notional Distinctions, Ways of Expression. In *Unity and Diversity of Languages*, Piet van Sterkenburg. ed., 123–135. Amsterdam, Philadelphia: Benjamins.

Foolen, Ad. 1983. Zur Semantik und Pragmatik der restriktiven Gradpartikeln: *only*, *nur* und *maar/alleen*. In *Partikeln und Interaktion*, Harald Weydt, ed., 188–199. Tübingen: Niemeyer.

Foolen, Ad. 1993. *De betekenis van partikels. Een documentatie van de stand van het onderzoek, met bijzondere aandacht voor* maar. Katholieke Universiteit Nijmegen.

Foolen, Ad, van Gerrevink, Richard, Hogeweg, Lotte and Prawiro-Atmodjo, Peia. 2009. The placement of focus particles in Dutch. In *Linguistics in the Netherlands 2009*, Bert Botma and Jacqueline van Kampen, eds., 51–63. Amsterdam, Philadelphia: Benjamins.

Francescotti, Robert M. 1995. Even: The Conventional Implicature Approach Reconsidered. *Linguistics and Philosophy* 18: 153–173.

Frascarelli, Mara and Hinterhölzl, Roland. 2007. Types of Topics in German and Italian. In *On Information Structure, Meaning and Form. Generalizations across languages*, Susanne Winkler and Kerstin Schwabe, eds., 87–116. Amsterdam, Philadelphia: Benjamins.

Frey, Werner. 1993. *Syntaktische Bedingungen für die semantische Interpretation. Über Bindung, implizite Argumente und Skopus*. Berlin: Akademie-Verlag.

Frey, Werner. 2000a. Syntactic Requirements on Adjuncts. *ZAS Papers in Linguistics* 17: 107–134.

Frey, Werner. 2000b. Über die syntaktische Position der Satztopiks im Deutschen. *ZAS Papers in Linguistics* 20: 137–172.

Frey, Werner. 2003. Syntactic conditions on adjunct classes. In *Modifying Adjuncts*, Ewald Lang, Claudia Maienborn and Catherine Fabricius-Hansen, eds., 163–209. Berlin, New York: Mouton de Gruyter.

Frey, Werner. 2004a. The grammar-pragmatics interface and the German prefield. *Sprache und Pragmatik* 52: 1–39.

Frey, Werner. 2004b. A medial topic position for German. *Linguistische Berichte* 198: 153–190.

Frey, Werner. 2006. Contrast and movement to the German prefield. In *The Architecture of Focus*, Valéria Molnár and Winkler Susanne Winkler, eds., 235–264. Berlin, New York: Mouton de Gruyter.

Frey, Werner and Pittner, Karin. 1998. Zur Positionierung der Adverbiale im deutschen Mittelfeld. *Linguistische Berichte* 176: 489–534.

Fries, Norbert. 1988. Über das Null-Topik im Deutschen. *Sprache und Pragmatik* 3: 19–49.

Fuchs, Anna. 1976. 'Normaler' und 'kontrastiver' Akzent. *Lingua* 38: 293–312.

Geach, Peter Thomas. 1962. *Reference and Generality: An Examination of Some Medieval and Modern Theories*. Ithaca: Cornell University Press.

Geilfuß-Wolfgang, Jochen. 1996. *Über gewisse Fälle von Assoziation mit Fokus*. Tübingen: Niemeyer.

Geurts, Bart and van der Sandt, Rob. 2004. Interpreting focus. *Theoretical Linguistics* 30: 1–44.

Gibbon, Dafydd. 1998. Intonation in German. In *Intonation Systems. A Survey of Twenty Languages*, Daniel Hirst and Albert di Christo, eds., 78–95. Cambridge: Cambridge University Press.

Glasberg, Brian R. and Moore, Brian C. J. 1990. Derivation of auditory filter shapes from notched-noise data. *Hearing Research* 47: 103–138.

Goldsmith, John A. 1976. Autosegmental phonology. Ph.D thesis, Massachusetts Institute of Technology, Cambridge, MA.

Greenwood, Donald D. 1961. Critical bandwidth and the frequency coordinates of the basilar membrane. *Journal of the Acoustical Society of America* 33: 1344–1356.

Greenwood, Donald D. 1990. A cochlear frequency-position function for several species. *Journal of the Acoustical Society of America* 87: 2592–2605.

Grice, Martine and Baumann, Stefan. 2002. Deutsche Intonation und GToBI. *Linguistische Berichte* 191: 267–298.

Grice, Martine, Baumann, Stefan and Benzmüller, Ralf. 2005. German Intonation in Autosegmental-Metrical Phonology. In *Prosodic Typology: The Phonology of Intonation and Phrasing*, Sun-Ah Jun, ed., 55–83. Oxford: Oxford University Press.

Grosjean, François. 1996. Gating. *Language and Cognitive Processes* 11: 597–604.

Grosjean, François and Hirt, Cendrine. 1996. Using Prosody to Predict the End of Sentences in English and French: Normal and Brain-damaged Subjects. *Language and Cognitive Processes* 11: 107–134.

Gussenhoven, Carlos. 1983. *On the Grammar and Semantics of Sentence Accents*. Dordrecht: Foris.

Gussenhoven, Carlos. 2004. *The Phonology of Tone and Intonation*. Cambridge: Cambridge University Press.

Gussenhoven, Carlos. 2006. Experimental Approaches to Establishing Discreteness of Intonational Contrasts. In *Methods in Empirical Prosody Research*, Stefan Sudhoff, Denisa Lenertová, Roland Meyer, Sandra Pappert, Petra Augurzky, Ina Mleinek, Nicole Richter and Johannes Schließer, eds., 321–334. Berlin, New York: de Gruyter.

Gussenhoven, Carlos and Rietveld, Antonius C. M. 1988. Fundamental frequency declination in Dutch: Testing three hypotheses. *Journal of Phonetics* 16: 355–369.

Haftka, Brigitta. 1994. Wie positioniere ich meine Position? Überlegungen zu funktionalen Phrasen im deutschen Mittelfeld. In *Was determiniert Wortstellungsvariation? Studien zu einem Interaktionsfeld von Grammatik, Pragmatik und Sprachtypologie*, Brigitta Haftka, ed., 139–159. Opladen: Westdeutscher Verlag.

Haftka, Brigitta. 1995. Syntactic Positions for Topic and Contrastive Focus in the German Middlefield. In *Proceedings of the Göttingen Focus Workshop, 17th DGfS, March 1–3, 1995*, Inga Kohlhoff, Susanne Winkler and Hans Bernhard Drubig, eds., 137–157. Heidelberg.

Haftka, Brigitta. 2003. Möglicherweise tatsächlich nicht immer. Beobachtungen zur Adverbialreihenfolge an der Spitze des Rhemas. In *Optionality in Syntax and Discourse Structure – Aspects of Word Order Variation in (West-) Germanic and Other Indo-European Languages. Folia Linguistica XXXVII*, Werner Abraham and László Molnárfi, eds., 103–128. Berlin, New York: Mouton de Gruyter.

Haftka, Brigitta. 2004. Topic Constraints in the German Middlefield. In *Information Structure. Theoretical and Empirical Aspects*, Anita Steube, ed., 125–162. Berlin, New York: de Gruyter.

Haider, Hubert. 1993. *Deutsche Syntax – generativ. Vorstudien zur Theorie einer projektiven Grammatik*. Tübingen: Narr.

Haider, Hubert. 1997. Projective Economy. On the minimal functional structure of the German clause. In *German: Syntactic Problems – Problematic Syntax*, Werner Abraham and Elly van Gelderen, eds., 83–103. Tübingen: Niemeyer.

Haider, Hubert. 2000. Adverb Placement – Convergence of Structure and Licensing. *Theoretical Linguistics* 26: 95–134.

Haider, Hubert and Rosengren, Inger. 1998. Scrambling. *Sprache und Pragmatik* 49: 1–104.

Hajičová, Eva, Partee, Barbara H. and Sgall, Petr. 1998a. Focus, Topic, and Semantics. In *Proceedings of the Workshop on Focus. University of Massachusetts Working Papers in Linguistics, 21*, Elena Benedicto, Maribel Romero and Satoshi Tomioka, eds., 101–124. Amherst: GLSA.

Hajičová, Eva, Partee, Barbara H. and Sgall, Petr. 1998b. *Topic-Focus Articulation, Tripartite Structures, and Semantic Content*. Dordrecht: Kluwer.

Hajičová, Eva and Sgall, Petr. 2004. Remarks on Focus Sensitive Particles (to Krifka's and von Fintel's Papers). In *Context-Dependence in the Analysis of Linguistic Meaning*, Hans Kamp and Barbara H. Partee, eds., 420–424. Amsterdam: Elsevier.

Hartmann, Katharina and Zimmermann, Malte. 2004. Focus Strategies in Chadic: The Case of Tangale Revisited. In *Interdisciplinary Studies on Information Structure 1*, Shinichiro Ishihara, Michaela Schmitz and Anne Schwarz, eds., 207–243. Potsdam: Universitätsverlag Potsdam.

Hartmann, Katharina and Zimmermann, Malte. 2006. Morphological Focus Marking in Gùrùntùm (West Chadic). In *Interdisciplinary Studies on Information Structure 5*. Shinichiro Ishihara, Michaela Schmitz and Anne Schwarz, eds., 61–105. Potsdam: Universitätsverlag Potsdam.

Hartmann, Katharina and Zimmermann, Malte. 2007. In place – out of place? Focus strategies in Hausa. In *On Information Structure, Meaning and Form. Generalizations across languages*, Susanne Winkler and Kerstin Schwabe, eds., 365–403. Amsterdam, Philadelphia: Benjamins.

Hayes, Bruce P. 1989. *Metrical stress theory: principles and case studies*. Chicago: University of Chicago Press.

Heim, Stefan and Alter, Kai. 2006. Prosodic pitch accents in language comprehension and production: ERP data and acoustic analyses. *Acta Neurobiologiae Experimentalis* 66: 55–68.

Heim, Stefan and Alter, Kai. 2007. Focus on focus: The brain's electrophysiological response to focus particles and accents in German. In *Interfaces and Interface Conditions*, Andreas Späth, ed., 277–297. Berlin, New York: de Gruyter.

Helbig, Gerhard. 1988. *Lexikon deutscher Partikeln*. Leipzig: Verlag Enzyklopädie.

Hendriks, Petra. 2004. Optimization in Focus Identification. In *Optimality Theory and Pragmatics*, Reinhard Blutner and Henk Zeevat, eds., 42–62. Basingstoke: Palgrave Macmillan.

Herburger, Elena. 2000. *What Counts: Focus and Quantification*. Cambridge: MIT Press.

Hermes, Dik. 2006. Stylization of Pitch Contours. In *Methods in Empirical Prosody Research*, Stefan Sudhoff, Denisa Lenertová, Roland Meyer, Sandra Pappert, Petra Augurzky, Ina Mleinek, Nicole Richter and Johannes Schließer, eds., 29–61. Berlin, New York: de Gruyter.

Hermes, Dik J. and van Gestel, Joost C. 1991. The frequency scale of speech intonation. *Journal of the Acoustical Society of America* 90: 97–102.

Hinterhölzl, Roland. 2004. Scrambling, Optionality and Non-Lexical Triggers. In *Triggers*, Anne Breitbarth and Henk van Riemsdijk, eds., 173–203. Berlin, New York: Mouton de Gruyter.

Hockett, Charles F. 1958. *A Course in Modern Linguistics*. New York: McMillan.

Hoeksema, Jack and Zwarts, Frans. 1991. Some Remarks on Focus Adverbs. *Journal of Semantics* 8: 51–70.

Hoffmann, Ludger. Ellipse. 1997. In *Grammatik der deutschen Sprache. Volume 1*, Gisela Zifonun, Ludger Hoffmann and Bruno Strecker, eds., 409–443. Berlin, New York: de Gruyter.

Höhle, Tilman N. 1982. Explikationen für 'normale Betonung' und 'normale Wortstellung'. In *Satzglieder im Deutschen: Vorschläge zur syntaktischen, semantischen und pragmatischen Fundierung*, Werner Abraham, ed., 75–153. Tübingen: Narr.

Horn, Laurence R. 1969. A Presuppositional Analysis of *Only* and *Even*. In *Papers from the 5th Regional Meeting of the Chicago Linguistics Society*, Robert I. Binnick, Alice Davison, Georgia Green and Jerry Morgan, eds., 98–107. University of Chicago.

Horn, Laurence R. 1992. The Said and the Unsaid. In *Proceedings of SALT 2*,Chris Barker and David Dowty, eds., 163–192. Columbus: Ohio State University.

Horn, Laurence R. 1996. Exclusive Company: *Only* and the Dynamics of Vertical Inference. *Journal of Semantics* 13: 1–40.

Huang, C.-T. James. 1984. On the Distribution and Reference of Empty Pronouns. *Linguistic Inquiry* 15: 531–574.

Ippolito, Michela. 2007. On the meaning of some focus sensitive particles. *Natural Language Semantics* 15: 1–34.

Ippolito, Michela. 2008. On the Meaning of *Only*. *Journal of Semantics* 25: 45–91.

Ito, Kiwako and Speer, Shari R. 2006. Using Interactive Tasks to Elicit Natural Dialogue. In *Methods in Empirical Prosody Research*, Stefan Sudhoff, Denisa Lenertová, Roland Meyer, Sandra Pappert, Petra Augurzky, Ina Mleinek, Nicole Richter and Johannes Schließer, eds., 229–257. Berlin, New York: de Gruyter.

Jackendoff, Ray S. 1972. *Semantic Interpretation in Generative Grammar*. Cambridge: MIT Press.

Jacobs, Joachim. 1982. *Syntax und Semantik der Negation im Deutschen*. München: Fink.

Jacobs, Joachim. 1983. *Fokus und Skalen. Zur Syntax und Semantik der Gradpartikeln im Deutschen*. Tübingen: Niemeyer.

Jacobs, Joachim. 1986. The Syntax of Focus and Adverbials in German. In *Topic, Focus, and Configurationality. Papers from the 6th Groningen Grammar Talks, Groningen, 1984*, Werner Abraham and Sjaak de Meij, eds., 103–127. Amsterdam, Philadelphia: Benjamins.

Jacobs, Joachim. 1988. Fokus-Hintergrund-Gliederung und Grammatik. In *Intonationsforschungen*, Hans Altmann, ed., 89–134. Tübingen: Niemeyer.

Jacobs, Joachim. 1991. Negation. In *Semantik. Ein internationales Handbuch der zeitgenössischen Forschung*, Arnim von Stechow and Dieter Wunderlich, eds., 560–596. Berlin, New York: de Gruyter.

Jacobs, Joachim. 1992. Neutral Stress and the Position of Heads. In *Informationsstruktur und Grammatik. Linguistische Berichte, Sonderheft 4*, Joachim Jacobs, ed., 220–244. Opladen: Westdeutscher Verlag.

Jacobs, Joachim. 1997. I-Topikalisierung. *Linguistische Berichte* 168: 91–133.

Jacobs, Joachim. 2001. The dimensions of topic-comment. *Linguistics* 39: 641–681.

Jaeger, T. Florian. 2004. Only always associates audibly. Even if only is repeated. The prosodic properties of second occurrence focus in English, manuscript, Stanford University.

Jaeger, T. Florian and Wagner, Michael. 2003. Association with Focus and Linear Order in German, manuscript, Stanford University.

Junghanns, Uwe. 2002. *Untersuchungen zur Syntax und Informationsstruktur slavischer Deklarativsätze. Linguistische Arbeitsberichte 80*. Leipzig.

Karttunen, Lauri and Peters, Stanley. 1979. Conventional Implicature. In *Presupposition*, Choon-Kyu Oh and David A. Dinneen, eds., 1–56. New York, San Francisco, London: Academic Press.

Kay, Paul. 1990. Even. *Linguistics and Philosophy* 13: 59–111.

Kayne, Richard. 1994. *The Antisymmetry of Syntax*. Cambridge: MIT Press.

Kleemann, Anja. 2006. The Syntax of Focus Particles in German Event vs. Result Nominals. In *Proceedings of CamLing 4, Cambridge*, 100–107.

Klein, Wolfgang and von Stutterheim, Christiane. 1987. Quaestio und referentielle Bewegung in Erzählungen. *Linguistische Berichte* 109: 163–183.

Klein, Wolfgang and von Stutterheim, Christiane. 1992. Textstruktur und referentielle Bewegung. *Zeitschrift für Literaturwissenschaft und Linguistik* 86: 67–92.

Kohler, Klaus J. 1990. Macro and micro F0 in the synthesis of intonation. In *Papers in Laboratory Phonology I. Between the Grammar and Physics of Speech*, John Kingston and Mary E. Beckman, eds., 115–138. Cambridge: Cambridge University Press.

Koktova, Eva. 1987. On the Scoping Properties of Negation, Focusing Particles and Sentence Adverbials. *Theoretical Linguistics* 14: 173–226.

König, Ekkehard. 1991a. Gradpartikeln. In *Semantik. Ein internationales Handbuch der zeitgenössischen Forschung*, Arnim von Stechow and Dieter Wunderlich, eds., 786–803. Berlin, New York: de Gruyter.

König, Ekkehard. 1991b. Identical values in conflicting roles: The use of German *ausgerechnet*, *eben*, *genau* and *gerade* as focus particles. In *Discourse Particles*, Werner Abraham, ed., 11–36. Amsterdam, Philadelphia: Benjamins.

König, Ekkehard. 1991c. *The Meaning of Focus Particles. A Comparative Perspective*. London, New York: Routledge.

König, Ekkehard. 1993. Focus Particles. In *Syntax: Ein internationales Handbuch zeitgenössischer Forschung*, Joachim Jacobs, ed., 978–987. Berlin, New York: de Gruyter.

Koster, Jan. 1987. *Domains and Dynasties. The Radical Autonomy of Syntax*. Dordrecht: Foris.

Kowalski, Andrea. 1992. Zur Syntax und Semantik von Gradpartikeln im Deutschen. Syntaktische Bedingungen für die Ausdehnung von Partikelskopus und -fokus, M.A. thesis, University of Wuppertal.

Krahmer, Emiel and Swerts, Marc. 2001. On the alleged existence of contrastive accents. *Speech Communication* 34: 391–405.

Kratzer, Angelika. 1991. The Representation of Focus. In *Semantik. Ein internationales Handbuch der zeitgenössischen Forschung*, Arnim von Stechow and Dieter Wunderlich, eds., 825–834. Berlin, New York: de Gruyter.

Krifka, Manfred. 1992a. A Compositional Semantics for Multiple Focus Constructions. In *Informationsstruktur und Grammatik. Linguistische Berichte, Sonderheft 4*, Joachim Jacobs, ed., 17–53. Opladen: Westdeutscher Verlag.

Krifka, Manfred. 1992b. A Framework for Focus-Sensitive Quantification. In *Proceedings of SALT 2*, Chris Barker and David Dowty, eds., 215–236. Columbus: Ohio State University.

Krifka, Manfred. 1993. Focus and Presupposition in Dynamic Interpretation. *Journal of Semantics* 10: 269–300.

Krifka, Manfred. 1999. Additive Particles under Stress. In *Proceedings of SALT 8*, Devon Strolovitch and Aaron Lawson, eds., 111–128. Cornell: CLC Publications.

Krifka, Manfred. 2004a. Focus and/or Context: A Second Look at Second Occurrence Expressions. In *Context-Dependence in the Analysis of Linguistic Meaning*, Hans Kamp and Barbara H. Partee, eds., 187–207. Amsterdam: Elsevier.

Krifka, Manfred. 2004b. Replies to Rooth, Bartels, Asher and Peregrin. In *Context-Dependence in the Analysis of Linguistic Meaning*, Hans Kamp and Barbara H. Partee, eds., 549–551. Amsterdam: Elsevier.

Krifka, Manfred. 2006. Association with focus phrases. In *The Architecture of Focus*, Valéria Molnár and Susanne Winkler, eds., 105–136. Berlin, New York: de Gruyter.

Ladd, D. Robert. 1983a. Even, Focus and Normal Stress. *Journal of Semantics* 2: 157–170.

Ladd, D. Robert. 1983b. Phonological Features of Intonational Peaks. *Language* 59: 721–759.

Ladd, D. Robert. 1996. *Intonational Phonology*. Cambridge: Cambridge University Press.

Ladd, D. Robert and Morton, Rachel. 1997. The perception of intonational emphasis: continuous or categorical? *Journal of Phonetics* 25: 313–342.

Ladd, D. Robert and Silverman, Kim E. A. 1984. Vowel Intrinsic Pitch in Connected Speech. *Phonetica* 41: 31–40.

Ladd, D. Robert, Verhoeven, Jo and Jacobs, Karen. 1994. Influence of adjacent pitch accents on each other's perceived prominence: Two contradictory effects. *Journal of Phonetics* 22: 87–99.

Lang, Ewald. 1977. *Semantik der koordinativen Verknüpfung*. Berlin: Akademie-Verlag.

Lang, Ewald. 1979. Zum Status der Satzadverbiale. *Slovo a Slovesnost* 40: 200–213.

Lang, Ewald. 1984. *The Semantics of Coordination*. Amsterdam, Philadelphia: Benjamins.

Lebeaux, David S. 1988. Language Acquisition and the Form of the Grammar. Ph.D. thesis, University of Massachusetts, Amherst, MA.

Lehiste, Ilse. 1970. *Suprasegmentals*. Cambridge: MIT Press.

Lenerz, Jürgen. 1977. *Zur Abfolge nominaler Satzglieder im Deutschen*. Tübingen: Narr.

Lenerz, Jürgen. 1993. Zu Syntax und Semantik deutscher Personalpronomina. In *Wortstellung und Informationsstruktur*, Marga Reis, ed., 117–153. Tübingen: Niemeyer.

Lenerz, Jürgen. 2001. Word Order Variation: Competition or Co-Operation? In *Competition in Syntax*, Gereon Müller and Wolfgang Sternefeld, eds., 249–281. Berlin, New York: Mouton de Gruyter.

Lenerz, Jürgen. 2002. Scrambling and Reference in German. In *Issues in Formal German(ic) Typology*, Werner Abraham and C. Jan-Wouter Zwart, eds., 179–192. Amsterdam, Philadelphia: Benjamins.

Levelt, Willem J. M. 1989. *Speaking. From Intention to Articulation*. Cambridge: MIT Press.

Levinson, Stephen C. 2000. *Presumptive Meanings. The Theory of Generalized Conversational Implicature*. Cambridge: MIT Press.

Liberman, Alvin M., Harris, Katherine S., Hoffman, Harold S. and Griffith, Belver C. 1957. The discrimination of speech sounds within and across phoneme boundaries. *Journal of Experimental Psychology* 54: 358–368.

Liberman, Mark and Prince, Alan. 1977. On Stress and Linguistic Rhythm. *Linguistic Inquiry* 8: 249–336.

Lindner, Katrin. 1991. 'Wir sind ja doch alte Bekannte.' The use of German *ja* and *doch* as modal particles. In *Discourse Particles*, Werner Abraham, ed., 163–201. Amsterdam, Philadelphia: Benjamins.

Marschall, Gottfried R. 2001. Semantik und konnektive Funktion der additiven Gradpartikeln: *auch* unter anderen. In *Textkonnektoren und andere textstrukturierende Einheiten*, Alain Cambourian, ed., 159–172. Tübingen: Stauffenburg.

Mayer, Jörg. 1997. Intonation und Bedeutung. Aspekte der Prosodie-Semantik-Schnittstelle im Deutschen. Ph.D. thesis, University of Stuttgart.

Mehlhorn, Grit. 2001. Produktion und Perzeption von Hutkonturen im Deutschen. In *Kontrast – lexikalisch, semantisch, intonatorisch. Linguistische Arbeitsberichte 77*, Anita Steube and Carla Umbach, eds., 31–57. Leipzig.

Mehlhorn, Grit. 2002. *Kontrastierte Konstituenten im Russischen. Experimentelle Untersuchungen zur Informationsstruktur*. Frankfurt am Main: Peter Lang.

Meinunger, André. 1996. *Discourse Dependent DP (De-)Placement. Groninger Arbeiten zur germanistischen Linguistik 39*. Groningen: Rijksuniversiteit Groningen.

Meinunger, André. 2000. *Syntactic Aspects of Topic and Comment.*Amsterdam, Philadelphia: Benjamins.

Molnár, Valéria. 1991. *Das TOPIK im Deutschen und im Ungarischen.*Stockholm: Almqvist & Wiksell International.

Molnár, Valéria. 2006. On different kinds of contrast. In *The Architecture of Focus*, Valéria Molnár and Susanne Winkler, eds., 197–233. Berlin, New York: Mouton de Gruyter.

Molnár, Valéria and Rosengren, Inger. 1997. Zu Jacobs' Explikation der I-Topikalisierung. *Linguistische Berichte* 169: 211–247.

Molnárfi, László. 2002. Focus and antifocus in modern Afrikaans and West Germanic. *Linguistics* 40: 1107–1130.

Molnárfi, László. 2003. On optional movement and feature checking in West Germanic. In *Optionality in Syntax and Discourse Structure – Aspects of Word Order Variation in (West-) Germanic and Other Indo-European Languages. Folia Linguistica XXXVII*, Werner Abraham and László Molnárfi, eds., 129–162. Berlin, New York: Mouton de Gruyter.

Molnárfi, László. 2004. On Scrambling as Defocusing in German and West Germanic. In *Triggers*, Anne Breitbarth and Henk van Riemsdijk, eds., 331–385. Berlin, New York: Mouton de Gruyter.

Molnárfi, László. 2007. Focus(ing) from a typological perspective. On the discourse configurationality of West Germanic. In *On Information Structure, Meaning and Form. Generalizations across languages*, Susanne Winkler and Kerstin Schwabe, eds., 155–181. Amsterdam, Philadelphia: Benjamins.

Moore, Brian C. J. 1997. Aspects of Auditory Processing, Related to Speech Perception. In *The Handbook of Phonetic Sciences*, William Hardcastle and John Laver, eds., 539–565. Oxford: Blackwell.

Mücke, Doris, Grice, Martine, Becker, Johannes, Hermes, Anne and Baumann, Stefan. 2006. Articulatory and acoustic correlates of prenuclear and nuclear accents. In *Proceedings of Speech Prosody 2006*, Rüdiger Hoffmann and Hansjörg Mixdorff, eds. Dresden: TUDpress.

Müller, Gereon. 1999. Optimality, Word Order, and Markedness in German. *Linguistics* 37: 777–818.

Müller, Karin. 1998. German Focus Particles and their Influence on Intonation. M.A. thesis, University of Stuttgart.

Müller, Karin. 1999. German Focus Particles and Intonation. In *Proceedings of the XIVth International Congress of Phonetic Sciences (ICPhS), San Francisco.*

Müller, Stefan. 2003. Mehrfache Vorfeldbesetzung. *Deutsche Sprache* 31: 29–62.

Müller, Stefan. 2005. Zur Analyse der scheinbar mehrfachen Vorfeldbesetzung. *Linguistische Berichte* 203: 297–330.

Nederstigt, Ulrike. 2001. Prosody: A clue for the interpretation of the additive focus particles *auch* and *noch*. *Linguistische Berichte* 188: 415–440.

Nederstigt, Ulrike. 2003. *Auch and noch in Child and Adult German*. Berlin, New York: Mouton de Gruyter.

Nederstigt, Ulrike. 2006. Additive Particles and Scope Marking in Child German. In *Semantics in Acquisition*, Veerle van Geenhoven, ed., 303–328. Dordrecht: Springer.

Neeleman, Ad and Reinhart, Tanya. 1998. Scrambling and the PF Interface. In *The Projection of Arguments. Lexical and Compositional Factors*, Miriam Butt and Wilhelm Geuder, eds., 309–353. Stanford: CSLI Publications.

Nespor, Marina and Vogel, Irene. 1986. *Prosodic Phonology*. Dordrecht: Foris.

Ni, Weijia, Crain, Stephen and Shankweiler, Donald. 1996. Sidestepping Garden Paths: Assessing the Contributions of Syntax, Semantics and Plausibility in Resolving Ambiguities. *Language and Cognitive Processes* 11: 283–334.

Niebuhr, Oliver. 2007. *Perzeption und kognitive Verarbeitung der Sprechmelodie. Theoretische Grundlagen und empirische Untersuchungen*. Berlin, New York: de Gruyter.

Pafel, Jürgen. 1998. *Skopus und logische Struktur. Studien zum Quantorenskopus im Deutschen. Arbeitsberichte des Sonderforschungsbereichs 340, 129*. Heidelberg: IBM.

Pafel, Jürgen. 2006. *Quantifier Scope in German*. Amsterdam, Philadelphia: Benjamins.

Partee, Barbara H. 1987. Noun Phrase Interpretation and Type-Shifting Principles. In *Studies in Discourse Re-presentation Theory and the Theory of Generalized Quantifiers*, Dordrecht: Foris. Jeroen Groenendijk, Dick de Jongh and Martin Stokhof, eds., 115–143.

Partee, Barbara H. 1992. Topic, Focus and Quantification. In *Proceedings of SALT 1*, Steven Moore and Adam Wyner, eds., 159–187. Cornell: CLC Publications.

Penner, Zvi, Tracy, Rosemarie and Wymann, Karin. 1999. Die Rolle der Fokuspartikel AUCH im frühen kindlichen Lexikon. Eine Studie zum Erwerb des Deutschen im Vergleich mit dem doppelten Erstspracherwerb Deutsch-Englisch und dem verspäteten Sprechbeginn. In *Das Lexikon im Spracherwerb*, Jörg Meibauer and Monika Rothweiler, eds., 229–251. Tübingen, Basel: Francke.

Pierrehumbert, Janet. 1980. The phonology and phonetics of English intonation. Ph.D. thesis, Massachusetts Institute of Technology, Cambridge, MA.

Pierrehumbert, Janet and Hirschberg, Julia. 1990. The Meaning of Intonational Contours in the Interpretation of Discourse. In *Intentions in Communication*, Philip R. Cohen, Jerry Morgan and Martha E. Pollack, eds., 271–311. Cambridge: MIT Press.

Pittner, Karin. 1999. *Adverbiale im Deutschen. Untersuchungen zu ihrer Stellung und Interpretation*. Tübingen: Stauffenburg.

Plank, Frans. 1979. Zur Affinität von *selbst* und *auch*. In *Die Partikeln der deutschen Sprache*, Harald Weydt, ed., 269–284. Berlin, New York: de Gruyter.

Poljakova, Svetlana. 2000. Fokusdomäne von Gradpartikeln im Deutschen und Russischen. *Linguistik Online* 6.

Pollock, Jean-Yves. 1989. Verb Movement, Universal Grammar, and the Structure of IP. *Linguistic Inquiry* 20: 365–424.

Primus, Beatrice. 1992. *Selbst* – Variants of a Scalar Adverb in German. In *Informationsstruktur und Grammatik. Linguistische Berichte, Sonderheft 4*, Joachim Jacobs, ed., 54–88. Opladen: Westdeutscher Verlag.

Reinhart, Tanya. 1981. Pragmatics and Linguistics: An Analysis of Sentence Topics. *Philosophica* 27: 53–93.

Reis, Marga. 1999. On Sentence Types in German: An Enquiry into the Relationship between Grammar and Pragmatics. *Interdisciplinary Journal for Germanic Linguistics and Semiotic Analysis* 4: 195–236.

Reis, Marga. 2005. On the Syntax of So-called Focus Particles in German – A Reply to Büring and Hartmann 2001. *Natural Language & Linguistic Theory* 23: 459–483.

Reis, Marga and Rosengren, Inger. 1997. A Modular Approach to the Grammar of Additive Particles: the Case of German Auch. *Journal of Semantics* 14: 237–309.

Repp, Bruno H. 1984. Categorical perception: Issues, methods, findings. In *Speech and Language: Advances in Basic Research and Practice, 10*, Norman J. Lass, ed., 243–335. New York: Academic Press.

Repp, Sophie. 2008. When the Negative Goes Missing: The Role of the Information Structure in Gapping Coordinations with *but*. In *The Discourse Potential of Underspecified Structures*, Anita Steube, ed., 359-388. Berlin, New York: de Gruyter.

Rooth, Mats. 1985. Association with Focus. Ph.D. thesis, University of Massachusetts, Amherst, MA.

Rooth, Mats. 1992. A Theory of Focus Interpretation. *Natural Language Semantics* 1: 75–116.

Rooth, Mats. 1996. Focus. In *The Handbook of Contemporary Semantic Theory*, Shalom Lappin, ed., 271–297. Oxford: Blackwell.

Rooth, Mats. 1999. Association with Focus or Association with Presupposition?. In *Focus. Linguistic, Cognitive, and Computational Perspectives*, Peter Bosch and Rob van der Sandt, eds., 232–244. Cambridge: Cambridge University Press.

Rooth, Mats. 2004. Comments on Krifka's Paper. In *Context-Dependence in the Analysis of Linguistic Meaning*, Hans Kamp and Barbara H. Partee, eds., 477–487. Amsterdam: Elsevier.

Rosengren, Inger. 1993a. Imperativsatz und "Wunschsatz" – zu ihrer Grammatik und Pragmatik. In *Satz und Illokution. Volume 2*, Inger Rosengren, ed., 1–47. Tübingen: Niemeyer.

Rosengren, Inger. 1993b. Wahlfreiheit mit Konsequenzen – Scrambling, Topikalisierung und FHG im Dienste der Informationsstrukturierung. In *Wortstellung und Informationsstruktur*, Marga Reis, ed., 251–312. Tübingen: Niemeyer.

Rosengren, Inger. 1994. Scrambling – was ist das? In *Was determiniert Wortstellungsvariation? Studien zu einem Interaktionsfeld von Grammatik, Pragmatik und Sprachtypologie*, Brigitta Haftka, ed., 175–196. Opladen: Westdeutscher Verlag.

Ross, John Robert. 1967. Constraints on Variables in Syntax. Ph.D. thesis, Massachusetts Institute of Technology, Cambridge, MA.

Rothstein, Susan. 1991. Heads, projections, and category determination. In *Views on Phrase Structure*, Katherine Leffel and Denis Bouchard, eds., 97–112. Dordrecht: Kluwer.

Rullmann, Hotze. 1997. *Even*, Polarity, and Scope. In *Papers in Experimental and Theoretical Linguistics, vol. 4*, Martha Gibson, Grace Wiebe and Gary Libben, eds., 40–64. Edmonton: University of Alberta.

Rullmann, Hotze. 2003. Additive Particles and Polarity. *Journal of Semantics* 20: 329–401.

Schafer, Amy J., Speer, Shari R. and Warren, Paul. 2004. Prosodic influences on the production and comprehension of syntactic ambiguity in a game-based conversation task. In *Approaches to Studying World-Situated Language Use*, John C. Trueswell and Michael K. Tanenhaus, eds., 209–225. Cambridge: MIT Press.

Schafer, Amy J., Speer, Shari R., Warren, Paul and White, S. David. 2000. Intonational Disambiguation in Sentence Production and Comprehension. *Journal of Psycholinuistic Research* 29: 169–182.

Schäfer, Martin. 2005. German Adverbial Adjectives: Syntactic Position and Semantic Interpretation. Ph.D. thesis, University of Leipzig.

Schneider, Katrin, Lintfert, Britta, Dogil, Grzegorz and Möbius, Bernd. 2006. Phonetic Grounding of Prosodic Categories. In *Methods in Empirical Prosody Research*, Stefan Sudhoff, Denisa Lenertová, Roland Meyer, Sandra Pappert, Petra Augurzky, Ina Mleinek, Nicole Richter and Johannes Schließer, eds., 335–361. Berlin, New York: de Gruyter.

Schulz, Barbara. 2006. Tune in, drop out: Harmonic alignment as a prerequisite for German topic-drop, manuscript, University of Hawai'i at Manoa.

Schwarz, Bernhard. 2005. Scalar Additive Particles in Negative Contexts. *Natural Language Semantics* 13: 125–168.

Sedivy, Julie C. 2002. Invoking Discourse-Based Contrast Sets and Resolving Syntactic Ambiguities. *Journal of Memory and Language* 46: 341–370.

Selkirk, Elisabeth. 1984. *Phonology and Syntax: The Relation between Sound and Structure*. Cambridge: MIT Press.

Selkirk, Elisabeth. 1995. Sentence Prosody: Intonation, Stress, and Phrasing. In *The Handbook of Phonological Theory*, John A. Goldsmith, ed., 550–569. Oxford: Blackwell.

Sgall, Petr, Hajičová, Eva and Panevová, Jarmila. 1986. *The Meaning of the Sentence in its Semantic and Pragmatic Aspects*. Dordrecht: Reidel.

Sgall, Petr. 1994. Focus and Focalizers. In *Focus & Natural Language Processing. Volume 2: Semantics*, Peter Bosch and Rob van der Sandt, eds., 409–414. Heidelberg: IBM.

Shaer, Benjamin. 2004. Left/right contrasts among English temporal adverbials. In *Adverbials. The interplay between meaning, context, and syntactic structure*, Jennifer R. Austin, Stefan Engelberg and Gisa Rauh, eds., 289–332. Amsterdam, Philadelphia: Benjamins.

Silverman, Kim E., Beckman, Mary E., Pitrelli, John, Ostendorf, Mari, Wightman, Colin, Price, Patti, Pierrehumbert, Janet and Hirschberg, Julia. 1992. ToBI: A Standard for Labeling English Prosody. In *Proceedings of the Second International Conference on Spoken Language Processing, Banff*, 867–870.

Sluijter, Agaath M. C and van Heuven, Vincent J. 1995. Effects of focus distribution, pitch accent and lexical stress on the temporal organization of syllables in Dutch. *Phonetica* 52: 71–89.

Späth, Andreas. 2007. On the Semantic Foundations of the Contrastive Focus within a Lexicalist Approach. In *Interfaces and Interface Conditions*, Andreas Späth, ed., 245–276. Berlin, New York: de Gruyter.

Späth, Andreas and Trautwein, Martin. 2004. Negative Descriptions of Events: Semantic and Conceptual Aspects of Sentence Negation and its Relevance for Information Structure. In *Information Structure. Theoretical and Empirical Aspects*, Anita Steube, ed., 41–73. Berlin, New York: de Gruyter.

Speyer, Augustin. 2004. Competing Constraints on Vorfeldbesetzung in German. *ZAS Papers in Linguistics* 35: 519–541.

Speyer, Augustin. 2007. Die Bedeutung der Centering Theory für Fragen der Vorfeldbesetzung im Deutschen. *Zeitschrift für Sprachwissenschaft* 26: 83–115.

Steedman, Mark. 2000. Information Structure and the Syntax-Phonology Interface. *Linguistic Inquiry* 31: 649–689.

Steedman, Mark. 2007. Information-Structural Semantics for English Intonation. In *Topic and Focus. Cross-Linguistic Perspectives on Meaning and Intonation*, Chungmin Lee, Matthew Gordon and Daniel Büring, eds., 245–264. Dordrecht: Springer.

Sternefeld, Wolfgang. 2006a. *Syntax. Eine morphologisch motivierte generative Beschreibung des Deutschen. Volume 1.* Tübingen: Stauffenburg.

Sternefeld, Wolfgang. 2006b. *Syntax. Eine morphologisch motivierte generative Beschreibung des Deutschen. Volume 2.* Tübingen: Stauffenburg.

Steube, Anita. 1995. Compositionally constructed epistemic meaning and reference in German. In *Deutsch als Fremdsprache. An den Quellen eines Faches. Festschrift für Gerhard Helbig zum 65. Geburtstag*, Heidrun Popp, ed., 117–127. München: Iudicum.

Steube, Anita. 1996. Informationsstrukturierung an der Nahtstelle zwischen Grammatik und Textlinguistik. In *Sprache und Kommunikation im Kulturkontext*, Volker Hertel, Irmhild Barz, Regine Metzler and Brigitte Uhlig, eds., 207–214. Frankfurt am Main: Peter Lang.

Steube, Anita. 2000. Ein kognitionswissenschaftlich basiertes Modell für Informationsstrukturierung (in Anwendung auf das Deutsche). In *Von der Philologie zur Grammatiktheorie. Peter Suchsland zum 65. Geburtstag*, Josef Bayer and Christine Römer, eds., 213–238. Tübingen: Niemeyer.

Steube, Anita. 2001. Correction by Contrastive Focus. *Theoretical Linguistics* 27: 215–249.

Steube, Anita. 2003. Bridge Contours in German assertive main clauses. In *Optionality in Syntax and Discourse Structure – Aspects of Word Order Variation in (West-) Germanic and Other Indo-European Languages. Folia Linguistica XXXVII*, Werner Abraham and László Molnárfi, eds., 163–190. Berlin, New York: Mouton de Gruyter.

Steube, Anita. 2005. A Short Survey of the Syntax of German Negation. In *Aleg(r)ace pro Evu. Papers in Honour of Eva Hajicová*, Jarmila Panevová and Barbora Vidová Hladká, eds., 133–139. Praha: MFF UK.

Steube, Anita. 2006. The Influence of Operators on the Interpretation of DPs and PPs in German Information Structure. In *The Architecture of Focus*, Valéria Molnár and Susanne Winkler, eds., 489–516. Berlin, New York: Mouton de Gruyter.

Steube, Anita. 2008. Semantic Composition of Information Structures with Operators. In *The Discourse Potential of Underspecified Structures*, Anita Steube, ed., 513–532. Berlin, New York: de Gruyter.

Steube, Anita, Alter, Kai and Späth, Andreas. 2004. Information Structure and Modular Grammar. In *Information Structure. Theoretical and Empirical Aspects*, Anita Steube, ed., 15–40. Berlin, New York: de Gruyter.

Steube, Anita and Späth, Andreas. 1998. DP-Semantik und Informationsstrukturierung im Russischen (auf der Basis eines Vergleichs mit dem Deutschen). *Sprache und Pragmatik* 46: 1–70.

Steube, Anita and Späth, Andreas. 2002. Semantik, Informationsstruktur und grammatische Modularität. In *Sprachtheoretische Grundlagen der Kognitionswissenschaft: Sprachliches und nichtsprachliches Wissen. Linguistische Arbeitsberichte 79*, Anita Steube, ed., 235–254. Leipzig.

Stolterfoht, Britta. 2005. *Processing word order variations and ellipses: the interplay of syntax and information structure during sentence comprehension.* Leipzig: Max Planck Institute for Human Cognitive and Brain Sciences.

Stolterfoht, Britta and Bader, Markus. 2004. Focus Structure and the Processing of Word Order Variations in German. In *Information Structure. Theoretical and Empirical Aspects*, Anita Steube, ed., 259–275. Berlin, New York: de Gruyter.

Stolterfoht, Britta, Friederici, Angela D., Alter, Kai and Steube, Anita. 2007. Processing focus structure and implicit prosody during reading: Differential ERP effects. *Cognition* 104: 565–590.

Sudhoff, Stefan. 2003. *Argumentsätze und es-Korrelate. Zur syntaktischen Struktur von Nebensatzeinbettungen im Deutschen.* Berlin: wvb.

Sudhoff, Stefan and Lenertová, Denisa. 2006. Prosodic Properties of Constituents Associated with Stressed *auch* in German. In *Proceedings of Speech Prosody 2006. Volume 1*, Rüdiger Hoffmann and Hansjörg Mixdorff, eds., 390–393. Dresden: TUDpress.

Sudhoff, Stefan, Steube, Anita and Hogrefe, Katharina. 2004. Syntaktische Positionen bewegungsbeschränkter I-Topiks im Deutschen. In *Grammatik und Kontext: Zur Interaktion von Syntax, Semantik und Prosodie bei der Informationsstrukturierung. Linguistische Arbeitsberichte 81*, Anita Steube, ed., 147–158. Leipzig.

Taglicht, Josef. 1984. *Message and Emphasis. On Focus and Scope in English.* London, New York: Longman.

Tanaka, Shin. 2000. Wir waren *auch* dabei. – Wir waren *nur* dabei?: *auch* als Topikpartikel. *Sprachwissenschaft* 25: 1–19.

Thiersch, Craig L. 1978. Topics in German Syntax. Ph.D. thesis, Massachusetts Institute of Technology, Cambridge, MA.

Toepel, Ulrike and Alter, Kai. 2004. On the Independence of Information Structural Processing from Prosody. In *Information Structure. Theoretical and Empirical Aspects.* Anita Steube, ed., 227–240. Berlin, New York: de Gruyter.

Toepel, Ulrike, Pannekamp, Ann and Alter, Kai. 2007. Catching the news: Processing strategies in listening to dialogs as measured by ERPs. *Behavioral and Brain Functions* 3: 53.

Tovena, Lucia M. 2005. Dealing with alternatives, handout, presented at *Sinn und Bedeutung*, Berlin, 13–15th October 2005.

Turk, Alice E. and Sawusch, James R. 1997. The domain of accentual lengthening in American English. *Journal of Phonetics* 25: 25–41.

Turk, Alice E. and White, Laurence. 1999. Structural influences on accentual lengthening in English. *Journal of Phonetics* 32: 171–206.

Uhmann, Susanne. 1991. *Fokusphonologie. Eine Analyse deutscher Intonationskonturen im Rahmen der nicht-linearen Phonologie.* Tübingen: Niemeyer.

Umbach, Carla. 2001. Restriktion der Alternativen. In *Kontrast – lexikalisch, semantisch, intonatorisch. Linguistische Arbeitsberichte 77*, Anita Steube and Carla Umbach, eds., 165–198. Leipzig.

Umbach, Carla. 2004. On the Notion of Contrast in Information Structure and Discourse Structure. *Journal of Semantics* 21: 155–175.

Vallduví, Enric and Vilkuna, Maria. 1998. On Rheme and Kontrast. In *The Limits of Syntax*, Peter W. Culicover and Louise McNally, eds., 79–108. San Diego: Academic Press.

van Bergen, Geertje and de Swart, Peter. 2009. Definiteness and Scrambling in Dutch: Where theory meets practice. In *Proceedings of NELS 38*, Anisa Schardl, Martin Walkow and Muhammad Abdurrahman, eds., 113–124. Amherst: GLSA.

van der Sandt, Rob. 1992. Presupposition Projection as Anaphora Resolution. *Journal of Semantics* 9: 333–377.

van Hoof, Hanneke. 2003. The rise in the rise-fall contour: does it evoke a contrastive topic or a contrastive focus?. *Linguistics* 41: 516–563.

von Fintel, Kai. 1994. Restrictions on Quantifier Domains. Ph.D. thesis, University of Massachusetts, Amherst, MA.

von Fintel, Kai. 2004. A Minimal Theory of Adverbial Quantification. In *Context-Dependence in the Analysis of Linguistic Meaning*, Hans Kamp and Barbara H. Partee, eds., 137–175. Amsterdam: Elsevier.

von Stechow, Arnim. 1991a. Current Issues in the Theory of Focus. In *Semantik. Ein internationales Handbuch der zeitgenössischen Forschung*, Arnim von Stechow and Dieter Wunderlich, eds., 804–825. Berlin, New York: de Gruyter.

von Stechow, Arnim. 1991b. Focusing and backgrounding operators. In *Discourse Particles*, Werner Abraham, ed., 37–84. Amsterdam, Philadelphia: Benjamins.

Wiese, Richard. 1996. *The Phonology of German*. Oxford: Clarendon Press.

Wilkinson, Karina. 1993. Towards a unified semantics of *Even*: A reply to Rooth. In *Proceedings of SALT 3*, Utpal Lahiri and Adam Zachary Wyner, eds., 182–201. Ithaca: DMLL Publications.

Wilkinson, Karina. 1996. The Scope of *Even*. *Natural Language Semantics* 4: 193–215.

Wunderlich, Dieter. 1988. Der Ton macht die Melodie – Zur Phonologie der Intonation des Deutschen. In *Intonationsforschungen*, Hans Altmann, ed., 1–40. Tübingen: Niemeyer.

Zeevat, Henk. 1992. Presupposition and Accommodation in Update Semantics. *Journal of Semantics* 9: 379–412.

Zimmermann, Ilse. 1985. Der syntaktische Parallelismus verbaler und adjektivischer Konstruktionen. Zu einigen Grundfragen der X-bar-Theorie. *Linguistische Studien des Zentralinstituts für Sprachwissenschaft der Akademie der Wissenschaften der DDR, Reihe A* 127: 159–213.

Zimmermann, Ilse. 1989. The Syntax of Comparative Constructions. In *Dimensional Adjectives. Grammatical Structure and Conceptual Interpretation*, Manfred Bierwisch and Ewald Lang, eds., 13–69. Berlin, Heidelberg: Springer.

Zimmermann, Ilse. 1999. Die Integration topikalischer DPs in die syntaktische und semantische Struktur von Sätzen. In *Sprachspezifische Aspekte der Informationsverteilung*, Monika Doherty, ed., 41–60. Berlin: Akademie-Verlag.

Zubizarreta, Maria Luisa. 1998. *Prosody, Focus, and Word Order*. Cambridge: MIT Press.

Name index

Subject index

Linguistik Aktuell/Linguistics Today

A complete list of titles in this series can be found on the publishers' website, *www.benjamins.com*

158 **DUGUINE, Maia, Susana HUIDOBRO and Nerea MADARIAGA (eds.):** Argument Structure and Syntactic Relations. A cross-linguistic perspective. *Expected June 2010*

157 **FISCHER, Susann:** Word-Order Change as a Source of Grammaticalisation. vii, 191 pp. + index. *Expected June 2010*

156 **DI SCIULLO, Anna Maria and Virginia HILL (eds.):** Edges, Heads, and Projections. Interface properties. vii, 262 pp. + index. *Expected May 2010*

155 **SATO, Yosuke:** Minimalist Interfaces. Evidence from Indonesian and Javanese. xiii, 155 pp. + index. *Expected May 2010*

154 **HORNSTEIN, Norbert and Maria POLINSKY (eds.):** Movement Theory of Control. vii, 327 pp. + index. *Expected April 2010*

153 **CABREDO HOFHERR, Patricia and Ora MATUSHANSKY (eds.):** Adjectives. Formal analyses in syntax and semantics. vii, 331 pp. + index. *Expected May 2010*

152 **GALLEGO, Ángel J.:** Phase Theory. xii, 360 pp. + index. *Expected April 2010*

151 **SUDHOFF, Stefan:** Focus Particles in German. Syntax, prosody, and information structure. 2010. xiii, 335 pp.

150 **EVERAERT, Martin, Tom LENTZ, Hannah de MULDER, Øystein NILSEN and Arjen ZONDERVAN (eds.):** The Linguistics Enterprise. From knowledge of language to knowledge in linguistics. 2010. ix, 379 pp.

149 **AELBRECHT, Lobke:** The Syntactic Licensing of Ellipsis. 2010. xii, 230 pp.

148 **HOGEWEG, Lotte, Helen de HOOP and Andrej MALCHUKOV (eds.):** Cross-linguistic Semantics of Tense, Aspect, and Modality. 2009. vii, 406 pp.

147 **GHOMESHI, Jila, Ileana PAUL and Martina WILTSCHKO (eds.):** Determiners. Universals and variation. 2009. vii, 247 pp.

146 **GELDEREN, Elly van (ed.):** Cyclical Change. 2009. viii, 329 pp.

145 **WESTERGAARD, Marit:** The Acquisition of Word Order. Micro-cues, information structure, and economy. 2009. xii, 245 pp.

144 **PUTNAM, Michael T. (ed.):** Towards a Derivational Syntax. Survive-minimalism. 2009. x, 269 pp.

143 **ROTHMAYR, Antonia:** The Structure of Stative Verbs. 2009. xv, 216 pp.

142 **NUNES, Jairo (ed.):** Minimalist Essays on Brazilian Portuguese Syntax. 2009. vi, 243 pp.

141 **ALEXIADOU, Artemis, Jorge HANKAMER, Thomas McFADDEN, Justin NUGER and Florian SCHAFER (eds.):** Advances in Comparative Germanic Syntax. 2009. xv, 395 pp.

140 **ROEHRS, Dorian:** Demonstratives and Definite Articles as Nominal Auxiliaries. 2009. xii, 196 pp.

139 **HICKS, Glyn:** The Derivation of Anaphoric Relations. 2009. xii, 309 pp.

138 **SIDDIQI, Daniel:** Syntax within the Word. Economy, allomorphy, and argument selection in Distributed Morphology. 2009. xii, 138 pp.

137 **PFAU, Roland:** Grammar as Processor. A Distributed Morphology account of spontaneous speech errors. 2009. xiii, 372 pp.

136 **KANDYBOWICZ, Jason:** The Grammar of Repetition. Nupe grammar at the syntax–phonology interface. 2008. xiii, 168 pp.

135 **LEWIS, William D., Simin KARIMI, Heidi HARLEY and Scott O. FARRAR (eds.):** Time and Again. Theoretical perspectives on formal linguistics. In honor of D. Terence Langendoen. 2009. xiv, 265 pp.

134 **ARMON-LOTEM, Sharon, Gabi DANON and Susan ROTHSTEIN (eds.):** Current Issues in Generative Hebrew Linguistics. 2008. vii, 393 pp.

133 **MACDONALD, Jonathan E.:** The Syntactic Nature of Inner Aspect. A minimalist perspective. 2008. xv, 241 pp.

132 **BIBERAUER, Theresa (ed.):** The Limits of Syntactic Variation. 2008. vii, 521 pp.

131 **DE CAT, Cécile and Katherine DEMUTH (eds.):** The Bantu–Romance Connection. A comparative investigation of verbal agreement, DPs, and information structure. 2008. xix, 355 pp.

130 **KALLULLI, Dalina and Liliane TASMOWSKI (eds.):** Clitic Doubling in the Balkan Languages. 2008. ix, 442 pp.

129 **STURGEON, Anne:** The Left Periphery. The interaction of syntax, pragmatics and prosody in Czech. 2008. xi, 143 pp.

128 **TALEGHANI, Azita H.:** Modality, Aspect and Negation in Persian. 2008. ix, 183 pp.

127 **DURRLEMAN-TAME, Stephanie:** The Syntax of Jamaican Creole. A cartographic perspective. 2008. xii, 190 pp.

126 **SCHÄFER, Florian:** The Syntax of (Anti-)Causatives. External arguments in change-of-state contexts. 2008. xi, 324 pp.

125 **ROTHSTEIN, Björn:** The Perfect Time Span. On the present perfect in German, Swedish and English. 2008. xi, 171 pp.

124 **IHSANE, Tabea:** The Layered DP. Form and meaning of French indefinites. 2008. ix, 260 pp.

123 **STOYANOVA, Marina:** Unique Focus. Languages without multiple wh-questions. 2008. xi, 184 pp.

122 **OOSTERHOF, Albert:** The Semantics of Generics in Dutch and Related Languages. 2008. xviii, 286 pp.

121 **TUNGSETH, Mai Ellin:** Verbal Prepositions and Argument Structure. Path, place and possession in Norwegian. 2008. ix, 187 pp.

120 **ASBURY, Anna, Jakub DOTLAČIL, Berit GEHRKE and Rick NOUWEN (eds.):** Syntax and Semantics of Spatial P. 2008. vi, 416 pp.

119 **FORTUNY, Jordi:** The Emergence of Order in Syntax. 2008. viii, 211 pp.

118 **JÄGER, Agnes:** History of German Negation. 2008. ix, 350 pp.

117 **HAUGEN, Jason D.:** Morphology at the Interfaces. Reduplication and Noun Incorporation in Uto-Aztecan. 2008. xv, 257 pp.

116 **ENDO, Yoshio:** Locality and Information Structure. A cartographic approach to Japanese. 2007. x, 235 pp.

115 **PUTNAM, Michael T.:** Scrambling and the Survive Principle. 2007. x, 216 pp.

114 **LEE-SCHOENFELD, Vera:** Beyond Coherence. The syntax of opacity in German. 2007. viii, 206 pp.

113 **EYTHÓRSSON, Thórhallur (ed.):** Grammatical Change and Linguistic Theory. The Rosendal papers. 2008. vi, 441 pp.

112 **AXEL, Katrin:** Studies on Old High German Syntax. Left sentence periphery, verb placement and verb-second. 2007. xii, 364 pp.

111 **EGUREN, Luis and Olga FERNÁNDEZ-SORIANO (eds.):** Coreference, Modality, and Focus. Studies on the syntax–semantics interface. 2007. xii, 239 pp.

110 **ROTHSTEIN, Susan (ed.):** Theoretical and Crosslinguistic Approaches to the Semantics of Aspect. 2008. viii, 453 pp.

109 **CHOCANO, Gema:** Narrow Syntax and Phonological Form. Scrambling in the Germanic languages. 2007. x, 333 pp.

108 **REULAND, Eric, Tanmoy BHATTACHARYA and Giorgos SPATHAS (eds.):** Argument Structure. 2007. xviii, 243 pp.

107 **CORVER, Norbert and Jairo NUNES (eds.):** The Copy Theory of Movement. 2007. vi, 388 pp.

106 **DEHÉ, Nicole and Yordanka KAVALOVA (eds.):** Parentheticals. 2007. xii, 314 pp.

105 **HAUMANN, Dagmar:** Adverb Licensing and Clause Structure in English. 2007. ix, 438 pp.

104 **JEONG, Youngmi:** Applicatives. Structure and interpretation from a minimalist perspective. 2007. vii, 144 pp.

103 **WURFF, Wim van der (ed.):** Imperative Clauses in Generative Grammar. Studies in honour of Frits Beukema. 2007. viii, 352 pp.

102 **BAYER, Josef, Tanmoy BHATTACHARYA and M.T. Hany BABU (eds.):** Linguistic Theory and South Asian Languages. Essays in honour of K. A. Jayaseelan. 2007. x, 282 pp.

101 **KARIMI, Simin, Vida SAMIIAN and Wendy K. WILKINS (eds.):** Phrasal and Clausal Architecture. Syntactic derivation and interpretation. In honor of Joseph E. Emonds. 2007. vi, 424 pp.

100 **SCHWABE, Kerstin and Susanne WINKLER (eds.):** On Information Structure, Meaning and Form. Generalizations across languages. 2007. vii, 570 pp.

99 **MARTÍNEZ-GIL, Fernando and Sonia COLINA (eds.):** Optimality-Theoretic Studies in Spanish Phonology. 2007. viii, 564 pp.

98 **PIRES, Acrisio:** The Minimalist Syntax of Defective Domains. Gerunds and infinitives. 2006. xiv, 188 pp.

97 **HARTMANN, Jutta M. and László MOLNÁRFI (eds.):** Comparative Studies in Germanic Syntax. From Afrikaans to Zurich German. 2006. vi, 332 pp.

96 **LYNGFELT, Benjamin and Torgrim SOLSTAD (eds.):** Demoting the Agent. Passive, middle and other voice phenomena. 2006. x, 333 pp.

95 **VOGELEER, Svetlana and Liliane TASMOWSKI (eds.):** Non-definiteness and Plurality. 2006. vi, 358 pp.